CW00832678

Daily Scriptures

The Eerdmans Language Resources series is a collection of textbooks, readers, reference books, and monographs pertaining to languages commonly used in biblical and theological studies. In these volumes, students and scholars will find indispensable help in understanding and mastering Hebrew, Aramaic, Greek, and other languages.

Other ELR Titles

N. Clayton Croy, *A Primer of Biblical Greek*

S. R. Driver, *A Treatise on the Use of the Tenses in Hebrew and Some Other Syntactical Questions*

Holger Gzella, *Aramaic: A History of the First World Language*

William L. Holladay, *A Concise Hebrew and Aramaic Lexicon of the Old Testament*

Page H. Kelley and Timothy G. Crawford, *Biblical Hebrew: An Introductory Grammar*, 2nd ed.

Page H. Kelley, Terry L. Burden, and Timothy G. Crawford, *A Handbook to "Biblical Hebrew: An Introductory Grammar,"* 2nd ed.

William Sanford Lasor, *Handbook of Biblical Hebrew*

Daily Scriptures

365 Readings in Hebrew, Greek, and Latin

Jacob N. Cerone and Matthew C. Fisher

William B. Eerdmans Publishing Company
Grand Rapids, Michigan

Wm. B. Eerdmans Publishing Co.
4035 Park East Court SE, Grand Rapids, Michigan 49546
www.eerdmans.com

Published 2021
Printed in the United States of America

27 26 25 24 23 22 21   1 2 3 4 5 6 7

ISBN 978-0-8028-7893-9

Library of Congress Cataloging-in-Publication Data

Names: Cerone, Jacob N. (Jacob Nathaniel), 1985– compiler. | Fisher, Matthew C., 1966– compiler.
Title: Daily scriptures : 365 readings in Hebrew, Greek, & Latin / Jacob N. Cerone and Matthew C. Fisher.
Other titles: Bible. Selections. Hebrew.
Description: Grand Rapids, Michigan : William B. Eerdmans Publishing Company, [2021] | Includes bibliographical references and index. | Summary: "A collection of daily Bible readings in Hebrew, Greek, and Latin with lexical aids, intended for use both as a devotional and as a way of maintaining knowledge of biblical languages"—Provided by publisher.
Identifiers: LCCN 2021016621 | ISBN 9780802878939 (hardcover)
Classification: LCC BS389 .C47 2021 | DDC 242/.2—dc23
LC record available at https://lccn.loc.gov/2021016621

For all students of the ancient languages

נָבִ֨יא מִקִּרְבְּךָ֤ מֵאַחֶ֙יךָ֙ כָּמֹ֔נִי יָקִ֥ים לְךָ֖ יְהוָ֣ה אֱלֹהֶ֑יךָ אֵלָ֖יו
תִּשְׁמָעֽוּן׃

Deuteronomy 18:15

Εἶπεν δὲ πρὸς αὐτούς· οὗτοι οἱ λόγοι μου οὓς ἐλάλησα πρὸς ὑμᾶς ἔτι ὢν σὺν ὑμῖν, ὅτι δεῖ πληρωθῆναι πάντα τὰ γεγραμμένα ἐν τῷ νόμῳ Μωϋσέως καὶ τοῖς προφήταις καὶ ψαλμοῖς περὶ ἐμοῦ.

Luke 24:44

et dixit ad eos haec sunt verba quae locutus sum ad vos cum adhuc essem vobiscum quoniam necesse est impleri omnia quae scripta sunt in lege Mosi et prophetis et psalmis de me.

Luke 24:44

Contents

Preface

A common thread woven throughout my studies has been the biblical languages. When I was a senior in high school, I started learning the Greek alphabet and some basic vocabulary. I was hooked. This was not because I had a natural talent for languages. I did not. What little I know I have fought for through persistent study, numerous courses, and a commitment to share what I have learned with others. I was hooked because I was convinced that it was necessary to study the biblical texts in their original languages because it would be the foundation for all further biblical studies and provide a deeper appreciation for the beauty and complexity of the original texts. During the first semester of Greek in my pastoral studies program, I was required to purchase a copy of the Nestle-Aland *Novum Testamentum*. Weeks later, I purchased the Rahlfs-Hanhart edition of the Septuagint along with the Latin *Vulgata* and the *Biblia Hebraica Stuttgartensia*. Never mind that, at the time, I could barely read the word λόγος, had never taken a lesson in Latin, and could not recognize the strange symbols in the *BHS*. I simply knew that I *needed* to be able to read these texts and these languages. As the years passed, Greek professors, like Michael Vanlaningham, Herbert Bateman, Scott Kellum, and especially David Alan Black, Hebrew professors, like Tim Sigler, Tracy McKenzie, and Heath Thomas, and Latin instructors, like Fred Williams and David Alan Black, cultivated my love of the languages and my love of both the Old and New Testaments. In fact, at the conclusion of my MDiv program, I could not decide whether I wanted to continue in Old Testament or New Testament studies. Instead of deciding, I enrolled in the New Testament department as a ThM student, performing a comparative discourse analysis between the Masoretic and Septuagint texts of Jonah. My ThM coursework consisted of New

Testament and Old Testament courses, which helped keep the relationship between the two Testaments constantly in mind, and my professors graciously permitted me the leeway to translate Greek, Latin, or Hebrew texts related to our studies in lieu of final papers. Professors like Black, McKenzie, and Thomas constantly reiterated the slogan: If you aren't using the languages, you're losing them.

However, learning and maintaining a language is no easy task. It requires discipline, convenient (even portable) access to texts, lexica, and a reading plan to keep you interested, engaged, and focused instead of floating aimlessly from book to book, passage to passage. The aim of this volume is to provide precisely these aids. We have carefully selected Hebrew, Greek, and Latin texts and arranged them within a salvation-historical framework, walking you through the biblical story from creation to God's culminating rule over all he has made. Contextual glosses are provided for infrequent vocabulary, and in some cases, translation or context aids are given in the footnotes to help orient you to better understand the material. The goal for this book is to provide a convenient, self-contained volume that helps readers keep up with their languages on a daily basis and simultaneously feed themselves spiritually on the whole counsel of God.

The conception for this book can only be described as providential. While conducting research for my doctoral dissertation in the theological library of the Friedrich Alexander University in Erlangen-Nuremberg, I stumbled upon a box of books that was being given away. Therein I found a volume of *Die Losungen 2011: Ursprachen*. Each year, the Evangelischen Brüder-Unität publishes a collection of Old Testament and New Testament readings for each day of the year. Although most editions available within the evangelische Kirche are printed in German, this edition was printed in the original languages. On the front cover, in Hebrew, were the words בְּרֵאשִׁית בָּרָא אֱלֹהִים ("in the beginning God created"), and below them in Greek were the words Ἐν ἀρχῇ ἦν ὁ λόγος ("in the beginning was the Word"). At the time, I was unfamiliar with *Die Losungen*, and I excitedly flipped through the volume to see whether the pairings had been selected based upon the New Testament author's usage of Old Testament texts. I was disappointed to find that this was not the case. This disappointment, however, inspired me to create the volume I had hoped already existed: an original languages devotional reader that contains short, manageable readings from the Old Testament and New Testament, which have been selected and paired together because New Testament authors had in some way received, relied upon, alluded to, cited, or shared thematic material with the Old Testament passage with which it has been paired.

I am thankful to a number of people who have helped along the way. First, I am especially grateful for those professors who taught me Greek, Hebrew, and Latin. This volume is, in the end, a fruit of their labors, of their commitment to their students, and their love for their craft. In the early stages of this book's conception, it was nonnegotiable to include the Hebrew Old Testament, Greek Old Testament, and Greek New Testament. Initially, I resisted the idea of including Latin, but in the end, I am thankful for the prodding from Tavis Bohlinger, Rick Brannan, and Natan de Carvalho. Without their insistence, this volume would not have taken its current form. I am also thankful to my wife, Mary Beth, who listened to me talk about this volume for countless hours and helped me think of numerous pairings to help fill out certain categories that were lacking, especially in the Advent section. Additionally, I would like to thank the following people for the encouragement they offered along the way: Todd Scacewater, Michael McEwen, and especially Nathaniel Cooley, who offered helpful suggestions that have only improved the overall quality of the reader. I am also grateful to my father, Joseph Cerone, for his help proofreading the preface and introduction to this book. The team at Eerdmans also deserves mention. It has been a pleasure working with them, especially Trevor Thompson, Laurel Draper, and Justin Howell. Finally, I am eternally grateful to my coauthor Matt Fisher. Matt and I steadily combed through both Testaments, looking for and documenting parallels. He helped refine the system for categorizing and arranging the passages, and he ensured nothing remained in the book that should not be there. He adjusted without complaint as the project morphed several times throughout the process and stepped up when I decided, after much waffling and hesitation, to aim for a more ambitious deadline than previously planned. It has been nothing but a pleasure to work with him on this, in every way, collaborative project.

Jacob N. Cerone

I still remember many years ago how my curiosity about Scripture's interpretation of Scripture was particularly piqued one day while reading F. F. Bruce's little book on the development of Old Testament themes in the New Testament. Bruce briefly reminded this reader that the New Testament authors occasionally equate Jesus with YHWH in the Old Testament. Pausing on Jude 5, he explained how, on the most likely reading, Jude understood Jesus Christ to be "the Lord" in the Exodus-wandering narratives. I was hooked.

Since that time, especially in my lectures on biblical theology at Saint Petersburg Christian University (Russia), I have explored ways various New Testament authors use Old Testament texts, and also the broader question of the relationship between the Testaments, and my interest in the subject has only grown.

Therefore, when, about a year ago, my friend Jacob invited me to participate in a book he was pitching to Eerdmans, seeking to pair relevant Old Testament passages with corresponding ones in the New Testament, I was pretty quickly onboard. A few months later, in the spring of 2020, when the COVID-19 crisis began spreading across the planet, I found that I had some extra time on my hands to search out several hundred pairings.

The very process of selecting the pairings is edifying, for it not only causes the researcher to identify what kind (or kinds) of connection there may be between the two passages (e.g., linguistic, thematic, typological) but also forces him to ponder surrounding texts and the often layers of subtle interpretational strategies used by the New Testament author. I am in awe of how our great God and Savior has so arranged and intertwined the texts of the canon to form an ever-deepening and seemingly never-ending well of intrabiblical connections.

Years ago, when Jacob and I lived in the same American town and went to the same American church, I'm sure we never thought that one day we'd be collaborating on a book while living out our lives with our families in Germany and Russia. I am, therefore, very grateful for how God has providentially arranged our comings and goings, and grateful to Jacob for inviting me into this project of his.

Matt Fisher

Introduction

The texts of the Old Testament were the sacred Scriptures of the early Christian communities. Christ's incarnation, death, resurrection, and ascension did not abrogate or even diminish their relevance. They were and continued to be the Word of God for his people. Through them Christians understood and interpreted the Christ event. This is evident the moment we reflect upon the language of the New Testament authors, the persistent allusions to Old Testament events and texts, as well as their explicit citations of them. Through them Christians found God's work of redemption throughout history and his will for their lives. Even after the composition and circulation of at least some of Paul's epistles, early Christian communities continued preaching, teaching, and citing Old Testament texts as instructive for Christian life and practice. For example, 25 percent of 1 Clement—one of the earliest, noncanonical Christian texts—consists of citations from the Old Testament, not to mention countless echoes and allusions. Commenting on the Christianity of Rome during the composition of 1 Clement, Adolf von Harnack writes, "It is a religion of the book . . . its valuable contents are God's commandments . . . in which his essence and his will are made evident."[1] Churches and Christians today, however, often intentionally or unintentionally neglect the Old Testament, viewing it as antiquated, irrelevant, or even problematic. But as this little daily reader explicitly demonstrates, the New Testament is tethered to its Jewish, Old Testament roots. It shares the same hopes, expectations, and history.

1. Adolf von Harnack, *The Letter of the Roman Church to the Corinthian Church from the Era of Domitian*, ed. and trans. Jacob N. Cerone (Eugene, OR: Pickwick, 2021), 57.

Purpose

Daily Scriptures has been designed for readers of the ancient languages who wish to maintain and improve their ability to read Greek, Hebrew,[2] or Latin by providing daily, devotional selections that connect the New Testament and the Old Testament. Statistically infrequent vocabulary for each of these languages appears in footnotes, enabling a seamless reading experience, while also familiarizing readers with a broader Hebrew, Greek, and Latin vocabulary. Our goal and our purpose for this volume is to keep you in the languages, keep you fed in the word, and hopefully spark a desire to explore more deeply how the New Testament at its core relies upon the Old Testament Scriptures.

Pedagogical Notes

Many original language readers are organized by the difficulty of the selected passages, enabling you to gradually build from less demanding texts (both syntactically speaking, as well as with regard to the vocabulary used) to more complicated texts. Unfortunately, the conceptual framework of this reader (see Organization and Criteria of Selection) did not afford the opportunity to choose and arrange passages based upon their perceived level of difficulty. Instead, you will find a broad selection of passages from every genre of literature within the biblical corpus, which represents almost every single book within the Protestant Old Testament and New Testament canon.[3] The fact that such a broad selection of literature has been included and the constant shift between different contexts and styles might make translation difficult at times. It will no doubt challenge your abilities in these languages.

2. And in two instances, Aramaic.

3. Excluding deuterocanonical books (which do not have extant Hebrew manuscripts), books that have no representation in this volume include Nehemiah, Song of Songs, Lamentations, Zephaniah, Haggai, Titus, Philemon, and 2–3 John. For an overview of which biblical books have been included and their respective representation/distribution, see the Old Testament to New Testament and the New Testament to Old Testament indexes.

However, there are a number of features in this reader that should help aid in your translation of these passages! First, the passages chosen are relatively familiar for those with a foundational knowledge of biblical history. Second, the shared themes and content between the passages should provide you with enough context to aid in translation. Third, one of the unique aspects of this volume is the inclusion of three different languages: Hebrew, Greek, and Latin (four if we count the two Aramaic passages from Daniel). If a certain passage proves to be a tough nut to crack, let your strengths in one language compensate for your weaknesses in another. Although there will certainly be text-critical differences between the texts, using Greek to help translate Hebrew or Hebrew to aid in translating the Greek text will ultimately strengthen your abilities in each of these languages. The last source of help is found in what might seem for some the most unlikely of places: the Latin *Vulgata*. Since English borrows extensively from Latin, there will often be terms in the *Vulgata* that you will recognize and that will help in the translation of a difficult phrase or in the recognition of forgotten vocabulary.

Texts and Editions Used

The texts used with permission from the Deutsche Bibelgesellschaft for this volume are the *Biblia Hebraica Stuttgartensia* (*BHS*), the Rahlfs-Hanhart *Septuaginta* (LXX), the Nestle-Aland *Novum Testamentum Graece* 28th ed. (NA28), and the Weber-Gryson *Biblia Sacra: Vulgata*.

The selections for this reader have been limited in the main to one verse from the Old Testament and one verse from the New Testament for each daily reading. There are some exceptions to this general rule wherein partial verses have been included. In such cases, ellipses indicate the use of a partial verse. *Caveat lector:* Versification follows that of the original languages and not the English versions of the Bible. Where the LXX diverges from the *BHS*, which regularly occurs within the Psalms, note is made of the appropriate LXX reference within brackets.

Finally, the text as it appears in each of these editions remains unchanged with the exception of the text-critical notes, which have been removed, the shift of accent marks for the Greek texts based upon the new context in which they appear, and other inconsequential alterations. In the infrequent instances where text-critical information is needed because the printed text is unintelligible, an alternate reading or explanation has been provided in the footnotes with the abbreviation TC.

Organization and Criteria of Selection

Organization

Old Testament and New Testament passages have been arranged within a salvation-historical framework (e.g., creation, fall, primeval history, patriarchs, exodus, conquest, judges, monarchies). The running foot for each day's reading indicates the category to which it belongs. Interspersed within this framework are a few systematic-theological topics. For instance, following creation, we have included a selection of readings about God and his attributes; reflections on sin, its nature, and its destructive force in creation follow naturally from readings about the fall; and a selection of pairings on the Holy Spirit are slotted between the resurrection and the apostolic age. An overview of the entire volume is as follows:

1. Creation
2. God
3. The Fall
4. Sin
5. Revelation
6. Primeval History
7. The Patriarchs
8. The Exodus
9. Wilderness Wanderings
10. Mosaic Covenant
11. Conquest
12. Judges
13. Monarchies

14. Exile
15. John the Baptist
16. Jesus's Infancy
17. Fulfillment of Prophecy
18. Jesus's Baptism and Temptation
19. Jesus and the Law
20. Jesus's Ministry
21. Opposition to Jesus
22. The Passion and Death of Jesus
23. Resurrection
24. Holy Spirit
25. Apostolic Age
26. Repentance
27. The Church
28. The Christian Life
29. The Last Days
30. Judgment
31. New Heavens and New Earth
32. Advent
33. God's Reign

It is important to note one prolonged interruption to the salvation-historical arrangement: December 1st until the 25th have readings related to Advent and Christmas. Since the timing of Advent remains the same from year to year, it has provided us with a fixed point in the church calendar around which we could plan a group of readings. Furthermore, it seemed altogether gloomy to reflect upon the last days and judgment during the Christmas season. With Christmas-related readings, however, we can celebrate the coming and arrival of the incarnate Christ during this joyous season and conclude the year with reflections on God's reign over all of creation on his eternal throne.

One additional feature concerning organization should be noted here. There are a handful of occasions where multiple verses should be read together across the span of multiple days. For instance, there are ten days in December in which Mary's ten-verse prayer (Magnificat) has been paired with Hannah's ten-verse prayer in 1 Samuel. In such instances, not every verse paired together will reflect a similar thought. Instead, the passages as a whole are related together and should be treated as a unit in and of themselves. These passages can be identified by the symbol of a chain link (🔗). In some instances, only the Old Testament or only the New Testament texts across multiple days will be chained together, and in other places, both Old Testament and New Testament texts will be chained together. Our hope is that this additional feature will aid you as you read the passages and seek out their relation to one another.

Process and Criteria for Selecting Pairings

Parallel passages between the Old and New Testaments were gathered from a number of sources. Among them were collections of parallels from personal studies and years of teaching, cross-references from the NA28, an edition of the NIV with Zondervan's "Center Column Reference System" (1984), Beale and Carson's *Commentary on the New Testament Use of the Old Testament*,[4] and Logos Bible Software's interactive "New Testament Use of the Old Testament." Potential parallels were recorded, summarized, and tagged according to their thematic material within a spreadsheet. Having gathered hundreds of passages, we then began structuring the volume salvation-historically and hand selecting the best options for the various topics covered.

Our goal in choosing pairings was to select passages from the New Testament that recollected stories, events, or narratives from the Old Testament. Allusions were preferred over direct citations, since a citation would mean that the same text would be repeated four times (Hebrew Bible, Septuagint, Greek New Testament, and *Vulgata*). Although citations were generally avoided, they were not entirely excluded from the volume. For example, while Rom 3:13 is very similar to its citation of

4. G. K. Beale and D. A. Carson, eds., *Commentary on the New Testament Use of the Old Testament* (Grand Rapids: Baker Academic; Nottingham: Apollos, 2007).

Ps 5:10, there are differences between the two texts, because Paul drew from multiple sources. Additionally, in the section "Jesus and the Law," there are a number of instances where Jesus cites an Old Testament prohibition and then interprets it. To avoid reproducing the same text four times, however, Jesus's citation of a law (e.g., "do not murder") is drawn directly from the Old Testament and his response to that law ("but I say to you") from the New Testament text. Finally, there are a few instances, like Acts 2:17 and its word-for-word citation of Joel 3:1, that have been included to help fill out certain sections of the reader.

Sometimes pairings do not reflect literary dependence but instead center on thematically related material. One example would be the pairing of Deut 7:9 with 1 Cor 10:13. The common point of intersection here is God's faithfulness and secondarily the necessity of following God's laws. Another example is God's statement in Jer 7:25 that he spoke to the fathers from the time they went out of Egypt up to Jeremiah's day through his prophets, and the New Testament text of Heb 1:1, where the author claims that God spoke to the fathers many times and in many ways through the prophets. Although there is no literary dependency, the texts share similar thematic content.

It is also important to note that some pairings have been made on the basis of traditional interpretations of a passage, even when those interpretations might not withstand the scrutiny of modern critical scholarship. One such example is the pairing of Isa 14:12 with Luke 10:18. Often, Isa 14:12 has been interpreted as a reference to the fall of Satan (the morning star) from heaven. Another example can be found in the early church's interpretation of Ps 87:6 [LXX 86:6] as a prophetic reference to the census Quirinius takes prior to Jesus's birth in Luke 2:1.

Throughout this reader, we attempted to confirm that the parallels we selected were included within the NA28 cross-references, commentary discussions, or the *Commentary on the New Testament's Use of the Old Testament*. By no means does this ensure the certainty of literary dependence. On the contrary, there exists at the very least a perceived connection between these passages. We encourage you to pick up both Testaments and investigate the broader contexts in which each of these pairings occurs. The daily selection should function as a springboard for deeper investigation in the New Testament's profound dependence upon the ever-relevant Old Testament.

Vocabulary and Morphological Aids

Criteria

The footnote section of this reader provides glosses for all words that occur one hundred times or less in the Hebrew Bible, one hundred times or less in the Greek Old Testament, thirty times or less in the Greek New Testament, and thirty times or less in the Latin *Vulgata*. For the select few Aramaic passages, glosses have been provided for all words, which will hopefully make them accessible even to readers with no knowledge of Aramaic. Since verbs can undergo radical changes throughout their respective stems/principal parts, we have also provided parsing information in addition to the glosses. Accordance Bible software functioned as the main search engine for determining the frequency of words in each passage.

In order to keep the size of the volume manageable, nouns are glossed only once per reading. If you do not recognize a word and there is no footnote, chances are you have already encountered that word on that day. Verbs receive parsing information and glosses for each occurrence unless the same inflection of that verb already has a note. We have also provided notes for proper nouns occurring under the stated thresholds to ensure that readers are not left scratching their heads, trying to translate a word that is in reality a proper noun.

Abbreviations

Although we attempted to use few and easily recognizable abbreviations, it is still helpful to provide a list of all abbreviations used within the footnotes:

1	first person	ind.	indicative
2	second person	inf.	infinitive
3	third person	juss.	jussive
a.	accusative	m.	masculine
abl.	ablative	mid.	middle
abs.	absolute	n.	neuter
act.	active	niph.	niphal
aor.	aorist	nom.	nominative
c.	common	opt.	optative
CH	Context Help	p.	plural
coh.	cohortative	PA	Pairing Aid
cons.	construct	pass.	passive
d.	dative	perf.	perfect
f.	feminine	pluperf.	pluperfect
fut.	future	pres.	present
futperf.	future perfect	ptcp.	participle
g.	genitive	s.	singular
ger.	gerund	sub.	subjunctive
hiph.	hiphil	TC	Textual Criticism
hoph.	hophal	TH	Translation Help
impf.	imperfect	v.	vocative
impv.	imperative	wcons.	waw consecutive

Glosses

We have relied upon the following lexica for the glosses provided within this reader. For Hebrew we used *HALOT*, BDB, and *DCH*;[5] for Greek

5. *HALOT* (Ludwig Koehler et al., *The Hebrew and Aramaic Lexicon of the Old Testament* [Leiden: Brill, 1994–2000]); BDB (Francis Brown, Samuel Rolles Driver, and Charles Augustus Briggs, *Enhanced Brown-Driver-Briggs Hebrew and English Lexicon* [Oxford: Clarendon, 1977]); and *DCH* (David J. A. Clines, ed., *The Dictionary of Classical Hebrew* [Sheffield: Sheffield Academic; Sheffield Phoenix, 1993–2011]).

we used BDAG, LSJ, Muraoka, and LEH;[6] and for Latin we used *OLD*, LSLD, and *CLDG*.[7]

The glosses provided within the footnotes are contextual. This means that the meaning given is dependent upon the specific context in which it occurs and does not represent the full semantic range of that word's meaning. Providing contextual glosses has both disadvantages and advantages. Learning a contextual gloss might give you the impression that you know the meaning of that word in all contexts, when in reality this is far from the truth. Lexica are indispensable resources for discovering the broader meaning of a word and how it can be used in various contexts. Nevertheless, the advantage of providing a contextual gloss in a reader such as this outweighs the disadvantages. Providing a noncontextual gloss defeats the aim of the reader: to read and comprehend more without the deflating and time-consuming hassle of constantly looking up unfamiliar words in a lexicon.

Conclusion

Our hope for this volume is that you grow in your knowledge and understanding of the Scriptures and of the ancient languages. We look forward to hearing about your experiences with it, as well as any ways it can be improved for future editions.

6. BDAG (Frederick William Danker et al., *A Greek-English Lexicon of the New Testament and Other Early Christian Literature* [Chicago: University of Chicago Press, 2000]); LSJ (Henry George Liddell et al., *A Greek-English Lexicon* [Oxford: Clarendon, 1996]); Muraoka (Takamitsu Muraoka, *A Greek-English Lexicon of the Septuagint* [Leuven: Peeters, 2009]); and LEH (Johan Lust, Erik Eynikel, and Katrin Hauspie, *A Greek-English Lexicon of the Septuagint*, rev. ed. [Deutsche Bibelgesellschaft: Stuttgart, 2003]).

7. *OLD* (P. G. W. Glare, *Oxford Latin Dictionary* [Oxford: Oxford University Press, 1968]); LSLD (Charlton T. Lewis and Charles Short, *Harper's Latin Dictionary* [New York: Harper & Brothers; Oxford: Clarendon, 1891]); and *CLDG* (*Collins Latin Dictionary Plus Grammar* [Glasgow: HarperCollins, 1997]).

Daily Readings

January 1

Genesis 1:1

בְּרֵאשִׁ֖ית[1] בָּרָ֣א[2] אֱלֹהִ֑ים אֵ֥ת הַשָּׁמַ֖יִם וְאֵ֥ת הָאָֽרֶץ׃

Ἐν ἀρχῇ ἐποίησεν ὁ θεὸς τὸν οὐρανὸν καὶ τὴν γῆν.

John 1:1

Ἐν ἀρχῇ ἦν ὁ λόγος, καὶ ὁ λόγος ἦν πρὸς τὸν θεόν, καὶ θεὸς ἦν ὁ λόγος.

in principio erat Verbum et Verbum erat apud Deum et Deus erat Verbum.

1. רֵאשִׁית, *beginning*
2. בָּרָא, qal perf. 3 m. s., *create*

January 2

Psalm 33:6 [LXX 32:6]

בִּדְבַ֣ר יְ֭הוָה שָׁמַ֣יִם נַעֲשׂ֑וּ וּבְר֥וּחַ פִּ֝֗יו כָּל־צְבָאָֽם׃

τῷ λόγῳ τοῦ κυρίου οἱ οὐρανοὶ ἐστερεώθησαν[1] καὶ τῷ πνεύματι τοῦ στόματος αὐτοῦ πᾶσα ἡ δύναμις[2] αὐτῶν·

Hebrews 11:3

Πίστει νοοῦμεν[3] κατηρτίσθαι[4] τοὺς αἰῶνας ῥήματι θεοῦ, εἰς τὸ μὴ ἐκ φαινομένων τὸ βλεπόμενον γεγονέναι.

fide intellegimus aptata[5] esse saecula verbo Dei ut ex invisibilibus[6] visibilia[7] fierent.

1. στερεόω, aor. pass. ind. 3 p., *make strong, firm*
2. δύναμις, *power;* here *host*
3. νοέω, pres. act. ind. 1 p., *understand*
4. καταρτίζω, perf. pass. inf., *create, strengthen*
5. apto, perf. pass. inf., *make ready, fit*
6. invisibilis, *invisible*
7. visibilis, *visible*

January 3

Genesis 1:3

וַיֹּ֥אמֶר אֱלֹהִ֖ים יְהִ֣י א֑וֹר וַֽיְהִי־אֽוֹר׃

καὶ εἶπεν ὁ θεός γενηθήτω φῶς. καὶ ἐγένετο φῶς.

2 Corinthians 4:6

ὅτι ὁ θεὸς ὁ εἰπών· ἐκ σκότους[1] φῶς λάμψει,[2] ὃς ἔλαμψεν[3] ἐν ταῖς καρδίαις ἡμῶν πρὸς φωτισμὸν[4] τῆς γνώσεως[5] τῆς δόξης τοῦ θεοῦ ἐν προσώπῳ [Ἰησοῦ] Χριστοῦ.

quoniam Deus, qui dixit de tenebris lucem splendescere[6] qui inluxit[7] in cordibus nostris ad inluminationem[8] scientiae claritatis[9] Dei in facie Christi Iesu.

1. σκότος, *darkness*
2. λάμπω, fut. act. ind. 3 s., *shine*
3. λάμπω, aor. act. ind. 3 s., *shine*
4. φωτισμός, *light, illumination*
5. γνῶσις, *knowledge*
6. splendesco, pres. act. inf., *become bright, shining*
7. inluceo, perf. act. ind. 3 s., *illuminate, shine*
8. inluminatio, *brightness, light, illumination*
9. claritas, *brightness, splendor, glory*

January 4

Genesis 1:27

וַיִּבְרָא[1] אֱלֹהִים׀ אֶת־הָאָדָם בְּצַלְמוֹ[2] בְּצֶלֶם אֱלֹהִים
בָּרָא[3] אֹתוֹ זָכָר[4] וּנְקֵבָה[5] בָּרָא אֹתָם׃

καὶ ἐποίησεν ὁ θεὸς τὸν ἄνθρωπον, κατʼ εἰκόνα[6] θεοῦ ἐποίησεν αὐτόν, ἄρσεν[7] καὶ θῆλυ[8] ἐποίησεν αὐτούς.

Acts 17:29

γένος[9] οὖν ὑπάρχοντες τοῦ θεοῦ οὐκ ὀφείλομεν νομίζειν[10] χρυσῷ[11] ἢ ἀργύρῳ[12] ἢ λίθῳ, χαράγματι[13] τέχνης[14] καὶ ἐνθυμήσεως[15] ἀνθρώπου, τὸ θεῖον[16] εἶναι ὅμοιον.

genus ergo cum simus Dei non debemus aestimare auro aut argento aut lapidi sculpturae[17] artis[18] et cogitationis hominis divinum[19] esse simile.

1. בָּרָא, qal wcons. 3 m. s., *create*
2. צֶלֶם, *image*
3. בָּרָא, qal perf. 3 m. s., *create*
4. זָכָר, *male*
5. נְקֵבָה, *female*
6. εἰκών, *image, likeness*
7. ἄρσην, *male*
8. θῆλυς, *female*
9. γένος, *descendant*
10. νομίζω, pres. act. inf., *think, consider*
11. χρυσός, *gold*
12. ἄργυρος, *silver*
13. χάραγμα, *thing formed, image*
14. τέχνη, *skill, trade*
15. ἐνθύμησις, *thought, reflection, idea*
16. θεῖος, *divine*
17. sculptura, *carving, sculpture*
18. ars, *skill, craft*
19. divinus, *divine*

January 5

Genesis 1:31

וַיַּ֤רְא אֱלֹהִים֙ אֶת־כָּל־אֲשֶׁ֣ר עָשָׂ֔ה וְהִנֵּה־ט֖וֹב מְאֹ֑ד
וַֽיְהִי־עֶ֥רֶב וַֽיְהִי־בֹ֖קֶר י֥וֹם הַשִּׁשִּֽׁי׃[1]

καὶ εἶδεν ὁ θεὸς τὰ πάντα, ὅσα ἐποίησεν, καὶ ἰδοὺ καλὰ λίαν.[2] καὶ ἐγένετο ἑσπέρα καὶ ἐγένετο πρωί, ἡμέρα ἕκτη.[3]

1 Timothy 4:4

ὅτι πᾶν κτίσμα[4] θεοῦ καλὸν καὶ οὐδὲν ἀπόβλητον[5] μετὰ εὐχαριστίας[6] λαμβανόμενον.

quia omnis creatura[7] Dei bona et nihil reiciendum[8] quod cum gratiarum actione[9] percipitur.[10]

1. שִׁשִּׁי, *sixth*
2. λίαν, *very, exceedingly*
3. ἕκτος, *sixth*
4. κτίσμα, *creature, that which is created*
5. ἀπόβλητος, *rejected*
6. εὐχαριστία, *thanksgiving*
7. creatura, *creature, creation*
8. reicio, ger. pass. n. nom. s., *reject, cast away*
9. actio, *action*; actio + gratia = *thanksgiving*
10. percipio, pres. pass. ind. 3 s., *receive*

January 6

Psalm 19:2 [LXX 18:2]

הַשָּׁמַיִם מְסַפְּרִים כְּבוֹד־אֵל וּמַעֲשֵׂה יָדָיו מַגִּיד הָרָקִיעַ׃[1]

Οἱ οὐρανοὶ διηγοῦνται[2] δόξαν θεοῦ, ποίησιν[3] δὲ χειρῶν αὐτοῦ ἀναγγέλλει τὸ στερέωμα.[4]

Romans 1:20

τὰ γὰρ ἀόρατα[5] αὐτοῦ ἀπὸ κτίσεως[6] κόσμου τοῖς ποιήμασιν[7] νοούμενα[8] καθορᾶται,[9] ἥ τε ἀΐδιος[10] αὐτοῦ δύναμις καὶ θειότης,[11] εἰς τὸ εἶναι αὐτοὺς ἀναπολογήτους.[12]

invisibilia[13] enim ipsius a creatura[14] mundi per ea quae facta sunt intellecta conspiciuntur[15] sempiterna[16] quoque[17] eius virtus et divinitas[18] ut sint inexcusabiles.[19]

1. רָקִיעַ, *expanse*

2. διηγέομαι, pres. mid. ind. 3 p., *tell, explain*

3. ποίησις, *work, creation*

4. στερέωμα, *firmament*

5. ἀόρατος, *invisible, unseen [attributes]*

6. κτίσις, *creation*

7. ποίημα, *created thing, that which is made*

8. νοέω, pres. mid. ptcp. n. nom. p., *understand*

9. καθοράω, pres. pass. ind. 3 s., *observe, perceive*

10. ἀΐδιος, *eternal*

11. θειότης, *divine nature*

12. ἀναπολόγητος, *without excuse*

13. invisibilis, *invisible*

14. creatura, *creation, creature*

15. conspicio, pres. pass. ind. 3 p., *see clearly*

16. sempiternus, *everlasting, eternal*

17. quoque, *also, too*

18. divinitas, *divinity.* **19.** inexcusabilis, *inexcusable*

January 7

Genesis 2:7

וַיִּיצֶר֩[1] יְהוָ֨ה אֱלֹהִ֜ים אֶת־הָֽאָדָ֗ם עָפָר֙ מִן־הָ֣אֲדָמָ֔ה
וַיִּפַּ֥ח[2] בְּאַפָּ֖יו נִשְׁמַ֣ת[3] חַיִּ֑ים וַֽיְהִ֥י הָֽאָדָ֖ם לְנֶ֥פֶשׁ חַיָּֽה׃

καὶ ἔπλασεν[4] ὁ θεὸς τὸν ἄνθρωπον χοῦν[5] ἀπὸ τῆς γῆς καὶ ἐνεφύσησεν[6] εἰς τὸ πρόσωπον αὐτοῦ πνοὴν[7] ζωῆς, καὶ ἐγένετο ὁ ἄνθρωπος εἰς ψυχὴν ζῶσαν.

1 Corinthians 15:47

ὁ πρῶτος ἄνθρωπος ἐκ γῆς χοϊκός,[8] ὁ δεύτερος ἄνθρωπος ἐξ οὐρανοῦ.

primus homo de terra terrenus[9] secundus homo de caelo caelestis.

1. יָצַר, qal wcons. 3 m. s., *form, fashion, create*
2. נָפַח, qal wcons. 3 m. s., *blow*
3. נְשָׁמָה, *breath*
4. πλάσσω, aor. act. ind. 3 s., *form, mold*
5. χοῦς, *soil, dust*
6. ἐμφυσάω, aor. act. ind. 3 s., *blow, breathe on*
7. πνοή, *breath, wind*
8. χοϊκός, *earth, dust*
9. terrenus, *earth, dust*

January 8

Genesis 2:2

וַיְכַ֤ל אֱלֹהִים֙ בַּיֹּ֣ום הַשְּׁבִיעִ֔י[1] מְלַאכְתֹּ֖ו אֲשֶׁ֣ר עָשָׂ֑ה
וַיִּשְׁבֹּת֙[2] בַּיֹּ֣ום הַשְּׁבִיעִ֔י מִכָּל־מְלַאכְתֹּ֖ו אֲשֶׁ֥ר עָשָֽׂה׃

καὶ συνετέλεσεν ὁ θεὸς ἐν τῇ ἡμέρᾳ τῇ ἕκτῃ[3] τὰ ἔργα αὐτοῦ, ἃ ἐποίησεν, καὶ κατέπαυσεν[4] τῇ ἡμέρᾳ τῇ ἑβδόμῃ ἀπὸ πάντων τῶν ἔργων αὐτοῦ, ὧν ἐποίησεν.

Hebrews 4:10

ὁ γὰρ εἰσελθὼν εἰς τὴν κατάπαυσιν[5] αὐτοῦ[6] καὶ αὐτὸς κατέπαυσεν ἀπὸ τῶν ἔργων αὐτοῦ ὥσπερ ἀπὸ τῶν ἰδίων ὁ θεός.

qui enim ingressus est in requiem eius[7] etiam ipse requievit ab operibus suis sicut a suis Deus.

1. שְׁבִיעִי, *seventh*
2. שָׁבַת, qal wcons. 3 m. s., *rest, cease*
3. ἕκτος, *sixth*
4. καταπαύω, aor. act. ind. 3 s., *cease*
5. κατάπαυσις, *place of rest*
6. CH: God is the referent of αὐτοῦ.
7. CH: God is the referent of eius.

January 9

Genesis 2:9

וַיַּצְמַ֞ח[1] יְהוָ֤ה אֱלֹהִים֙ מִן־הָ֣אֲדָמָ֔ה כָּל־עֵ֛ץ נֶחְמָ֥ד[2]
לְמַרְאֶ֖ה וְט֣וֹב לְמַאֲכָ֑ל[3] וְעֵ֤ץ הַֽחַיִּים֙ בְּת֣וֹךְ הַגָּ֔ן[4] וְעֵ֕ץ
הַדַּ֖עַת[5] ט֥וֹב וָרָֽע׃

καὶ ἐξανέτειλεν[6] ὁ θεὸς ἔτι ἐκ τῆς γῆς πᾶν ξύλον[7] ὡραῖον[8] εἰς ὅρασιν καὶ καλὸν εἰς βρῶσιν[9] καὶ τὸ ξύλον τῆς ζωῆς ἐν μέσῳ τῷ παραδείσῳ[10] καὶ τὸ ξύλον τοῦ εἰδέναι γνωστὸν[11] καλοῦ καὶ πονηροῦ.

Revelation 2:7

Ὁ ἔχων οὖς ἀκουσάτω τί τὸ πνεῦμα λέγει ταῖς ἐκκλησίαις. Τῷ νικῶντι[12] δώσω αὐτῷ φαγεῖν ἐκ τοῦ ξύλου τῆς ζωῆς, ὅ ἐστιν ἐν τῷ παραδείσῳ τοῦ θεοῦ.

qui habet aurem audiat quid Spiritus dicat ecclesiis vincenti[13] dabo ei edere[14] de ligno[15] vitae quod est in paradiso[16] Dei mei.

1. צָמַח, hiph. wcons. 3 m. s., *spring up, sprout*

2. חָמַד, niph. ptcp. m. s. abs., *desire, take pleasure in*

3. מַאֲכָל, *food*

4. גַּן, *garden*

5. דַּ֫עַת, *knowledge*

6. ἐξανατέλλω, aor. act. ind. 3 s., *cause to spring up*

7. ξύλον, *tree*

8. ὡραῖος, *beautiful*

9. βρῶσις, *food*

10. παράδεισος, *garden*

11. γνωστός, *knowledge*

12. νικάω, pres. act. ptcp. m. d. s., *conquer*

13. vinco, pres. act. ptcp. m. d. s., *conquer, overcome*

14. edo, pres. act. inf., *eat*

15. lignum, *tree*

16. paradisus, *paradise*

January 10

1. הֹ֗וי, *woe*
2. רִיב, qal ptcp. m. s. abs., *strive, contend*
3. יָצַר, qal ptcp. m. s. cons., *form*
4. חֶ֫רֶשׂ, *earthenware*
5. חֹ֫מֶר, *clay*
6. יָצַר, qal ptcp. m. s. cons., *form*
7. פֹּ֫עַל, *work*
8. ποῖος, *what kind of?*
9. κατασκευάζω, aor. act. ind. 1 s., *create, form*
10. πηλός, *clay*
11. κεραμεύς, *potter*
12. ἀροτριάω, pres. act. ptcp. m. nom. s., *plow*
13. ἀροτριάω, fut. act. ind. 3 s., *plow*
14. ὦ, *woe*
15. μενοῦνγε, *but, rather*
16. ἀνταποκρίνομαι, pres. mid. ptcp. m. nom. s., *answer back, talk back*
17. πλάσμα, *what is formed*
18. πλάσσω, aor. act. ptcp. m. d. s., *to form*
19. o, *oh, woe*

Isaiah 45:9

הֹ֗וי[1] רָ֚ב[2] אֶת־יֹ֣צְרֹ֔ו[3] חֶ֖רֶשׂ[4] אֶת־חַרְשֵׂ֣י אֲדָמָ֑ה הֲיֹאמַ֨ר
חֹ֤מֶר[5] לְיֹֽצְרֹו֙[6] מַֽה־תַּעֲשֶׂ֔ה וּפָעָלְךָ֖[7] אֵין־יָדַ֥יִם לֹֽו׃

Ποῖον[8] βέλτιον κατεσκεύασα[9] ὡς πηλὸν[10] κεραμέως;[11] μὴ ὁ ἀροτριῶν[12] ἀροτριάσει[13] τὴν γῆν ὅλην τὴν ἡμέραν; μὴ ἐρεῖ ὁ πηλὸς τῷ κεραμεῖ Τί ποιεῖς, ὅτι οὐκ ἐργάζῃ οὐδὲ ἔχεις χεῖρας;

Romans 9:20

ὦ[14] ἄνθρωπε, μενοῦνγε[15] σὺ τίς εἶ ὁ ἀνταποκρινόμενος[16] τῷ θεῷ; *μὴ ἐρεῖ τὸ πλάσμα*[17] *τῷ πλάσαντι·*[18] *τί με ἐποίησας* οὕτως;

o[19] homo tu quis es qui respondeas Deo numquid dicit figmentum[20] ei qui se finxit[21] quid me fecisti sic.

20. figmentum, *anything made or formed.* **21.** fingo, perf. act. ind. 3 s., *form, fashion*

January 11

Exodus 3:14

וַיֹּ֤אמֶר אֱלֹהִים֙ אֶל־מֹשֶׁ֔ה אֶֽהְיֶ֖ה אֲשֶׁ֣ר אֶֽהְיֶ֑ה וַיֹּ֗אמֶר
כֹּ֤ה תֹאמַר֙ לִבְנֵ֣י יִשְׂרָאֵ֔ל אֶֽהְיֶ֖ה שְׁלָחַ֥נִי אֲלֵיכֶֽם׃

καὶ εἶπεν ὁ θεὸς πρὸς Μωυσῆν Ἐγώ εἰμι ὁ ὤν·
καὶ εἶπεν Οὕτως ἐρεῖς τοῖς υἱοῖς Ισραηλ Ὁ ὢν
ἀπέσταλκέν με πρὸς ὑμᾶς.

Revelation 1:8

Ἐγώ εἰμι τὸ ἄλφα[1] καὶ τὸ ὦ,[2] λέγει κύριος ὁ θεός,
ὁ ὢν καὶ ὁ ἦν καὶ ὁ ἐρχόμενος, ὁ παντοκράτωρ.[3]

ego sum Alpha[4] et Omega[5] principium[6] et finis
dicit Dominus Deus qui est et qui erat et qui
venturus est Omnipotens.[7]

1. ἄλφα, *Alpha*
2. ὦ, *Omega*
3. παντοκράτωρ, *almighty*
4. alpha, *Alpha*
5. omega, *Omega*
6. principium, *beginning*
7. omnipotens, *almighty*

January 12

Psalm 86:9 [LXX 85:9]

כָּל־גּוֹיִ֤ם ׀ אֲשֶׁ֥ר עָשִׂ֗יתָ יָב֤וֹאוּ ׀ וְיִשְׁתַּחֲו֣וּ לְפָנֶ֣יךָ אֲדֹנָ֑י
וִֽיכַבְּד֖וּ לִשְׁמֶֽךָ׃

πάντα τὰ ἔθνη, ὅσα ἐποίησας, ἥξουσιν[1] καὶ προσκυνήσουσιν ἐνώπιόν σου, κύριε, καὶ δοξάσουσιν τὸ ὄνομά σου.

Revelation 15:4

τίς οὐ μὴ φοβηθῇ, κύριε, καὶ δοξάσει τὸ ὄνομά σου; ὅτι μόνος ὅσιος,[2] ὅτι *πάντα τὰ ἔθνη ἥξουσιν καὶ προσκυνήσουσιν ἐνώπιόν σου,* ὅτι τὰ δικαιώματά[3] σου ἐφανερώθησαν.

quis non timebit Domine et magnificabit[4] nomen tuum quia solus pius[5] quoniam omnes gentes venient et adorabunt in conspectu tuo quoniam iudicia tua manifestata sunt.

1. ἥκω, fut. act. ind. 3 p., *come, be present*
2. ὅσιος, *holy*
3. δικαίωμα, *righteous act*
4. magnifico, fut. act. ind. 3 s., *magnify, make great*
5. pius, *holy*

January 13

Isaiah 6:3

וְקָרָא זֶה[1] אֶל־זֶה וְאָמַר קָדוֹשׁ ׀ קָדוֹשׁ קָדוֹשׁ יְהוָה
צְבָאוֹת מְלֹא[2] כָל־הָאָרֶץ כְּבוֹדוֹ׃

καὶ ἐκέκραγον ἕτερος[3] πρὸς τὸν ἕτερον καὶ ἔλεγον Ἅγιος ἅγιος ἅγιος κύριος σαβαωθ,[4] πλήρης πᾶσα ἡ γῆ τῆς δόξης αὐτοῦ.

Revelation 4:8

καὶ τὰ τέσσαρα ζῷα,[5] ἓν καθ᾽ ἓν αὐτῶν ἔχων ἀνὰ[6] πτέρυγας[7] ἕξ,[8] κυκλόθεν[9] καὶ ἔσωθεν[10] γέμουσιν[11] ὀφθαλμῶν, καὶ ἀνάπαυσιν[12] οὐκ ἔχουσιν ἡμέρας καὶ νυκτὸς λέγοντες· ἅγιος ἅγιος *ἅγιος κύριος ὁ θεὸς ὁ παντοκράτωρ,*[13] ὁ ἦν καὶ ὁ ὢν καὶ ὁ ἐρχόμενος.

et quattuor animalia[14] singula eorum habebant alas[15] senas[16] et in circuitu[17] et intus[18] plena sunt oculis et requiem[19] non habent die et nocte dicentia sanctus sanctus sanctus Dominus Deus omnipotens[20] qui erat et qui est et qui venturus est.

1. CH: The referent of זֶה here and following are the seraphim.
2. מָלֵא, *full*
3. CH: The referent of ἕτερος here and following are the seraphim.
4. σαβαωθ, *Sabaoth*
5. ζῷον, *living being, animal*
6. ἀνά, *each*
7. πτέρυξ, *wing*
8. ἕξ, *six*
9. κυκλόθεν, *from all around*
10. ἔσωθεν, *within*
11. γέμω, pres. act. ind. 3 p., *be full*
12. ἀνάπαυσις, *rest*
13. παντοκράτωρ, *almighty*
14. animal, *living being, animal*
15. ala, *wing*
16. seni, *six each*
17. circuitus, *encircling*
18. intus, *within*
19. requies, *rest*
20. omnipotens, *almighty*

January 14

Proverbs 20:27

נֵ֣ר[1] יְ֭הוָה נִשְׁמַ֣ת[2] אָדָ֑ם חֹ֝פֵ֗שׂ[3] כָּל־חַדְרֵי־בָֽטֶן׃

φῶς κυρίου πνοὴ[4] ἀνθρώπων, ὃς ἐρευνᾷ[5] ταμιεῖα[6] κοιλίας.

1 Corinthians 2:11

τίς γὰρ οἶδεν ἀνθρώπων τὰ τοῦ ἀνθρώπου εἰ μὴ τὸ πνεῦμα τοῦ ἀνθρώπου τὸ ἐν αὐτῷ; οὕτως καὶ τὰ τοῦ θεοῦ οὐδεὶς ἔγνωκεν εἰ μὴ τὸ πνεῦμα τοῦ θεοῦ.

quis enim scit hominum quae sint hominis nisi spiritus hominis qui in ipso est ita et quae Dei sunt nemo cognovit nisi Spiritus Dei.

1. נֵר, *lamp*
2. נְשָׁמָה, *breath, spirit*
3. חָפַשׂ, qal ptcp. m. s. abs., *search*
4. πνοή, *breath*
5. ἐρευνάω, pres. act. ind. 3 s., *search*
6. ταμιεῖον, *chamber*

January 15

Deuteronomy 6:4

שְׁמַ֖ע יִשְׂרָאֵ֑ל יְהוָ֥ה אֱלֹהֵ֖ינוּ יְהוָ֥ה ׀ אֶחָֽד׃

Ἄκουε, Ισραηλ· κύριος ὁ θεὸς ἡμῶν κύριος εἷς ἐστιν.

1 Corinthians 8:4

Περὶ τῆς βρώσεως[1] οὖν τῶν εἰδωλοθύτων,[2] οἴδαμεν ὅτι οὐδὲν εἴδωλον[3] ἐν κόσμῳ καὶ ὅτι οὐδεὶς θεὸς εἰ μὴ εἷς.

de escis[4] autem quae idolis[5] immolantur[6] scimus quia nihil est idolum in mundo et quod nullus Deus nisi unus.

1. βρῶσις, *food*
2. εἰδωλόθυτος, *meat sacrificed to idols*
3. εἴδωλον, *idol*
4. esca, *food*
5. idolum, *idol*
6. immolo, pres. pass. ind. 3 p., *sacrifice*

January 16

Deuteronomy 7:9

וְיָדַעְתָּ֕ כִּֽי־יְהוָ֥ה אֱלֹהֶ֖יךָ ה֣וּא הָאֱלֹהִ֑ים הָאֵל֙ הַנֶּאֱמָ֔ן[1]
שֹׁמֵ֤ר הַבְּרִית֙ וְהַחֶ֔סֶד לְאֹהֲבָ֥יו וּלְשֹׁמְרֵ֛י מִצְוֺתָ֖ו
לְאֶ֥לֶף דּֽוֹר׃

καὶ γνώσῃ ὅτι κύριος ὁ θεός σου, οὗτος θεός, θεὸς πιστός,[2] ὁ φυλάσσων διαθήκην καὶ ἔλεος τοῖς ἀγαπῶσιν αὐτὸν καὶ τοῖς φυλάσσουσιν τὰς ἐντολὰς αὐτοῦ εἰς χιλίας γενεάς.

1 Corinthians 10:13

πειρασμὸς[3] ὑμᾶς οὐκ εἴληφεν εἰ μὴ ἀνθρώπινος·[4] πιστὸς δὲ ὁ θεός, ὃς οὐκ ἐάσει[5] ὑμᾶς πειρασθῆναι ὑπὲρ ὃ δύνασθε ἀλλὰ ποιήσει σὺν τῷ πειρασμῷ καὶ τὴν ἔκβασιν[6] τοῦ δύνασθαι ὑπενεγκεῖν.[7]

temptatio[8] vos non adprehendat nisi humana[9] fidelis autem Deus qui non patietur vos temptari super id quod potestis sed faciet cum temptatione etiam proventum[10] ut possitis sustinere.

1. אָמַן, niph. ptcp. m. s. abs., *faithful*
2. πιστός, *faithful*
3. πειρασμός, *temptation*
4. ἀνθρώπινος, *human*; TH: that which is common to humankind
5. ἐάω, fut. act. ind. 3 s., *permit*
6. ἔκβασις, *way of escape*
7. ὑποφέρω, aor. act. inf., *endure*
8. temptatio, *temptation*
9. humanus, *human*; TH: that which is common to humankind
10. proventus, *way of escape*

January 17

Isaiah 44:25

מֵפֵר֙[1] אֹת֣וֹת[2] בַּדִּ֔ים[3] וְקֹסְמִ֖ים[4] יְהוֹלֵ֑ל[5] מֵשִׁ֧יב חֲכָמִ֛ים אָח֖וֹר[6] וְדַעְתָּ֥ם[7] יְשַׂכֵּֽל׃[8]

διασκεδάσει[9] σημεῖα ἐγγαστριμύθων[10] καὶ μαντείας[11] ἀπὸ καρδίας, ἀποστρέφων φρονίμους[12] εἰς τὰ ὀπίσω καὶ τὴν βουλὴν αὐτῶν μωρεύων.[13]

1 Corinthians 1:20

ποῦ σοφός;[14] ποῦ γραμματεύς; ποῦ συζητητὴς[15] τοῦ αἰῶνος τούτου; οὐχὶ ἐμώρανεν[16] ὁ θεὸς τὴν σοφίαν τοῦ κόσμου;

ubi sapiens[17] ubi scriba ubi conquisitor[18] huius saeculi nonne stultam[19] fecit Deus sapientiam huius mundi.

1. פָּרַר, hiph. ptcp. m. s. abs., *frustrate*
2. אוֹת, *sign*
3. בַּד, *liar*
4. קסם, qal ptcp. m. p. abs., *practice divination*
5. הָלַל, poel impf. 3 m. s., *make into a fool*
6. אָחוֹר, *back*
7. דַּ֫עַת, *knowledge*
8. סָכַל, piel impf. 3 m. s., *make foolish*
9. διασκεδάζω, fut. act. ind. 3 s., *scatter, break*
10. ἐγγαστρίμυθος, *ventriloquist*
11. μαντεία, *divination*
12. φρόνιμος, *wise*
13. μωρεύω, pres. act. ptcp. m. nom. s., *turn into folly*
14. σοφός, *wise*
15. συζητητής, *debater*
16. μωρεύω, aor. act. ind. 3 s., *turn into folly*
17. sapiens, *wise*
18. conquisitor, *disputer*
19. stultus, *foolish*

January 18

Exodus 34:6

וַיַּעֲבֹ֨ר יְהוָ֥ה ׀ עַל־פָּנָיו֮ וַיִּקְרָא֒ יְהוָ֣ה ׀ יְהוָ֔ה אֵ֥ל רַח֖וּם[1]
וְחַנּ֑וּן[2] אֶ֥רֶךְ[3] אַפַּ֖יִם וְרַב־חֶ֥סֶד וֶאֱמֶֽת׃

καὶ παρῆλθεν κύριος πρὸ προσώπου αὐτοῦ καὶ ἐκάλεσεν Κύριος ὁ θεὸς οἰκτίρμων[4] καὶ ἐλεήμων,[5] μακρόθυμος[6] καὶ πολυέλεος[7] καὶ ἀληθινὸς.[8]

James 5:11

ἰδοὺ μακαρίζομεν[9] τοὺς ὑπομείναντας·[10] τὴν ὑπομονὴν Ἰὼβ[11] ἠκούσατε καὶ τὸ τέλος κυρίου εἴδετε, ὅτι πολύσπλαγχνός[12] ἐστιν ὁ κύριος καὶ οἰκτίρμων.

ecce beatificamus[13] qui sustinuerunt sufferentiam[14] Iob[15] audistis et finem Domini vidistis quoniam misericors[16] est Dominus et miserator.[17]

1. רַחוּם, *merciful, compassionate*

2. חַנּוּן, *gracious*

3. אָרֵךְ, *slow, patient*

4. οἰκτίρμων, *compassionate, merciful*

5. ἐλεήμων, *merciful*

6. μακρόθυμος, *patient, long-suffering*

7. πολυέλεος, *very merciful*

8. ἀληθινός, *true*

9. μακαρίζω, pres. act. ind. 1 p., *bless*

10. ὑπομένω, aor. act. ptcp. m. a. p., *steadfast*

11. Ἰώβ, *Job*

12. πολύσπλαγχνός, *very compassionate*

13. beatifico, pres. act. ind. 1 p., *consider happy*

14. sufferentia, *patience*

15. Iob, *Job*

16. misericors, *merciful*

17. miserator, *compassionate*

January 19

Deuteronomy 32:21

הֵ֚ם קִנְא֣וּנִי[1] בְלֹא־אֵ֔ל כִּעֲס֖וּנִי[2] בְּהַבְלֵיהֶ֑ם[3] וַאֲנִי֙
אַקְנִיאֵ֣ם[4] בְּלֹא־עָ֔ם בְּג֥וֹי נָבָ֖ל[5] אַכְעִיסֵֽם׃[6]

αὐτοὶ παρεζήλωσάν[7] με ἐπ᾽ οὐ θεῷ, παρώργισάν[8] με ἐν τοῖς εἰδώλοις αὐτῶν· κἀγὼ παραζηλώσω[9] αὐτοὺς ἐπ᾽ οὐκ ἔθνει, ἐπ᾽ ἔθνει ἀσυνέτῳ[10] παροργιῶ[11] αὐτούς.

1 Corinthians 10:22

ἢ παραζηλοῦμεν[12] τὸν κύριον; μὴ ἰσχυρότεροι[13] αὐτοῦ ἐσμεν;

an aemulamur[14] Dominum numquid fortiores[15] illo sumus?

1. קנא, piel perf. 3 c. p., *be jealous*
2. כָּעַס, piel perf. 3 c. p., *be angry*
3. הֶ֫בֶל, *idol*
4. קנא, hiph. impf. 1 c. s., *be jealous*
5. נָבָל, *foolish*
6. כָּעַס, hiph. perf. 1 c. s., *be angry*
7. παραζηλόω, aor. act. ind. 3 p., *make jealous*
8. παροργίζω, aor. act. ind. 3 p., *make angry*
9. παραζηλόω, fut. act. ind. 1 s., *make jealous*
10. ἀσύνετος, *without understanding, foolish*
11. παροργίζω, fut. act. ind. 1 s., *make angry*
12. παραζηλόω, pres. act. ind. 1 p., *make jealous*
13. ἰσχυρός, *strong, mighty*
14. aemulor, pres. dep. ind. 1 p., *make jealous*
15. fortis, *strong*

The Fall

January 20

Isaiah 14:12

אֵיךְ[1] נָפַלְתָּ מִשָּׁמַיִם הֵילֵל[2] בֶּן־שָׁחַר[3] נִגְדַּעְתָּ[4] לָאָרֶץ
חוֹלֵשׁ[5] עַל־גּוֹיִם׃

πῶς ἐξέπεσεν[6] ἐκ τοῦ οὐρανοῦ ὁ ἑωσφόρος[7] ὁ πρωὶ ἀνατέλλων;[8] συνετρίβη[9] εἰς τὴν γῆν ὁ ἀποστέλλων πρὸς πάντα τὰ ἔθνη.[10]

Luke 10:18

εἶπεν δὲ αὐτοῖς· ἐθεώρουν τὸν σατανᾶν ὡς ἀστραπὴν[11] ἐκ τοῦ οὐρανοῦ πεσόντα.

et ait illis videbam Satanan sicut fulgur[12] de caelo cadentem.

1. אֵיךְ, *how*

2. הֵילֵל, *shining one, morning star*

3. שַׁחַר, *dawn*

4. גָּדַע, niph. perf. 2 m. s., *be hewn down*

5. חָלַשׁ, qal ptcp. m. s. abs., *lay low, prostrate*

6. ἐκπίπτω, aor. act. ind. 3 s., *fall*

7. ἑωσφόρος, *morning star*

8. ἀνατέλλω, pres. act. ptcp. m. nom. s., *rise*

9. συντρίβω, aor. pass. ind. 3 s., *crush, break*

10. TH: NETS supplies "star" as the direct object.

11. ἀστραπή, *lightning*

12. fulgur, *lightning*

January 21

Genesis 3:4

וַיֹּאמֶר הַנָּחָשׁ[1] אֶל־הָאִשָּׁה לֹא־מוֹת תְּמֻתוּן׃

καὶ εἶπεν ὁ ὄφις[2] τῇ γυναικί Οὐ θανάτῳ ἀποθανεῖσθε.

John 8:44

ὑμεῖς ἐκ τοῦ πατρὸς τοῦ διαβόλου ἐστὲ καὶ τὰς ἐπιθυμίας τοῦ πατρὸς ὑμῶν θέλετε ποιεῖν. ἐκεῖνος ἀνθρωποκτόνος[3] ἦν ἀπ' ἀρχῆς καὶ ἐν τῇ ἀληθείᾳ οὐκ ἔστηκεν,[4] ὅτι οὐκ ἔστιν ἀλήθεια ἐν αὐτῷ. ὅταν λαλῇ τὸ ψεῦδος,[5] ἐκ τῶν ἰδίων λαλεῖ, ὅτι ψεύστης[6] ἐστὶν καὶ ὁ πατὴρ αὐτοῦ.

vos ex patre diabolo estis et desideria[7] patris vestri vultis facere ille homicida[8] erat ab initio et in veritate non stetit quia non est veritas in eo cum loquitur mendacium[9] ex propriis[10] loquitur quia mendax[11] est et pater eius.

1. נָחָשׁ, *snake*
2. ὄφις, *snake*
3. ἀνθρωποκτόνος, *murderer*
4. στήκω, impf. act. ind. 3 s., *stand*
5. ψεῦδος, *lie*
6. ψεύστης, *liar*
7. desiderium, *desire*
8. homicida, *murderer*
9. mendacium, *lie*
10. proprius, *one's own (character)*
11. mendax, *liar*

January 22

1. מַאֲכָל, *food*
2. תַּאֲוָה, *desirable*
3. חָמַד, niph. ptcp. m. abs. s., *be desirable, pleasing*
4. שָׂכַל, hiph. inf. cons., *make wise*
5. βρῶσις, *food*
6. ἀρεστός, *pleasing*
7. ὡραῖος, *beautiful*
8. κατανοέω, aor. act. inf., *perceive, contemplate*
9. βασιλεύω, aor. act. ind. 3 s., *rule, reign*
10. Ἀδάμ, *Adam*
11. μέχρι, *up till, until*
12. ὁμοίωμα, *like, similar to*
13. παράβασις, *transgression*
14. τύπος, *type*
15. regno, perf. act. ind. 3 s., *rule, reign*
16. Adam, *Adam*
17. similitudo, *like*
18. prevaricatio, *transgression, disobedience*
19. forma, *example, form*

Genesis 3:6

וַתֵּרֶא הָאִשָּׁה כִּי טוֹב הָעֵץ לְמַאֲכָל[1] וְכִי תַאֲוָה[2]־הוּא
לָעֵינַיִם וְנֶחְמָד[3] הָעֵץ לְהַשְׂכִּיל[4] וַתִּקַּח מִפִּרְיוֹ וַתֹּאכַל
וַתִּתֵּן גַּם־לְאִישָׁהּ עִמָּהּ וַיֹּאכַל׃

καὶ εἶδεν ἡ γυνὴ ὅτι καλὸν τὸ ξύλον εἰς βρῶσιν[5] καὶ ὅτι ἀρεστὸν[6] τοῖς ὀφθαλμοῖς ἰδεῖν καὶ ὡραῖόν[7] ἐστιν τοῦ κατανοῆσαι,[8] καὶ λαβοῦσα τοῦ καρποῦ αὐτοῦ ἔφαγεν· καὶ ἔδωκεν καὶ τῷ ἀνδρὶ αὐτῆς μετ᾽ αὐτῆς, καὶ ἔφαγον.

Romans 5:14

ἀλλ᾽ ἐβασίλευσεν[9] ὁ θάνατος ἀπὸ Ἀδὰμ[10] μέχρι[11] Μωϋσέως καὶ ἐπὶ τοὺς μὴ ἁμαρτήσαντας ἐπὶ τῷ ὁμοιώματι[12] τῆς παραβάσεως[13] Ἀδὰμ ὅς ἐστιν τύπος[14] τοῦ μέλλοντος.

sed regnavit[15] mors ab Adam[16] usque ad Mosen etiam in eos qui non peccaverunt in similitudinem[17] praevaricationis[18] Adae qui est forma[19] futuri.

January 23

Genesis 3:13

וַיֹּ֨אמֶר יְהוָ֧ה אֱלֹהִ֛ים לָאִשָּׁ֖ה מַה־זֹּ֣את עָשִׂ֑ית וַתֹּ֨אמֶר֙
הָֽאִשָּׁ֔ה הַנָּחָ֥שׁ[1] הִשִּׁיאַ֖נִי[2] וָאֹכֵֽל׃

καὶ εἶπεν κύριος ὁ θεὸς τῇ γυναικί Τί τοῦτο ἐποίησας; καὶ εἶπεν ἡ γυνή Ὁ ὄφις[3] ἠπάτησέν[4] με, καὶ ἔφαγον.

2 Corinthians 11:3

φοβοῦμαι δὲ μή πως,[5] ὡς ὁ ὄφις ἐξηπάτησεν[6] Εὕαν[7] ἐν τῇ πανουργίᾳ[8] αὐτοῦ, φθαρῇ[9] τὰ νοήματα[10] ὑμῶν ἀπὸ τῆς ἁπλότητος[11] [καὶ τῆς ἁγνότητος][12] τῆς εἰς τὸν Χριστόν.

timeo autem ne sicut serpens[13] Evam[14] seduxit astutia[15] sua ita corrumpantur[16] sensus[17] vestri et excidant[18] a simplicitate[19] quae est in Christo.

1. נָחָשׁ, *snake*

2. נָשָׁא, hiph. perf. 3 m. s., *deceive*

3. ὄφις, *snake*

4. ἀπατάω, aor. act. ind. 3 s., *deceive*

5. πώς, *somehow*; TH: μή + πώς = *lest somehow*

6. ἐξαπατάω, aor. act. ind. 3 s., *deceive*

7. Εὕα, *Eve*

8. πανουργία, *cunning*

9. φθείρω, aor. pass. subj. 3 s., *lead astray*

10. νόημα, *thought*

11. ἁπλότης, *sincere*

12. ἁγνότης, *pure*

13. serpens, *snake*

14. Eva, *Eve*

15. astutia, *craftiness, guile*

16. corrumpo, pres. pass. subj. 3 p., *corrupt, spoil*

17. sensus, *mind, understanding*

18. excido, pres. act. subj. 3 p., *fall away*

19. simplicitas, *simplicity, candor*

January 24

Genesis 3:16

אֶל־הָאִשָּׁה אָמַר הַרְבָּה אַרְבֶּה עִצְּבוֹנֵךְ[1] וְהֵרֹנֵךְ[2]
בְּעֶצֶב[3] תֵּלְדִי בָנִים וְאֶל־אִישֵׁךְ תְּשׁוּקָתֵךְ[4] וְהוּא
יִמְשָׁל[5]־בָּךְ׃

καὶ τῇ γυναικὶ εἶπεν Πληθύνων πληθυνῶ τὰς λύπας[6] σου καὶ τὸν στεναγμόν[7] σου, ἐν λύπαις τέξῃ τέκνα· καὶ πρὸς τὸν ἄνδρα σου ἡ ἀποστροφή[8] σου, καὶ αὐτός σου κυριεύσει.[9]

1 Corinthians 11:3

Θέλω δὲ ὑμᾶς εἰδέναι ὅτι παντὸς ἀνδρὸς ἡ κεφαλὴ ὁ Χριστός ἐστιν, κεφαλὴ δὲ γυναικὸς ὁ ἀνήρ, κεφαλὴ δὲ τοῦ Χριστοῦ ὁ θεός.

volo autem vos scire quod omnis viri caput Christus est caput autem mulieris vir caput vero Christi Deus.

1. עִצָּבוֹן, *pain, toil*
2. הֵרוֹן, *childbearing*
3. עֶ֫צֶב, *pain, toil*
4. תְּשׁוּקָה, *desire*
5. מָשַׁל, qal impf. 3 m. s., *rule, have dominion*
6. λύπη, *pain, grief*
7. στεναγμός, *groaning*
8. ἀποστροφή, *turning, return*
9. κυριεύω, fut. act. ind. 3 s., *rule over, dominate*

January 25

Genesis 3:17

וּלְאָדָ֣ם[1] אָמַ֗ר כִּֽי־שָׁמַעְתָּ֮ לְק֣וֹל אִשְׁתֶּךָ֒ וַתֹּ֙אכַל֙ מִן־
הָעֵ֔ץ אֲשֶׁ֤ר צִוִּיתִ֙יךָ֙ לֵאמֹ֔ר לֹ֥א תֹאכַ֖ל מִמֶּ֑נּוּ אֲרוּרָ֤ה[2]
הָֽאֲדָמָה֙ בַּעֲבוּרֶ֔ךָ[3] בְּעִצָּבוֹן֙[4] תֹּֽאכֲלֶ֔נָּה כֹּ֖ל יְמֵ֥י חַיֶּֽיךָ׃

τῷ δὲ Αδαμ[5] εἶπεν Ὅτι ἤκουσας τῆς φωνῆς τῆς γυναικός σου καὶ ἔφαγες ἀπὸ τοῦ ξύλου, οὗ ἐνετειλάμην σοι τούτου μόνου μὴ φαγεῖν ἀπ᾽ αὐτοῦ, ἐπικατάρατος[6] ἡ γῆ ἐν τοῖς ἔργοις σου· ἐν λύπαις[7] φάγῃ αὐτὴν πάσας τὰς ἡμέρας τῆς ζωῆς σου.

Romans 8:20

τῇ γὰρ ματαιότητι[8] ἡ κτίσις[9] ὑπετάγη,[10] οὐχ ἑκοῦσα[11] ἀλλὰ διὰ τὸν ὑποτάξαντα.[12]

vanitati[13] enim creatura[14] subiecta[15] est non volens sed propter eum qui subiecit.[16]

1. אָדָם, *Adam*

2. אָרַר, qal pass. ptcp. f. s. abs., *curse*

3. עֲבוּר, *because of*

4. עִצָּבוֹן, *pain, toil*

5. Αδαμ, *Adam*

6. ἐπικατάρατος, *cursed*

7. λύπη, *pain, grief*

8. ματαιότης, *futility*

9. κτίσις, *creation*

10. ὑποτάσσω, aor. pass. ind. 3 s., *subject, submit*

11. ἑκών, *willingly*

12. ὑποτάσσω, aor. act. ptcp. m. a. s., *subject, submit*

13. vanitas, *vanity, emptiness*

14. creatura, *creature, creation*

15. subicio, perf. pass. ind. 3 s., *subdue, subject*

16. subicio, perf. act. ind. 3 s., *subdue, subject*

January 26

Ecclesiastes 5:15

וְגַם־זֹה[1] רָעָה חוֹלָה[2] כָּל־עֻמַּת[3] שֶׁבָּא כֵּן יֵלֵךְ וּמַה־יִּתְרוֹן[4] לוֹ שֶׁיַּעֲמֹל[5] לָרוּחַ׃

καί γε τοῦτο πονηρὰ ἀρρωστία·[6] ὥσπερ γὰρ παρεγένετο, οὕτως καὶ ἀπελεύσεται, καὶ τίς περισσεία[7] αὐτῷ, ᾗ μοχθεῖ[8] εἰς ἄνεμον;[9]

1 Timothy 6:7

οὐδὲν γὰρ εἰσηνέγκαμεν[10] εἰς τὸν κόσμον, ὅτι[11] οὐδὲ ἐξενεγκεῖν[12] τι δυνάμεθα.

nihil enim intulimus[13] in mundum haut[14] dubium[15] quia nec auferre[16] quid possumus.

1. זֹה, *this*

2. חָלָה, qal ptcp. f. s. abs., *be sick, experience misfortune*

3. עֻמָּה, *just as*

4. יִתְרוֹן, *profit, gain*

5. עָמַל, qal impf. 3 m. s., *toil*

6. ἀρρωστία, *sickness*

7. περισσεία, *abundance*

8. μοχθέω, pres. act. ind. 3 s., *labor, toil*

9. ἄνεμος, *wind*

10. εἰσφέρω, aor. act. ind. 1 p., *bring in*

11. TC: Some MSS insert ἀληθές ("it is certain") in order to eliminate the awkwardness of ὅτι. See the Vulgata addition of haut dubium, for example. TH: Translate with "it is certain that" or "and."

12. ἐκφέρω, aor. act. inf., *go out*

13. infero, perf. act. ind. 1 p., *bring in*

14. haut, *by no means*

15. dubius, *uncertain*

16. aufero, pres. act. inf., *take away*

January 27

Genesis 3:15

וְאֵיבָ֣ה ׀[1] אָשִׁ֗ית[2] בֵּֽינְךָ֙ וּבֵ֣ין הָֽאִשָּׁ֔ה וּבֵ֥ין זַרְעֲךָ֖ וּבֵ֣ין
זַרְעָ֑הּ ה֚וּא יְשׁוּפְךָ֣[3] רֹ֔אשׁ וְאַתָּ֖ה תְּשׁוּפֶ֥נּוּ[4] עָקֵֽב׃[5]

καὶ ἔχθραν[6] θήσω ἀνὰ μέσον σου καὶ ἀνὰ μέσον τῆς γυναικὸς καὶ ἀνὰ μέσον τοῦ σπέρματός σου καὶ ἀνὰ μέσον τοῦ σπέρματος αὐτῆς· αὐτός σου τηρήσει[7] κεφαλήν, καὶ σὺ τηρήσεις[8] αὐτοῦ πτέρναν.[9]

Romans 16:20

ὁ δὲ θεὸς τῆς εἰρήνης συντρίψει[10] τὸν σαταναν[11] ὑπὸ τοὺς πόδας ὑμῶν ἐν τάχει.[12] Ἡ χάρις τοῦ κυρίου ἡμῶν Ἰησοῦ μεθ᾽ ὑμῶν.

Deus autem pacis conteret[13] Satanan sub pedibus vestris velociter[14] gratia Domini nostri Iesu Christi vobiscum.

1. אֵיבָה, *enmity*
2. שִׁית, qal impf. 1 c. s., *put, set*
3. שׁוּף, qal impf. 3 m. s., *bruise*
4. שׁוּף, qal impf. 2 m. s., *bruise*
5. עָקֵב, *heel*
6. ἔχθρα, *enmity*
7. τηρέω, fut. act. ind. 3 s., *watch; lie in wait for*
8. τηρέω, fut. act. ind. 2 s., *watch; lie in wait for*
9. πτέρνα, *heel*
10. συντρίβω, fut. act. ind. 3 s., *crush, break*
11. σατανᾶς, *Satan*
12. ταχύς, *quickly*
13. contero, pres. act. subj. 3 s., *crush, break*
14. velociter, *swiftly, speedily*

Sin

January 28

Genesis 2:17

וּמֵעֵ֗ץ הַדַּ֙עַת֙[1] ט֣וֹב וָרָ֔ע לֹ֥א תֹאכַ֖ל מִמֶּ֑נּוּ כִּ֗י בְּי֛וֹם אֲכָלְךָ֥ מִמֶּ֖נּוּ מ֥וֹת תָּמֽוּת׃

ἀπὸ δὲ τοῦ ξύλου τοῦ γινώσκειν καλὸν καὶ πονηρόν, οὐ φάγεσθε ἀπ᾽ αὐτοῦ· ᾗ δ᾽ ἂν ἡμέρᾳ φάγητε ἀπ᾽ αὐτοῦ, θανάτῳ ἀποθανεῖσθε.

Romans 5:12

Διὰ τοῦτο ὥσπερ δι᾽ ἑνὸς ἀνθρώπου ἡ ἁμαρτία εἰς τὸν κόσμον εἰσῆλθεν καὶ διὰ τῆς ἁμαρτίας ὁ θάνατος, καὶ οὕτως εἰς πάντας ἀνθρώπους ὁ θάνατος διῆλθεν, ἐφ᾽ ᾧ πάντες ἥμαρτον.

propterea[2] sicut per unum hominem in hunc mundum peccatum intravit et per peccatum mors et ita in omnes homines mors pertransiit[3] in quo omnes peccaverunt.

1. דַּעַת, *knowledge*
2. propterea, *therefore*
3. pertranseo, perf. act. ind. 3 s., *pass through, enter into*

January 29

Psalm 106:20 [LXX 105:20]

וַיָּמִ֥ירוּ[1] אֶת־כְּבוֹדָ֑ם בְּתַבְנִ֥ית[2] שׁ֝֗וֹר[3] אֹכֵ֥ל עֵֽשֶׂב׃[4]

καὶ ἠλλάξαντο[5] τὴν δόξαν αὐτῶν ἐν ὁμοιώματι[6] μόσχου ἔσθοντος[7] χόρτον.[8]

Romans 1:23

καὶ ἤλλαξαν[9] τὴν δόξαν τοῦ ἀφθάρτου[10] θεοῦ ἐν ὁμοιώματι εἰκόνος[11] φθαρτοῦ[12] ἀνθρώπου καὶ πετεινῶν[13] καὶ τετραπόδων[14] καὶ ἑρπετῶν.[15]

et mutaverunt[16] gloriam incorruptibilis[17] Dei in similitudinem[18] imaginis[19] corruptibilis[20] hominis et volucrum[21] et quadrupedum[22] et serpentium.[23]

1. מוּר, hiph. wcons. 3 m. p., *exchange*

2. תַּבְנִית, *image*

3. שׁוֹר, *ox*

4. עֵשֶׂב, *grass*

5. ἀλλάσσω, aor. mid. ind. 3 p., *exchange*

6. ὁμοίωμα, *likeness, image*

7. ἔσθω, pres. act. ptcp. m. g. s., *eat*

8. χόρτος, *grass*

9. ἀλλάσσω, aor. act. ind. 3 p., *exchange*

10. ἄφθαρτος, *immortal*

11. εἰκών, *image*

12. φθαρτός, *perishable, mortal*

13. πετεινόν, *bird*

14. τετράπους, *four-footed animal*

15. ἑρπετόν, *reptile, creeping thing*

16. muto, perf. act. ind. 3 p., *exchange*

17. incorruptibilis, *incorruptible*

18. similitudo, *likeness*

19. imago, *image*

20. corruptibilis, *corruptible, mortal*

21. volucris, *bird*

22. quadrupes, *four-footed animal.* **23.** serpens, *snake*

January 30

1. נָבָל, *foolish, fool*

2. תעב, hiph. perf. 3 c. p., *do something abominable*

3. עֲלִילָה, *abominable deed*

4. διαφθείρω, aor. act. ind. 3 p., *destroy, cause corruption*

5. βδελύσσω, aor. pass. ind. 3 p., *be detestable*

6. ἐπιτήδευμα, *practice*

7. χρηστότης, *kindness*

8. προέχω, pres. mid. ind. 1 p., *be better off*

9. πάντως, *by all means*

10. προαιτιάομαι, aor. mid. ind. 1 p., *accuse, charge*

11. Ἕλληνας, *gentile*

12. praecello, pres. act. ind. 1 p., *excel, surpass*

13. nequaquam, *by no means*

14. causor, perf. dep. ind. 3 p., *plead, charge*

15. Graeci, *Greek*

Psalm 14:1 [LXX 13:1]

אָמַר נָבָל[1] בְּלִבּוֹ אֵין אֱלֹהִים הִשְׁחִיתוּ הִתְעִיבוּ[2] עֲלִילָה[3] אֵין עֹשֵׂה־טוֹב׃

Εἶπεν ἄφρων ἐν καρδίᾳ αὐτοῦ Οὐκ ἔστιν θεός· διέφθειραν[4] καὶ ἐβδελύχθησαν[5] ἐν ἐπιτηδεύμασιν,[6] οὐκ ἔστιν ποιῶν χρηστότητα,[7] οὐκ ἔστιν ἕως ἑνός.

Romans 3:9

Τί οὖν; προεχόμεθα;[8] οὐ πάντως·[9] προῃτιασάμεθα[10] γὰρ Ἰουδαίους τε καὶ Ἕλληνας[11] πάντας ὑφ᾽ ἁμαρτίαν εἶναι.

quid igitur praecellimus[12] eos nequaquam[13] causati[14] enim sumus Iudaeos et Graecos[15] omnes sub peccato esse.

January 31

Psalm 5:10

כִּי אֵין בְּפִיהוּ נְכוֹנָה קִרְבָּם הַוּוֹת[1] קֶבֶר[2]־פָּתוּחַ
גְּרוֹנָם[3] לְשׁוֹנָם יַחֲלִיקוּן׃[4]

ὅτι οὐκ ἔστιν ἐν τῷ στόματι αὐτῶν
ἀλήθεια, ἡ καρδία αὐτῶν ματαία·[5] τάφος[6]
ἀνεῳγμένος ὁ λάρυγξ[7] αὐτῶν, ταῖς γλώσσαις
αὐτῶν ἐδολιοῦσαν.[8]

Romans 3:13

τάφος ἀνεῳγμένος ὁ λάρυγξ αὐτῶν, ταῖς γλώσσαις αὐτῶν ἐδολιοῦσαν, ἰὸς[9] ἀσπίδων[10] ὑπὸ τὰ χείλη[11] αὐτῶν·

sepulchrum[12] patens[13] est guttur[14] eorum
linguis suis dolose[15] agebant venenum[16]
aspidum[17] sub labiis[18] eorum.

1. הַוָּה, *destruction*
2. קֶבֶר, *grave*
3. גָּרוֹן, *throat*
4. חָלַק, hiph. impf. 3 m. p., *be smooth, flatter*
5. μάταιος, *empty, vain*
6. τάφος, *grave*
7. λάρυγξ, *throat*
8. δολιόω, impf. act. ind. 3 p., *deceive*
9. ἰός, *poison*
10. ἀσπίς, *asp, snake*
11. χεῖλος, *lip*
12. sepulchrum, *grave*
13. pateo, pres. act. ptcp. n. nom. s., *be open*
14. guttur, *throat*
15. dolose, *deceitfully*
16. venenum, *poison*
17. aspis, *asp, viper*
18. labium, *lip*

February 1

Isaiah 53:11[1]

מֵעֲמַ֤ל[2] נַפְשׁוֹ֙ יִרְאֶ֣ה יִשְׂבָּ֔ע[3] בְּדַעְתּ֕וֹ[4] יַצְדִּ֥יק צַדִּ֛יק
עַבְדִּ֖י לָֽרַבִּ֑ים וַעֲוֺנֹתָ֖ם ה֥וּא יִסְבֹּֽל׃[5]

καὶ βούλεται κύριος ἀφελεῖν ἀπὸ τοῦ πόνου[6] τῆς ψυχῆς αὐτοῦ, δεῖξαι αὐτῷ φῶς καὶ πλάσαι[7] τῇ συνέσει, δικαιῶσαι[8] δίκαιον εὖ[9] δουλεύοντα πολλοῖς, καὶ τὰς ἁμαρτίας αὐτῶν αὐτὸς ἀνοίσει.

Romans 5:19

ὥσπερ γὰρ διὰ τῆς παρακοῆς[10] τοῦ ἑνὸς ἀνθρώπου ἁμαρτωλοὶ κατεστάθησαν[11] οἱ πολλοί, οὕτως καὶ διὰ τῆς ὑπακοῆς[12] τοῦ ἑνὸς δίκαιοι κατασταθήσονται[13] οἱ πολλοί.

sicut enim per inoboedientiam[14] unius hominis peccatores constituti sunt multi ita et per unius oboeditionem[15] iusti constituentur multi.

1. CH: This verse is a part of the Suffering Servant text in Isa 53 and speaks of the servant taking on the sins of the many.
2. עָמָל, *anguish*
3. שָׂבַע, qal impf. 3 m. s., *be satisfied*
4. דַּעַת, *knowledge*
5. סָבַל, qal impf. 3 m. s., *bear a load*
6. πόνος, *pain, labor*
7. πλάσσω, aor. act. inf., *form*
8. δικαιόω, aor. act. inf., *justify*
9. εὖ, *well*
10. παρακοή, *disobedience*
11. καθίστημι, aor. pass. ind. 3 p., *make, put down*
12. ὑπακοή, *obedience*
13. καθίστημι, fut. pass. ind. 3 p., *make, put down*
14. inoboedientia, *disobedience*
15. oboeditio, *obedience*

February 2

Hosea 10:12

זִרְע֨וּ[1] לָכֶ֤ם לִצְדָקָה֙ קִצְר֣וּ[2] לְפִי־חֶ֔סֶד נִ֥ירוּ[3] לָכֶ֖ם נִ֑יר[4]
וְעֵת֙ לִדְר֣וֹשׁ אֶת־יְהוָ֔ה עַד־יָב֕וֹא וְיֹרֶ֥ה[5] צֶ֖דֶק לָכֶֽם׃

σπείρατε[6] ἑαυτοῖς εἰς δικαιοσύνην, τρυγήσατε[7] εἰς καρπὸν ζωῆς, φωτίσατε[8] ἑαυτοῖς φῶς γνώσεως,[9] ἐκζητήσατε τὸν κύριον ἕως τοῦ ἐλθεῖν γενήματα[10] δικαιοσύνης ὑμῖν.

Galatians 6:8

ὅτι ὁ σπείρων[11] εἰς τὴν σάρκα ἑαυτοῦ ἐκ τῆς σαρκὸς θερίσει[12] φθοράν,[13] ὁ δὲ σπείρων εἰς τὸ πνεῦμα ἐκ τοῦ πνεύματος θερίσει ζωὴν αἰώνιον.

quae enim seminaverit homo haec et metet[14] quoniam qui seminat in carne sua de carne et metet corruptionem[15] qui autem seminat in spiritu de spiritu metet vitam aeternam.

1. זָרַע, qal impv. m. p., *sow*
2. קָצַר, qal impv. m. p., *reap*
3. נִיר, qal impv. m. p., *break up*
4. נִיר, *fallow ground*
5. יָרָה, hiph. impf. 3 m. s., *rain*
6. σπείρω, aor. act. impv. 2 p., *sow*
7. τρυγάω, aor. act. impv. 2 p., *gather, reap*
8. φωτίζω, aor. act. impv. 2 p., *give light, enlighten*
9. γνῶσις, *knowledge*
10. γένημα, *produce, harvest*
11. σπείρω, pres. act. ptcp. m. nom. s., *sow*
12. θερίζω, fut. act. ind. 3 s., *reap*
13. φθορά, *corruption*
14. meto, fut. act. ind. 3 s., *reap*
15. corruptio, *corruption*

February 3

Psalm 4:5

רִגְזוּ[1] וְאַל־תֶּחֱטָאוּ אִמְרוּ בִלְבַבְכֶם עַל־מִשְׁכַּבְכֶם[2]
וְדֹמּוּ[3] . . .

ὀργίζεσθε[4] καὶ μὴ ἁμαρτάνετε· λέγετε ἐν
ταῖς καρδίαις ὑμῶν καὶ ἐπὶ ταῖς κοίταις[5] ὑμῶν
κατανύγητε.[6] . . .

Ephesians 4:26

ὀργίζεσθε καὶ μὴ ἁμαρτάνετε· ὁ ἥλιος μὴ ἐπιδυέτω[7]
ἐπὶ [τῷ] παροργισμῷ[8] ὑμῶν.

irascimini[9] et nolite peccare sol non occidat[10]
super iracundiam[11] vestram.

1. רָגַז, qal impv. m. p., *be angry*
2. מִשְׁכָּב, *bed*
3. דָּמַם, qal impv. m. p., *be silent*
4. ὀργίζω, pres. pass. impv. 2 p., *be angry*
5. κοίτη, *bed*
6. κατανύσσομαι, aor. pass. impv. 2 p., *be pained, feel anxiety*
7. ἐπιδύω, pres. act. impv. 3 s., *go down*
8. παροργισμός, *wrath*
9. irascor, pres. dep. impv. 2 p., *be angry*
10. occido, pres. act. subj. 3 s., *fall, go down*
11. iracundia, *wrath*

February 4

Psalm 22:14 [LXX 21:14]

פָּצ֣וּ[1] עָלַ֣י פִּיהֶ֑ם אַ֝רְיֵ֗ה[2] טֹרֵ֥ף[3] וְשֹׁאֵֽג׃[4]

ἤνοιξαν ἐπ᾽ ἐμὲ τὸ στόμα αὐτῶν ὡς λέων[5] ὁ ἁρπάζων[6] καὶ ὠρυόμενος.[7]

1 Peter 5:8

νήψατε,[8] γρηγορήσατε.[9] ὁ ἀντίδικος[10] ὑμῶν διάβολος *ὡς λέων ὠρυόμενος* περιπατεῖ ζητῶν τινα καταπιεῖν.[11]

sobrii[12] estote vigilate[13] quia adversarius[14] vester diabolus tamquam leo[15] rugiens[16] circuit[17] quaerens quem devoret.[18]

1. פָּצָה, qal perf. 3 c. p., *open*
2. אַרְיֵה, *lion*
3. טָרַף, qal ptcp. m. s. abs., *tear*
4. שָׁאַג, qal ptcp. m. s. abs., *roar*
5. λέων, *lion*
6. ἁρπάζω, pres. act. ptcp. m. nom. s., *snatch away*
7. ὠρύομαι, pres. mid. ptcp. m. nom. s., *roar*
8. νήφω, aor. act. impv. 2 p., *be sober, self-controlled*
9. γρηγορέω, aor. act. impv. 2 p., *be awake, watchful*
10. ἀντίδικος, *adversary*
11. καταπίνω, aor. act. inf., *devour*
12. sobrius, *sober*
13. vigilo, pres. act. impv. 2 p., *keep watch*
14. adversarius, *adversary*
15. leo, *lion*
16. rugio, pres. act. ptcp. m. nom. s., *roar*
17. circuo, pres. act. ind. 3 s., *go around*
18. devoro, pres. act. subj. 3 s., *devour*

February 5

Genesis 4:7

הֲל֤וֹא אִם־תֵּיטִיב֙ שְׂאֵ֔ת וְאִם֙ לֹ֣א תֵיטִ֔יב לַפֶּ֖תַח
חַטָּ֣את רֹבֵ֑ץ[1] וְאֵלֶ֙יךָ֙ תְּשׁ֣וּקָת֔וֹ[2] וְאַתָּ֖ה תִּמְשָׁל[3]־בּֽוֹ׃

οὐκ, ἐὰν ὀρθῶς[4] προσενέγκῃς, ὀρθῶς δὲ μὴ διέλῃς,[5] ἥμαρτες; ἡσύχασον·[6] πρὸς σὲ ἡ ἀποστροφὴ[7] αὐτοῦ, καὶ σὺ ἄρξεις[8] αὐτοῦ.

Romans 6:12

Μὴ οὖν βασιλευέτω[9] ἡ ἁμαρτία ἐν τῷ θνητῷ[10] ὑμῶν σώματι εἰς τὸ ὑπακούειν[11] ταῖς ἐπιθυμίαις αὐτοῦ.

non ergo regnet[12] peccatum in vestro mortali[13] corpore ut oboediatis[14] concupiscentiis[15] eius.

1. רָבַץ, qal ptcp. m. s. abs., *lie down, stretch out*
2. תְּשׁוּקָה, *desire*
3. מָשַׁל, qal impf. 2 m. s., *rule over*
4. ὀρθός, *rightly, correctly*
5. διαιρέω, aor. act. subj. 2 s., *divide, separate*
6. ἡσυχάζω, aor. act. impv. 2 s., *be at rest, remain quiet*
7. ἀποστροφή, *return, turning away*
8. ἄρχω, fut. act. ind. 2 s., *rule over*
9. βασιλεύω, pres. act. impv. 3 s., *reign, rule over*
10. θνητός, *mortal*
11. ὑπακούω, pres. act. inf., *obey*
12. regno, pres. act. subj. 3 s., *reign*
13. mortalis, *mortal*
14. oboedio, pres. act. subj. 2 p., *obey*
15. concupiscentia, *desire*

February 6

Isaiah 53:5

וְהוּא֙ מְחֹלָ֣ל[1] מִפְּשָׁעֵ֔נוּ[2] מְדֻכָּ֖א[3] מֵעֲוֺנֹתֵ֑ינוּ מוּסַ֤ר
שְׁלוֹמֵ֙נוּ֙ עָלָ֔יו וּבַחֲבֻרָתֹ֖ו[4] נִרְפָּא[5]־לָֽנוּ׃

αὐτὸς δὲ ἐτραυματίσθη[6] διὰ τὰς ἀνομίας ἡμῶν καὶ μεμαλάκισται[7] διὰ τὰς ἁμαρτίας ἡμῶν· παιδεία εἰρήνης ἡμῶν ἐπ᾽ αὐτόν, τῷ μώλωπι[8] αὐτοῦ ἡμεῖς ἰάθημεν.[9]

1 Peter 2:24

ὃς τὰς ἁμαρτίας ἡμῶν αὐτὸς ἀνήνεγκεν[10] *ἐν τῷ σώματι αὐτοῦ ἐπὶ τὸ ξύλον,*[11] *ἵνα ταῖς ἁμαρτίαις ἀπογενόμενοι*[12] *τῇ δικαιοσύνῃ ζήσωμεν, οὗ τῷ μώλωπι ἰάθητε.*[13]

qui peccata nostra ipse pertulit[14] in corpore suo super lignum[15] ut peccatis mortui iustitiae viveremus cuius livore[16] sanati[17] estis.

1. חָלַל, polal ptcp. m. s. abs., *pierce*
2. פֶּשַׁע, *transgression*
3. דָּכָא, pual ptcp. m. s. abs., *crush*
4. חַבּוּרָה, *stripe*
5. רָפָא, niph. perf. 3 m. s., *heal*
6. τραυματίζω, aor. pass. ind. 3 s., *wound*
7. μαλακίζομαι, perf. pass. ind. 3 s., *be sick, weak*
8. μώλωψ, *wound*
9. ἰάομαι, aor. pass. ind. 1 p., *heal*
10. ἀναφέρω, aor. act. ind. 3 s., *bear*
11. ξύλον, *tree, wood*
12. ἀπογίνομαι, aor. mid. ptcp. m. nom. p., *die*
13. ἰάομαι, aor. pass. ind. 2 p., *heal*
14. perfero, perf. act. ind. 3 s., *bear*
15. lignum, *wood, tree*
16. livor, *stripe, bruise*
17. sano, perf. pass. ind. 2 p., *heal*

February 7

Isaiah 53:10

וַֽיהוָ֞ה חָפֵ֤ץ[1] דַּכְּאוֹ֙[2] הֶֽחֱלִ֔י[3] אִם־תָּשִׂ֤ים אָשָׁם֙[4] נַפְשׁ֔וֹ
יִרְאֶ֥ה זֶ֖רַע יַאֲרִ֣יךְ[5] יָמִ֑ים וְחֵ֥פֶץ[6] יְהוָ֖ה בְּיָד֥וֹ יִצְלָֽח׃[7]

καὶ κύριος βούλεται καθαρίσαι αὐτὸν τῆς πληγῆς·[8] ἐὰν δῶτε περὶ ἁμαρτίας, ἡ ψυχὴ ὑμῶν ὄψεται σπέρμα μακρόβιον.[9]

Matthew 20:28

. . . ὁ υἱὸς τοῦ ἀνθρώπου οὐκ ἦλθεν διακονηθῆναι ἀλλὰ διακονῆσαι καὶ δοῦναι τὴν ψυχὴν αὐτοῦ λύτρον[10] ἀντὶ[11] πολλῶν.

. . . Filius hominis non venit ministrari sed ministrare et dare animam suam redemptionem[12] pro multis.

1. חָפֵץ, qal perf. 3 m. s., *delight*
2. דָּכָא, piel inf. cons., *crush*
3. חָלָה, hiph. perf. 3 m. s., *make sick, bring to grief*
4. אָשָׁם, *guilt*
5. אָרַךְ, hiph. impf. 3 m. s., *prolong*
6. חֵפֶץ, *will*
7. צָלַח, qal impf. 3 m. s., *prosper*
8. πληγή, *blow, wound*
9. μακρόβιος, *long-lived*
10. λύτρον, *ransom*
11. ἀντί, *in place of, for*
12. redemptio, *ransom, redemption*

February 8

Exodus 31:18

וַיִּתֵּ֣ן אֶל־מֹשֶׁ֗ה כְּכַלֹּתוֹ֙ לְדַבֵּ֤ר אִתּוֹ֙ בְּהַ֣ר סִינַ֔י[1] שְׁנֵ֖י
לֻחֹ֣ת[2] הָעֵדֻ֑ת[3] לֻחֹ֣ת אֶ֔בֶן כְּתֻבִ֖ים בְּאֶצְבַּ֥ע[4] אֱלֹהִֽים׃

Καὶ ἔδωκεν Μωυσεῖ, ἡνίκα κατέπαυσεν[5] λαλῶν αὐτῷ ἐν τῷ ὄρει τῷ Σινα,[6] τὰς δύο πλάκας[7] τοῦ μαρτυρίου, πλάκας λιθίνας[8] γεγραμμένας τῷ δακτύλῳ[9] τοῦ θεοῦ.

John 1:17

ὅτι ὁ νόμος διὰ Μωϋσέως ἐδόθη, ἡ χάρις καὶ ἡ ἀλήθεια διὰ Ἰησοῦ Χριστοῦ ἐγένετο.

quia lex per Mosen data est gratia et veritas per Iesum Christum facta est.

1. סִינַי, *Sinai*
2. לוּחַ, *tablet*
3. עֵדוּת, *testimony*
4. אֶצְבַּע, *finger*
5. καταπαύω, aor. act. ind. 3 s., *finish, stop*
6. Σινα, *Sinai*
7. πλάξ, *tablet*
8. λίθινος, *made of stone*
9. δάκτυλος, *finger*

February 9

Jeremiah 7:25

לְמִן־הַיּ֗וֹם אֲשֶׁ֨ר יָצְא֤וּ אֲבֽוֹתֵיכֶם֙ מֵאֶ֣רֶץ מִצְרַ֔יִם עַ֖ד
הַיּ֣וֹם הַזֶּ֑ה וָאֶשְׁלַ֤ח אֲלֵיכֶם֙ אֶת־כָּל־עֲבָדַ֣י הַנְּבִיאִ֔ים
י֖וֹם הַשְׁכֵּ֥ם[1] וְשָׁלֹֽחַ׃

ἀφ᾽ ἧς ἡμέρας ἐξήλθοσαν οἱ πατέρες αὐτῶν ἐκ γῆς Αἰγύπτου καὶ ἕως τῆς ἡμέρας ταύτης καὶ ἐξαπέστειλα πρὸς ὑμᾶς πάντας τοὺς δούλους μου τοὺς προφήτας ἡμέρας καὶ ὄρθρου[2] καὶ ἀπέστειλα.

Hebrews 1:1

Πολυμερῶς[3] καὶ πολυτρόπως[4] πάλαι[5] ὁ θεὸς λαλήσας τοῖς πατράσιν ἐν τοῖς προφήταις.

multifariam[6] et multis modis olim[7] Deus loquens patribus in prophetis.

1. שָׁכַם, hiph. inf. abs., *rise early*
2. ὄρθρος, *early in the morning*
3. πολυμερῶς, *many times*
4. πολυτρόπως, *in many ways*
5. πάλαι, *long ago*
6. multifariam, *in many ways*
7. olim, *long ago*

February 10

Psalm 2:8

שְׁאַ֤ל מִמֶּ֗נִּי וְאֶתְּנָ֣ה ג֭וֹיִם נַחֲלָתֶ֑ךָ וַ֝אֲחֻזָּתְךָ֗[1]
אַפְסֵי[2]־אָֽרֶץ׃

αἴτησαι[3] παρ᾽ ἐμοῦ, καὶ δώσω σοι ἔθνη τὴν κληρονομίαν σου καὶ τὴν κατάσχεσίν[4] σου τὰ πέρατα[5] τῆς γῆς.

Hebrews 1:2

ἐπ᾽ ἐσχάτου τῶν ἡμερῶν τούτων ἐλάλησεν ἡμῖν ἐν υἱῷ, ὃν ἔθηκεν κληρονόμον[6] πάντων, δι᾽ οὗ καὶ ἐποίησεν τοὺς αἰῶνας.

novissime[7] diebus istis locutus est nobis in Filio quem constituit heredem[8] universorum per quem fecit et saecula.

1. אֲחֻזָּה, *possession*
2. אֶ֫פֶס, *end*
3. αἰτέω, aor. mid. impv. 2 s., *ask*
4. κατάσχεσις, *possession*
5. πέρας, *end*
6. κληρονόμος, *heir*
7. nove, *finally, afterward*
8. heres, *heir*

February 11

Deuteronomy 18:15

נָבִ֨יא מִקִּרְבְּךָ֤ מֵאַחֶ֙יךָ֙ כָּמֹ֔נִי יָקִ֥ים לְךָ֖ יְהוָ֣ה אֱלֹהֶ֑יךָ
אֵלָ֖יו תִּשְׁמָעֽוּן׃

προφήτην ἐκ τῶν ἀδελφῶν σου ὡς ἐμὲ ἀναστήσει σοι κύριος ὁ θεός σου, αὐτοῦ ἀκούσεσθε.

Acts 3:22

Μωϋσῆς μὲν εἶπεν ὅτι *προφήτην ὑμῖν ἀναστήσει κύριος ὁ θεὸς ὑμῶν ἐκ τῶν ἀδελφῶν ὑμῶν ὡς ἐμέ· αὐτοῦ ἀκούσεσθε κατὰ πάντα ὅσα ἂν λαλήσῃ* πρὸς ὑμᾶς.

Moses quidem dixit quia prophetam vobis suscitabit Dominus Deus vester de fratribus vestris tamquam me ipsum audietis iuxta[1] omnia quaecumque locutus fuerit vobis.

1. iuxta, *according to*

February 12

Deuteronomy 18:19

וְהָיָ֗ה הָאִישׁ֙ אֲשֶׁ֤ר לֹֽא־יִשְׁמַע֙ אֶל־דְּבָרַ֔י אֲשֶׁ֥ר יְדַבֵּ֖ר בִּשְׁמִ֑י אָנֹכִ֖י אֶדְרֹ֥שׁ מֵעִמּֽוֹ׃

καὶ ὁ ἄνθρωπος, ὃς ἐὰν μὴ ἀκούσῃ ὅσα ἐὰν λαλήσῃ ὁ προφήτης ἐπὶ τῷ ὀνόματί μου, ἐγὼ ἐκδικήσω[1] ἐξ αὐτοῦ.

Acts 3:23

ἔσται δὲ πᾶσα ψυχὴ ἥτις ἐὰν μὴ ἀκούσῃ τοῦ προφήτου ἐκείνου ἐξολεθρευθήσεται[2] ἐκ τοῦ λαοῦ.

erit autem omnis anima quae non audierit prophetam illum exterminabitur[3] de plebe.

1. ἐκδικέω, fut. act. ind. 1 s., *avenge*

2. ἐξολεθρεύω, fut. pass. ind. 3 s., *destroy completely*

3. extermino, fut. pass. ind. 3 s., *drive out, destroy*

February 13

Exodus 25:8

וְעָ֥שׂוּ לִ֖י מִקְדָּ֑שׁ[1] וְשָׁכַנְתִּ֖י בְּתוֹכָֽם׃

καὶ ποιήσεις μοι ἁγίασμα,[2] καὶ ὀφθήσομαι ἐν ὑμῖν.

John 1:14

Καὶ ὁ λόγος σὰρξ ἐγένετο καὶ ἐσκήνωσεν[3] ἐν ἡμῖν, καὶ ἐθεασάμεθα[4] τὴν δόξαν αὐτοῦ, δόξαν ὡς μονογενοῦς[5] παρὰ πατρός, πλήρης[6] χάριτος καὶ ἀληθείας.

et Verbum[7] caro factum est et habitavit in nobis et vidimus gloriam eius gloriam quasi unigeniti[8] a Patre plenum gratiae et veritatis.

1. מִקְדָּשׁ, *sanctuary*
2. ἁγίασμα, *sacred place, sanctuary*
3. σκηνόω, aor. act. ind. 3 s., *dwell in a tent*
4. θεάομαι, aor. mid. ind. 1 p., *see*
5. μονογενής, *only, unique*
6. πλήρης, *full*
7. verbum, *word*
8. unigenitus, *only, unique*

February 14

Exodus 33:20

וַיֹּ֕אמֶר לֹ֥א תוּכַ֖ל לִרְאֹ֣ת אֶת־פָּנָ֑י כִּ֛י לֹֽא־יִרְאַ֥נִי הָאָדָ֖ם
וָחָֽי׃

καὶ εἶπεν Οὐ δυνήσῃ ἰδεῖν μου τὸ πρόσωπον· οὐ γὰρ μὴ ἴδῃ ἄνθρωπος τὸ πρόσωπόν μου καὶ ζήσεται.

John 1:18

Θεὸν οὐδεὶς ἑώρακεν πώποτε·[1] μονογενὴς[2] θεὸς ὁ ὢν εἰς τὸν κόλπον[3] τοῦ πατρὸς ἐκεῖνος ἐξηγήσατο.[4]

Deum nemo vidit umquam[5] unigenitus[6] Filius qui est in sinu[7] Patris ipse enarravit.[8]

1. πώποτε, *ever, at any time*
2. μονογενής, *only, unique*
3. κόλπος, *side, breast, chest*
4. ἐξηγέομαι, aor. mid. ind. 3 s., *explain, interpret, exposit, make known*
5. umquam, *ever, at any time*
6. unigenitus, *only, unique*
7. sinus, *bosom*
8. enarro, perf. act. ind. 3 s., *declare, narrate*

Primeval History

February 15

Genesis 4:4–5a

וְהֶ֨בֶל[1] הֵבִ֥יא גַם־ה֛וּא מִבְּכֹר֥וֹת צֹאנ֖וֹ וּמֵֽחֶלְבֵהֶ֑ן[2]
וַיִּ֣שַׁע[3] יְהוָ֔ה אֶל־הֶ֖בֶל וְאֶל־מִנְחָתֽוֹ׃ וְאֶל־קַ֥יִן[4] וְאֶל־
מִנְחָת֖וֹ לֹ֣א שָׁעָ֑ה[5]

καὶ Αβελ[6] ἤνεγκεν καὶ αὐτὸς ἀπὸ τῶν πρωτοτόκων τῶν προβάτων αὐτοῦ καὶ ἀπὸ τῶν στεάτων[7] αὐτῶν. καὶ ἐπεῖδεν ὁ θεὸς ἐπὶ Αβελ καὶ ἐπὶ τοῖς δώροις αὐτοῦ, ἐπὶ δὲ Καιν[8] καὶ ἐπὶ ταῖς θυσίαις αὐτοῦ οὐ προσέσχεν.

Hebrews 11:4

Πίστει πλείονα θυσίαν[9] Ἄβελ παρὰ Κάϊν προσήνεγκεν[10] τῷ θεῷ, δι᾽ ἧς ἐμαρτυρήθη εἶναι δίκαιος, μαρτυροῦντος ἐπὶ τοῖς δώροις[11] αὐτοῦ τοῦ θεοῦ, καὶ δι᾽ αὐτῆς ἀποθανὼν ἔτι λαλεῖ.

fide plurimam hostiam[12] Abel[13] quam Cain[14] obtulit Deo per quam testimonium consecutus[15] est esse iustus testimonium perhibente muneribus[16] eius Deo et per illam defunctus[17] adhuc loquitur.

1. הֶ֫בֶל, *Abel*
2. חֵ֫לֶב, *fat portions*
3. שָׁעָה, qal wcons. 3 m. s., *regard*
4. קַ֫יִן, *Cain*
5. שָׁעָה, qal perf. 3 m. s., *regard*
6. Αβελ, *Abel*
7. στέαρ, *fat*
8. Καιν, *Cain*
9. θυσία, *sacrifice, offering*
10. προσφέρω, aor. act. ind. 3 s., *offer, sacrifice*
11. δῶρον, *gift*
12. hostia, *sacrifice, offering*
13. Abel, *Abel*
14. Cain, *Cain*
15. consequor, perf. dep. ind. 3 s., *obtain, attain*
16. munus, *gift*
17. defungor, perf. dep. ptcp. m. nom. s., *die*

February 16

Genesis 5:24

וַיִּתְהַלֵּךְ חֲנוֹךְ[1] אֶת־הָאֱלֹהִים וְאֵינֶנּוּ כִּי־לָקַח אֹתוֹ
אֱלֹהִים׃

καὶ εὐηρέστησεν[2] Ενωχ[3] τῷ θεῷ καὶ οὐχ ηὑρίσκετο, ὅτι μετέθηκεν[4] αὐτὸν ὁ θεός.

Hebrews 11:5

Πίστει Ἑνὼχ μετετέθη[5] τοῦ μὴ ἰδεῖν θάνατον, καὶ οὐχ ηὑρίσκετο[6] διότι[7] μετέθηκεν αὐτὸν ὁ θεός. πρὸ[8] γὰρ τῆς μεταθέσεως[9] μεμαρτύρηται εὐαρεστηκέναι[10] τῷ θεῷ.

fide Enoch[11] translatus[12] est ne videret mortem et non inveniebatur quia transtulit[13] illum Deus ante translationem[14] enim testimonium habebat placuisse Deo.

1. חֲנוֹךְ, *Enoch*

2. εὐαρεστέω, aor. act. ind. 3 s., *please, be pleasing*

3. Ἑνώχ, *Enoch*

4. μετατίθημι, aor. act. ind. 3 s., *transfer, move*

5. μετατίθημι, aor. pass. ind. 3 s., *transfer, move*

6. εὑρίσκω, impf. pass. ind. 3 s., *find*

7. διότι, *for*

8. πρό, *before*

9. μετάθεσις, *transferred, moved*

10. εὐαρεστέω, perf. act. inf., *please, be pleasing*

11. Enoch, *Enoch*

12. transfero, perf. pass. ind. 3 s., *cross over, transfer*

13. transfero, perf. act. ind. 3 s., *cross over, transfer*

14. translatio, *transfer, translation*

February 17

Genesis 7:1

וַיֹּאמֶר יְהוָה לְנֹחַ[1] בֹּא־אַתָּה וְכָל־בֵּיתְךָ אֶל־הַתֵּבָה[2]
כִּי־אֹתְךָ רָאִיתִי צַדִּיק לְפָנַי בַּדּוֹר הַזֶּה׃

Καὶ εἶπεν κύριος ὁ θεὸς πρὸς Νωε[3] Εἴσελθε σὺ καὶ πᾶς ὁ οἶκός σου εἰς τὴν κιβωτόν,[4] ὅτι σὲ εἶδον δίκαιον ἐναντίον μου ἐν τῇ γενεᾷ ταύτῃ.

Hebrews 11:7

Πίστει χρηματισθεὶς[5] Νῶε περὶ τῶν μηδέπω[6] βλεπομένων, εὐλαβηθεὶς[7] κατεσκεύασεν[8] κιβωτὸν εἰς σωτηρίαν[9] τοῦ οἴκου αὐτοῦ δι᾽ ἧς κατέκρινεν[10] τὸν κόσμον, καὶ τῆς κατὰ πίστιν δικαιοσύνης ἐγένετο κληρονόμος.[11]

fide Noe[12] responso[13] accepto de his quae adhuc non videbantur metuens[14] aptavit[15] arcam[16] in salutem domus suae per quam damnavit[17] mundum et iustitiae quae per fidem est heres[18] est institutus.[19]

1. נֹחַ, *Noah*
2. תֵּבָה, *ark*
3. Νωε, *Noah*
4. κιβωτός, *ark*
5. χρηματίζω, aor. pass. ptcp. m. nom. s., *warn, direct*
6. μηδέπω, *not yet*
7. εὐλαβέομαι, aor. pass. ptcp. m. nom. s., *fear*
8. κατασκευάζω, aor. act. ind. 3 s., *construct, prepare*
9. σωτηρία, *salvation*
10. κατακρίνω, aor. act. ind. 3 s., *condemn*
11. κληρονόμος, *heir*
12. Noe, *Noah*
13. responsum, *answer*
14. metuo, pres. act. ptcp. m. nom. s., *fear*
15. apto, perf. act. ind. 3 s., *fit, frame, fashion*
16. arca, *ark*
17. damno, perf. act. ind. 3 s., *judge, condemn*
18. heres, *heir*
19. instituo, perf. pass. ind. 3 s., *institute, appoint*

February 18

Genesis 7:7

וַיָּבֹא נֹחַ[1] וּבָנָיו וְאִשְׁתּוֹ וּנְשֵׁי־בָנָיו אִתּוֹ אֶל־הַתֵּבָה[2]
מִפְּנֵי מֵי הַמַּבּוּל׃[3]

εἰσῆλθεν δὲ Νωε[4] καὶ οἱ υἱοὶ αὐτοῦ καὶ ἡ γυνὴ αὐτοῦ καὶ αἱ γυναῖκες τῶν υἱῶν αὐτοῦ μετ᾽ αὐτοῦ εἰς τὴν κιβωτὸν[5] διὰ τὸ ὕδωρ τοῦ κατακλυσμοῦ.[6]

Matthew 24:38–39

ὡς γὰρ ἦσαν ἐν ταῖς ἡμέραις [ἐκείναις] ταῖς πρὸ[7] τοῦ κατακλυσμοῦ τρώγοντες[8] καὶ πίνοντες, γαμοῦντες[9] καὶ γαμίζοντες,[10] ἄχρι[11] ἧς ἡμέρας εἰσῆλθεν Νῶε εἰς τὴν κιβωτόν, καὶ οὐκ ἔγνωσαν ἕως ἦλθεν ὁ κατακλυσμὸς καὶ ἦρεν ἅπαντας, οὕτως ἔσται [καὶ] ἡ παρουσία[12] τοῦ υἱοῦ τοῦ ἀνθρώπου.

sicut enim erant in diebus ante diluvium[13] comedentes[14] et bibentes nubentes[15] et nuptum[16] tradentes usque ad eum diem quo introivit in arcam[17] Noe[18] et non cognoverunt donec venit diluvium et tulit omnes ita erit et adventus[19] Filii hominis.

1. נֹחַ, *Noah*
2. תֵּבָה, *ark*
3. מַבּוּל, *flood*
4. Νωε, *Noah*
5. κιβωτός, *ark*
6. κατακλυσμός, *flood*
7. πρό, *before*
8. τρώγω, pres. act. ptcp. m. nom. p., *eat*
9. γαμέω, pres. act. ptcp. m. nom. p., *marry*
10. γαμίζω, pres. act. ptcp. m. nom. p., *give in marriage*
11. ἄχρι, *until*
12. παρουσία, *coming*
13. diluvium, *flood*
14. comedo, pres. act. ptcp. m. nom. p., *eat up, consume*
15. nubo, pres. act. ptcp. f. nom. p., *marry*
16. nubo, perf. pass. ptcp. n. nom. s., *marrying*
17. arca, *ark*
18. Noe, *Noah*
19. adventus, *coming*

February 19

Genesis 9:4

אַךְ־בָּשָׂר בְּנַפְשׁוֹ דָמוֹ לֹא תֹאכֵלוּ׃

πλὴν κρέας[1] ἐν αἵματι ψυχῆς οὐ φάγεσθε.

Acts 15:29

ἀπέχεσθαι[2] εἰδωλοθύτων[3] καὶ αἵματος καὶ πνικτῶν[4] καὶ πορνείας,[5] ἐξ ὧν διατηροῦντες[6] ἑαυτοὺς εὖ[7] πράξετε.[8]

ut abstineatis[9] vos ab immolatis[10] simulacrorum[11] et sanguine suffocato[12] et fornicatione[13] a quibus custodientes vos bene agetis.

1. κρέας, *meat*
2. ἀπέχω, pres. mid. inf., *abstain, be far off*
3. εἰδωλόθυτος, *(meat) offered to idols*
4. πνικτός, *strangled, choked*
5. πορνεία, *(sexual) immorality*
6. διατηρέω, pres. act. ptcp. m. nom. p., *keep*
7. εὖ, *well, good*
8. πράσσω, fut. act. ind. 2 p., *do*
9. abstineo, pres. act. subj. 2 p., *abstain, hold back*
10. immolo, perf. pass. ptcp. n. abl. p., *sacrifice*
11. simulacrum, *idol, image*
12. suffoco, perf. pass. ptcp. n. abl. s., *strangle*
13. fornicatio, *fornication*

February 20

Genesis 12:5

וַיִּקַּח אַבְרָם[1] אֶת־שָׂרַי[2] אִשְׁתּוֹ וְאֶת־לוֹט[3] בֶּן־
אָחִיו וְאֶת־כָּל־רְכוּשָׁם[4] אֲשֶׁר רָכָשׁוּ[5] וְאֶת־הַנֶּפֶשׁ
אֲשֶׁר־עָשׂוּ בְחָרָן[6] וַיֵּצְאוּ לָלֶכֶת אַרְצָה כְּנַעַן וַיָּבֹאוּ
אַרְצָה כְּנָעַן׃

καὶ ἔλαβεν Αβραμ[7] τὴν Σαραν[8] γυναῖκα αὐτοῦ καὶ τὸν Λωτ[9] υἱὸν τοῦ ἀδελφοῦ αὐτοῦ καὶ πάντα τὰ ὑπάρχοντα αὐτῶν, ὅσα ἐκτήσαντο, καὶ πᾶσαν ψυχήν, ἣν ἐκτήσαντο ἐν Χαρραν,[10] καὶ ἐξήλθοσαν πορευθῆναι εἰς γῆν Χανααν[11] καὶ ἦλθον εἰς γῆν Χανααν.

Acts 7:4

τότε ἐξελθὼν ἐκ γῆς Χαλδαίων[12] κατῴκησεν ἐν Χαρράν.[13] κἀκεῖθεν μετὰ τὸ ἀποθανεῖν τὸν πατέρα αὐτοῦ μετῴκισεν[14] αὐτὸν εἰς τὴν γῆν ταύτην εἰς ἣν ὑμεῖς νῦν κατοικεῖτε.

tunc exiit de terra Chaldeorum[15] et habitavit in Charram[16] et inde postquam[17] mortuus est pater eius transtulit[18] illum in terram istam in qua nunc vos habitatis.

1. אַבְרָם, *Abram*
2. שָׂרַי, *Sarai*
3. לוֹט, *Lot*
4. רְכוּשׁ, *possession, property*
5. רָכַשׁ, qal perf. 3 c. p., *acquire*
6. חָרָן, *Haran*
7. Αβραμ, *Abram*
8. Σαρα, *Sara*
9. Λωτ, *Lot*
10. Χαρράν, *Haran*
11. Χανααν, *Canaan*
12. Χαλδαῖος, *Chaldean*
13. Χαρράν, *Haran*
14. μετοικίζω, aor. act. ind. 3 s., *remove, deport*
15. Chaldeus, *Chaldean*
16. Charram, *Haran*
17. postquam, *after, when*
18. transfero, perf. act. ind. 3 s., *transport, transfer*

February 21

Genesis 12:3

וַאֲבָרְכָה מְבָרְכֶיךָ וּמְקַלֶּלְךָ אָאֹר[1] וְנִבְרְכוּ בְךָ כֹּל מִשְׁפְּחֹת הָאֲדָמָה׃

καὶ εὐλογήσω τοὺς εὐλογοῦντάς σε, καὶ τοὺς καταρωμένους[2] σε καταράσομαι·[3] καὶ ἐνευλογηθήσονται[4] ἐν σοὶ πᾶσαι αἱ φυλαὶ τῆς γῆς.

Galatians 3:8

προϊδοῦσα[5] δὲ ἡ γραφὴ[6] ὅτι ἐκ πίστεως δικαιοῖ[7] τὰ ἔθνη ὁ θεός, προευηγγελίσατο[8] τῷ Ἀβραὰμ ὅτι *ἐνευλογηθήσονται ἐν σοὶ πάντα τὰ ἔθνη.*

providens[9] autem scriptura quia ex fide iustificat gentes Deus praenuntiavit[10] Abrahae quia benedicentur in te omnes gentes.

1. אָרַר, qal impf. 1 c. s., *curse*
2. καταράομαι, pres. mid. ptcp. m. a. p., *curse*
3. καταράομαι, fut. mid. ind. 1 s., *curse*
4. ἐνευλογέω, fut. pass. ind. 3 p., *bless*
5. προοράω, aor. act. ptcp. f. nom. s., *see ahead of time, foresee*
6. γραφή, *Scripture*
7. δικαιόω, pres. act. ind. 3 s., *justify, pronounce righteous*
8. προευαγγελίζομαι, aor. mid. ind. 3 s., *preach the gospel*
9. providens, pres. act. ptcp. f. nom. s., *foresee*
10. praenuntio, perf. act. ind. 3 s., *announce/tell in advance*

February 22

Genesis 12:7

וַיֵּרָא יְהוָה אֶל־אַבְרָם[1] וַיֹּאמֶר לְזַרְעֲךָ אֶתֵּן אֶת־
הָאָרֶץ הַזֹּאת וַיִּבֶן שָׁם מִזְבֵּחַ לַיהוָה הַנִּרְאֶה אֵלָיו׃

καὶ ὤφθη κύριος τῷ Αβραμ[2] καὶ εἶπεν αὐτῷ Τῷ σπέρματί[3] σου δώσω τὴν γῆν ταύτην. καὶ ᾠκοδόμησεν ἐκεῖ Αβραμ θυσιαστήριον κυρίῳ τῷ ὀφθέντι αὐτῷ.

Galatians 3:16

τῷ δὲ Ἀβραὰμ ἐρρέθησαν αἱ ἐπαγγελίαι[4] καὶ τῷ σπέρματι αὐτοῦ. οὐ λέγει· καὶ τοῖς σπέρμασιν, ὡς ἐπὶ πολλῶν ἀλλ᾽ ὡς ἐφ᾽ ἑνός· *καὶ τῷ σπέρματί σου,* ὅς ἐστιν Χριστός.

Abrahae dictae sunt promissiones[5] et semini eius non dicit et seminibus quasi in multis sed quasi in uno et semini tuo qui est Christus.

1. אַבְרָם, *Abram*
2. Αβραμ, *Abram*
3. σπέρμα, *offspring, seed*
4. ἐπαγγελία, *promise*
5. promissio, *promise*

February 23

Genesis 14:18–19a

וּמַלְכִּי־צֶ֙דֶק֙[1] מֶ֣לֶךְ שָׁלֵ֔ם[2] הוֹצִ֖יא לֶ֣חֶם וָיָ֑יִן וְה֥וּא כֹהֵ֖ן
לְאֵ֥ל עֶלְיֽוֹן׃[3] וַֽיְבָרְכֵ֖הוּ

καὶ Μελχισεδεκ[4] βασιλεὺς Σαλημ[5] ἐξήνεγκεν ἄρτους καὶ οἶνον· ἦν δὲ ἱερεὺς τοῦ θεοῦ τοῦ ὑψίστου.[6] καὶ ηὐλόγησεν τὸν Αβραμ.[7]

Hebrews 7:1

Οὗτος γὰρ ὁ *Μελχισέδεκ,*[8] *βασιλεὺς Σαλήμ, ἱερεὺς τοῦ θεοῦ τοῦ ὑψίστου, ὁ συναντήσας*[9] *Ἀβραὰμ ὑποστρέφοντι ἀπὸ τῆς κοπῆς*[10] *τῶν βασιλέων καὶ εὐλογήσας αὐτόν.*

hic enim Melchisedech[11] rex Salem[12] sacerdos Dei summi qui obviavit[13] Abrahae regresso[14] a caede[15] regum et benedixit ei

1. מַלְכִּי־צֶדֶק, *Melchizedek*
2. שָׁלֵם, *Salem*
3. עֶלְיוֹן, *Highest, Most High*
4. Μελχισεδεκ, *Melchizedek*
5. Σαλημ, *Salem*
6. ὕψιστος, *Most High*
7. Αβραμ, *Abram*
8. Μελχισέδεκ, *Melchizedek*
9. συναντάω, aor. act. ptcp. m. nom. s., *meet, come upon*
10. κοπή, *slaughter*
11. Melchisedech, *Melchizedek*
12. Salem, *Salem*
13. obvio, perf. act. ind. 3 s., *meet*
14. regredior, perf. dep. ptcp. m. d. s., *return*
15. caedes, *slaughter*

February 24

Genesis 15:6

וְהֶאֱמִ֖ן[1] בַּֽיהוָ֑ה וַיַּחְשְׁבֶ֥הָ לּ֖וֹ צְדָקָֽה׃

καὶ ἐπίστευσεν[2] Αβραμ[3] τῷ θεῷ, καὶ ἐλογίσθη[4] αὐτῷ εἰς δικαιοσύνην.

Romans 4:9

Ὁ μακαρισμὸς[5] οὖν οὗτος ἐπὶ τὴν περιτομὴν[6] ἢ καὶ ἐπὶ τὴν ἀκροβυστίαν;[7] λέγομεν γάρ· ἐλογίσθη τῷ Ἀβραὰμ ἡ πίστις εἰς δικαιοσύνην.

beatitudo[8] ergo haec in circumcisione an etiam in praeputio[9] dicimus enim quia reputata[10] est Abrahae fides ad iustitiam.

1. אָמַן, hiph. perf. 3 m. s., *believe*
2. πιστεύω, aor. act. ind. 3 s., *believe*
3. Αβραμ, *Abram*
4. λογίζομαι, aor. pass. ind. 3 s., *count, calculate*
5. μακαρισμός, *blessedness*
6. περιτομή, *circumcision*
7. ἀκροβυστία, *uncircumcision, foreskin*
8. beatitudo, *blessedness, happiness*
9. praeputium, *uncircumcision, foreskin*
10. reputo, perf. pass. ind. 3 s., *reckon, account*

February 25

Genesis 17:11

וּנְמַלְתֶּ֕ם[1] אֵ֖ת בְּשַׂ֣ר עָרְלַתְכֶ֑ם[2] וְהָיָה֙ לְא֣וֹת[3] בְּרִ֔ית
בֵּינִ֖י וּבֵינֵיכֶֽם׃

καὶ περιτμηθήσεσθε[4] τὴν σάρκα τῆς
ἀκροβυστίας[5] ὑμῶν, καὶ ἔσται ἐν σημείῳ
διαθήκης ἀνὰ μέσον ἐμοῦ καὶ ὑμῶν.

Romans 4:11

καὶ σημεῖον ἔλαβεν περιτομῆς[6] σφραγῖδα[7] τῆς
δικαιοσύνης τῆς πίστεως τῆς ἐν τῇ ἀκροβυστίᾳ,
εἰς τὸ εἶναι αὐτὸν πατέρα πάντων τῶν
πιστευόντων δι᾽ ἀκροβυστίας, εἰς τὸ λογισθῆναι[8]
[καὶ] αὐτοῖς [τὴν] δικαιοσύνην.

et signum accepit circumcisionis signaculum[9]
iustitiae fidei quae est in praeputio[10] ut sit
pater omnium credentium per praeputium ut
reputetur[11] et illis ad iustitiam.

1. מוּל, niph. perf. 2 m. p., *circumcise*
2. עָרְלָה, *foreskin*
3. אוֹת, *sign*
4. περιτέμνω, fut. pass. ind. 2 p., *circumcise*
5. ἀκροβυστία, *foreskin, uncircumcision*
6. περιτομή, *circumcision*
7. σφραγίς, *seal*
8. λογίζομαι, aor. pass. inf., *count, calculate*
9. signaculum, *seal*
10. praeputium, *foreskin, uncircumcision*
11. reputo, pres. pass. subj. 3 s., *reckon, account*

February 26

Genesis 18:11

וְאַבְרָהָ֤ם וְשָׂרָה֙[1] זְקֵנִ֔ים בָּאִ֖ים בַּיָּמִ֑ים חָדַל֙[2] לִהְי֣וֹת
לְשָׂרָ֔ה אֹ֖רַח כַּנָּשִֽׁים׃

Αβρααμ δὲ καὶ Σαρρα[3] πρεσβύτεροι προβεβηκότες[4] ἡμερῶν, ἐξέλιπεν δὲ Σαρρα γίνεσθαι τὰ γυναικεῖα.[5]

Luke 1:7

καὶ οὐκ ἦν αὐτοῖς τέκνον, καθότι[6] ἦν ἡ Ἐλισάβετ[7] στεῖρα,[8] καὶ ἀμφότεροι[9] προβεβηκότες ἐν ταῖς ἡμέραις αὐτῶν ἦσαν.

et non erat illis filius eo quod esset Elisabeth[10] sterilis[11] et ambo[12] processissent in diebus suis.

1. שָׂרָה, *Sarah*
2. חָדַל, qal perf. 3 m. s., *cease*
3. Σάρρα, *Sarah*
4. προβαίνω, perf. act. ptcp. m. nom. p., *advance, be old*
5. γυναικεῖος, *of or belonging to a woman*
6. καθότι, *because*
7. Ἐλισάβετ, *Elizabeth*
8. στεῖρα, *barren, infertile*
9. ἀμφότεροι, *both*
10. Elisabeth, *Elizabeth*
11. sterilis, *barren, infertile*
12. ambo, *both*

February 27

1. הָרָה, qal wcons. 3 f. s., *conceive*
2. שָׂרָה, *Sarah*
3. זְקֻנִים, *old age*
4. Σάρρα, *Sarah*
5. γῆρας, *old age*
6. στεῖρα, *barren, infertile*
7. καταβολή, *foundation*; TH: εἰς καταβολὴν σπέρματος = *found a posterity* or *received power to conceive*
8. σπέρμα, *seed, posterity*
9. ἡλικία, *age*
10. ἐπεί, *since*
11. πιστός, *faith*
12. ἡγέομαι, aor. mid. ind. 3 s., *consider, lead*
13. ἐπαγγέλλομαι, aor. mid. ptcp. m. a. s., *promise*
14. Sarra, *Sarah*
15. sterilis, *barren, infertile*
16. conceptio, *conception*
17. praeter, *beyond, past*
18. aetas, *age*
19. promitto, plu-perf. act. ind. 3 s., *promise*

Genesis 21:2

וַתַּ֨הַר[1] וַתֵּ֨לֶד שָׂרָ֧ה[2] לְאַבְרָהָ֛ם בֵּ֖ן לִזְקֻנָ֑יו[3] לַמּוֹעֵ֕ד
אֲשֶׁר־דִּבֶּ֥ר אֹת֖וֹ אֱלֹהִֽים׃

καὶ συλλαβοῦσα ἔτεκεν Σαρρα[4] τῷ Αβρααμ υἱὸν εἰς τὸ γῆρας[5] εἰς τὸν καιρόν, καθὰ ἐλάλησεν αὐτῷ κύριος.

Hebrews 11:11

Πίστει καὶ αὐτὴ Σάρρα στεῖρα[6] δύναμιν εἰς καταβολὴν[7] σπέρματος[8] ἔλαβεν καὶ παρὰ καιρὸν ἡλικίας,[9] ἐπεὶ[10] πιστὸν[11] ἡγήσατο[12] τὸν ἐπαγγειλάμενον.[13]

fide et ipsa Sarra[14] sterilis[15] virtutem in conceptionem[16] seminis accepit etiam praeter[17] tempus aetatis[18] quoniam fidelem credidit esse qui promiserat.[19]

February 28

Genesis 22:9

וַיָּבֹאוּ אֶֽל־הַמָּקוֹם֮ אֲשֶׁ֣ר אָֽמַר־ל֣וֹ הָאֱלֹהִים֒ וַיִּ֨בֶן שָׁ֤ם אַבְרָהָם֙ אֶת־הַמִּזְבֵּ֔חַ וַֽיַּעֲרֹ֖ךְ[1] אֶת־הָעֵצִ֑ים וַֽיַּעֲקֹד֙[2] אֶת־יִצְחָ֣ק בְּנ֔וֹ וַיָּ֤שֶׂם אֹתוֹ֙ עַל־הַמִּזְבֵּ֔חַ מִמַּ֖עַל לָעֵצִֽים׃

ἦλθον ἐπὶ τὸν τόπον, ὃν εἶπεν αὐτῷ ὁ θεός. καὶ ᾠκοδόμησεν ἐκεῖ Αβρααμ θυσιαστήριον[3] καὶ ἐπέθηκεν τὰ ξύλα καὶ συμποδίσας[4] Ισαακ τὸν υἱὸν αὐτοῦ ἐπέθηκεν αὐτὸν ἐπὶ τὸ θυσιαστήριον ἐπάνω τῶν ξύλων.

James 2:21

Ἀβραὰμ ὁ πατὴρ ἡμῶν οὐκ ἐξ ἔργων ἐδικαιώθη[5] ἀνενέγκας[6] Ἰσαὰκ[7] τὸν υἱὸν αὐτοῦ ἐπὶ τὸ θυσιαστήριον;

Abraham pater noster nonne ex operibus iustificatus est offerens Isaac[8] filium suum super altare?[9]

1. עָרַךְ, qal wcons. 3 m. s., *arrange*
2. עָקַד, qal wcons. 3 m. s., *bind*
3. θυσιαστήριον, *altar*
4. συμποδίζω, aor. act. ptcp. m. nom. s., *bind*
5. δικαιόω, aor. pass. ind. 3 s., *justify, pronounce righteous*
6. ἀναφέρω, aor. act. ptcp. m. nom. s., *offer, bring up*
7. Ἰσαάκ, *Isaac*
8. Isaac, *Isaac*
9. altare, *altar*

1. בֶּ֫טֶן, *womb*

2. לְאֹם, *nation*

3. מֵעֶה, *belly*

4. פָּרַד, niph. impf. 3 m. p., *divide, separate*

5. אָמֵץ, qal impf. 3 m. s., *be strong*

6. צָעִיר, *younger, little*

7. γαστήρ, *womb*

8. διαστέλλω, fut. pass. ind. 3 p., *divide*

9. ὑπερέχω, fut. act. ind. 3 s., *excel, exceed*

10. δουλεύω, fut. act. ind. 3 s., *serve*

11. ἐλάσσων, *least, little*

12. μήπω, *not yet*

13. μηδέ, *but not, nothing*

14. πράσσω, aor. act. ptcp. m. g. p., *do, accomplish*

15. φαῦλος, *evil, bad*

16. ἐκλογή, *election, choice*

17. πρόθεσις, *purpose*

18. nondum, *not yet*

19. electio, *choice, election*

20. propositum, *purpose*

21. parvus, *small*

March 1

Genesis 25:23

וַיֹּאמֶר יְהוָה לָהּ שְׁנֵי גֹיִים בְּבִטְנֵךְ[1] וּשְׁנֵי לְאֻמִּים[2] מִמֵּעַיִךְ[3] יִפָּרֵדוּ[4] וּלְאֹם מִלְאֹם יֶאֱמָץ[5] וְרַב יַעֲבֹד צָעִיר[6]׃

καὶ εἶπεν κύριος αὐτῇ Δύο ἔθνη ἐν τῇ γαστρί[7] σού εἰσιν, καὶ δύο λαοὶ ἐκ τῆς κοιλίας σου διασταλήσονται·[8] καὶ λαὸς λαοῦ ὑπερέξει,[9] καὶ ὁ μείζων δουλεύσει[10] τῷ ἐλάσσονι.[11]

Romans 9:11–12

μήπω[12] γὰρ γεννηθέντων μηδὲ[13] πραξάντων[14] τι ἀγαθὸν ἢ φαῦλον,[15] ἵνα ἡ κατ᾽ ἐκλογὴν[16] πρόθεσις[17] τοῦ θεοῦ μένῃ, οὐκ ἐξ ἔργων ἀλλ᾽ ἐκ τοῦ καλοῦντος, ἐρρέθη αὐτῇ ὅτι *ὁ μείζων δουλεύσει τῷ ἐλάσσονι.*

cum enim nondum[18] nati fuissent aut aliquid egissent bonum aut malum ut secundum electionem[19] propositum[20] Dei maneret non ex operibus sed ex vocante dictum est ei quia maior serviet minori.[21]

March 2

Genesis 27:34

כִּשְׁמֹ֤עַ עֵשָׂו֙[1] אֶת־דִּבְרֵ֣י אָבִ֔יו וַיִּצְעַ֣ק[2] צְעָקָ֔ה[3] גְּדֹלָ֥ה
וּמָרָ֖ה[4] עַד־מְאֹ֑ד וַיֹּ֣אמֶר לְאָבִ֔יו בָּרְכֵ֥נִי גַם־אָ֖נִי אָבִֽי׃

ἐγένετο δὲ ἡνίκα[5] ἤκουσεν Ησαυ τὰ ῥήματα Ισαακ τοῦ πατρὸς αὐτοῦ, ἀνεβόησεν[6] φωνὴν μεγάλην καὶ πικρὰν[7] σφόδρα καὶ εἶπεν Εὐλόγησον δὴ κἀμέ, πάτερ.

Hebrews 12:17

ἴστε γὰρ ὅτι καὶ μετέπειτα[8] θέλων κληρονομῆσαι[9] τὴν εὐλογίαν[10] ἀπεδοκιμάσθη,[11] μετανοίας[12] γὰρ τόπον οὐχ εὗρεν καίπερ[13] μετὰ δακρύων[14] ἐκζητήσας[15] αὐτήν.

scitote enim quoniam et postea[16] cupiens[17] hereditare[18] benedictionem[19] reprobatus[20] est non enim invenit paenitentiae locum quamquam[21] cum lacrimis[22] inquisisset[23] eam.

1. עֵשָׂו, *Esau*
2. צָעַק, qal wcons. 3 m. s., *cry out*
3. צְעָקָה, *cry*
4. מַר, *bitter*
5. ἡνίκα, *when*
6. ἀναβοάω, aor. act. ind. 3 s., *cry*
7. πικρός, *bitter*
8. μετέπειτα, *afterward*
9. κληρονομέω, aor. act. inf., *inherit*
10. εὐλογία, *blessing*
11. ἀποδοκιμάζω, aor. pass. ind. 3 s., *reject*
12. μετάνοια, *repentance*
13. καίπερ, *though*
14. δάκρυον, *tear*
15. ἐκζητέω, aor. act. ptcp. m. nom. s., *search, seek*
16. postea, *thereafter, afterward*
17. cupio, pres. act. ptcp. m. nom. s., *desire*
18. heredito, pres. act. inf., *inherit*
19. benedictio, *blessing, benediction*
20. reprobo, perf. pass. ind. 3 s., *reject*
21. quamquam, *although*
22. lacrima, *tear*
23. inquiro, pluperf. act. subj. 3 s., *seek, look for*

March 3

Genesis 28:12

וַיַּחֲלֹ֗ם[1] וְהִנֵּ֤ה סֻלָּם֙[2] מֻצָּ֣ב[3] אַ֔רְצָה וְרֹאשׁ֖וֹ מַגִּ֣יעַ
הַשָּׁמָ֑יְמָה וְהִנֵּה֙ מַלְאֲכֵ֣י אֱלֹהִ֔ים עֹלִ֥ים וְיֹרְדִ֖ים בּֽוֹ׃

καὶ ἐνυπνιάσθη,[4] καὶ ἰδοὺ κλίμαξ[5] ἐστηριγμένη[6] ἐν τῇ γῇ, ἧς ἡ κεφαλὴ ἀφικνεῖτο[7] εἰς τὸν οὐρανόν, καὶ οἱ ἄγγελοι τοῦ θεοῦ ἀνέβαινον καὶ κατέβαινον ἐπ᾽ αὐτῆς.

John 1:51

καὶ λέγει αὐτῷ· ἀμὴν ἀμὴν λέγω ὑμῖν, ὄψεσθε *τὸν οὐρανὸν ἀνεῳγότα καὶ τοὺς ἀγγέλους τοῦ θεοῦ ἀναβαίνοντας καὶ καταβαίνοντας ἐπὶ* τὸν υἱὸν τοῦ ἀνθρώπου.

et dicit ei amen amen dico vobis videbitis caelum apertum et angelos Dei ascendentes et descendentes supra Filium hominis.

1. חָלַם, qal wcons. 3 m. s., *dream*
2. סֻלָּם, *ladder*
3. נָצַב, hoph. ptcp. m. s. abs., *stand*
4. ἐνυπνιάζομαι, aor. mid. ind. 3 s., *dream*
5. κλῖμαξ, *ladder*
6. στηρίζω, perf. pass. ptcp. f. nom. s., *fix, set*
7. ἀφικνέομαι, impf. mid. ind. 3 s., *reach, arrive at*

March 4

Genesis 30:23

וַתַּ֥הַר[1] וַתֵּ֖לֶד בֵּ֑ן וַתֹּ֕אמֶר אָסַ֥ף אֱלֹהִ֖ים אֶת־חֶרְפָּתִֽי׃[2]

καὶ συλλαβοῦσα ἔτεκεν τῷ Ιακωβ υἱόν. εἶπεν δὲ Ραχηλ[3] Ἀφεῖλεν[4] ὁ θεός μου τὸ ὄνειδος.[5]

Luke 1:25

ὅτι οὕτως μοι πεποίηκεν κύριος ἐν ἡμέραις αἷς ἐπεῖδεν[6] ἀφελεῖν[7] ὄνειδός μου[8] ἐν ἀνθρώποις.

quia sic mihi fecit Dominus in diebus quibus respexit[9] auferre[10] obprobrium[11] meum[12] inter homines.

1. הָרָה, qal wcons. 3 f. s., *conceive*

2. חֶרְפָּה, *reproach*

3. Ραχήλ, *Rachel*

4. ἀφαιρέω, aor. act. ind. 3 s., *take away*

5. ὄνειδος, *reproach*

6. ἐφοράω, aor. act. ind. 3 s., *watch over*

7. ἀφαιρέω, aor. act. inf., *take away*

8. CH: The referent of μου is Elizabeth.

9. respicio, perf. act. ind. 3 s., *regard*

10. aufero, pres. act. inf., *take away, remove*

11. obprobrium, *reproach*

12. CH: The referent of meum is Elizabeth.

March 5

Genesis 39:23

אֵ֣ין ׀ שַׂ֣ר בֵּית־הַסֹּ֗הַר[1] רֹאֶ֤ה אֶֽת־כָּל־מְא֨וּמָה֙[2] בְּיָד֔וֹ[3]
בַּאֲשֶׁ֥ר יְהוָ֖ה אִתּ֑וֹ וַֽאֲשֶׁר־ה֥וּא עֹשֶׂ֖ה יְהוָ֥ה מַצְלִֽיחַ׃[4]

οὐκ ἦν ὁ ἀρχιδεσμοφύλαξ[5] τοῦ δεσμωτηρίου[6] γινώσκων δι᾽ αὐτὸν[7] οὐθέν·[8] πάντα γὰρ ἦν διὰ χειρὸς Ιωσηφ διὰ τὸ τὸν κύριον μετ᾽ αὐτοῦ εἶναι, καὶ ὅσα αὐτὸς ἐποίει, κύριος εὐώδου[9] ἐν ταῖς χερσὶν αὐτοῦ.

Acts 7:9

Καὶ οἱ πατριάρχαι[10] ζηλώσαντες[11] τὸν Ἰωσὴφ[12] ἀπέδοντο[13] εἰς Αἴγυπτον.[14] καὶ ἦν ὁ θεὸς μετ᾽ αὐτοῦ.

et patriarchae[15] aemulantes[16] Ioseph vendiderunt[17] in Aegyptum[18] et erat Deus cum eo.

1. סֹהַר, *prison, round house*
2. מְאוּמָה, *anything*
3. CH: The referent of the pronoun is Joseph; TH = *in Joseph's hands.*
4. צָלַח, hiph. ptcp. m. s. abs., *prosper, succeed*
5. ἀρχιδεσμοφύλαξ, *chief prison guard*
6. δεσμωτήριον, *prison*
7. CH: The referent of the pronoun is Joseph.
8. οὐθείς, *nothing*
9. εὐοδόω, impf. act. ind. 3 s., *prosper*
10. πατριάρχης, *patriarch*
11. ζηλόω, aor. act. ptcp. m. nom. p., *be jealous*
12. Ιωσηφ, *Joseph*
13. ἀποδίδωμι, aor. mid. ind. 3 p., *sell*
14. Αἴγυπτος, *Egypt*
15. patriarcha, *patriarch*
16. aemulor, pres. act. ptcp. m. nom. p., *envy*
17. vendo, perf. act. ind. 3 p., *sell*
18. Aegyptus, *Egypt*

March 6

Genesis 41:55

וַתִּרְעַב֙[1] כָּל־אֶ֣רֶץ מִצְרַ֔יִם וַיִּצְעַ֥ק[2] הָעָ֛ם אֶל־פַּרְעֹ֖ה
לַלָּ֑חֶם וַיֹּ֨אמֶר פַּרְעֹ֤ה לְכָל־מִצְרַ֙יִם֙ לְכ֣וּ אֶל־יוֹסֵ֔ף
אֲשֶׁר־יֹאמַ֥ר לָכֶ֖ם תַּעֲשֽׂוּ׃

καὶ ἐπείνασεν[3] πᾶσα ἡ γῆ Αἰγύπτου, ἐκέκραξεν δὲ ὁ λαὸς πρὸς Φαραω περὶ ἄρτων· εἶπεν δὲ Φαραω πᾶσι τοῖς Αἰγυπτίοις Πορεύεσθε πρὸς Ιωσηφ, καὶ ὃ ἐὰν εἴπῃ ὑμῖν, ποιήσατε.

John 2:5

λέγει ἡ μήτηρ αὐτοῦ τοῖς διακόνοις·[4] ὅ τι ἂν λέγῃ ὑμῖν ποιήσατε.

dicit mater eius ministris quodcumque dixerit vobis facite.

1. רָעֵב, qal wcons. 3 f. s., *be hungry*
2. צָעַק, qal wcons. 3 m. s., *cry out*
3. πεινάω, aor. act. ind. 3 s., *be hungry*
4. διάκονος, *servant*

March 7

Deuteronomy 10:22

בְּשִׁבְעִים נֶפֶשׁ יָרְדוּ אֲבֹתֶיךָ מִצְרָיְמָה וְעַתָּה שָׂמְךָ
יְהוָה אֱלֹהֶיךָ כְּכוֹכְבֵי[1] הַשָּׁמַיִם לָרֹב׃

ἐν ἑβδομήκοντα[2] ψυχαῖς κατέβησαν οἱ πατέρες σου εἰς Αἴγυπτον, νυνὶ[3] δὲ ἐποίησέν σε κύριος ὁ θεός σου ὡσεὶ τὰ ἄστρα[4] τοῦ οὐρανοῦ τῷ πλήθει.

Acts 7:14

ἀποστείλας δὲ Ἰωσὴφ[5] μετεκαλέσατο[6] Ἰακὼβ[7] τὸν πατέρα αὐτοῦ καὶ πᾶσαν τὴν συγγένειαν[8] ἐν ψυχαῖς ἑβδομήκοντα πέντε.[9]

mittens autem Ioseph accersivit[10] Iacob[11] patrem suum et omnem cognationem[12] in animabus septuaginta[13] quinque.

1. כּוֹכָב, *star*
2. ἑβδομήκοντα, *seventy*
3. νυνί, *now*
4. ἄστρον, *star*
5. Ἰωσήφ, *Joseph*
6. μετακαλέω, aor. mid. ind. 3 s., *call*
7. Ἰακώβ, *Jacob*
8. συγγένεια, *family, kindred*
9. πέντε, *five*
10. accerso, perf. act. ind. 3 s., *call for, send for*
11. Iacob, *Jacob*
12. cognatio, *family, kindred*
13. septuaginta, *seventy*

March 8

Genesis 50:24

וַיֹּ֤אמֶר יוֹסֵף֙ אֶל־אֶחָ֔יו אָנֹכִ֖י מֵ֑ת וֵֽאלֹהִ֞ים פָּקֹ֧ד יִפְקֹ֣ד
אֶתְכֶ֗ם וְהֶעֱלָ֤ה אֶתְכֶם֙ מִן־הָאָ֣רֶץ הַזֹּ֔את אֶל־הָאָ֕רֶץ
אֲשֶׁ֥ר נִשְׁבַּ֛ע לְאַבְרָהָ֥ם לְיִצְחָ֖ק וּֽלְיַעֲקֹֽב׃

καὶ εἶπεν Ιωσηφ τοῖς ἀδελφοῖς αὐτοῦ λέγων Ἐγὼ ἀποθνήσκω· ἐπισκοπῇ[1] δὲ ἐπισκέψεται ὑμᾶς ὁ θεὸς καὶ ἀνάξει ὑμᾶς ἐκ τῆς γῆς ταύτης εἰς τὴν γῆν, ἣν ὤμοσεν ὁ θεὸς τοῖς πατράσιν ἡμῶν Αβρααμ καὶ Ισαακ καὶ Ιακωβ.

Hebrews 11:22

Πίστει Ἰωσὴφ[2] τελευτῶν[3] περὶ τῆς ἐξόδου[4] τῶν υἱῶν Ἰσραὴλ[5] ἐμνημόνευσεν[6] καὶ περὶ τῶν ὀστέων[7] αὐτοῦ ἐνετείλατο.[8]

fide Ioseph moriens de profectione[9] filiorum Israhel memoratus[10] est et de ossibus[11] suis mandavit.[12]

1. ἐπισκοπή, *visitation*
2. Ἰωσήφ, *Joseph*
3. τελευτάω, pres. act. ptcp. m. nom. s., *die*
4. ἔξοδος, *departure, exodus*
5. Ἰσραήλ, *Israel*
6. μνημονεύω, aor. act. ind. 3 s., *mention*
7. ὀστέον, *bone*
8. ἐντέλλω, aor. mid. ind. 3 s., *command*
9. profectio, *departure, going out*
10. memoror, perf. dep. ind. 3 s., *mention*
11. os, *bone*
12. mando, perf. act. ind. 3 s., *command*

The Exodus

March 9

Exodus 2:14

וַיֹּאמֶר מִי שָׂמְךָ לְאִישׁ שַׂר וְשֹׁפֵט עָלֵינוּ הַלְהָרְגֵנִי
אַתָּה אֹמֵר כַּאֲשֶׁר הָרַגְתָּ אֶת־הַמִּצְרִי[1] וַיִּירָא מֹשֶׁה
וַיֹּאמַר אָכֵן[2] נוֹדַע הַדָּבָר׃

ὁ δὲ εἶπεν Τίς σε κατέστησεν ἄρχοντα καὶ δικαστὴν[3] ἐφ᾽ ἡμῶν; μὴ ἀνελεῖν[4] με σὺ θέλεις, ὃν τρόπον ἀνεῖλες[5] ἐχθὲς[6] τὸν Αἰγύπτιον; ἐφοβήθη δὲ Μωυσῆς καὶ εἶπεν Εἰ οὕτως ἐμφανὲς[7] γέγονεν τὸ ῥῆμα τοῦτο;

Acts 7:35

Τοῦτον τὸν Μωϋσῆν ὃν ἠρνήσαντο[8] εἰπόντες· *τίς σε κατέστησεν*[9] *ἄρχοντα*[10] *καὶ δικαστήν*; τοῦτον ὁ θεὸς [καὶ] ἄρχοντα καὶ λυτρωτὴν[11] ἀπέσταλκεν σὺν χειρὶ ἀγγέλου τοῦ ὀφθέντος αὐτῷ ἐν τῇ βάτῳ.[12]

hunc Mosen quem negaverunt dicentes quis te constituit principem et iudicem[13] hunc Deus principem et redemptorem[14] misit cum manu angeli qui apparuit illi in rubo.[15]

1. מִצְרִי, *Egyptian*
2. אָכֵן, *surely*
3. δικαστής, *judge*
4. ἀναιρέω, aor. act. inf., *kill, destroy*
5. ἀναιρέω, aor. act. ind. 2 s., *kill, destroy*
6. ἐχθές, *yesterday*
7. ἐμφανής, *visible*
8. ἀρνέομαι, aor. mid. ind. 3 p., *reject*
9. καθίστημι, aor. act. ind. 3 s., *put in charge*
10. ἄρχων, *ruler*
11. λυτρωτής, *redeemer, ransomer*
12. βάτος, *thorn-bush*
13. iudex, *judge*
14. redemptor, *savior, redeemer*
15. rubus, *bramble/bush*

March 10

Exodus 4:21

וַיֹּאמֶר יְהוָה אֶל־מֹשֶׁה בְּלֶכְתְּךָ לָשׁוּב מִצְרַיְמָה רְאֵה
כָּל־הַמֹּפְתִים[1] אֲשֶׁר־שַׂמְתִּי בְיָדֶךָ וַעֲשִׂיתָם לִפְנֵי
פַרְעֹה וַאֲנִי אֲחַזֵּק אֶת־לִבּוֹ וְלֹא יְשַׁלַּח אֶת־הָעָם׃

εἶπεν δὲ κύριος πρὸς Μωυσῆν Πορευομένου σου καὶ ἀποστρέφοντος εἰς Αἴγυπτον ὅρα πάντα τὰ τέρατα,[2] ἃ ἔδωκα ἐν ταῖς χερσίν σου, ποιήσεις αὐτὰ ἐναντίον Φαραω· ἐγὼ δὲ σκληρυνῶ[3] τὴν καρδίαν αὐτοῦ, καὶ οὐ μὴ ἐξαποστείλῃ τὸν λαόν.

Romans 9:18

ἄρα[4] οὖν ὃν θέλει ἐλεεῖ,[5] ὃν δὲ θέλει σκληρύνει.[6]

ergo cuius vult miseretur et quem vult indurat.[7]

1. מוֹפֵת, *wonder, marvel*
2. τέρας, *wonder, marvel*
3. σκληρύνω, fut. act. ind. 1 s., *harden*
4. ἄρα, *therefore, for*
5. ἐλεέω, pres. act. ind. 3 s., *have/show mercy*
6. σκληρύνω, pres. act. ind. 3 s., *harden*
7. induro, pres. act. ind. 3 s., *harden*

March 11

Exodus 6:6

לָכֵ֞ן אֱמֹ֣ר לִבְנֵֽי־יִשְׂרָאֵל֮ אֲנִ֣י יְהוָה֒ וְהוֹצֵאתִ֣י אֶתְכֶ֗ם
מִתַּ֙חַת֙ סִבְלֹ֣ת[1] מִצְרַ֔יִם וְהִצַּלְתִּ֥י אֶתְכֶ֖ם מֵעֲבֹדָתָ֑ם
וְגָאַלְתִּ֤י אֶתְכֶם֙ בִּזְר֣וֹעַ[2] נְטוּיָ֔ה וּבִשְׁפָטִ֖ים[3] גְּדֹלִֽים׃

βάδιζε[4] εἰπὸν τοῖς υἱοῖς Ισραηλ λέγων Ἐγὼ κύριος καὶ ἐξάξω[5] ὑμᾶς ἀπὸ τῆς δυναστείας[6] τῶν Αἰγυπτίων[7] καὶ ῥύσομαι ὑμᾶς ἐκ τῆς δουλείας[8] καὶ λυτρώσομαι ὑμᾶς ἐν βραχίονι[9] ὑψηλῷ[10] καὶ κρίσει μεγάλῃ.

Acts 13:17

ὁ θεὸς τοῦ λαοῦ τούτου Ἰσραὴλ ἐξελέξατο[11] τοὺς πατέρας ἡμῶν καὶ τὸν λαὸν ὕψωσεν[12] ἐν τῇ παροικίᾳ[13] ἐν γῇ Αἰγύπτου καὶ μετὰ βραχίονος ὑψηλοῦ ἐξήγαγεν[14] αὐτοὺς ἐξ αὐτῆς.

Deus plebis Israhel elegit patres nostros et plebem exaltavit[15] cum essent incolae[16] in terra Aegypti[17] et in brachio[18] excelso[19] eduxit[20] eos ex ea.

1. סִבְלָה, *burden*
2. זְרוֹעַ, *arm*
3. שֶׁפֶט, *judgment*
4. βαδίζω, pres. act. impv. 2 s., *go, walk*
5. ἐξάγω, fut. act. ind. 1 s., *lift up, exalt*
6. δυναστεία, *sovereignty, power*
7. Αἰγύπτος, *Egypt*
8. δουλεία, *slavery*
9. βραχίων, *arm*
10. ὑψηλός, *high*
11. ἐκλέγομαι, aor. mid. ind. 3 s., *choose, select*
12. ὑψόω, aor. act. ind. 3 s., *lift up, exalt*
13. παροικία, *stay, lodging, journeying*
14. ἐξάγω, aor. act. ind. 3 s., *lead/bring out*
15. exalto, perf. act. ind. 3 s., *lift up, exalt*
16. incola, *stranger, sojourner*
17. Aegyptus, *Egypt*
18. bracchium, *arm*
19. excelsus, *high*
20. educo, perf. act. ind. 3 s., *lead/bring out*

March 12

Exodus 7:11

וַיִּקְרָא֙ גַּם־פַּרְעֹ֔ה לַחֲכָמִ֖ים וְלַֽמְכַשְּׁפִ֑ים[1] וַיַּֽעֲשׂ֨וּ גַם־
הֵ֜ם חַרְטֻמֵּ֥י[2] מִצְרַ֛יִם בְּלַהֲטֵיהֶ֖ם[3] כֵּֽן׃

συνεκάλεσεν[4] δὲ Φαραω τοὺς σοφιστὰς[5] Αἰγύπτου καὶ τοὺς φαρμάκους,[6] καὶ ἐποίησαν καὶ οἱ ἐπαοιδοὶ[7] τῶν Αἰγυπτίων ταῖς φαρμακείαις[8] αὐτῶν ὡσαύτως.[9]

2 Timothy 3:8

ὃν τρόπον[10] δὲ Ἰάννης[11] καὶ Ἰαμβρῆς[12] ἀντέστησαν[13] Μωϋσεῖ, οὕτως καὶ οὗτοι ἀνθίστανται[14] τῇ ἀληθείᾳ, ἄνθρωποι κατεφθαρμένοι[15] τὸν νοῦν,[16] ἀδόκιμοι[17] περὶ τὴν πίστιν.

quemadmodum autem Iannes[18] et Mambres[19] restiterunt[20] Mosi ita et hii resistunt[21] veritati homines corrupti[22] mente[23] reprobi[24] circa fidem.

1. כשׁף, piel ptcp. m. p. abs., *practice sorcery*

2. חַרְטֹם, *magician, diviner*

3. לְהָטִים, *secret art*

4. συγκαλέω, aor. act. ind. 3 s., *call together*

5. σοφιστής, *wise man*

6. φάρμακος, *sorcerer*

7. ἐπαοιδός, *enchanter*

8. φάρμακεία, *magic*

9. ὡσαύτως, *likewise*

10. τρόπος, *as, in the manner*

11. Ἰάννης, *Jannes*

12. Ἰαμβρῆς, *Jambres*

13. ἀνθίστημι, aor. act. ind. 3 p., *resist, oppose*

14. ἀνθίστημι, pres. mid. ind. 3 p., *resist, oppose*

15. καταφθείρω, perf. mid. ptcp. m. nom. p., *corrupt*

16. νοῦς, *mind*

17. ἀδόκιμος, *worthless, disreputable*

18. Iannes, *Jannes*

19. Mambres, *Jambres*

20. resto, perf. act. ind. 3 p., *resist.* **21.** resisto, pres. act. ind. 3 p., *resist.* **22.** corrumpo, perf. pass. ptcp. m. nom. p., *corrupt.* **23.** mens, *mind.* **24.** reprobus, *reprobate, rejected*

March 13

1. יְאֹר, *Nile*
2. הָפַךְ, niph. perf. 3 c. p., *turn*
3. τύπτω, pres. act. ind. 1 s., *strike, beat*
4. μεταβάλλω, fut. act. ind. 3 s., *change, turn*
5. κλείω, aor. act. inf., *close, shut*
6. ὑετός, *rain*
7. βρέχω, pres. act. subj. 3 s., *rain, drench*
8. προφητεία, *prophecy*
9. στρέφω, pres. act. inf., *turn*
10. πατάσσω, aor. act. inf., *strike*
11. πληγή, *plague*
12. ὁσάκις, *as (often as)*
13. ἐάν, conditional particle
14. cludo, ger. act. n. g. s., *shut*
15. pluo, pres. act. subj. 3 s., *rain*
16. prophetia, *prophecy*
17. plaga, *plague*
18. quotienscumque, *as often as*

Exodus 7:17

כֹּ֚ה אָמַ֣ר יְהוָ֔ה בְּזֹ֣את תֵּדַ֔ע כִּ֖י אֲנִ֣י יְהוָ֑ה הִנֵּ֨ה אָנֹכִ֜י מַכֶּ֣ה ׀ בַּמַּטֶּ֣ה אֲשֶׁר־בְּיָדִ֗י עַל־הַמַּ֛יִם אֲשֶׁ֥ר בַּיְאֹ֖ר[1] וְנֶהֶפְכ֥וּ[2] לְדָֽם׃

τάδε λέγει κύριος Ἐν τούτῳ γνώσῃ ὅτι ἐγὼ κύριος· ἰδοὺ ἐγὼ τύπτω[3] τῇ ῥάβδῳ τῇ ἐν τῇ χειρί μου ἐπὶ τὸ ὕδωρ τὸ ἐν τῷ ποταμῷ, καὶ μεταβαλεῖ[4] εἰς αἷμα.

Revelation 11:6

οὗτοι ἔχουσιν τὴν ἐξουσίαν κλεῖσαι[5] τὸν οὐρανόν, ἵνα μὴ ὑετὸς[6] βρέχῃ[7] τὰς ἡμέρας τῆς προφητείας[8] αὐτῶν, καὶ ἐξουσίαν ἔχουσιν ἐπὶ τῶν ὑδάτων στρέφειν[9] αὐτὰ εἰς αἷμα καὶ πατάξαι[10] τὴν γῆν ἐν πάσῃ πληγῇ[11] ὁσάκις[12] ἐὰν[13] θελήσωσιν.

hii habent potestatem cludendi[14] caelum ne pluat[15] diebus prophetiae[16] ipsorum et potestatem habent super aquas convertendi eas in sanguinem et percutere terram omni plaga[17] quotienscumque[18] voluerint.

March 14

Exodus 9:10

וַיִּקְח֞וּ אֶת־פִּ֣יחַ[1] הַכִּבְשָׁ֗ן[2] וַיַּֽעַמְדוּ֙ לִפְנֵ֣י פַרְעֹ֔ה וַיִּזְרֹ֥ק[3]
אֹת֛וֹ מֹשֶׁ֖ה הַשָּׁמָ֑יְמָה וַיְהִ֗י שְׁחִין֙[4] אֲבַעְבֻּעֹ֔ת[5] פֹּרֵ֖חַ[6]
בָּאָדָ֥ם וּבַבְּהֵמָֽה׃

καὶ ἔλαβεν τὴν αἰθάλην[7] τῆς καμιναίας[8] ἐναντίον Φαραω καὶ ἔπασεν[9] αὐτὴν Μωυσῆς εἰς τὸν οὐρανόν, καὶ ἐγένετο ἕλκη,[10] φλυκτίδες[11] ἀναζέουσαι,[12] ἐν τοῖς ἀνθρώποις καὶ ἐν τοῖς τετράποσιν.[13]

Revelation 16:2

Καὶ ἀπῆλθεν ὁ πρῶτος καὶ ἐξέχεεν[14] τὴν φιάλην[15] αὐτοῦ εἰς τὴν γῆν, καὶ ἐγένετο ἕλκος κακὸν[16] καὶ πονηρὸν ἐπὶ τοὺς ἀνθρώπους τοὺς ἔχοντας τὸ χάραγμα[17] τοῦ θηρίου[18] καὶ τοὺς προσκυνοῦντας[19] τῇ εἰκόνι[20] αὐτοῦ.

et abiit primus et effudit[21] fialam[22] suam in terram et factum est vulnus[23] saevum[24] ac pessimum in homines qui habent caracterem[25] bestiae et eos qui adoraverunt imaginem[26] eius.

1. פִּיחַ, *soot*
2. כִּבְשָׁן, *furnace*
3. זָרַק, qal wcons. 3 m. s., *sprinkle*
4. שְׁחִין, *boil*
5. אֲבַעְבֻּעֹת, *sore*
6. פָּרַח, qal ptcp. m. s. abs., *break out*
7. αἰθάλη, *soot*
8. καμιναία, *furnace*
9. πάσσω, aor. act. ind. 3 s., *scatter*
10. ἕλκος, *sore*
11. φλυκτίς, *blister*
12. ἀναζέω, pres. act. ptcp. f. nom. p., *break out*
13. τετράπους, *four-footed*
14. ἐκχέω, aor. act. ind. 3 s., *pour out*
15. φιάλη, *bowl*
16. κακός, *harm, evil, bad*
17. χάραγμα, *mark*
18. θηρίον, *beast*
19. προσκυνέω, pres. act. ptcp. m. a. p., *worship*
20. εἰκών, *image*
21. effundo, perf. act. ind. 3 s., *pour out*
22. fiala, *bowl*
23. vulnus, *wound*
24. saevus, *sore*
25. caracter, *mark*. **26.** imago, *image*

March 15

Exodus 9:24

וַיְהִי בָרָד[1] וְאֵשׁ מִתְלַקַּחַת בְּתוֹךְ הַבָּרָד כָּבֵד[2]
מְאֹד אֲשֶׁר לֹא־הָיָה כָמֹהוּ בְּכָל־אֶרֶץ מִצְרַיִם מֵאָז
הָיְתָה לְגוֹי׃

ἦν δὲ ἡ χάλαζα[3] καὶ τὸ πῦρ φλογίζον[4] ἐν τῇ χαλάζῃ· ἡ δὲ χάλαζα πολλὴ σφόδρα[5] σφόδρα, ἥτις τοιαύτη[6] οὐ γέγονεν ἐν Αἰγύπτῳ ἀφ᾽ οὗ γεγένηται ἐπ᾽ αὐτῆς ἔθνος.

Revelation 16:21

καὶ χάλαζα μεγάλη ὡς ταλαντιαία[7] καταβαίνει ἐκ τοῦ οὐρανοῦ ἐπὶ τοὺς ἀνθρώπους, καὶ ἐβλασφήμησαν[8] οἱ ἄνθρωποι τὸν θεὸν ἐκ τῆς πληγῆς[9] τῆς χαλάζης, ὅτι μεγάλη ἐστὶν ἡ πληγὴ αὐτῆς σφόδρα.

et grando[10] magna sicut talentum[11] descendit de caelo in homines et blasphemaverunt homines Deum propter plagam[12] grandinis[13] quoniam magna facta est vehementer.[14]

1. בָּרָד, *hail*
2. כָּבֵד, *heavy*
3. χάλαζα, *hail*
4. φλογίζω, pres. act. ptcp. n. nom. s., *set on fire*
5. σφόδρα, *exceedingly*
6. τοιοῦτος, *such, such a kind*
7. ταλαντιαῖος, *talent*
8. βλασφημέω, aor. act. ind. 3 p., *blaspheme*
9. πληγή, *plague*
10. grando, *hail*
11. talentum, *talent*
12. plaga, *plague*
13. grando, *hailstorm*
14. vehementer, *greatly, exceedingly*

March 16

Exodus 10:12

וַיֹּ֨אמֶר יְהוָ֜ה אֶל־מֹשֶׁ֗ה נְטֵ֨ה יָדְךָ֜ עַל־אֶ֤רֶץ מִצְרַ֙יִם֙
בָּֽאַרְבֶּ֔ה[1] וְיַ֖עַל עַל־אֶ֣רֶץ מִצְרָ֑יִם וְיֹאכַל֙ אֶת־כָּל־
עֵ֣שֶׂב[2] הָאָ֔רֶץ אֵ֛ת כָּל־אֲשֶׁ֥ר הִשְׁאִ֖יר הַבָּרָֽד׃[3]

εἶπεν δὲ κύριος πρὸς Μωυσῆν Ἔκτεινον τὴν χεῖρα ἐπὶ γῆν Αἰγύπτου, καὶ ἀναβήτω ἀκρὶς[4] ἐπὶ τὴν γῆν καὶ κατέδεται[5] πᾶσαν βοτάνην[6] τῆς γῆς καὶ πάντα τὸν καρπὸν τῶν ξύλων, ὃν ὑπελίπετο[7] ἡ χάλαζα.[8]

Revelation 9:3

καὶ ἐκ τοῦ καπνοῦ[9] ἐξῆλθον ἀκρίδες εἰς τὴν γῆν, καὶ ἐδόθη αὐταῖς ἐξουσία ὡς ἔχουσιν ἐξουσίαν οἱ σκορπίοι[10] τῆς γῆς.

et de fumo[11] exierunt lucustae[12] in terram et data est illis potestas sicut habent potestatem scorpiones[13] terrae.

1. אַרְבֶּה, *locust*
2. עֵשֶׂב, *plant*
3. בָּרָד, *hail*
4. ἀκρίς, *locust*
5. κατεσθίω, aor. act. ind. 3 s., *devour, eat*
6. βοτάνη, *plant*
7. ὑπολείπω, aor. mid. ind. 3 s., *leave behind*
8. χάλαζα, *hail*
9. καπνός, *smoke*
10. σκορπίος, *scorpion*
11. fumus, *smoke*
12. lucusta, *locust*
13. scorpio, *scorpion*

March 17

1. חֹ֑שֶׁךְ, *dark*
2. מָשַׁשׁ, hiph. impf. 3 m. s. juss., *feel, that which can be felt*
3. ψηλαφητός, *felt, palpable*
4. πέμπτος, *fifth*
5. ἐκχέω, aor. act. ind. 3 s., *pour out*
6. φιάλη, *bowl*
7. θρόνος, *throne*
8. θηρίον, *animal*
9. σκοτόω, perf. pass. ptcp. f. nom. s., *darken, blind*
10. μασάομαι, impf. mid. ind. 3 p., *gnaw, chew*
11. γλῶσσα, *tongue*
12. πόνος, *pain*
13. quintus, *fifth*
14. effundo, perf. act. ind. 3 s., *pour out*
15. fiala, *bowl*
16. tenebrosus, *dark*
17. conmanduco, perf. act. ind. 3 p., *gnaw*
18. prae, *before, in front of, for*
19. dolor, *pain, grief*

Exodus 10:21

וַיֹּ֨אמֶר יְהוָ֜ה אֶל־מֹשֶׁ֗ה נְטֵ֤ה יָֽדְךָ֙ עַל־הַשָּׁמַ֔יִם וִ֥יהִי
חֹ֖שֶׁךְ[1] עַל־אֶ֣רֶץ מִצְרָ֑יִם וְיָמֵ֖שׁ[2] חֹֽשֶׁךְ׃

Εἶπεν δὲ κύριος πρὸς Μωυσῆν Ἔκτεινον τὴν χεῖρά σου εἰς τὸν οὐρανόν, καὶ γενηθήτω σκότος ἐπὶ γῆν Αἰγύπτου, ψηλαφητὸν[3] σκότος.

Revelation 16:10

Καὶ ὁ πέμπτος[4] ἐξέχεεν[5] τὴν φιάλην[6] αὐτοῦ ἐπὶ τὸν θρόνον[7] τοῦ θηρίου,[8] καὶ ἐγένετο ἡ βασιλεία αὐτοῦ ἐσκοτωμένη,[9] καὶ ἐμασῶντο[10] τὰς γλώσσας[11] αὐτῶν ἐκ τοῦ πόνου.[12]

et quintus[13] effudit[14] fialam[15] suam super sedem bestiae et factum est regnum eius tenebrosum[16] et conmanducaverunt[17] linguas suas prae[18] dolore.[19]

March 18

Exodus 12:41

וַיְהִ֗י מִקֵּץ֙[1] שְׁלֹשִׁ֣ים שָׁנָ֔ה וְאַרְבַּ֥ע מֵא֖וֹת שָׁנָ֑ה
וַיְהִ֗י בְּעֶ֙צֶם֙ הַיּ֣וֹם הַזֶּ֔ה יָֽצְא֛וּ כָּל־צִבְא֥וֹת יְהוָ֖ה
מֵאֶ֥רֶץ מִצְרָֽיִם׃

καὶ ἐγένετο μετὰ τὰ τετρακόσια[2] τριάκοντα[3] ἔτη[4] ἐξῆλθεν πᾶσα ἡ δύναμις[5] κυρίου ἐκ γῆς Αἰγύπτου.

Galatians 3:17

τοῦτο δὲ λέγω· διαθήκην[6] προκεκυρωμένην[7] ὑπὸ τοῦ θεοῦ ὁ μετὰ τετρακόσια καὶ τριάκοντα ἔτη γεγονὼς νόμος οὐκ ἀκυροῖ[8] εἰς τὸ καταργῆσαι[9] τὴν ἐπαγγελίαν.[10]

hoc autem dico testamentum confirmatum[11] a Deo quae post quadringentos[12] et triginta[13] annos facta est lex non irritam[14] facit ad evacuandam[15] promissionem.[16]

1. קֵץ, *end*

2. τετρακόσιοι, *four hundred*

3. τριάκοντα, *thirty*

4. ἔτος, *year*

5. TH: here *host.*

6. διαθήκη, *covenant, testament*

7. προκυρόω, perf. mid. ptcp. f. a. s., *determine previously/earlier*

8. ἀκυρόω, pres. act. ind. 3 s., *cancel, nullify*

9. καταργέω, aor. act. inf., *make void, nullify*

10. ἐπαγγελία, *good news*

11. confirmo, perf. pass. ptcp. n. a. s., *make firm, strengthen*

12. quadringenti, *four hundred*

13. triginta, *thirty*

14. irritus, *void, of no effect*

15. evacuo, ger. f. a. s., *make void, empty*

16. promissio, *promise*

March 19

Exodus 12:51

וַיְהִ֕י בְּעֶ֖צֶם הַיּ֣וֹם הַזֶּ֑ה הוֹצִ֨יא יְהוָ֜ה אֶת־בְּנֵ֧י יִשְׂרָאֵ֛ל מֵאֶ֥רֶץ מִצְרַ֖יִם עַל־צִבְאֹתָֽם׃

καὶ ἐγένετο ἐν τῇ ἡμέρᾳ ἐκείνῃ ἐξήγαγεν κύριος τοὺς υἱοὺς Ισραηλ ἐκ γῆς Αἰγύπτου[1] σὺν δυνάμει[2] αὐτῶν.

Jude 5

Ὑπομνῆσαι[3] δὲ ὑμᾶς βούλομαι, εἰδότας ὑμᾶς ἅπαξ[4] πάντα ὅτι Ἰησοῦς λαὸν ἐκ γῆς Αἰγύπτου σώσας τὸ δεύτερον τοὺς μὴ πιστεύσαντας ἀπώλεσεν.

commonere[5] autem vos volo scientes semel[6] omnia quoniam Iesus populum de terra Aegypti[7] salvans[8] secundo eos qui non crediderunt perdidit.

1. Αἴγυπτος, *Egypt*
2. TH: here *host*
3. ὑπομιμνῄσκω, aor. act. inf., *remind*
4. ἅπαξ, *once*
5. commoneo, pres. act. inf., *remind, admonish*
6. semel, *once*
7. Aegyptus, *Egypt*
8. salvo, pres. act. ptcp. m. nom. s., *save*

March 20

Exodus 13:21

וַיהוָ֡ה הֹלֵךְ֩ לִפְנֵיהֶ֨ם יוֹמָ֜ם[1] בְּעַמּ֤וּד עָנָן֙[2] לַנְחֹתָ֣ם[3]
הַדֶּ֔רֶךְ וְלַ֛יְלָה בְּעַמּ֥וּד אֵ֖שׁ לְהָאִ֣יר[4] לָהֶ֑ם לָלֶ֖כֶת
יוֹמָ֥ם וָלָֽיְלָה׃

ὁ δὲ θεὸς ἡγεῖτο αὐτῶν, ἡμέρας μὲν ἐν στύλῳ νεφέλης[5] δεῖξαι αὐτοῖς τὴν ὁδόν, τὴν δὲ νύκτα ἐν στύλῳ πυρός.

1 Corinthians 10:1

Οὐ θέλω γὰρ ὑμᾶς ἀγνοεῖν,[6] ἀδελφοί, ὅτι οἱ πατέρες ἡμῶν πάντες ὑπὸ τὴν νεφέλην ἦσαν καὶ πάντες διὰ τῆς θαλάσσης διῆλθον.

nolo enim vos ignorare[7] fratres quoniam patres nostri omnes sub nube[8] fuerunt et omnes mare transierunt.

1. יוֹמָם, *day*
2. עָנָן, *cloud*
3. נָחָה, hiph. inf. cons., *lead*
4. אוֹר, hiph. inf. cons., *be a light*
5. νεφέλη, *cloud*
6. ἀγνοέω, pres. act. inf., *be ignorant*
7. ignoro, pres. act. inf., *be ignorant of*
8. nubes, *cloud*

March 21

Exodus 14:29

וּבְנֵ֧י יִשְׂרָאֵ֛ל הָלְכ֥וּ בַיַּבָּשָׁ֖ה[1] בְּת֣וֹךְ הַיָּ֑ם וְהַמַּ֤יִם לָהֶם֙ חֹמָ֔ה מִֽימִינָ֖ם וּמִשְּׂמֹאלָֽם׃[2]

οἱ δὲ υἱοὶ Ισραηλ ἐπορεύθησαν διὰ ξηρᾶς[3] ἐν μέσῳ τῆς θαλάσσης, τὸ δὲ ὕδωρ αὐτοῖς τεῖχος ἐκ δεξιῶν καὶ τεῖχος ἐξ εὐωνύμων.[4]

1 Corinthians 10:2

καὶ πάντες εἰς τὸν Μωϋσῆν ἐβαπτίσθησαν ἐν τῇ νεφέλῃ[5] καὶ ἐν τῇ θαλάσσῃ.

et omnes in Mose baptizati sunt in nube[6] et in mari.

1. יַבָּשָׁה, *dry ground*
2. שְׂמֹאל, *left*
3. ξηρός, *dry land*
4. εὐώνυμος, *left*
5. νεφέλη, *cloud*
6. nubes, *cloud*

March 22

Exodus 15:11

מִֽי־כָמֹ֤כָה בָּֽאֵלִם֙ יְהוָ֔ה מִ֥י כָּמֹ֖כָה נֶאְדָּ֣ר[1] בַּקֹּ֑דֶשׁ
נוֹרָ֥א תְהִלֹּ֖ת[2] עֹ֥שֵׂה פֶֽלֶא׃[3]

τίς ὅμοιός[4] σοι ἐν θεοῖς, κύριε; τίς ὅμοιός σοι, δεδοξασμένος ἐν ἁγίοις, θαυμαστὸς[5] ἐν δόξαις, ποιῶν τέρατα;[6]

Revelation 15:3

καὶ ᾄδουσιν[7] τὴν ᾠδὴν[8] Μωϋσέως τοῦ δούλου τοῦ θεοῦ καὶ τὴν ᾠδὴν τοῦ ἀρνίου[9] λέγοντες· *μεγάλα καὶ θαυμαστὰ τὰ ἔργα σου, κύριε ὁ θεὸς ὁ παντοκράτωρ·*[10] *δίκαιαι καὶ ἀληθιναὶ*[11] *αἱ ὁδοί σου, ὁ βασιλεὺς τῶν ἐθνῶν.*

et cantant[12] canticum[13] Mosi servi Dei et canticum agni dicentes magna et mirabilia[14] opera tua Domine Deus omnipotens[15] iustae et verae viae tuae rex saeculorum.

1. אָדַר, niph. ptcp. m. s. abs., *be glorious, majestic*
2. תְּהִלָּה, *deed*
3. פֶּ֫לֶא, *wonder, marvel*
4. ὅμοιος, *like*
5. θαυμαστός, *wonderful*
6. τέρας, *marvel, wonder*
7. ᾄδω, pres. act. ind. 3 p., *sing*
8. ᾠδή, *song*
9. ἀρνίον, *lamb*
10. παντοκράτωρ, *almighty*
11. ἀληθινός, *true*
12. canto, pres. act. ind. 3 p., *sing*
13. canticum, *song*
14. mirabilia, *wonderful*
15. omnipotens, *almighty*

Wilderness Wanderings

March 23

Exodus 16:4

וַיֹּ֤אמֶר יְהוָה֙ אֶל־מֹשֶׁ֔ה הִנְנִ֨י מַמְטִ֥יר[1] לָכֶ֛ם לֶ֖חֶם מִן־
הַשָּׁמָ֑יִם וְיָצָ֨א הָעָ֤ם וְלָֽקְטוּ֙[2] דְּבַר־י֣וֹם בְּיוֹמ֔וֹ לְמַ֧עַן
אֲנַסֶּ֛נּוּ[3] הֲיֵלֵ֥ךְ בְּתוֹרָתִ֖י אִם־לֹֽא׃

εἶπεν δὲ κύριος πρὸς Μωυσῆν Ἰδοὺ ἐγὼ ὕω[4] ὑμῖν ἄρτους ἐκ τοῦ οὐρανοῦ, καὶ ἐξελεύσεται ὁ λαὸς καὶ συλλέξουσιν[5] τὸ τῆς ἡμέρας εἰς ἡμέραν, ὅπως πειράσω[6] αὐτοὺς εἰ πορεύσονται τῷ νόμῳ μου ἢ οὔ.

John 6:33

ὁ γὰρ ἄρτος τοῦ θεοῦ ἐστιν ὁ καταβαίνων ἐκ τοῦ οὐρανοῦ καὶ ζωὴν διδοὺς τῷ κόσμῳ.

panis enim Dei est qui descendit de caelo et dat vitam mundo.

1. מָטַר, hiph. ptcp. m. s. abs., *rain*
2. לָקַט, qal perf. 3 c. p., *gather*
3. נָסָה, piel impf. 1 c. s., *test, try*
4. ὕω, pres. act. ind. 1 s., *send rain*
5. συλλέγω, fut. act. ind. 3 p., *gather, collect*
6. πειράζω, aor. act. subj. 1 s., *tempt, test*

March 24

Exodus 17:6

הִנְנִ֣י עֹמֵד֩ לְפָנֶ֨יךָ שָּׁ֥ם ׀ עַֽל־הַצּוּר֮[1] בְּחֹרֵב֒[2] וְהִכִּ֣יתָ
בַצּוּר֙ וְיָצְא֥וּ מִמֶּ֛נּוּ מַ֖יִם וְשָׁתָ֣ה הָעָ֑ם וַיַּ֤עַשׂ כֵּן֙ מֹשֶׁ֔ה
לְעֵינֵ֖י זִקְנֵ֥י יִשְׂרָאֵֽל׃

ὅδε ἐγὼ ἕστηκα πρὸ τοῦ σὲ ἐκεῖ ἐπὶ τῆς πέτρας[3] ἐν Χωρηβ·[4] καὶ πατάξεις τὴν πέτραν, καὶ ἐξελεύσεται ἐξ αὐτῆς ὕδωρ, καὶ πίεται ὁ λαός μου. ἐποίησεν δὲ Μωυσῆς οὕτως ἐναντίον τῶν υἱῶν Ισραηλ.

1 Corinthians 10:4

καὶ πάντες τὸ αὐτὸ πνευματικὸν[5] ἔπιον πόμα·[6] ἔπινον γὰρ ἐκ πνευματικῆς ἀκολουθούσης πέτρας, ἡ πέτρα δὲ ἦν ὁ Χριστός.

et omnes eundem potum[7] spiritalem[8] biberunt bibebant autem de spiritali consequenti[9] eos petra[10] petra autem erat Christus.

1. צוּר, *rock*
2. חֹרֵב, *Horeb*
3. πέτρα, *rock, stone*
4. Χωρηβ, *Horeb*
5. πνευματικός, *spiritual*
6. πόμα, *drink*
7. potus, *drink*
8. spiritalis, *spiritual*
9. consequor, pres. act. ptcp. f. abl. s., *follow*
10. petra, *rock, stone*

March 25

Numbers 12:7

לֹא־כֵן עַבְדִּי מֹשֶׁה בְּכָל־בֵּיתִי נֶאֱמָן[1] הוּא׃

οὐχ οὕτως ὁ θεράπων[2] μου Μωυσῆς· ἐν ὅλῳ τῷ οἴκῳ μου πιστός[3] ἐστιν.

Hebrews 3:3

πλείονος γὰρ οὗτος[4] δόξης παρὰ Μωϋσῆν ἠξίωται,[5] καθ᾽ ὅσον πλείονα τιμὴν ἔχει τοῦ οἴκου ὁ κατασκευάσας[6] αὐτόν.

amplioris[7] enim gloriae iste[8] prae[9] Mose dignus habitus est quanto[10] ampliorem honorem habet domus qui fabricavit[11] illam.

1. אָמַן, niph. ptcp. m. s. abs., *be faithful*
2. θεράπων, *servant*
3. πιστός, *faithful*
4. CH: οὗτος refers to Jesus
5. ἀξιόω, perf. pass. ind. 3 s., *deem worthy*
6. κατασκευάζω, aor. act. ptcp. m. nom. s., *build*
7. amplus, *more*
8. CH: iste refers to Jesus
9. prae, *than, in comparison with*
10. quanto, *by how much*
11. fabrico, perf. act. ind. 3 s., *build*

March 26

Numbers 14:29

בַּמִּדְבָּר הַזֶּה יִפְּלוּ פִגְרֵיכֶם[1] וְכָל־פְּקֻדֵיכֶם
לְכָל־מִסְפַּרְכֶם מִבֶּן עֶשְׂרִים שָׁנָה וָמָעְלָה אֲשֶׁר
הֲלִינֹתֶם[2] עָלָי׃

ἐν τῇ ἐρήμῳ ταύτῃ πεσεῖται τὰ κῶλα[3] ὑμῶν καὶ πᾶσα ἡ ἐπισκοπὴ[4] ὑμῶν καὶ οἱ κατηριθμημένοι[5] ὑμῶν ἀπὸ εἰκοσαετοῦς[6] καὶ ἐπάνω, ὅσοι ἐγόγγυσαν[7] ἐπ᾽ ἐμοί.

1 Corinthians 10:5

Ἀλλ᾽ οὐκ ἐν τοῖς πλείοσιν αὐτῶν εὐδόκησεν[8] ὁ θεός, κατεστρώθησαν[9] γὰρ ἐν τῇ ἐρήμῳ.

sed non in pluribus eorum beneplacitum[10] est Deo nam prostrati[11] sunt in deserto.

1. פֶּגֶר, *dead (body)*
2. לוּן, hiph. perf. 2 m. p., *grumble*
3. κῶλον, *corpse*
4. ἐπισκοπή, *census*
5. καταριθμέω, perf. pass. ptcp. m. nom. p., *enumerate, number*
6. εἰκοσαετής, *twenty years old*
7. γογγύζω, aor. act. ind. 3 p., *grumble*
8. εὐδοκέω, aor. act. ind. 3 s., *be pleased*
9. καταστρώννυμι, aor. pass. ind. 3 p., *lay low, scatter*
10. beneplaceo, perf. pass. ind. 3 s., *please*
11. prosterno, perf. pass. ptcp. m. nom. p., *cast down, debase*

March 27

Exodus 17:7

וַיִּקְרָא֙ שֵׁ֣ם הַמָּק֔וֹם מַסָּ֖ה[1] וּמְרִיבָ֑ה[2] עַל־רִ֣יב׀[3] בְּנֵ֣י
יִשְׂרָאֵ֗ל וְעַ֨ל נַסֹּתָ֤ם[4] אֶת־יְהוָה֙ לֵאמֹ֔ר הֲיֵ֧שׁ יְהוָ֛ה
בְּקִרְבֵּ֖נוּ אִם־אָֽיִן׃

καὶ ἐπωνόμασεν[5] τὸ ὄνομα τοῦ τόπου ἐκείνου Πειρασμὸς[6] καὶ Λοιδόρησις[7] διὰ τὴν λοιδορίαν[8] τῶν υἱῶν Ισραηλ καὶ διὰ τὸ πειράζειν[9] κύριον λέγοντας Εἰ ἔστιν κύριος ἐν ἡμῖν ἢ οὔ;

Hebrews 3:8

μὴ σκληρύνητε[10] τὰς καρδίας ὑμῶν ὡς ἐν τῷ παραπικρασμῷ[11] κατὰ τὴν ἡμέραν τοῦ πειρασμοῦ ἐν τῇ ἐρήμῳ.

nolite obdurare[12] corda vestra sicut in exacerbatione[13] secundum diem temptationis[14] in deserto.

1. מַסָּה, *Massah*
2. מְרִיבָה, *Meribah*
3. רִיב, *quarreling, dispute*
4. נָסָה, piel inf. cons., *test*
5. ἐπονομάζω, aor. act. ind. 3 s., *name, call*
6. πειρασμός, *Testing*
7. λοιδόρησις, *Insulting*
8. λοιδορία, *railing, reviling*
9. πειράζω, pres. act. inf., *test, tempt*
10. σκληρύνω, aor. act. subj. 2 p., *harden*
11. παραπικρασμός, *rebellion, provocation*
12. obduro, pres. act. inf., *harden*
13. exacerbatio, *provocation*
14. temptatio, *temptation*

March 28

Numbers 21:6

וַיְשַׁלַּ֨ח יְהוָ֜ה בָּעָ֗ם אֵ֚ת הַנְּחָשִׁ֣ים[1] הַשְּׂרָפִ֔ים[2] וַֽיְנַשְּׁכ֖וּ[3]
אֶת־הָעָ֑ם וַיָּ֥מָת עַם־רָ֖ב מִיִּשְׂרָאֵֽל׃

καὶ ἀπέστειλεν κύριος εἰς τὸν λαὸν τοὺς ὄφεις[4] τοὺς θανατοῦντας, καὶ ἔδακνον[5] τὸν λαόν, καὶ ἀπέθανεν λαὸς πολὺς τῶν υἱῶν Ισραηλ.

1 Corinthians 10:9

μηδὲ ἐκπειράζωμεν[6] τὸν Χριστόν, καθώς τινες αὐτῶν ἐπείρασαν καὶ ὑπὸ τῶν ὄφεων ἀπώλλυντο.

neque temptemus Christum sicut quidam eorum temptaverunt et a serpentibus[7] perierunt.

1. נָחָשׁ, *snake*
2. שָׂרָף, *fiery*
3. נָשַׁךְ, piel wcons. 3 m. p., *bite*
4. ὄφις, *snake*
5. δάκω, impf. act. ind. 3 p., *bite*
6. ἐκπειράζω, pres. act. subj. 1 p., *test, tempt*
7. serpens, *snake*

March 29

Numbers 21:9

וַיַּ֤עַשׂ מֹשֶׁה֙ נְחַ֣שׁ[1] נְח֔שֶׁת וַיְשִׂמֵ֖הוּ עַל־הַנֵּ֑ס[2] וְהָיָ֗ה
אִם־נָשַׁ֤ךְ[3] הַנָּחָשׁ֙ אֶת־אִ֔ישׁ וְהִבִּ֛יט[4] אֶל־נְחַ֥שׁ
הַנְּחֹ֖שֶׁת וָחָֽי׃

καὶ ἐποίησεν Μωυσῆς ὄφιν[5] χαλκοῦν καὶ ἔστησεν αὐτὸν ἐπὶ σημείου, καὶ ἐγένετο ὅταν ἔδακνεν[6] ὄφις ἄνθρωπον, καὶ ἐπέβλεψεν ἐπὶ τὸν ὄφιν τὸν χαλκοῦν καὶ ἔζη.

John 3:14

Καὶ καθὼς Μωϋσῆς ὕψωσεν[7] τὸν ὄφιν ἐν τῇ ἐρήμῳ, οὕτως ὑψωθῆναι[8] δεῖ τὸν υἱὸν τοῦ ἀνθρώπου.

et sicut Moses exaltavit[9] serpentem[10] in deserto ita exaltari[11] oportet Filium hominis.

1. נָחָשׁ, *snake*
2. נֵס, *pole*
3. נָשַׁךְ, qal perf. 3 m. s., *bite*
4. נָבַט, hiph. perf. 3 m. s., *look at*
5. ὄφις, *snake*
6. δάκνω, impf. act. ind. 3 s., *bite, wound*
7. ὑψόω, aor. act. ind. 3 s., *lift up*
8. ὑψόω, aor. pass. inf., *lift up*
9. exalto, perf. act. ind. 3 s., *lift up, exalt*
10. serpens, *snake*
11. exalto, pres. pass. inf., *lift up, exalt*

March 30

Numbers 25:9

וַיִּהְי֕וּ הַמֵּתִ֖ים בַּמַּגֵּפָ֑ה[1] אַרְבָּעָ֥ה וְעֶשְׂרִ֖ים אָֽלֶף׃

καὶ ἐγένοντο οἱ τεθνηκότες[2] ἐν τῇ πληγῇ[3]
τέσσαρες καὶ εἴκοσι[4] χιλιάδες.[5]

1 Corinthians 10:8

μηδὲ πορνεύωμεν,[6] καθώς τινες αὐτῶν
ἐπόρνευσαν[7] καὶ ἔπεσαν μιᾷ ἡμέρᾳ εἴκοσι τρεῖς
χιλιάδες.

neque fornicemur[8] sicut quidam ex ipsis
fornicati[9] sunt et ceciderunt una die viginti[10]
tria milia.

1. מַגֵּפָה, *plague*
2. θνῄσκω, perf. act. ptcp. m. nom. p., *die*
3. πληγή, *blow, wound*
4. εἴκοσι, *twenty*
5. χιλιάς, *thousand*
6. πορνεύω, pres. act. subj. 1 p., *commit sexual immorality*
7. πορνεύω, aor. act. ind. 3 p., *commit sexual immorality*
8. fornicor, pres. dep. subj. 1 p., *fornicate*
9. fornicor, perf. dep. ind. 3 p., *fornicate*
10. viginti, *twenty*

March 31

Numbers 14:2

וַיִּלֹּנוּ[1] עַל־מֹשֶׁה וְעַל־אַהֲרֹן כֹּל בְּנֵי יִשְׂרָאֵל וַיֹּאמְרוּ
אֲלֵהֶם כָּל־הָעֵדָה לוּ[2]־מַתְנוּ בְּאֶרֶץ מִצְרַיִם אוֹ
בַּמִּדְבָּר הַזֶּה לוּ־מָתְנוּ׃

καὶ διεγόγγυζον[3] ἐπὶ Μωυσῆν καὶ Ααρων πάντες οἱ υἱοὶ Ισραηλ, καὶ εἶπαν πρὸς αὐτοὺς πᾶσα ἡ συναγωγή Ὄφελον[4] ἀπεθάνομεν ἐν γῇ Αἰγύπτῳ, ἢ ἐν τῇ ἐρήμῳ ταύτῃ εἰ ἀπεθάνομεν.

1 Corinthians 10:10

μηδὲ γογγύζετε,[5] καθάπερ[6] τινὲς αὐτῶν ἐγόγγυσαν[7] καὶ ἀπώλοντο ὑπὸ τοῦ ὀλοθρευτοῦ.[8]

neque murmuraveritis[9] sicut quidam eorum murmuraverunt[10] et perierunt ab exterminatore.[11]

1. לון, niph. wcons. 3 m. p., *grumble*

2. לוּ, *if only*

3. διαγογγύζω, impf. act. ind. 3 p., *grumble*

4. ὄφελον, *We wish*

5. γογγύζω, pres. act. impv. 2 p., *grumble*

6. καθάπερ, *as, just as*

7. γογγύζω, aor. act. ind. 3 p., *grumble*

8. ὀλοθρευτής, *destroyer (angel)*

9. murmuro, perf. act. subj. 2 p., *murmur, grumble*

10. murmuro, perf. act. ind. 3 p., *murmur, grumble*

11. exterminator, *destroyer*

April 1

Numbers 27:17

אֲשֶׁר[1]־יֵצֵא לִפְנֵיהֶם וַאֲשֶׁר יָבֹא לִפְנֵיהֶם וַאֲשֶׁר
יוֹצִיאֵם וַאֲשֶׁר יְבִיאֵם וְלֹא תִהְיֶה עֲדַת יְהוָה כַּצֹּאן
אֲשֶׁר אֵין־לָהֶם רֹעֶה׃

ὅστις[2] ἐξελεύσεται πρὸ προσώπου αὐτῶν καὶ ὅστις εἰσελεύσεται πρὸ προσώπου αὐτῶν καὶ ὅστις ἐξάξει αὐτοὺς καὶ ὅστις εἰσάξει αὐτούς, καὶ οὐκ ἔσται ἡ συναγωγὴ κυρίου ὡσεὶ πρόβατα, οἷς οὐκ ἔστιν ποιμήν.[3]

Mark 6:34

Καὶ ἐξελθὼν εἶδεν πολὺν ὄχλον καὶ ἐσπλαγχνίσθη[4] ἐπ᾽ αὐτούς, ὅτι ἦσαν *ὡς πρόβατα μὴ ἔχοντα ποιμένα*, καὶ ἤρξατο διδάσκειν αὐτοὺς πολλά.

et exiens vidit multam turbam Iesus et misertus est super eos quia erant sicut oves non habentes pastorem[5] et coepit docere illos multa.

1. CH: This relative pronoun refers to the man Moses hopes God will appoint for Israel.
2. CH: This relative pronoun refers to the man Moses hopes God will appoint for Israel.
3. ποιμήν, *shepherd*
4. σπλαγχνίζομαι, aor. pass. ind. 3 s., *have compassion*
5. pastor, *shepherd*

Mosaic Covenant

April 2

Deuteronomy 9:10

וַיִּתֵּ֨ן יְהוָ֜ה אֵלַ֗י אֶת־שְׁנֵי֙ לוּחֹ֣ת[1] הָאֲבָנִ֔ים כְּתֻבִ֖ים בְּאֶצְבַּ֣ע[2] אֱלֹהִ֑ים וַעֲלֵיהֶ֗ם כְּֽכָל־הַדְּבָרִ֡ים אֲשֶׁר֩ דִּבֶּ֨ר יְהוָ֧ה עִמָּכֶ֛ם בָּהָ֖ר מִתּ֥וֹךְ הָאֵ֖שׁ בְּי֥וֹם הַקָּהָֽל׃

καὶ ἔδωκεν κύριος ἐμοὶ τὰς δύο πλάκας[3] τὰς λιθίνας[4] γεγραμμένας ἐν τῷ δακτύλῳ[5] τοῦ θεοῦ, καὶ ἐπ᾽ αὐταῖς ἐγέγραπτο πάντες οἱ λόγοι, οὓς ἐλάλησεν κύριος πρὸς ὑμᾶς ἐν τῷ ὄρει ἡμέρᾳ ἐκκλησίας.[6]

1. לוּחַ, *tablet*
2. אֶצְבַּע, *finger*
3. πλάξ, *tablet*
4. λίθινος, *made of stone*
5. δάκτυλος, *finger*
6. ἐκκλησία, *assembly*
7. ἐγγράφω, perf. mid. ptcp. f. nom. s., *inscribe, write*
8. μέλας, *black ink*
9. σάρκινος, *flesh, mortal*
10. epistula, *letter*
11. atramentum, *ink*
12. tabula, *tablet*
13. lapideus, *made of stone*
14. carnalis, *of the flesh, carnal*

2 Corinthians 3:3

φανερούμενοι ὅτι ἐστὲ ἐπιστολὴ Χριστοῦ διακονηθεῖσα ὑφ᾽ ἡμῶν, ἐγγεγραμμένη[7] οὐ μέλανι[8] ἀλλὰ πνεύματι θεοῦ ζῶντος, οὐκ ἐν πλαξὶν λιθίναις ἀλλ᾽ ἐν πλαξὶν καρδίαις σαρκίναις.[9]

manifestati quoniam epistula[10] estis Christi ministrata a nobis et scripta non atramento[11] sed Spiritu Dei vivi non in tabulis[12] lapideis[13] sed in tabulis cordis carnalibus.[14]

April 3

Deuteronomy 5:1

וַיִּקְרָ֣א מֹשֶׁה֮ אֶל־כָּל־יִשְׂרָאֵל֒ וַיֹּ֣אמֶר אֲלֵהֶ֗ם שְׁמַ֤ע
יִשְׂרָאֵל֙ אֶת־הַחֻקִּ֣ים וְאֶת־הַמִּשְׁפָּטִ֔ים אֲשֶׁ֧ר אָנֹכִ֛י
דֹּבֵ֥ר בְּאָזְנֵיכֶ֖ם הַיּ֑וֹם וּלְמַדְתֶּ֣ם[1] אֹתָ֔ם וּשְׁמַרְתֶּ֖ם
לַעֲשֹׂתָֽם׃

Καὶ ἐκάλεσεν Μωυσῆς πάντα Ισραηλ καὶ εἶπεν πρὸς αὐτούς Ἄκουε, Ισραηλ, τὰ δικαιώματα καὶ τὰ κρίματα, ὅσα ἐγὼ λαλῶ ἐν τοῖς ὠσὶν ὑμῶν ἐν τῇ ἡμέρᾳ ταύτῃ, καὶ μαθήσεσθε[2] αὐτὰ καὶ φυλάξεσθε ποιεῖν αὐτά.

Mark 10:19

τὰς ἐντολὰς οἶδας· *μὴ φονεύσῃς,*[3] *μὴ μοιχεύσῃς,*[4] *μὴ κλέψῃς,*[5] *μὴ ψευδομαρτυρήσῃς,*[6] *μὴ ἀποστερήσῃς,*[7] *τίμα*[8] *τὸν πατέρα σου καὶ τὴν μητέρα.*

praecepta[9] nosti ne adulteres[10] ne occidas ne fureris[11] ne falsum[12] testimonium dixeris ne fraudem[13] feceris honora[14] patrem tuum et matrem.

1. לָמַד, qal perf. 2 m. p., *learn*

2. μανθάνω, fut. mid. ind. 2 p., *learn*

3. φονεύω, aor. act. subj. 2 s., *murder*

4. μοιχεύω, aor. act. subj. 2 s., *commit adultery*

5. κλέπτω, aor. act. subj. 2 s., *steal*

6. ψευδομαρτυρέω, aor. act. subj. 2 s., *bear false testimony*

7. ἀποστερέω, aor. act. subj. 2 s., *defraud*

8. τιμάω, pres. act. impv. 2 s., *honor*

9. praeceptum, *commandment, precept*

10. adultero, pres. act. subj. 2 s., *commit adultery*

11. furor, pres. dep. subj. 2 s., *steal*

12. fallo, perf. pass. ptcp. n. a. s., *deceive*

13. fraus, *deceit, fraud*

14. honoro, pres. act. impv. 2 s., *honor*

April 4

Habakkuk 2:19

הֹ֣וי[1] אֹמֵ֤ר לָעֵץ֙ הָקִ֔יצָה[2] ע֖וּרִי[3] לְאֶ֣בֶן דּוּמָ֑ם[4] ה֣וּא
יוֹרֶ֔ה[5] הִנֵּה־ה֗וּא תָּפוּשׂ֙[6] זָהָ֣ב וָכֶ֔סֶף וְכָל־ר֖וּחַ אֵ֥ין
בְּקִרְבּֽוֹ׃

οὐαὶ[7] ὁ λέγων τῷ ξύλῳ Ἔκνηψον[8] ἐξεγέρθητι,[9] καὶ τῷ λίθῳ Ὑψώθητι· καὶ αὐτό ἐστιν φαντασία,[10] τοῦτο δέ ἐστιν ἔλασμα[11] χρυσίου καὶ ἀργυρίου, καὶ πᾶν πνεῦμα οὐκ ἔστιν ἐν αὐτῷ.

1 Corinthians 12:2

Οἴδατε ὅτι ὅτε ἔθνη ἦτε πρὸς τὰ εἴδωλα[12] τὰ ἄφωνα[13] ὡς ἂν ἤγεσθε ἀπαγόμενοι.[14]

scitis quoniam cum gentes essetis ad simulacra[15] muta[16] prout[17] ducebamini euntes.

1. הוֹי, *woe*
2. קִיץ, hiph. impv. m. s., *awake*
3. עוּר, qal impv. f. s., *arise*
4. דּוּמָם, *dumb, silent*
5. יָרָה, hiph. impf. 3 m. s., *teach*
6. תָּפַשׂ, qal ptcp. m. s. abs., *overlaid, sheathed*
7. οὐαί, *woe*
8. ἐκνήφω, aor. act. impv. 2 s., *sober up*
9. ἐξεγείρω, aor. pass. impv. 2 s., *arise, wake up*
10. φαντασία, *fantasy, appearance*
11. ἔλασμα, *beaten metal*
12. εἴδωλον, *idol*
13. ἄφωνος, *speechless*
14. ἀπάγω, pres. pass. ptcp. m. nom. p., *lead astray*
15. simulacrum, *idol, image*
16. mutus, *mute, dumb*
17. prout, *just as*

April 5

Deuteronomy 5:7

לֹ֣א יִהְיֶ֥ה־לְךָ֛ אֱלֹהִ֥ים אֲחֵרִ֖ים עַל־פָּנָֽיַ׃

οὐκ ἔσονταί σοι θεοὶ ἕτεροι πρὸ προσώπου μου.

1 John 5:21

Τεκνία,[1] φυλάξατε ἑαυτὰ ἀπὸ τῶν εἰδώλων.[2]

filioli[3] custodite vos a simulacris.[4]

1. τεκνίον, *little child*

2. εἴδωλον, *idol, false god*

3. filiolus, *little child*

4. simulacrum, *idol, image*

April 6

***Deuteronomy* 5:12**

שָׁמ֛וֹר אֶת־י֥וֹם הַשַּׁבָּ֖ת לְקַדְּשׁ֑וֹ כַּאֲשֶׁ֥ר צִוְּךָ֖ ׀ יְהוָ֥ה
אֱלֹהֶֽיךָ׃

φύλαξαι τὴν ἡμέραν τῶν σαββάτων ἁγιάζειν αὐτήν, ὃν τρόπον ἐνετείλατό σοι κύριος ὁ θεός σου.

***Mark* 2:27**

Καὶ ἔλεγεν αὐτοῖς· τὸ σάββατον διὰ τὸν ἄνθρωπον ἐγένετο καὶ οὐχ ὁ ἄνθρωπος διὰ τὸ σάββατον.

et dicebat eis sabbatum propter hominem factum est et non homo propter sabbatum.

April 7

Deuteronomy 18:1

לֹֽא־יִהְיֶה לַכֹּהֲנִים הַלְוִיִּם כָּל־שֵׁבֶט לֵוִי חֵלֶק[1] וְנַחֲלָה
עִם־יִשְׂרָאֵל אִשֵּׁי[2] יְהוָה וְנַחֲלָתוֹ יֹאכֵלֽוּן׃

Οὐκ ἔσται τοῖς ἱερεῦσιν τοῖς Λευίταις, ὅλῃ φυλῇ Λευι,[3] μερὶς οὐδὲ κλῆρος μετὰ Ισραηλ· καρπώματα[4] κυρίου ὁ κλῆρος αὐτῶν, φάγονται αὐτά.

1 Corinthians 9:13

Οὐκ οἴδατε ὅτι οἱ τὰ ἱερὰ[5] ἐργαζόμενοι [τὰ] ἐκ τοῦ ἱεροῦ ἐσθίουσιν, οἱ τῷ θυσιαστηρίῳ[6] παρεδρεύοντες[7] τῷ θυσιαστηρίῳ συμμερίζονται;[8]

nescitis quoniam qui in sacrario[9] operantur quae de sacrario sunt edunt[10] qui altario[11] deserviunt[12] cum altario participantur?[13]

1. חֵ֫לֶק, *portion*
2. אִשֶּׁה, *offering (made by fire)*
3. Λευι, *Levites*
4. κάρπωμα, *offering, burnt offering*
5. ἱερός, *temple*
6. θυσιαστήριον, *altar*
7. παρεδρεύω, pres. act. ptcp. m. nom. p., *serve*
8. συμμερίζω, pres. mid. ind. 3 p., *share with*
9. sacrarium, *sanctuary*
10. edo, pres. act. ind. 3 p., *eat*
11. altartium, *altar*
12. deservio, pres. act. ind. 3 p., *serve*
13. participor, pres. dep. ind. 3 p., *partake of*

April 8

Isaiah 55:11

כֵּ֣ן יִהְיֶ֤ה דְבָרִי֙ אֲשֶׁ֣ר יֵצֵ֣א מִפִּ֔י לֹֽא־יָשׁ֥וּב אֵלַ֖י רֵיקָ֑ם[1]
כִּ֤י אִם־עָשָׂה֙ אֶת־אֲשֶׁ֣ר חָפַ֔צְתִּי[2] וְהִצְלִ֖יחַ[3] אֲשֶׁ֥ר
שְׁלַחְתִּֽיו׃

οὕτως ἔσται τὸ ῥῆμά μου, ὃ ἐὰν ἐξέλθῃ ἐκ τοῦ στόματός μου, οὐ μὴ ἀποστραφῇ, ἕως ἂν συντελεσθῇ ὅσα ἠθέλησα καὶ εὐοδώσω[4] τὰς ὁδούς σου καὶ τὰ ἐντάλματά[5] μου.

Matthew 5:18

ἀμὴν γὰρ λέγω ὑμῖν· ἕως ἂν παρέλθῃ[6] ὁ οὐρανὸς καὶ ἡ γῆ, ἰῶτα[7] ἓν ἢ μία κεραία[8] οὐ μὴ παρέλθῃ ἀπὸ τοῦ νόμου, ἕως ἂν πάντα γένηται.

amen quippe[9] dico vobis donec transeat caelum et terra iota[10] unum aut unus apex[11] non praeteribit[12] a lege donec omnia fiant.

1. רֵיקָם, *empty*
2. חָפֵץ, qal perf. 1 c. s., *delight in, take pleasure in*
3. צָלַח, hiph. perf. 3 m. s., *prosper, succeed*
4. εὐοδόω, fut. act. ind. 1 s., *prosper*
5. ἔνταλμα, *commandment*
6. παρέρχομαι, aor. act. subj. 3 s., *pass by*
7. ἰῶτα, *iota*
8. κεραία, *small stroke (of a letter)*
9. quippe, *for*
10. iota, *iota*
11. apex, *point (of a letter)*
12. praetereo, fut. act. ind. 3 s., *go by, pass by*

April 9

Leviticus 8:15

וַיִּשְׁחָ֗ט[1] וַיִּקַּח֩ מֹשֶׁ֨ה אֶת־הַדָּ֜ם וַ֠יִּתֵּן עַל־קַרְנ֨וֹת[2]
הַמִּזְבֵּ֤חַ סָבִיב֙ בְּאֶצְבָּע֔וֹ[3] וַיְחַטֵּ֖א אֶת־הַמִּזְבֵּ֑חַ וְאֶת־
הַדָּ֗ם יָצַק֙[4] אֶל־יְס֣וֹד[5] הַמִּזְבֵּ֔חַ וַֽיְקַדְּשֵׁ֖הוּ לְכַפֵּ֥ר עָלָֽיו׃

καὶ ἔσφαξεν[6] αὐτὸν καὶ ἔλαβεν Μωυσῆς ἀπὸ τοῦ αἵματος καὶ ἐπέθηκεν ἐπὶ τὰ κέρατα τοῦ θυσιαστηρίου[7] κύκλῳ τῷ δακτύλῳ[8] καὶ ἐκαθάρισεν τὸ θυσιαστήριον· καὶ τὸ αἷμα ἐξέχεεν ἐπὶ τὴν βάσιν[9] τοῦ θυσιαστηρίου καὶ ἡγίασεν αὐτὸ τοῦ ἐξιλάσασθαι ἐπ᾽ αὐτοῦ.

Hebrews 9:21

καὶ τὴν σκηνὴν[10] δὲ καὶ πάντα τὰ σκεύη[11] τῆς λειτουργίας[12] τῷ αἵματι ὁμοίως[13] ἐρράντισεν.[14]

etiam tabernaculum[15] et omnia vasa[16] ministerii sanguine similiter aspersit.[17]

1. שׁחט, qal wcons. 3 m. s., *slaughter*

2. קֶ֫רֶן, *horn*

3. אֶצְבַּע, *finger*

4. יָצַק, qal perf. 3 m. s., *pour*

5. יְסוֹד, *base, foundation*

6. σφάζω, aor. act. ind. 3 s., *slaughter*

7. θυσιαστήριον, *altar*

8. δάκτυλος, *finger*

9. βάσις, *foundation, base*

10. σκηνή, *tabernacle*

11. σκεῦος, *vessel*

12. λειτουργία, *service*

13. ὁμοίως, *same manner/way*

14. ῥαντίζω, aor. act. ind. 3 s., *sprinkle*

15. tabernaculum, *tabernacle*

16. vas, *vessel*

17. aspergo, perf. act. ind. 3 s., *sprinkle*

April 10

Leviticus 9:7

וַיֹּ֨אמֶר מֹשֶׁ֜ה אֶֽל־אַהֲרֹ֗ן קְרַ֤ב אֶל־הַמִּזְבֵּ֙חַ֙ וַעֲשֵׂ֞ה אֶת־
חַטָּֽאתְךָ֙ וְאֶת־עֹ֣לָתֶ֔ךָ וְכַפֵּ֥ר בַּֽעַדְךָ֖ וּבְעַ֣ד הָעָ֑ם וַעֲשֵׂ֞ה
אֶת־קָרְבַּ֤ן[1] הָעָם֙ וְכַפֵּ֣ר בַּֽעֲדָ֔ם כַּאֲשֶׁ֖ר צִוָּ֥ה יְהוָֽה׃

καὶ εἶπεν Μωυσῆς τῷ Ααρων Πρόσελθε πρὸς τὸ θυσιαστήριον[2] καὶ ποίησον τὸ περὶ τῆς ἁμαρτίας σου καὶ τὸ ὁλοκαύτωμά[3] σου καὶ ἐξίλασαι[4] περὶ σεαυτοῦ καὶ τοῦ οἴκου σου· καὶ ποίησον τὰ δῶρα τοῦ λαοῦ καὶ ἐξίλασαι περὶ αὐτῶν, καθάπερ[5] ἐνετείλατο κύριος τῷ Μωυσῇ.

Hebrews 5:3

καὶ δι᾽ αὐτὴν ὀφείλει, καθὼς περὶ τοῦ λαοῦ, οὕτως καὶ περὶ αὐτοῦ προσφέρειν περὶ ἁμαρτιῶν.

et propter eam debet quemadmodum et pro populo ita etiam pro semet ipso offerre pro peccatis.

1. קָרְבָּן, *offering*
2. θυσιαστήριον, *altar*
3. ὁλοκαύτωμα, *whole burnt offering*
4. ἐξιλάσκομαι, aor. mid. impv. 2 s., *make atonement*
5. καθάπερ, *just as*

April 11

Leviticus 16:2

וַיֹּ֨אמֶר יְהוָ֜ה אֶל־מֹשֶׁ֗ה דַּבֵּר֮ אֶל־אַהֲרֹ֣ן אָחִיךָ֒ וְאַל־
יָבֹ֤א בְכָל־עֵת֙ אֶל־הַקֹּ֔דֶשׁ מִבֵּ֖ית לַפָּרֹ֑כֶת[1] אֶל־פְּנֵ֨י
הַכַּפֹּ֜רֶת[2] אֲשֶׁ֤ר עַל־הָאָרֹן֙ וְלֹ֣א יָמ֔וּת כִּ֚י בֶּֽעָנָ֔ן[3] אֵרָאֶ֖ה
עַל־הַכַּפֹּֽרֶת׃

καὶ εἶπεν κύριος πρὸς Μωυσῆν Λάλησον πρὸς Ααρων τὸν ἀδελφόν σου καὶ μὴ εἰσπορευέσθω πᾶσαν ὥραν[4] εἰς τὸ ἅγιον ἐσώτερον[5] τοῦ καταπετάσματος[6] εἰς πρόσωπον τοῦ ἱλαστηρίου,[7] ὅ ἐστιν ἐπὶ τῆς κιβωτοῦ τοῦ μαρτυρίου, καὶ οὐκ ἀποθανεῖται· ἐν γὰρ νεφέλῃ ὀφθήσομαι ἐπὶ τοῦ ἱλαστηρίου.

Hebrews 9:6

Τούτων δὲ οὕτως κατεσκευασμένων[8] εἰς μὲν τὴν πρώτην σκηνὴν[9] διὰ παντὸς εἰσίασιν[10] οἱ ἱερεῖς τὰς λατρείας[11] ἐπιτελοῦντες.[12]

his vero ita conpositis[13] in priori[14] quidem tabernaculo[15] semper introibant sacerdotes sacrificiorum[16] officia[17] consummantes.

1. פָּרֹ֫כֶת, *curtain, veil*

2. כַּפֹּ֫רֶת, *mercy seat, atonement lid*

3. עָנָן, *cloud*

4. ὥρα, *hour, time*

5. ἐσώτερος, *inside*

6. καταπέτασμα, *curtain, veil*

7. ἱλαστήριον, *place of propitiation/forgiveness*

8. κατασκευάζω, perf. pass. ptcp. n. g. p., *prepare*

9. σκηνή, *tabernacle*

10. εἴσειμι, pres. act. ind. 3 p., *enter*

11. λατρεία, *service, worship*

12. ἐπιτελέω, pres. act. ptcp. m. nom. p., *complete, perform*

13. conpono, perf. pass. ptcp. n. abl. p., *prepare*

14. prior, *first*

15. tabernaculum, *tabernacle*

16. sacrificium, *sacrifice*

17. officium, *office*

April 12

Leviticus 16:34

וְהָֽיְתָה־זֹּ֨את לָכֶ֜ם לְחֻקַּ֣ת עוֹלָ֗ם לְכַפֵּ֞ר עַל־בְּנֵ֤י
יִשְׂרָאֵל֙ מִכָּל־חַטֹּאתָ֔ם אַחַ֖ת בַּשָּׁנָ֑ה וַיַּ֕עַשׂ כַּאֲשֶׁ֛ר
צִוָּ֥ה יְהוָ֖ה אֶת־מֹשֶֽׁה׃

καὶ ἔσται τοῦτο ὑμῖν νόμιμον[1] αἰώνιον ἐξιλάσκεσθαι περὶ τῶν υἱῶν Ισραηλ ἀπὸ πασῶν τῶν ἁμαρτιῶν αὐτῶν· ἅπαξ[2] τοῦ ἐνιαυτοῦ[3] ποιηθήσεται, καθάπερ[4] συνέταξεν κύριος τῷ Μωυσῇ.

Hebrews 9:7

εἰς δὲ τὴν δευτέραν ἅπαξ τοῦ ἐνιαυτοῦ μόνος ὁ ἀρχιερεύς, οὐ χωρὶς αἵματος ὃ προσφέρει ὑπὲρ ἑαυτοῦ καὶ τῶν τοῦ λαοῦ ἀγνοημάτων.[5]

in secundo autem semel[6] in anno solus pontifex non sine sanguine quem offert pro sua et populi ignorantia.[7]

1. νόμιμος, *statute, ordinance*
2. ἅπαξ, *once*
3. ἐνιαυτός, *year*
4. καθάπερ, *just as*
5. ἀγνόημα, *ignorant*; TH: *unintentional sin*
6. semel, *once*
7. ignorantia, *ignorant*; TH: *unintentional sin*

April 13

Leviticus 17:11

כִּ֣י נֶ֣פֶשׁ הַבָּשָׂר֮ בַּדָּ֣ם הִוא֒ וַאֲנִ֞י נְתַתִּ֤יו לָכֶם֙ עַל־
הַמִּזְבֵּ֔חַ לְכַפֵּ֖ר עַל־נַפְשֹׁתֵיכֶ֑ם כִּֽי־הַדָּ֥ם ה֖וּא
בַּנֶּ֥פֶשׁ יְכַפֵּֽר׃

ἡ γὰρ ψυχὴ πάσης σαρκὸς αἷμα αὐτοῦ ἐστιν, καὶ ἐγὼ δέδωκα αὐτὸ ὑμῖν ἐπὶ τοῦ θυσιαστηρίου ἐξιλάσκεσθαι[1] περὶ τῶν ψυχῶν ὑμῶν· τὸ γὰρ αἷμα αὐτοῦ ἀντὶ τῆς ψυχῆς ἐξιλάσεται.[2]

Hebrews 9:22

καὶ σχεδὸν[3] ἐν αἵματι πάντα καθαρίζεται κατὰ τὸν νόμον καὶ χωρὶς αἱματεκχυσίας[4] οὐ γίνεται ἄφεσις.[5]

et omnia paene[6] in sanguine mundantur[7] secundum legem et sine sanguinis fusione[8] non fit remissio.[9]

1. ἐξιλάσκομαι, pres. mid. inf., *make atonement*
2. ἐξιλάσκομαι, fut. mid. ind. 3 s., *make atonement*
3. σχεδόν, *almost*
4. αἱματεκχυσία, *shedding of blood*
5. ἄφεσις, *forgiveness*
6. paene, *almost*
7. mundo, pres. pass. ind. 3 p., *cleanse*
8. fusio, *shedding*
9. remissio, *forgiveness*

April 14

Leviticus 18:5

וּשְׁמַרְתֶּ֤ם אֶת־חֻקֹּתַי֙ וְאֶת־מִשְׁפָּטַ֔י אֲשֶׁ֨ר יַעֲשֶׂ֥ה
אֹתָ֛ם הָאָדָ֖ם וָחַ֣י בָּהֶ֑ם אֲנִ֖י יְהוָֽה׃

καὶ φυλάξεσθε πάντα τὰ προστάγματά μου καὶ πάντα τὰ κρίματά μου καὶ ποιήσετε αὐτά, ἃ ποιήσας ἄνθρωπος ζήσεται ἐν αὐτοῖς· ἐγὼ κύριος ὁ θεὸς ὑμῶν.

Matthew 19:17

ὁ δὲ εἶπεν αὐτῷ· τί με ἐρωτᾷς περὶ τοῦ ἀγαθοῦ; εἷς ἐστιν ὁ ἀγαθός· εἰ δὲ θέλεις εἰς τὴν ζωὴν εἰσελθεῖν, τήρησον τὰς ἐντολάς.

qui dixit ei quid me interrogas de bono unus est bonus Deus si autem vis ad vitam ingredi serva mandata.

April 15

Leviticus 18:8

עֶרְוַ֥ת[1] אֵֽשֶׁת־אָבִ֖יךָ לֹ֣א תְגַלֵּ֑ה עֶרְוַ֥ת אָבִ֖יךָ הִֽוא׃

ἀσχημοσύνην[2] γυναικὸς πατρός σου οὐκ ἀποκαλύψεις·[3] ἀσχημοσύνη πατρός σού ἐστιν.

1 Corinthians 5:1

Ὅλως[4] ἀκούεται ἐν ὑμῖν πορνεία,[5] καὶ τοιαύτη πορνεία ἥτις οὐδὲ ἐν τοῖς ἔθνεσιν, ὥστε γυναῖκά τινα τοῦ πατρὸς ἔχειν.

omnino[6] auditur inter vos fornicatio[7] et talis fornicatio qualis[8] nec inter gentes ita ut uxorem patris aliquis habeat.

1. עֶרְוָה, *nakedness*
2. ἀσχημοσύνη, *shame*
3. ἀποκαλύπτω, fut. act. ind. 2 s., *uncover, reveal*
4. ὅλως, *actually*
5. πορνεία, *sexual immorality*
6. omnino, *actually, altogether*
7. fornicatio, *fornication*
8. qualis, *of what kind?*

April 16

Leviticus 19:17

לֹא־תִשְׂנָא אֶת־אָחִיךָ בִּלְבָבֶךָ הוֹכֵחַ[1] תּוֹכִיחַ[2] אֶת־
עֲמִיתֶךָ[3] וְלֹא־תִשָּׂא עָלָיו חֵטְא׃[4]

οὐ μισήσεις τὸν ἀδελφόν σου τῇ διανοίᾳ[5] σου, ἐλεγμῷ[6] ἐλέγξεις[7] τὸν πλησίον σου καὶ οὐ λήμψῃ δι᾽ αὐτὸν ἁμαρτίαν.

Matthew 18:15

Ἐὰν δὲ ἁμαρτήσῃ [εἰς σὲ] ὁ ἀδελφός σου, ὕπαγε ἔλεγξον[8] αὐτὸν μεταξὺ[9] σοῦ καὶ αὐτοῦ μόνου. ἐάν σου ἀκούσῃ, ἐκέρδησας[10] τὸν ἀδελφόν σου.

si autem peccaverit in te frater tuus vade et corripe[11] eum inter te et ipsum solum si te audierit lucratus[12] es fratrem tuum.

1. יָכַח, hiph. inf. abs., *correct, reprove*
2. יָכַח, hiph. impf. 2 m. s., *correct, reprove*
3. עָמִית, *fellow, associate, neighbor*
4. חֵטְא, *sin*
5. διάνοια, *mind, thought*
6. ἐλεγμός, *correction, reproof*
7. ἐλέγχω, fut. act. ind. 2 s., *reprove*
8. ἐλέγχω, aor. act. impv. 2 s., *reprove*
9. μεταξύ, *between*
10. κερδαίνω, aor. act. ind. 2 s., *gain*
11. corripio, pres. act. impv. 2 s., *reprove*
12. lucror, perf. dep. ind. 2 s., *gain, profit*

April 17

Psalm 143:2 [LXX 142:2]

וְאַל־תָּבוֹא בְמִשְׁפָּט אֶת־עַבְדֶּךָ כִּי לֹא־יִצְדַּק[1] לְפָנֶיךָ
כָל־חָי׃

καὶ μὴ εἰσέλθῃς εἰς κρίσιν μετὰ τοῦ δούλου σου,
ὅτι οὐ δικαιωθήσεται[2] ἐνώπιόν σου πᾶς ζῶν.

Galatians 2:16

εἰδότες [δὲ] ὅτι οὐ δικαιοῦται[3] ἄνθρωπος ἐξ ἔργων νόμου ἐὰν μὴ διὰ πίστεως Ἰησοῦ Χριστοῦ, καὶ ἡμεῖς εἰς Χριστὸν Ἰησοῦν ἐπιστεύσαμεν, ἵνα δικαιωθῶμεν[4] ἐκ πίστεως Χριστοῦ καὶ οὐκ ἐξ ἔργων νόμου, ὅτι ἐξ ἔργων νόμου οὐ δικαιωθήσεται πᾶσα σάρξ.

scientes autem quod non iustificatur homo ex operibus legis nisi per fidem Iesu Christi et nos in Christo Iesu credidimus ut iustificemur ex fide Christi et non ex operibus legis propter quod ex operibus legis non iustificabitur omnis caro.

1. צֶדֶק, *righteous*
2. δικαιόω, fut. pass. ind. 3 s., *pronounce righteous*
3. δικαιόω, pres. pass. ind., *pronounce righteous*
4. δικαιόω, aor. pass. subj. 1 p., *pronounce righteous*

Conquest

April 18

Joshua 2:4

וַתִּקַּ֧ח הָאִשָּׁ֛ה אֶת־שְׁנֵ֥י הָאֲנָשִׁ֖ים וַֽתִּצְפְּנ֑וֹ[1] וַתֹּ֣אמֶר ׀
כֵּ֗ן[2] בָּ֤אוּ אֵלַי֙ הָֽאֲנָשִׁ֔ים וְלֹ֥א יָדַ֖עְתִּי מֵאַ֥יִן[3] הֵֽמָּה׃

καὶ λαβοῦσα ἡ γυνὴ τοὺς ἄνδρας ἔκρυψεν αὐτοὺς καὶ εἶπεν αὐτοῖς λέγουσα Εἰσεληλύθασιν πρός με οἱ ἄνδρες.

James 2:25

ὁμοίως[4] δὲ καὶ Ῥαὰβ[5] ἡ πόρνη[6] οὐκ ἐξ ἔργων ἐδικαιώθη ὑποδεξαμένη[7] τοὺς ἀγγέλους καὶ ἑτέρᾳ ὁδῷ ἐκβαλοῦσα;

similiter autem et Raab[8] meretrix[9] nonne ex operibus iustificata est suscipiens nuntios[10] et alia via eiciens?

1. צָפַן, qal wcons. 3 f. s., *hide*
2. כֵּן, *right, true*
3. אַיִן, *whence, from where*
4. ὁμοίως, *likewise*
5. Ῥαάβ, *Rahab*
6. πόρνη, *prostitute*
7. ὑποδέχομαι, aor. mid. ptcp. f. nom. s., *receive*
8. Raab, *Rahab*
9. meretrix, *prostitute, harlot*
10. nuntius, *messenger*

April 19

Joshua 2:12

וְעַתָּה הִשָּׁבְעוּ־נָא לִי בַּיהוָה כִּי־עָשִׂיתִי עִמָּכֶם חָסֶד
וַעֲשִׂיתֶם גַּם־אַתֶּם עִם־בֵּית אָבִי חֶסֶד וּנְתַתֶּם לִי
אוֹת[1] אֱמֶת׃

καὶ νῦν ὀμόσατέ μοι κύριον τὸν θεόν, ὅτι ποιῶ ὑμῖν ἔλεος καὶ ποιήσετε καὶ ὑμεῖς ἔλεος ἐν τῷ οἴκῳ τοῦ πατρός μου.

Hebrews 11:31

Πίστει Ῥαὰβ[2] ἡ πόρνη[3] οὐ συναπώλετο[4] τοῖς ἀπειθήσασιν[5] δεξαμένη τοὺς κατασκόπους[6] μετ᾽ εἰρήνης.

fide Raab[7] meretrix[8] non periit cum incredulis[9] excipiens[10] exploratores[11] cum pace.

1. אוֹת, *sign*
2. Ῥαάβ, *Rahab*
3. πόρνη, *prostitute*
4. συναπόλλυμι, aor. mid. ind. 3 s., *perish together with*
5. ἀπειθέω, aor. act. ptcp. m. d. s., *disobey, disobedient*
6. κατάσκοπος, *spy*
7. Raab, *Rahab*
8. meretrix, *prostitute, harlot*
9. incredulus, *unbeliever, faithless*
10. excipio, pres. act. ptcp. f. nom. s., *welcome, rescue*
11. explorator, *spy, explorer*

April 20

Joshua 7:1

וַיִּמְעֲל֧וּ[1] בְנֵֽי־יִשְׂרָאֵ֛ל מַ֖עַל[2] בַּחֵ֑רֶם[3] וַיִּקַּ֡ח עָכָ֣ן[4] בֶּן־
כַּרְמִי֩[5] בֶן־זַבְדִּ֨י[6] בֶן־זֶ֜רַח[7] לְמַטֵּ֤ה יְהוּדָה֙ מִן־הַחֵ֔רֶם
וַיִּֽחַר[8]־אַ֥ף יְהוָ֖ה בִּבְנֵ֥י יִשְׂרָאֵֽל׃

Καὶ ἐπλημμέλησαν[9] οἱ υἱοὶ Ισραηλ πλημμέλειαν[10] μεγάλην καὶ ἐνοσφίσαντο[11] ἀπὸ τοῦ ἀναθέματος·[12] καὶ ἔλαβεν Αχαρ[13] υἱὸς Χαρμι[14] υἱοῦ Ζαμβρι[15] υἱοῦ Ζαρα[16] ἐκ τῆς φυλῆς Ιουδα ἀπὸ τοῦ ἀναθέματος· καὶ ἐθυμώθη[17] ὀργῇ κύριος τοῖς υἱοῖς Ισραηλ.

Acts 5:4[18]

οὐχὶ μένον σοὶ ἔμενεν καὶ πραθὲν[19] ἐν τῇ σῇ[20] ἐξουσίᾳ ὑπῆρχεν; τί ὅτι ἔθου ἐν τῇ καρδίᾳ σου τὸ πρᾶγμα[21] τοῦτο; οὐκ ἐψεύσω[22] ἀνθρώποις ἀλλὰ τῷ θεῷ.

nonne manens tibi manebat et venundatum[23] in tua erat potestate quare posuisti in corde tuo hanc rem[24] non es mentitus[25] hominibus sed Deo.

1. מָעַל, qal wcons. 3 m. p., *act unfaithfully*
2. מַעַל, *unfaithful act*
3. חֵרֶם, *devoted thing (to the ban)*
4. עָכָן, *Achan*
5. כַּרְמִי, *Carmi*
6. זַבְדִּי, *Zabdi*
7. זֶרַח, *Zerah*
8. חָרָה, qal wcons. 3 m. s., *be angry*
9. πλημμελέω, aor. act. ind. 3 p., *err, sin*
10. πλημμέλεια, *sin*
11. νοσφίζω, aor. mid. ind. 3 p., *steal, pilfer*
12. ἀνάθεμα, *accursed*
13. Αχαρ, *Achan*
14. Χαρμι, *Carmi*
15. Ζαμβρι, *Zambri*
16. Ζαρα, *Zerah*
17. θυμόω, aor. pass. ind. 3 s., *be angry*
18. CH: In this passage, Peter is speaking to Ananias.
19. πιπράσκω, aor. pass. ptcp. n. nom. s., *sell*
20. σός, *your*

21. πρᾶγμα, *thing, deed.* **22.** ψεύδομαι, aor. mid. ind. 2 s., *lie.* **23.** venundo, perf. pass. ptcp. n. nom. s., *sell.* **24.** res, *thing.* **25.** mentior, perf. dep. ind. 2 s., *lie, deceive*

April 21

Joshua 7:19

וַיֹּ֨אמֶר יְהוֹשֻׁ֜עַ אֶל־עָכָ֗ן[1] בְּנִי֙ שִׂים־נָ֨א כָב֜וֹד לַֽיהוָ֨ה
אֱלֹהֵ֧י יִשְׂרָאֵ֛ל וְתֶן־ל֥וֹ תוֹדָ֖ה[2] וְהַגֶּד־נָ֣א לִ֗י מֶ֣ה עָשִׂ֔יתָ
אַל־תְּכַחֵ֖ד[3] מִמֶּֽנִּי׃

καὶ εἶπεν Ἰησοῦς τῷ Αχαρ[4] Δὸς δόξαν σήμερον τῷ κυρίῳ θεῷ Ισραηλ καὶ δὸς τὴν ἐξομολόγησιν[5] καὶ ἀνάγγειλόν μοι τί ἐποίησας, καὶ μὴ κρύψῃς ἀπ᾽ ἐμοῦ.

John 9:24

Ἐφώνησαν οὖν τὸν ἄνθρωπον ἐκ δευτέρου ὃς ἦν τυφλὸς καὶ εἶπαν αὐτῷ· δὸς δόξαν τῷ θεῷ· ἡμεῖς οἴδαμεν ὅτι οὗτος ὁ ἄνθρωπος ἁμαρτωλός ἐστιν.

vocaverunt ergo rursum[6] hominem qui fuerat caecus et dixerunt ei da gloriam Deo nos scimus quia hic homo peccator est.

1. עָכָן, *Achan*
2. תּוֹדָה, *praise, thanksgiving*
3. כָּחַד, piel impf. 2 m. s. juss., *hide*
4. Αχαρ, *Achan*
5. ἐξομολόγησις, *confession*
6. rursum, *again*

April 22

Joshua 14:1

וְאֵ֛לֶּה אֲשֶׁר־נָחֲל֥וּ[1] בְנֵֽי־יִשְׂרָאֵ֖ל בְּאֶ֣רֶץ כְּנָ֑עַן[2] אֲשֶׁ֨ר
נִחֲל֜וּ[3] אוֹתָ֗ם אֶלְעָזָ֤ר[4] הַכֹּהֵן֙ וִיהוֹשֻׁ֣עַ בִּן־נ֔וּן[5] וְרָאשֵׁ֛י
אֲב֥וֹת הַמַּטּ֖וֹת לִבְנֵ֥י יִשְׂרָאֵֽל׃

Καὶ οὗτοι οἱ κατακληρονομήσαντες[6] υἱῶν Ισραηλ ἐν τῇ γῇ Χανααν,[7] οἷς κατεκληρονόμησεν[8] αὐτοῖς Ελεαζαρ[9] ὁ ἱερεὺς καὶ Ἰησοῦς ὁ τοῦ Ναυη[10] καὶ οἱ ἄρχοντες πατριῶν φυλῶν τῶν υἱῶν Ισραηλ.

Acts 13:19

καὶ καθελὼν[11] ἔθνη ἑπτὰ ἐν γῇ Χανάαν κατεκληρονόμησεν τὴν γῆν αὐτῶν.

et destruens[12] gentes septem in terra Chanaan[13] sorte[14] distribuit[15] eis terram eorum.

1. נחל, qal perf. 3 c. p., *inherit*

2. כְּנַ֫עַן, *Canaan*

3. נחל, piel perf. 3 c. p., *inherit*

4. אֶלְעָזָר, *Eleazar*

5. נוּן, *Nun*

6. κατακληρονομέω, aor. act. ptcp. m. nom. p., *divide by lot*

7. Χανααν, *Canaan*

8. κατακληρονομέω, aor. act. ind. 3 s., *divide by lot*

9. Ελεαζαρ, *Eleazar*

10. Ναυη, *Nun*

11. καθαιρέω, aor. act. ptcp. m. nom. s., *destroy*

12. destruo, pres. act. ptcp. m. nom. s., *destroy*

13. Chanaan, *Canaan*

14. sors, *lot*

15. distribuo, perf. act. ind. 3 s., *divide*

April 23

Joshua 18:1

וַיִּקָּהֲלוּ[1] כָּל־עֲדַת בְּנֵי־יִשְׂרָאֵל שִׁלֹה[2] וַיַּשְׁכִּינוּ שָׁם
אֶת־אֹהֶל מוֹעֵד וְהָאָרֶץ נִכְבְּשָׁה[3] לִפְנֵיהֶם׃

Καὶ ἐξεκκλησιάσθη[4] πᾶσα συναγωγὴ υἱῶν Ισραηλ εἰς Σηλω[5] καὶ ἔπηξαν[6] ἐκεῖ τὴν σκηνὴν τοῦ μαρτυρίου, καὶ ἡ γῆ ἐκρατήθη ὑπ᾽ αὐτῶν.

Acts 7:45

ἣν[7] καὶ εἰσήγαγον[8] διαδεξάμενοι[9] οἱ πατέρες ἡμῶν μετὰ Ἰησοῦ ἐν τῇ κατασχέσει[10] τῶν ἐθνῶν, ὧν ἐξῶσεν[11] ὁ θεὸς ἀπὸ προσώπου τῶν πατέρων ἡμῶν ἕως τῶν ἡμερῶν Δαυίδ.

quod[12] et induxerunt[13] suscipientes patres nostri cum Iesu in possessionem[14] gentium quas expulit[15] Deus a facie patrum nostrorum usque in diebus David.

1. קהל, niph. wcons. 3 m. p., *assemble*
2. שִׁילוֹ, *Shiloh*
3. כָּבַשׁ, niph. perf. 3 f. s., *subdue*
4. ἐξεκκλησιάζω, aor. pass. ind. 3 s., *gather, assemble*
5. Σηλω, *Shiloh*
6. πήγνυμι, aor. act. ind. 3 p., *fasten, set up*
7. CH: This pronoun is a referent to the tabernacle.
8. εἰσάγω, aor. act. ind. 3 p., *bring in*
9. διαδέχομαι, aor. mid. ptcp. m. nom. p., *take possession of*
10. κατάσχεσις, *possession*
11. ἐξωθέω, aor. act. ind. 3 s., *expel, drive out*
12. CH: This pronoun is a referent to the tabernacle.
13. induco, perf. act. ind. 3 p., *bring in*
14. possessio, *possession*
15. expello, perf. act. ind. 3 s., *drive out, expel*

April 24

Joshua 22:4

וְעַתָּ֗ה הֵנִ֨יחַ יְהוָ֤ה אֱלֹֽהֵיכֶם֙ לַאֲחֵיכֶ֔ם כַּאֲשֶׁ֖ר דִּבֶּ֣ר
לָהֶ֑ם וְעַתָּ֡ה פְּנוּ֩ וּלְכ֨וּ לָכֶ֜ם לְאָהֳלֵיכֶ֗ם אֶל־אֶ֙רֶץ֙
אֲחֻזַּתְכֶ֔ם[1] אֲשֶׁ֣ר ׀ נָתַ֣ן לָכֶ֗ם מֹשֶׁה֙ עֶ֣בֶד יְהוָ֔ה בְּעֵ֖בֶר[2]
הַיַּרְדֵּֽן׃

νῦν δὲ κατέπαυσεν[3] κύριος ὁ θεὸς ἡμῶν τοὺς ἀδελφοὺς ἡμῶν, ὃν τρόπον εἶπεν αὐτοῖς· νῦν οὖν ἀποστραφέντες ἀπέλθατε εἰς τοὺς οἴκους ὑμῶν καὶ εἰς τὴν γῆν τῆς κατασχέσεως[4] ὑμῶν, ἣν ἔδωκεν ὑμῖν Μωυσῆς ἐν τῷ πέραν[5] τοῦ Ιορδάνου.

Hebrews 4:8

εἰ γὰρ αὐτοὺς Ἰησοῦς κατέπαυσεν, οὐκ ἂν περὶ ἄλλης ἐλάλει μετὰ ταῦτα ἡμέρας.

nam si eis Iesus requiem[6] praestitisset[7] numquam[8] de alio loqueretur posthac[9] die.

1. אֲחֻזָּה, *own, possession*
2. עֵבֶר, *east side, beyond*
3. καταπαύω, aor. act. ind. 3 s., *rest*
4. κατάσχεσις, *possession*
5. πέραν, *beyond, on the other side*
6. requies, *rest*
7. praesto, pluperf. act. subj. 3 s., *give*
8. numquam, *never*
9. posthac, *afterward*

April 25

Joshua 24:32

וְאֶת־עַצְמ֣וֹת יוֹסֵ֡ף אֲשֶׁר־הֶעֱל֣וּ בְנֵֽי־יִשְׂרָאֵ֣ל ׀
מִמִּצְרַ֡יִם קָבְר֣וּ בִשְׁכֶם֒[1] בְּחֶלְקַ֣ת[2] הַשָּׂדֶ֗ה אֲשֶׁ֨ר קָנָ֧ה[3]
יַעֲקֹ֛ב מֵאֵ֛ת בְּנֵֽי־חֲמ֥וֹר[4] אֲבִֽי־שְׁכֶ֖ם בְּמֵאָ֣ה קְשִׂיטָ֑ה[5]
וַיִּהְי֥וּ לִבְנֵֽי־יוֹסֵ֖ף לְנַחֲלָֽה׃

καὶ τὰ ὀστᾶ Ιωσηφ ἀνήγαγον οἱ υἱοὶ Ισραηλ ἐξ Αἰγύπτου καὶ κατώρυξαν[6] ἐν Σικιμοις[7] ἐν τῇ μερίδι τοῦ ἀγροῦ, οὗ ἐκτήσατο Ιακωβ παρὰ τῶν Αμορραίων[8] τῶν κατοικούντων ἐν Σικιμοις ἀμνάδων[9] ἑκατὸν καὶ ἔδωκεν αὐτὴν Ιωσηφ ἐν μερίδι.

John 4:5

Ἔρχεται οὖν εἰς πόλιν τῆς Σαμαρείας[10] λεγομένην Συχὰρ[11] πλησίον[12] τοῦ χωρίου[13] ὃ ἔδωκεν Ἰακὼβ[14] [τῷ] Ἰωσὴφ τῷ υἱῷ αὐτοῦ.

venit ergo in civitatem Samariae[15] quae dicitur Sychar[16] iuxta[17] praedium[18] quod dedit Iacob[19] Ioseph filio suo.

1. שְׁכֶם, *Shechem*
2. חֶלְקָה, *portion of land*
3. קנה, qal perf. 3 m. s., *buy*
4. חֲמוֹר, *Hamor*
5. קְשִׂיטָה, *piece of money*
6. κατορύσσω, aor. act. ind. 3 p., *bury*
7. Σικιμα, *Shechem*
8. Ἀμορραῖος, *Amorite*
9. ἀμνάς, *ewe lamb*
10. Σαμάρεια, *Samaria*
11. Συχάρ, *Sychar*
12. πλησίον, *near*
13. χωρίον, *field*
14. Ἰακώβ, *Jacob*
15. Samaria, *Samaria*
16. Sychar, *Sychar*
17. iuxta, *near*
18. praedium, *estate, land*
19. Iacob, *Jacob*

Judges

April 26

Judges 2:16

וַיָּ֥קֶם יְהוָ֖ה שֹֽׁפְטִ֑ים וַיּ֣וֹשִׁיע֔וּם מִיַּ֖ד שֹׁסֵיהֶֽם׃[1]

καὶ ἤγειρεν[2] αὐτοῖς κύριος κριτὰς[3] καὶ ἔσωσεν αὐτοὺς ἐκ χειρὸς τῶν προνομευόντων[4] αὐτούς.

Acts 13:20

ὡς ἔτεσιν τετρακοσίοις[5] καὶ πεντήκοντα.[6] καὶ μετὰ ταῦτα ἔδωκεν κριτὰς ἕως Σαμουὴλ[7] [τοῦ] προφήτου.

quasi post quadringentos[8] et quinquaginta[9] annos et post haec dedit iudices[10] usque ad Samuhel[11] prophetam.

1. שָׁסָה, qal ptcp. m. p. cons., *plunder*
2. ἐγείρω, aor. act. ind. 3 s., *raise*
3. κριτής, *judge*
4. προνομεύω, pres. act. ptcp. m. g. p., *plunder*
5. τετρακόσιοι, *four hundred*
6. πεντήκοντα, *fifty*
7. Σαμουήλ, *Samuel*
8. quadringenti, *four hundred*
9. quinquaginta, *fifty*
10. iudex, *judge*
11. Samuhel, *Samuel*

April 27

Judges 5:19

בָּ֤אוּ מְלָכִים֙ נִלְחָ֔מוּ אָ֤ז נִלְחֲמוּ֙ מַלְכֵ֣י כְנַ֔עַן[1] בְּתַעְנַ֖ךְ[2]
עַל־מֵ֣י מְגִדּ֑וֹ[3] בֶּ֥צַע[4] כֶּ֖סֶף לֹ֥א לָקָֽחוּ׃

ἦλθον βασιλεῖς καὶ παρετάξαντο.[5] τότε ἐπολέμησαν βασιλεῖς Χαναʼαν[6] ἐν Θενναχ[7] ἐπὶ ὕδατος Μαγεδδω·[8] πλεονεξίαν[9] ἀργυρίου οὐκ ἔλαβον.

Revelation 16:16

Καὶ συνήγαγεν αὐτοὺς εἰς τὸν τόπον τὸν καλούμενον Ἑβραϊστὶ[10] Ἁρμαγεδών.[11]

et congregavit illos in locum qui vocatur hebraice[12] Hermagedon.[13]

1. כְּנַעַן, *Canaan*
2. תַּעְנַךְ, *Taanach*
3. מְגִדּוֹ, *Megiddo*
4. בֶּצַע, *plunder*
5. παρατάσσω, aor. mid. ind. 3 p., *muster, array for battle*
6. Χαναʼαν, *Canaan*
7. Θενναχ, *Taanach*
8. Μαγεδδω, *Megiddo*
9. πλεονεξία, *gain*
10. Ἑβραϊστί, *in Hebrew*
11. Ἁρμαγεδών, *Armageddon*
12. hebraice, *in Hebrew*
13. Hermagedon, *Armageddon*

April 28

Judges 5:24

תְּבֹרַךְ֙ מִנָּשִׁ֔ים יָעֵ֕ל[1] אֵ֖שֶׁת חֶ֣בֶר[2] הַקֵּינִ֑י[3] מִנָּשִׁ֥ים
בָּאֹ֖הֶל תְּבֹרָֽךְ׃

εὐλογηθείη ἐκ γυναικῶν Ιαηλ[4] γυνὴ Χαβερ[5] τοῦ Κιναίου,[6] ἐκ γυναικῶν ἐν σκηνῇ εὐλογηθείη.

Luke 1:42

καὶ ἀνεφώνησεν[7] κραυγῇ[8] μεγάλῃ καὶ εἶπεν· εὐλογημένη σὺ[9] ἐν γυναιξὶν καὶ εὐλογημένος ὁ καρπὸς τῆς κοιλίας[10] σου.

et exclamavit[11] voce magna et dixit benedicta tu[12] inter mulieres et benedictus fructus ventris[13] tui.

1. יָעֵל, *Jael*
2. חֶבֶר, *Heber*
3. קֵינִי, *Kenite*
4. Ιαηλ, *Jael*
5. Χαβερ, *Heber*
6. Κιναῖος, *Kenite*
7. ἀναφωνέω, aor. act. ind. 3 s., *exclaim*
8. κραυγή, *voice*
9. CH: The referent is Mary, the mother of Jesus. The speaker is Elizabeth, the mother of John the Baptist.
10. κοιλία, *womb*
11. exclamo, perf. act. ind. 3 s., *cry aloud, shout*
12. CH: The referent is Mary, the mother of Jesus. The speaker is Elizabeth, the mother of John the Baptist.
13. venter, *womb*

April 29

Judges 7:2

וַיֹּ֨אמֶר יְהוָ֜ה אֶל־גִּדְע֗וֹן[1] רַב֙ הָעָ֣ם אֲשֶׁ֣ר אִתָּ֔ךְ מִתִּתִּ֥י
אֶת־מִדְיָ֖ן[2] בְּיָדָ֑ם פֶּן־יִתְפָּאֵ֨ר[3] עָלַ֤י יִשְׂרָאֵל֙ לֵאמֹ֔ר יָדִ֖י
הוֹשִׁ֥יעָה לִּֽי׃

καὶ εἶπεν κύριος πρὸς Γεδεων[4] Πολὺς ὁ λαὸς ὁ μετὰ σοῦ ὥστε μὴ παραδοῦναί με τὴν Μαδιαμ[5] ἐν χειρὶ αὐτῶν, μήποτε καυχήσηται[6] Ισραηλ ἐπ᾽ ἐμὲ λέγων Ἡ χείρ μου ἔσωσέν με.

Ephesians 2:8–9

Τῇ γὰρ χάριτί ἐστε σεσῳσμένοι διὰ πίστεως· καὶ τοῦτο οὐκ ἐξ ὑμῶν, θεοῦ τὸ δῶρον·[7] οὐκ ἐξ ἔργων, ἵνα μή τις καυχήσηται.

gratia enim estis salvati[8] per fidem et hoc non ex vobis Dei enim donum[9] est non ex operibus ut ne quis glorietur.

1. גִּדְעוֹן, *Gideon*
2. מִדְיָן, *Midian*
3. פָּאַר, hitpael impf. 3 m. s., *glorify oneself, boast*
4. Γεδεών, *Gideon*
5. Μαδιάμ, *Midian*
6. καυχάομαι, aor. mid. subj. 3 s., *boast*
7. δῶρον, *gift*
8. salvo, perf. pass. ind. 2 p., *save*
9. donum, *gift*

Monarchies

April 30

1 Samuel 8:5

וַיֹּאמְר֣וּ אֵלָ֗יו הִנֵּה֙ אַתָּ֣ה זָקַ֔נְתָּ[1] וּבָנֶ֕יךָ לֹ֥א הָלְכ֖וּ
בִּדְרָכֶ֑יךָ עַתָּ֗ה שִׂימָה־לָּ֥נוּ מֶ֛לֶךְ לְשָׁפְטֵ֖נוּ כְּכָל־הַגּוֹיִֽם׃

καὶ εἶπαν αὐτῷ Ἰδοὺ σὺ γεγήρακας,[2] καὶ οἱ υἱοί σου οὐ πορεύονται ἐν τῇ ὁδῷ σου· καὶ νῦν κατάστησον ἐφ᾽ ἡμᾶς βασιλέα δικάζειν[3] ἡμᾶς καθὰ καὶ τὰ λοιπὰ ἔθνη.

Acts 13:21

κἀκεῖθεν ᾐτήσαντο βασιλέα καὶ ἔδωκεν αὐτοῖς ὁ θεὸς τὸν Σαοὺλ[4] υἱὸν Κίς,[5] ἄνδρα ἐκ φυλῆς Βενιαμίν,[6] ἔτη τεσσεράκοντα.[7]

et exinde[8] postulaverunt[9] regem et dedit illis Deus Saul[10] filium Cis[11] virum de tribu Beniamin[12] annis quadraginta.[13]

1. זָקֵן, qal perf. 2 m. s., *be old*
2. γηράσκω, perf. act. ind. 2 s., *be/grow old*
3. δικάζω, pres. act. inf., *judge*
4. Σαούλ, *Saul*
5. Κίς, *Cis*
6. Βενιαμίν, *Benjamin*
7. τεσσεράκοντα, *forty*
8. exinde, *then, after that*
9. postulo, perf. act. ind. 3 p., *ask, plead*
10. Saul, *Saul*
11. Cis, *Cis*
12. Beniamin, *Benjamin*
13. quadraginta, *forty*

May 1

1 Samuel 12:3[1]

הִנְנִי עֲנוּ בִי נֶגֶד יְהוָה וְנֶגֶד מְשִׁיחוֹ[2] אֶת־שׁוֹר[3] ׀ מִי
לָקַחְתִּי וַחֲמוֹר[4] מִי לָקַחְתִּי וְאֶת־מִי עָשַׁקְתִּי[5] אֶת־
מִי רַצּוֹתִי[6] וּמִיַּד־מִי לָקַחְתִּי כֹפֶר[7] וְאַעְלִים[8] עֵינַי בּוֹ
וְאָשִׁיב לָכֶם׃

ἰδοὺ ἐγώ, ἀποκρίθητε κατ᾽ ἐμοῦ ἐνώπιον κυρίου καὶ ἐνώπιον χριστοῦ[9] αὐτοῦ· μόσχον τίνος εἴληφα ἢ ὄνον τίνος εἴληφα ἢ τίνα κατεδυνάστευσα[10] ὑμῶν ἢ τίνα ἐξεπίεσα[11] ἢ ἐκ χειρὸς τίνος εἴληφα ἐξίλασμα[12] καὶ ὑπόδημα;[13] ἀποκρίθητε κατ᾽ ἐμοῦ, καὶ ἀποδώσω ὑμῖν.

Acts 20:33[14]

ἀργυρίου[15] ἢ χρυσίου[16] ἢ ἱματισμοῦ[17] οὐδενὸς ἐπεθύμησα.[18]

argentum[19] aut aurum[20] aut vestem[21] nullius concupivi.[22]

1. CH: The first person pronoun refers to Samuel. He calls upon the people of Israel to testify before the Lord about his character and dealings with Israel.

2. מָשִׁיחַ, *appointed one*

3. שׁוֹר, *ox*

4. חֲמוֹר, *donkey*

5. עָשַׁק, qal perf. 1 c. s., *wrong*

6. רָצַץ, qal perf. 1 c. s., *crush*

7. כֹּפֶר, *ransom*

8. עָלַם, hiph. impf. 1 c. s., *conceal, be hidden*

9. χριστός, *anointed one*

10. καταδυναστεύω, aor. act. ind. 1 s., *take, oppress*

11. ἐκπιέζω, aor. act. ind. 1 s., *take, force out*

12. ἐξίλασμα, *propitiatory offering*

13. ὑπόδημα, *sandal, shoe*

14. CH: Paul testifies before the Ephesian elders that he did not covet these things.

15. ἀργύριον, *silver*

16. χρυσίον, *gold.* **17.** ἱματισμός, *clothing.* **18.** ἐπιθυμέω, aor. act. ind. 1 s., *desire, covet.* **19.** argentum, *silver.* **20.** aurum, *gold.* **21.** vestes, *garment, clothing.* **22.** concupisco, perf. act. ind. 1 s., *desire, covet*

May 2

1 Samuel 13:14

וְעַתָּ֖ה מַמְלַכְתְּךָ֣ לֹא־תָק֑וּם בִּקֵּשׁ֩ יְהוָ֨ה ל֜וֹ אִ֣ישׁ
כִּלְבָב֗וֹ וַיְצַוֵּ֨הוּ יְהוָ֤ה לְנָגִיד֙[1] עַל־עַמּ֔וֹ כִּ֚י לֹ֣א שָׁמַ֔רְתָּ
אֵ֥ת אֲשֶׁר־צִוְּךָ֖ יְהוָֽה׃

καὶ νῦν ἡ βασιλεία σου οὐ στήσεται, καὶ ζητήσει κύριος ἑαυτῷ ἄνθρωπον κατὰ τὴν καρδίαν αὐτοῦ, καὶ ἐντελεῖται κύριος αὐτῷ εἰς ἄρχοντα ἐπὶ τὸν λαὸν αὐτοῦ, ὅτι οὐκ ἐφύλαξας ὅσα ἐνετείλατό σοι κύριος.

Acts 13:22

καὶ μεταστήσας[2] αὐτὸν ἤγειρεν τὸν Δαυὶδ αὐτοῖς εἰς βασιλέα ᾧ καὶ εἶπεν μαρτυρήσας· εὗρον Δαυὶδ τὸν τοῦ Ἰεσσαί,[3] ἄνδρα κατὰ τὴν καρδίαν μου, ὃς ποιήσει πάντα τὰ θελήματά μου.

et amoto[4] illo suscitavit illis David regem cui et testimonium perhibens dixit inveni David filium Iesse[5] virum secundum cor meum qui faciet omnes voluntates meas.

1. נָגִיד, *leader*
2. μεθίστημι, aor. act. ptcp. m. nom. s., *remove*
3. Ἰεσσαί, *Jesse*
4. amoveo, perf. pass. ptcp. m. abl. s., *remove, put away*
5. Iesse, *Jesse*

May 3

2 Samuel 7:16

וְנֶאְמַ֨ן[1] בֵּיתְךָ֧ וּמַֽמְלַכְתְּךָ֛ עַד־עוֹלָ֖ם לְפָנֶ֑יךָ כִּסְאֲךָ֕
יִהְיֶ֥ה נָכ֖וֹן עַד־עוֹלָֽם׃

καὶ πιστωθήσεται[2] ὁ οἶκος αὐτοῦ καὶ ἡ βασιλεία αὐτοῦ ἕως αἰῶνος ἐνώπιον ἐμοῦ, καὶ ὁ θρόνος αὐτοῦ ἔσται ἀνωρθωμένος[3] εἰς τὸν αἰῶνα.

Luke 1:32

οὗτος ἔσται μέγας καὶ υἱὸς ὑψίστου[4] κληθήσεται καὶ δώσει αὐτῷ κύριος ὁ θεὸς τὸν θρόνον Δαυὶδ τοῦ πατρὸς αὐτοῦ.

hic erit magnus et Filius Altissimi[5] vocabitur et dabit illi Dominus Deus sedem David patris eius.

1. אָמַן, niph. perf. 3 m. s., *establish*
2. πιστόω, fut. pass. ind. 3 s., *guarantee, establish*
3. ἀνορθόω, perf. pass. ptcp. m. nom. s., *build anew, restore*
4. ὕψιστος, *Most High*
5. altus, *Most High*

May 4

1 Kings 2:10

וַיִּשְׁכַּב דָּוִד עִם־אֲבֹתָיו וַיִּקָּבֵר בְּעִיר דָּוִד׃

καὶ ἐκοιμήθη[1] Δαυιδ μετὰ τῶν πατέρων αὐτοῦ καὶ ἐτάφη ἐν πόλει Δαυιδ.

Acts 13:36

Δαυὶδ μὲν γὰρ ἰδίᾳ γενεᾷ ὑπηρετήσας[2] τῇ τοῦ θεοῦ βουλῇ[3] ἐκοιμήθη καὶ προσετέθη[4] πρὸς τοὺς πατέρας αὐτοῦ καὶ εἶδεν διαφθοράν.[5]

David enim sua generatione cum administrasset[6] voluntati Dei dormivit et adpositus[7] est ad patres suos et vidit corruptionem.[8]

1. κοιμάω, aor. pass. ind. 3 s., *sleep*
2. ὑπηρετέω, aor. act. ptcp. m. nom. s., *serve*
3. βουλή, *will*
4. προστίθημι, aor. pass. ind. 3 s., *place*
5. διαφθορά, *decay, rot*
6. administro, plu-perf. act. subj. 3 s., *administer, direct*
7. adpono, perf. pass. ind. 3 s., *place beside*
8. corruptio, *corruption*

May 5

1 Kings 8:17

וַיְהִ֕י עִם־לְבַ֖ב דָּוִ֣ד אָבִ֑י לִבְנ֣וֹת בַּ֔יִת לְשֵׁ֖ם יְהוָ֥ה אֱלֹהֵ֖י יִשְׂרָאֵֽל׃

καὶ ἐγένετο ἐπὶ τῆς καρδίας Δαυιδ τοῦ πατρός μου οἰκοδομῆσαι οἶκον τῷ ὀνόματι κυρίου θεοῦ Ισραηλ.

Acts 7:45

ἣν[1] καὶ εἰσήγαγον[2] διαδεξάμενοι[3] οἱ πατέρες ἡμῶν μετὰ Ἰησοῦ ἐν τῇ κατασχέσει[4] τῶν ἐθνῶν, ὧν ἐξῶσεν[5] ὁ θεὸς ἀπὸ προσώπου τῶν πατέρων ἡμῶν ἕως τῶν ἡμερῶν Δαυίδ.

quod[6] et induxerunt[7] suscipientes patres nostri cum Iesu in possessionem[8] gentium quas expulit[9] Deus a facie patrum nostrorum usque in diebus David.

1. CH: This is a reference to the tabernacle.

2. εἰσάγω, aor. act. ind. 3 p., *bring in*

3. διαδέχομαι, aor. mid. ptcp. m. nom. p., *take possession of*

4. κατάσχεσις, *possession*

5. ἐξωθέω, aor. act. ind. 3 s., *expel, drive out*

6. CH: This is a reference to the tabernacle.

7. induco, perf. act. ind. 3 p., *bring in*

8. possessio, *possession*

9. expello, perf. act. ind. 3 s., *drive out, expel*

May 6

1 Kings 8:18

וַיֹּ֣אמֶר יְהוָה֮ אֶל־דָּוִ֣ד אָבִי֒ יַ֗עַן[1] אֲשֶׁ֤ר הָיָה֙ עִם־לְבָ֣בְךָ֔
לִבְנ֥וֹת בַּ֖יִת לִשְׁמִ֑י הֱטִֽיבֹ֔תָ[2] כִּ֥י הָיָ֖ה עִם־לְבָבֶֽךָ׃

καὶ εἶπεν κύριος πρὸς Δαυιδ τὸν πατέρα μου Ἀνθ᾽ ὧν ἦλθεν ἐπὶ τὴν καρδίαν σου τοῦ οἰκοδομῆσαι οἶκον τῷ ὀνόματί μου, καλῶς[3] ἐποίησας ὅτι ἐγενήθη ἐπὶ τὴν καρδίαν σου.

Acts 7:46

ὃς εὗρεν χάριν ἐνώπιον τοῦ θεοῦ καὶ ᾐτήσατο εὑρεῖν σκήνωμα[4] τῷ οἴκῳ Ἰακώβ.[5]

qui invenit gratiam ante Deum et petiit ut inveniret tabernaculum[6] Deo Iacob.[7]

1. יַעַן, *because of*
2. טוֹב, hiph. perf. 2 m. s., *be good, be pleasing*
3. καλῶς, *well*
4. σκήνωμα, *tent, tabernacle*
5. Ἰακώβ, *Jacob*
6. tabernaculum, *tent, tabernacle*
7. Iacob, *Jacob*

May 7

1 Kings 8:19

רַ֣ק אַתָּ֔ה לֹ֥א תִבְנֶ֖ה הַבָּ֑יִת כִּ֤י אִם־בִּנְךָ֙ הַיֹּצֵ֣א
מֵחֲלָצֶ֔יךָ[1] הֽוּא־יִבְנֶ֥ה הַבַּ֖יִת לִשְׁמִֽי׃

πλὴν σὺ οὐκ οἰκοδομήσεις τὸν οἶκον, ἀλλ᾽ ἢ ὁ υἱός σου ὁ ἐξελθὼν ἐκ τῶν πλευρῶν[2] σου, οὗτος οἰκοδομήσει τὸν οἶκον τῷ ὀνόματί μου.

Acts 7:47

Σολομὼν[3] δὲ οἰκοδόμησεν αὐτῷ οἶκον.

Salomon[4] autem aedificavit illi domum.

1. חָלָץ, *loins*
2. πλευρά, *side, rib*
3. Σολομών, *Solomon*
4. Salomon, *Solomon*

May 8

2 Chronicles 5:7

וַיָּבִ֣יאוּ הַכֹּהֲנִ֩ים אֶת־אֲר֨וֹן בְּרִית־יְהוָ֧ה אֶל־מְקוֹמ֛וֹ
אֶל־דְּבִ֥יר[1] הַבַּ֖יִת אֶל־קֹ֣דֶשׁ הַקֳּדָשִׁ֑ים אֶל־תַּ֖חַת כַּנְפֵ֥י
הַכְּרוּבִֽים׃[2]

καὶ εἰσήνεγκαν[3] οἱ ἱερεῖς τὴν κιβωτὸν διαθήκης κυρίου εἰς τὸν τόπον αὐτῆς εἰς τὸ δαβιρ[4] τοῦ οἴκου εἰς τὰ ἅγια τῶν ἁγίων ὑποκάτω[5] τῶν πτερύγων[6] τῶν χερουβιν.[7]

Revelation 11:19

Καὶ ἠνοίγη ὁ ναὸς τοῦ θεοῦ ὁ ἐν τῷ οὐρανῷ καὶ ὤφθη ἡ κιβωτὸς[8] τῆς διαθήκης αὐτοῦ ἐν τῷ ναῷ αὐτοῦ, καὶ ἐγένοντο ἀστραπαὶ[9] καὶ φωναὶ καὶ βρονταὶ[10] καὶ σεισμὸς[11] καὶ χάλαζα[12] μεγάλη.

et apertum est templum Dei in caelo et visa est arca[13] testamenti eius in templo eius et facta sunt fulgora[14] et voces et terraemotus[15] et grando[16] magna.

1. דְּבִיר, *inner sanctuary*
2. כְּרוּב, *cherub*
3. εἰσφέρω, aor. act. ind. 3 p., *bring*
4. δαβιρ, transliteration of Hebrew; *inner sanctuary*
5. ὑποκάτω, *under*
6. πτέρυξ, *wing*
7. χερούβ, *cherub*
8. κιβωτός, *ark*
9. ἀστραπή, *lightning*
10. βροντή, *thunder*
11. σεισμός, *earthquake*
12. χάλαζα, *hail*
13. arca, *ark*
14. fulgur, *lightning*
15. terraemotus, *earthquake*
16. grando, *hail*

May 9

1 Kings 8:27

כִּ֚י הַֽאֻמְנָ֔ם[1] יֵשֵׁ֥ב אֱלֹהִ֖ים עַל־הָאָ֑רֶץ הִ֠נֵּה הַשָּׁמַ֜יִם
וּשְׁמֵ֤י הַשָּׁמַ֙יִם֙ לֹ֣א יְכַלְכְּל֔וּךָ[2] אַ֕ף כִּֽי־הַבַּ֥יִת הַזֶּ֖ה
אֲשֶׁ֥ר בָּנִֽיתִי׃

ὅτι εἰ ἀληθῶς[3] κατοικήσει ὁ θεὸς μετὰ ἀνθρώπων ἐπὶ τῆς γῆς; εἰ ὁ οὐρανὸς καὶ ὁ οὐρανὸς τοῦ οὐρανοῦ οὐκ ἀρκέσουσίν[4] σοι, πλὴν καὶ ὁ οἶκος οὗτος, ὃν ᾠκοδόμησα τῷ ὀνόματί σου;

Acts 17:24

ὁ θεὸς ὁ ποιήσας τὸν κόσμον καὶ πάντα τὰ ἐν αὐτῷ, οὗτος οὐρανοῦ καὶ γῆς ὑπάρχων κύριος οὐκ ἐν χειροποιήτοις[5] ναοῖς κατοικεῖ.

Deus qui fecit mundum et omnia quae in eo sunt hic caeli et terrae cum sit Dominus non in manufactis[6] templis inhabitat.[7]

1. אָמְנָם, *truly*
2. כּוּל, pilpel impf. 3 m. p., *contain*
3. ἀληθῶς, *truly*
4. ἀρκέω, fut. act. ind. 3 p., *be enough, be sufficient*
5. χειροποίητος, *made by hands*
6. manufactus, *made by hands*
7. inhabito, pres. act. ind. 3 s., *inhabit*

May 10

1 Kings 10:1

וּמַֽלְכַּת[1]־שְׁבָא[2] שֹׁמַעַת אֶת־שֵׁמַע[3] שְׁלֹמֹה לְשֵׁם
יְהוָה וַתָּבֹא לְנַסֹּתוֹ[4] בְּחִידוֹת׃[5]

Καὶ βασίλισσα[6] Σαβα[7] ἤκουσεν τὸ ὄνομα Σαλωμων[8] καὶ τὸ ὄνομα κυρίου καὶ ἦλθεν πειράσαι[9] αὐτὸν ἐν αἰνίγμασιν.[10]

Luke 11:31

βασίλισσα νότου[11] ἐγερθήσεται ἐν τῇ κρίσει μετὰ τῶν ἀνδρῶν τῆς γενεᾶς ταύτης καὶ κατακρινεῖ[12] αὐτούς, ὅτι ἦλθεν ἐκ τῶν περάτων[13] τῆς γῆς ἀκοῦσαι τὴν σοφίαν Σολομῶνος, καὶ ἰδοὺ πλεῖον Σολομῶνος ὧδε.

regina[14] austri[15] surget in iudicio cum viris generationis huius et condemnabit[16] illos quia venit a finibus terrae audire sapientiam Salomonis et ecce plus Salomone hic.

1. מַלְכָּה, *queen*
2. שְׁבָא, *Sheba*
3. שֵׁמַע, *news, report, fame*
4. נָסָה, piel inf. cons., *test*
5. חִידָה, *riddle, question*
6. βασίλισσα, *queen*
7. Σαβα, *Sheba*
8. Σολομών, *Solomon*
9. πειράζω, aor. act. inf., *test*
10. αἴνιγμα, *enigma, riddle, question*
11. νότος, *south*
12. κατακρίνω, fut. act. ind. 3 s., *condemn*
13. πέρας, *end*
14. regina, *queen*
15. auster, *south*
16. condemno, fut. act. ind. 3 s., *condemn*

May 11

1 Kings 10:7

וְלֹא־הֶאֱמַנְתִּי[1] לַדְּבָרִים עַד אֲשֶׁר־בָּאתִי וַתִּרְאֶינָה
עֵינַי וְהִנֵּה לֹא־הֻגַּד־לִי הַחֵצִי הוֹסַפְתָּ חָכְמָה וָטוֹב
אֶל־הַשְּׁמוּעָה[2] אֲשֶׁר שָׁמָעְתִּי׃

καὶ οὐκ ἐπίστευσα[3] τοῖς λαλοῦσίν μοι, ἕως ὅτου παρεγενόμην καὶ ἑωράκασιν οἱ ὀφθαλμοί μου, καὶ ἰδοὺ οὐκ ἔστιν τὸ ἥμισυ[4] καθὼς ἀπήγγειλάν μοι, προστέθεικας ἀγαθὰ πρὸς αὐτὰ ἐπὶ πᾶσαν τὴν ἀκοήν,[5] ἣν ἤκουσα ἐν τῇ γῇ μου.

Luke 12:27

κατανοήσατε[6] τὰ κρίνα[7] πῶς αὐξάνει·[8] οὐ κοπιᾷ[9] οὐδὲ νήθει·[10] λέγω δὲ ὑμῖν, οὐδὲ Σολομὼν[11] ἐν πάσῃ τῇ δόξῃ αὐτοῦ περιεβάλετο[12] ὡς ἓν τούτων.

considerate[13] lilia[14] quomodo crescunt[15] non laborant[16] non nent[17] dico autem vobis nec Salomon in omni gloria sua vestiebatur[18] sicut unum ex istis.

1. אָמַן, hiph. perf. 1 c. s., *believe, trust*

2. שְׁמוּעָה, *report*

3. πιστεύω, aor. act. ind. 1 s., *believe*

4. ἥμισυς, *half*

5. ἀκοή, *report*

6. κατανοέω, aor. act. impv. 2 p., *consider*

7. κρίνον, *lily*

8. αὐξάνω, pres. act. ind. 3 s., *grow*

9. κοπιάω, pres. act. ind. 3 s., *work*

10. νήθω, pres. act. ind. 3 s., *spin*

11. Σολομών, *Solomon*

12. περιβάλλω, aor. mid. ind. 3 s., *clothe, put on*

13. considero, pres. act. impv. 2 p., *examine, consider*

14. lilium, *lily*

15. cresco, pres. act. ind. 3 p., *grow*

16. laboro, pres. act. ind. 3 p., *work*

17. neo, pres. act. ind. 3 p., *spin*

18. vestio, impf. pass. ind. 3 s., *clothe, dress*

May 12

1 Kings 16:31

וַיְהִי֙ הֲנָקֵ֣ל[1] לֶכְתּ֔וֹ בְּחַטֹּ֖אות יָרָבְעָ֣ם בֶּן־נְבָ֑ט[2] וַיִּקַּ֨ח
אִשָּׁ֜ה אֶת־אִיזֶ֣בֶל[3] בַּת־אֶתְבַּ֗עַל[4] מֶ֚לֶךְ צִידֹנִ֔ים[5] וַיֵּ֗לֶךְ
וַיַּֽעֲבֹד֙ אֶת־הַבַּ֔עַל וַיִּשְׁתַּ֖חוּ לֽוֹ׃

καὶ οὐκ ἦν αὐτῷ ἱκανὸν[6] τοῦ πορεύεσθαι ἐν ταῖς ἁμαρτίαις Ιεροβοαμ υἱοῦ Ναβατ,[7] καὶ ἔλαβεν γυναῖκα τὴν Ιεζαβελ[8] θυγατέρα Ιεθεβααλ[9] βασιλέως Σιδωνίων[10] καὶ ἐπορεύθη καὶ ἐδούλευσεν τῷ Βααλ[11] καὶ προσεκύνησεν αὐτῷ.

Revelation 2:20

ἀλλ᾽ ἔχω κατὰ σοῦ ὅτι ἀφεῖς τὴν γυναῖκα Ἰεζάβελ, ἡ λέγουσα ἑαυτὴν προφῆτιν[12] καὶ διδάσκει καὶ πλανᾷ τοὺς ἐμοὺς δούλους πορνεῦσαι[13] καὶ φαγεῖν εἰδωλόθυτα.[14]

sed habeo adversus te quia permittis[15] mulierem Hiezabel[16] quae se dicit propheten[17] docere et seducere servos meos fornicari[18] et manducare de idolothytis.[19]

1. קָלַל, niph. perf. 3 m. s., *be trifling*
2. נְבָט, *Nebat*
3. אִיזֶבֶל, *Jezebel*
4. אֶתְבַּעַל, *Ethbaal*
5. צִידֹנִי, *Sidonian*
6. ἱκανός, *sufficient*
7. Ναβατ, *Nabat*
8. Ιεζαβελ, *Jezebel*
9. Ιεθεβααλ, *Ethbaal*
10. Σιδώνιος, *Sidonian*
11. Βααλ, *Baal*
12. προφῆτις, *prophetess*
13. πορνεύω, *commit sexual immorality*
14. εἰδωλόθυτος, *(meat) sacrificed to idols*
15. permitto, pres. act. ind. 2 s., *permit, allow*
16. Hiezabel, *Jezebel*
17. prophetes, *prophetess*
18. fornicor, pres. dep. inf., *fornicate*
19. idolothytum, *(meat) sacrificed to idols*

May 13

1 Kings 17:1

וַיֹּאמֶר֩ אֵלִיָּ֨הוּ[1] הַתִּשְׁבִּ֜י[2] מִתֹּשָׁבֵ֣י[3] גִלְעָד֮ אֶל־אַחְאָב֒[4] חַי־יְהוָ֞ה אֱלֹהֵ֤י יִשְׂרָאֵל֙ אֲשֶׁ֣ר עָמַ֣דְתִּי לְפָנָ֔יו אִם־יִהְיֶ֛ה הַשָּׁנִ֥ים הָאֵ֖לֶּה טַ֣ל[5] וּמָטָ֑ר[6] כִּ֖י אִם־לְפִ֥י דְבָרִֽי׃

Καὶ εἶπεν Ηλιου[7] ὁ προφήτης ὁ Θεσβίτης[8] ἐκ Θεσβων[9] τῆς Γαλααδ πρὸς Αχααβ[10] Ζῇ κύριος ὁ θεὸς τῶν δυνάμεων ὁ θεὸς Ισραηλ, ᾧ παρέστην[11] ἐνώπιον αὐτοῦ, εἰ ἔσται τὰ ἔτη ταῦτα δρόσος[12] καὶ ὑετὸς[13] ὅτι εἰ μὴ διὰ στόματος λόγου μου.

James 5:17

Ἠλίας ἄνθρωπος ἦν ὁμοιοπαθὴς[14] ἡμῖν καὶ προσευχῇ προσηύξατο τοῦ μὴ βρέξαι,[15] καὶ οὐκ ἔβρεξεν[16] ἐπὶ τῆς γῆς ἐνιαυτοὺς[17] τρεῖς καὶ μῆνας[18] ἕξ.[19]

Helias[20] homo erat similis nobis passibilis[21] et oratione oravit ut non plueret[22] super terram et non pluit[23] annos tres et menses[24] sex.[25]

1. אֵלִיָּהוּ, *Elijah*
2. תִּשְׁבִּי, *Tishbite*
3. תִּשָׁבִי, *Tishbe*
4. אַחְאָב, *Ahab*
5. טַל, *dew*
6. מָטָר, *rain*
7. Ηλιου, *Elijah*
8. Θεσβίτης, *Tishbite*
9. Θεσβων, *Tishbe*
10. Αχααβ, *Ahab*
11. παρίστημι, aor. act. ind. 1 s., *stand*
12. δρόσος, *dew*
13. ὑετός, *rain*
14. ὁμοιοπαθής, *of the same nature*
15. βρέχω, aor. act. inf., *rain*
16. βρέχω, aor. act. ind. 3 s., *rain*
17. ἐνιαυτός, *year*
18. μήν, *month*
19. ἕξ, *six*
20. Helias, *Elijah*
21. passibilis, *capable of suffering*
22. pluo, impf. act. subj. 3 s., *rain*
23. pluo, perf. act. ind. 3 s., *rain*
24. mensis, *month*
25. sex, *six*

May 14

2 Kings 1:10

וַיַּעֲנֶה אֵלִיָּהוּ[1] וַיְדַבֵּר אֶל־שַׂר הַחֲמִשִּׁים וְאִם־אִישׁ
אֱלֹהִים אָנִי תֵּרֶד אֵשׁ מִן־הַשָּׁמַיִם וְתֹאכַל אֹתְךָ
וְאֶת־חֲמִשֶּׁיךָ וַתֵּרֶד אֵשׁ מִן־הַשָּׁמַיִם וַתֹּאכַל אֹתוֹ
וְאֶת־חֲמִשָּׁיו׃

καὶ ἀπεκρίθη Ηλιου[2] καὶ εἶπεν πρὸς τὸν πεντηκόνταρχον[3] Καὶ εἰ ἄνθρωπος τοῦ θεοῦ ἐγώ, καταβήσεται πῦρ ἐκ τοῦ οὐρανοῦ καὶ καταφάγεταί σε καὶ τοὺς πεντήκοντά σου· καὶ κατέβη πῦρ ἐκ τοῦ οὐρανοῦ καὶ κατέφαγεν αὐτὸν καὶ τοὺς πεντήκοντα αὐτοῦ.

Luke 9:54

ἰδόντες δὲ οἱ μαθηταὶ Ἰάκωβος καὶ Ἰωάννης εἶπαν· κύριε, θέλεις εἴπωμεν *πῦρ καταβῆναι ἀπὸ τοῦ οὐρανοῦ καὶ ἀναλῶσαι*[4] *αὐτούς;*

cum vidissent autem discipuli eius Iacobus et Iohannes dixerunt Domine vis dicimus ut ignis descendat de caelo et consumat[5] illos.

1. אֵלִיָּהוּ, *Elijah*
2. Ηλιου, *Elijah*
3. πεντηκόνταρχος, *officer over fifty men*
4. ἀναλόω, aor. act. inf., *consume*
5. consumo, pres. act. subj. 3 s., *consume*

May 15

2 Kings 2:11

וַיְהִ֗י הֵ֤מָּה הֹלְכִים֙ הָל֣וֹךְ וְדַבֵּ֔ר וְהִנֵּ֤ה רֶֽכֶב־אֵשׁ֙ וְס֣וּסֵי
אֵ֔שׁ וַֽיַּפְרִ֖דוּ[1] בֵּ֣ין שְׁנֵיהֶ֑ם וַיַּ֙עַל֙ אֵֽלִיָּ֔הוּ[2] בַּסְּעָרָ֖ה[3]
הַשָּׁמָֽיִם׃

καὶ ἐγένετο αὐτῶν πορευομένων ἐπορεύοντο καὶ ἐλάλουν, καὶ ἰδοὺ ἅρμα πυρὸς καὶ ἵπποι πυρὸς καὶ διέστειλαν[4] ἀνὰ μέσον ἀμφοτέρων, καὶ ἀνελήμφθη[5] Ηλιου[6] ἐν συσσεισμῷ[7] ὡς εἰς τὸν οὐρανόν.

Revelation 11:12

καὶ ἤκουσαν φωνῆς μεγάλης ἐκ τοῦ οὐρανοῦ λεγούσης αὐτοῖς· ἀνάβατε ὧδε. καὶ ἀνέβησαν εἰς τὸν οὐρανὸν ἐν τῇ νεφέλῃ,[8] καὶ ἐθεώρησαν αὐτοὺς οἱ ἐχθροὶ αὐτῶν.

et audierunt vocem magnam de caelo dicentem illis ascendite huc[9] et ascenderunt in caelum in nube[10] et viderunt illos inimici eorum.

1. פָּרַד, hiph. wcons. 3 m. p., *separate*
2. אֵלִיָּהוּ, *Elijah*
3. סְעָרָה, *wind-storm, whirlwind*
4. διαστέλλω, aor. act. ind. 3 p., *divide*
5. ἀναλαμβάνω, aor. pass. ind. 3 s., *take up*
6. Ηλιου, *Elijah*
7. συσσεισμός, *commotion of air*
8. νεφέλη, *cloud*
9. huc, *to this place*
10. nubes, *cloud*

May 16

2 Kings 5:14

וַיֵּ֗רֶד וַיִּטְבֹּ֤ל[1] בַּיַּרְדֵּן֙ שֶׁ֣בַע פְּעָמִ֔ים כִּדְבַ֖ר אִ֣ישׁ הָאֱלֹהִ֑ים וַיָּ֣שָׁב בְּשָׂר֗וֹ כִּבְשַׂ֛ר נַ֥עַר קָטֹ֖ן[2] וַיִּטְהָֽר׃[3]

καὶ κατέβη Ναιμαν[4] καὶ ἐβαπτίσατο[5] ἐν τῷ Ιορδάνῃ ἑπτάκι[6] κατὰ τὸ ῥῆμα Ελισαιε,[7] καὶ ἐπέστρεψεν ἡ σὰρξ αὐτοῦ ὡς σὰρξ παιδαρίου μικροῦ, καὶ ἐκαθαρίσθη.

Luke 4:27

καὶ πολλοὶ λεπροὶ[8] ἦσαν ἐν τῷ Ἰσραὴλ ἐπὶ Ἐλισαίου τοῦ προφήτου, καὶ οὐδεὶς αὐτῶν ἐκαθαρίσθη εἰ μὴ Ναιμὰν ὁ Σύρος.[9]

et multi leprosi[10] erant in Israhel sub Heliseo[11] propheta et nemo eorum mundatus[12] est nisi Neman[13] Syrus.[14]

1. טָבַל, qal wcons. 3 m. s., *dip, bathe*
2. קָטֹן, *little, small*
3. טָהֵר, qal wcons. 3 m. s., *clean, purify*
4. Ναιμαν, *Naaman*
5. βαπτίζω, aor. mid. ind. 3 s., *wash, dip*
6. ἑπτάκις, *seven*
7. Ελισαιε, *Elisha*
8. λεπρός, *leper*
9. Σύρος, *Syrian*
10. leprosus, *leper*
11. Heliseus, *Elisha*
12. mundo, perf. pass. ind. 3 s., *cleanse*
13. Neman, *Naaman*
14. Syrus, *Syrian*

May 17

2 Kings 8:11[1]

וַיַּעֲמֵד אֶת־פָּנָיו וַיָּשֶׂם עַד־בֹּשׁ וַיֵּבְךְּ אִישׁ הָאֱלֹהִים׃

καὶ παρέστη[2] τῷ προσώπῳ αὐτοῦ καὶ ἔθηκεν ἕως αἰσχύνης,[3] καὶ ἔκλαυσεν ὁ ἄνθρωπος τοῦ θεοῦ.

Luke 19:41

Καὶ ὡς ἤγγισεν ἰδὼν τὴν πόλιν ἔκλαυσεν ἐπ᾽ αὐτὴν.

et ut adpropinquavit videns civitatem flevit[4] super illam dicens.

1. CH: Elisha is the subject of this verse.

2. παρίστημι, aor. act. ind. 3 s., *stand by*

3. αἰσχύνη, *shame*

4. fleo, perf. act. ind. 3 s., *weep*

May 18

2 Chronicles 36:15

וַיִּשְׁלַח יְהוָה אֱלֹהֵי אֲבוֹתֵיהֶם עֲלֵיהֶם בְּיַד מַלְאָכָיו הַשְׁכֵּם[1] וְשָׁלוֹחַ כִּי־חָמַל[2] עַל־עַמּוֹ וְעַל־מְעוֹנוֹ׃[3]

καὶ ἐξαπέστειλεν κύριος ὁ θεὸς τῶν πατέρων αὐτῶν ἐν χειρὶ προφητῶν ὀρθρίζων[4] καὶ ἀποστέλλων τοὺς ἀγγέλους αὐτοῦ, ὅτι ἦν φειδόμενος[5] τοῦ λαοῦ αὐτοῦ καὶ τοῦ ἁγιάσματος[6] αὐτοῦ.

Matthew 21:34

ὅτε δὲ ἤγγισεν ὁ καιρὸς τῶν καρπῶν, ἀπέστειλεν τοὺς δούλους αὐτοῦ πρὸς τοὺς γεωργοὺς[7] λαβεῖν τοὺς καρποὺς αὐτοῦ.

cum autem tempus fructuum adpropinquasset misit servos suos ad agricolas[8] ut acciperent fructus eius.

1. שׁכם, hiph. inf. cons., *rise early*
2. חָמַל, qal perf. 3 m. s., *pity, have compassion*
3. מָעוֹן, *place of dwelling*
4. ὀρθρίζω, pres. act. ptcp. m. nom. s., *rise*
5. φείδομαι, pres. mid. ptcp. m. nom. s., *spare*
6. ἁγίασμα, *sacred place, sanctuary*
7. γεωργός, *farmer, tenant*
8. agricola, *farmer*

May 19

2 Chronicles 36:16

וַיִּהְי֤וּ מַלְעִבִים֙[1] בְּמַלְאֲכֵ֣י הָאֱלֹהִ֔ים וּבוֹזִ֣ים[2] דְּבָרָ֔יו וּמִֽתַּעְתְּעִ֖ים[3] בִּנְבִאָ֑יו עַ֣ד עֲל֧וֹת חֲמַת־יְהוָ֛ה בְּעַמּ֖וֹ עַד־לְאֵ֥ין מַרְפֵּֽא׃[4]

καὶ ἦσαν μυκτηρίζοντες[5] τοὺς ἀγγέλους αὐτοῦ καὶ ἐξουδενοῦντες[6] τοὺς λόγους αὐτοῦ καὶ ἐμπαίζοντες[7] ἐν τοῖς προφήταις αὐτοῦ, ἕως ἀνέβη ὁ θυμὸς κυρίου ἐν τῷ λαῷ αὐτοῦ, ἕως οὐκ ἦν ἴαμα.[8]

Matthew 21:35

καὶ λαβόντες οἱ γεωργοὶ[9] τοὺς δούλους αὐτοῦ ὃν μὲν ἔδειραν,[10] ὃν δὲ ἀπέκτειναν, ὃν δὲ ἐλιθοβόλησαν.[11]

et agricolae[12] adprehensis servis eius alium ceciderunt[13] alium occiderunt alium vero lapidaverunt.[14]

1. לָעַב, hiph. ptcp. m. p. abs., *mock*
2. בָּזָה, qal ptcp. m. p. abs., *despise*
3. תָּעַע, hithpalel ptcp. m. p. abs., *ridicule, mock*
4. מַרְפֵּא, *remedy*
5. μυκτηρίζω, pres. act. ptcp. m. nom. p., *mock*
6. ἐξουδενέω, pres. act. ptcp. m. nom. p., *despise, treat with contempt*
7. ἐμπαίζω, pres. act. ptcp. m. nom. p., *mock*
8. ἴαμα, *remedy, cure*
9. γεωργός, *farmer, tenant*
10. δέρω, aor. act. ind. 3 p., *beat*
11. λιθοβολέω, aor. act. ind. 3 p., *throw stones at*
12. agricola, *farmer*
13. caedo, perf. act. ind. 3 p., *beat*
14. lapido, perf. act. ind. 3 p., *throw stones at*

May 20

Ezekiel 1:1

וַיְהִ֣י ׀ בִּשְׁלֹשִׁ֣ים שָׁנָ֗ה בָּֽרְבִיעִי֙[1] בַּחֲמִשָּׁ֣ה לַחֹ֔דֶשׁ
וַאֲנִ֥י בְתוֹךְ־הַגּוֹלָ֖ה[2] עַל־נְהַר־כְּבָ֑ר[3] נִפְתְּחוּ֙ הַשָּׁמַ֔יִם
וָאֶרְאֶ֖ה מַרְא֥וֹת[4] אֱלֹהִֽים׃

Καὶ ἐγένετο ἐν τῷ τριακοστῷ[5] ἔτει ἐν τῷ τετάρτῳ[6] μηνὶ πέμπτῃ[7] τοῦ μηνὸς καὶ ἐγὼ ἤμην ἐν μέσῳ τῆς αἰχμαλωσίας ἐπὶ τοῦ ποταμοῦ τοῦ Χοβαρ,[8] καὶ ἠνοίχθησαν οἱ οὐρανοί, καὶ εἶδον ὁράσεις θεοῦ.

Revelation 19:11

Καὶ εἶδον τὸν οὐρανὸν ἠνεῳγμένον, καὶ ἰδοὺ ἵππος[9] λευκὸς[10] καὶ ὁ καθήμενος ἐπ᾽ αὐτὸν [καλούμενος] πιστὸς καὶ ἀληθινός,[11] καὶ ἐν δικαιοσύνῃ κρίνει καὶ πολεμεῖ.[12]

et vidi caelum apertum et ecce equus[13] albus[14] et qui sedebat super eum vocabatur Fidelis et Verax[15] vocatur et iustitia iudicat et pugnat.[16]

1. רְבִיעִי, *fourth*
2. גּוֹלָה, *exile*
3. כְּבָר, *Chebar*
4. מַרְאָה, *vision*
5. τριακοστός, *thirtieth*
6. τέταρτος, *fourth*
7. πέμπτος, *fifth*
8. Χοβαρ, *Chebar*
9. ἵππος, *horse*
10. λευκός, *white*
11. ἀληθινός, *true*
12. πολεμέω, pres. act. ind. 3 s., *wage war*
13. equus, *horse*
14. albus, *white*
15. verax, *true*
16. pugno, pres. act. ind. 3 s., *fight*

May 21

Ezekiel 3:1

וַיֹּ֣אמֶר אֵלַ֔י בֶּן־אָדָ֕ם אֵ֥ת אֲשֶׁר־תִּמְצָ֖א אֱכ֑וֹל אֱכוֹל֙ אֶת־הַמְּגִלָּ֣ה[1] הַזֹּ֔את וְלֵ֥ךְ דַּבֵּ֖ר אֶל־בֵּ֥ית יִשְׂרָאֵֽל׃

καὶ εἶπεν πρός με Υἱὲ ἀνθρώπου, κατάφαγε τὴν κεφαλίδα[2] ταύτην καὶ πορεύθητι καὶ λάλησον τοῖς υἱοῖς Ισραηλ.

Revelation 10:9

καὶ ἀπῆλθα πρὸς τὸν ἄγγελον λέγων αὐτῷ δοῦναί μοι τὸ βιβλαρίδιον.[3] καὶ λέγει μοι· λάβε καὶ κατάφαγε[4] αὐτό, καὶ πικρανεῖ[5] σου τὴν κοιλίαν,[6] ἀλλ᾽ ἐν τῷ στόματί σου ἔσται γλυκὺ[7] ὡς μέλι.[8]

et abii ad angelum dicens ei ut daret mihi librum et dicit mihi accipe et devora[9] illum et faciet amaricare[10] ventrem[11] tuum sed in ore tuo erit dulce[12] tamquam mel.[13]

1. מְגִלָּה, *scroll*
2. κεφαλίς, *volume, scroll*
3. βιβλαρίδιον, *small scroll, book*
4. κατεσθίω, aor. act. impv. 2 s., *devour*
5. πικραίνω, fut. act. ind. 3 s., *make bitter*
6. κοιλία, *stomach*
7. γλυκύς, *sweet*
8. μέλι, *honey*
9. devoro, pres. act. impv. 2 s., *devour, eat up*
10. amarico, pres. act. inf., *be/make bitter*
11. venter, *stomach*
12. dulcis, *sweet*
13. mel, *honey*

May 22

Ezekiel 9:4

וַיֹּ֤אמֶר יְהוָה֙ אֵלָ֔ו עֲבֹר֙ בְּת֣וֹךְ הָעִ֔יר בְּת֖וֹךְ יְרֽוּשָׁלָ֑͏ִם
וְהִתְוִ֨יתָ[1] תָּ֜ו[2] עַל־מִצְח֣וֹת[3] הָאֲנָשִׁ֗ים הַנֶּֽאֱנָחִים֙[4]
וְהַנֶּ֣אֱנָקִ֔ים[5] עַ֚ל כָּל־הַתּ֣וֹעֵב֔וֹת הַֽנַּעֲשׂ֖וֹת בְּתוֹכָֽהּ׃

καὶ εἶπεν πρὸς αὐτόν Δίελθε μέσην τὴν Ιερουσαλημ καὶ δὸς τὸ σημεῖον ἐπὶ τὰ μέτωπα[6] τῶν ἀνδρῶν τῶν καταστεναζόντων[7] καὶ τῶν κατωδυνωμένων[8] ἐπὶ πάσαις ταῖς ἀνομίαις ταῖς γινομέναις ἐν μέσῳ αὐτῆς.

Revelation 9:4

καὶ ἐρρέθη αὐταῖς ἵνα μὴ ἀδικήσουσιν[9] τὸν χόρτον[10] τῆς γῆς οὐδὲ πᾶν χλωρὸν[11] οὐδὲ πᾶν δένδρον,[12] εἰ μὴ τοὺς ἀνθρώπους οἵτινες οὐκ ἔχουσιν τὴν σφραγῖδα[13] τοῦ θεοῦ ἐπὶ τῶν μετώπων.

et praeceptum est illis ne laederent[14] faenum[15] terrae neque omne viride[16] neque omnem arborem nisi tantum homines qui non habent signum Dei in frontibus.[17]

1. תוה, hiph. perf. 2 m. s., *mark*
2. תָּו, *mark*
3. מֵ֫צַח, *forehead*
4. אָנַח, niph. ptcp. m. p. abs., *sigh*
5. אָנַק, niph. ptcp. m. p. abs., *groan*
6. μέτωπον, *forehead*
7. καταστενάζω, pres. act. ptcp. m. g. p., *sigh*
8. κατοδυνάω, perf. pass. ptcp. m. g. p., *make bitter*
9. ἀδικέω, fut. act. ind. 3 p., *harm*
10. χόρτον, *grass*
11. χλωρός, *green*
12. δένδρον, *tree*
13. σφραγίς, *seal*
14. laedo, impf. act. subj. 3 p., *strike*
15. faenum, *grass*
16. viridis, *green*
17. frons, *forehead*

May 23

Ezekiel 12:2

בֶּן־אָדָ֕ם בְּת֥וֹךְ בֵּֽית־הַמֶּ֖רִי[1] אַתָּ֣ה יֹשֵׁ֑ב אֲשֶׁ֣ר עֵינַ֩יִם֩ לָהֶ֨ם לִרְא֜וֹת וְלֹ֣א רָא֗וּ אָזְנַ֨יִם לָהֶ֤ם לִשְׁמֹ֙עַ֙ וְלֹ֣א שָׁמֵ֔עוּ כִּ֛י בֵּ֥ית מְרִ֖י הֵֽם׃

Υἱὲ ἀνθρώπου, ἐν μέσῳ τῶν ἀδικιῶν αὐτῶν σὺ κατοικεῖς, οἳ ἔχουσιν ὀφθαλμοὺς τοῦ βλέπειν καὶ οὐ βλέπουσιν καὶ ὦτα ἔχουσιν τοῦ ἀκούειν καὶ οὐκ ἀκούουσιν, διότι οἶκος παραπικραίνων[2] ἐστίν.

Mark 8:18

ὀφθαλμοὺς ἔχοντες οὐ βλέπετε καὶ ὦτα ἔχοντες οὐκ ἀκούετε; καὶ οὐ μνημονεύετε.[3]

oculos habentes non videtis et aures habentes non auditis nec recordamini.[4]

1. מְרִי, *rebellious*
2. παραπικραίνω, pres. act. ptcp. m. nom. s., *provoke*
3. μνημονεύω, pres. act. ind. 2 p., *remember*
4. recordor, pres. dep. ind. 2 p., *remember*

May 24

Ezekiel 36:20

וַיָּב֗וֹא אֶל־הַגּוֹיִם֙ אֲשֶׁר־בָּ֣אוּ שָׁ֔ם וַֽיְחַלְּל֖וּ אֶת־שֵׁ֣ם
קָדְשִׁ֑י בֶּאֱמֹ֤ר לָהֶם֙ עַם־יְהוָ֣ה אֵ֔לֶּה וּמֵאַרְצ֖וֹ יָצָֽאוּ׃

καὶ εἰσήλθοσαν εἰς τὰ ἔθνη, οὗ εἰσήλθοσαν ἐκεῖ, καὶ ἐβεβήλωσαν[1] τὸ ὄνομά μου τὸ ἅγιον ἐν τῷ λέγεσθαι αὐτούς Λαὸς κυρίου οὗτοι καὶ ἐκ τῆς γῆς αὐτοῦ ἐξεληλύθασιν.

Romans 2:24

τὸ γὰρ ὄνομα τοῦ θεοῦ δι᾽ ὑμᾶς βλασφημεῖται[2] ἐν τοῖς ἔθνεσιν, καθὼς γέγραπται.

nomen enim Dei per vos blasphematur inter gentes sicut scriptum est.

1. βεβηλόω, aor. act. ind. 3 p., *profane*

2. βλασφημέω, pres. pass. ind. 3 s., *profane*

May 25

Ezekiel 14:21

כִּי כֹה אָמַר אֲדֹנָי יְהוִה אַף כִּי־אַרְבַּעַת שְׁפָטַי ׀[1]
הָרָעִים חֶרֶב וְרָעָב וְחַיָּה[2] רָעָה וָדֶבֶר[3] שִׁלַּחְתִּי אֶל־
יְרוּשָׁלָ͏ִם לְהַכְרִית מִמֶּנָּה אָדָם וּבְהֵמָה׃

τάδε λέγει κύριος Ἐὰν δὲ καὶ τὰς τέσσαρας ἐκδικήσεις[4] μου τὰς πονηράς, ῥομφαίαν[5] καὶ λιμὸν[6] καὶ θηρία πονηρὰ καὶ θάνατον, ἐξαποστείλω ἐπὶ Ιερουσαλημ τοῦ ἐξολεθρεῦσαι ἐξ αὐτῆς ἄνθρωπον καὶ κτῆνος.

Revelation 6:8

καὶ εἶδον, καὶ ἰδοὺ ἵππος[7] χλωρός,[8] καὶ ὁ καθήμενος ἐπάνω[9] αὐτοῦ ὄνομα αὐτῷ [ὁ] θάνατος, καὶ ὁ ᾅδης[10] ἠκολούθει μετ᾽ αὐτοῦ καὶ ἐδόθη αὐτοῖς ἐξουσία ἐπὶ τὸ τέταρτον[11] τῆς γῆς ἀποκτεῖναι ἐν ῥομφαίᾳ καὶ ἐν λιμῷ καὶ ἐν θανάτῳ καὶ ὑπὸ τῶν θηρίων τῆς γῆς.

et ecce equus[12] pallidus[13] et qui sedebat desuper[14] nomen illi Mors[15] et inferus[16] sequebatur eum et data est illi potestas super quattuor partes terrae interficere gladio fame[17] et morte et bestiis terrae.

1. שֶׁפֶט, *judgment*
2. חַיָּה, *animal, living thing*
3. דֶּבֶר, *pestilence*
4. ἐκδίκησις, *vengeance*
5. ῥομφαία, *sword*
6. λιμός, *famine*
7. ἵππος, *horse*
8. χλωρός, *pale*
9. ἐπάνω, *upon*
10. ᾅδης, *Hades*
11. τέταρτος, *fourth*
12. equus, *horse*
13. pallidus, *pale*
14. desuper, *above*
15. mors, *death*
16. inferus, *hell, Hades*
17. fames, *famine, hunger*

May 26

Ezekiel 18:20

הַנֶּ֥פֶשׁ הַחֹטֵ֖את הִ֣יא תָמ֑וּת בֵּ֞ן לֹא־יִשָּׂ֣א ׀ בַּעֲוֺ֣ן הָאָ֗ב
וְאָב֙ לֹ֤א יִשָּׂא֙ בַּעֲוֺ֣ן הַבֵּ֔ן צִדְקַ֤ת הַצַּדִּיק֙ עָלָ֣יו תִּֽהְיֶ֔ה
וְרִשְׁעַ֥ת[1] רָשָׁ֖ע עָלָ֥יו תִּֽהְיֶֽה׃

ἡ δὲ ψυχὴ ἡ ἁμαρτάνουσα ἀποθανεῖται· ὁ δὲ υἱὸς οὐ λήμψεται τὴν ἀδικίαν τοῦ πατρὸς αὐτοῦ, οὐδὲ ὁ πατὴρ λήμψεται τὴν ἀδικίαν τοῦ υἱοῦ αὐτοῦ· δικαιοσύνη δικαίου ἐπ᾽ αὐτὸν ἔσται, καὶ ἀνομία ἀνόμου ἐπ᾽ αὐτὸν ἔσται.

John 9:2

καὶ ἠρώτησαν αὐτὸν οἱ μαθηταὶ αὐτοῦ λέγοντες· ῥαββί,[2] τίς ἥμαρτεν, οὗτος ἢ οἱ γονεῖς[3] αὐτοῦ, ἵνα τυφλὸς γεννηθῇ;

et interrogaverunt eum discipuli sui rabbi[4] quis peccavit hic aut parentes[5] eius ut caecus nasceretur?

1. רִשְׁעָה, *wickedness*
2. ῥαββί, *rabbi*
3. γονεύς, *parent*
4. rabbi, *rabbi*
5. parens, *parent*

May 27

Ezekiel 20:34

וְהוֹצֵאתִ֤י אֶתְכֶם֙ מִן־הָ֣עַמִּ֔ים וְקִבַּצְתִּ֣י אֶתְכֶ֔ם מִן־
הָ֣אֲרָצ֔וֹת אֲשֶׁ֥ר נְפוֹצֹתֶ֖ם[1] בָּ֑ם בְּיָ֤ד חֲזָקָה֙[2] וּבִזְר֣וֹעַ[3]
נְטוּיָ֔ה וּבְחֵמָ֖ה שְׁפוּכָֽה׃

καὶ ἐξάξω ὑμᾶς ἐκ τῶν λαῶν καὶ εἰσδέξομαι[4] ὑμᾶς ἐκ τῶν χωρῶν, οὗ διεσκορπίσθητε[5] ἐν αὐταῖς, ἐν χειρὶ κραταιᾷ[6] καὶ ἐν βραχίονι ὑψηλῷ καὶ ἐν θυμῷ κεχυμένῳ.[7]

2 Corinthians 6:17

διὸ ἐξέλθατε ἐκ μέσου αὐτῶν καὶ ἀφορίσθητε,[8] *λέγει κύριος, καὶ ἀκαθάρτου μὴ ἅπτεσθε· κἀγὼ εἰσδέξομαι ὑμᾶς.*

propter quod exite de medio eorum et separamini[9] dicit Dominus et inmundum[10] ne tetigeritis.

1. פּוּץ, niph. perf. 2 m. p., *scatter*
2. חָזָק, *strong*
3. זְרוֹעַ, *arm*
4. εἰσδέχομαι, fut. mid. ind. 1 s., *receive*
5. διασκορπίζω, aor. pass. ind. 2 p., *scatter*
6. κραταιός, *strong*
7. χέω, perf. pass. ptcp. m. d. s., *pour out*
8. ἀφορίζω, aor. pass. impv. 2 p., *separate*
9. separo, pres. pass. impv. 2 p., *separate*
10. immundus, *unclean*

May 28

Ezekiel 34:11

כִּ֣י כֹּ֤ה אָמַר֙ אֲדֹנָ֣י יְהוִ֔ה הִנְנִי־אָ֕נִי וְדָרַשְׁתִּ֥י אֶת־צֹאנִ֖י
וּבִקַּרְתִּֽים׃[1]

διότι τάδε λέγει κύριος Ἰδοὺ ἐγὼ ἐκζητήσω τὰ πρόβατά μου καὶ ἐπισκέψομαι αὐτά.

Luke 15:4

τίς ἄνθρωπος ἐξ ὑμῶν ἔχων ἑκατὸν[2] πρόβατα καὶ ἀπολέσας ἐξ αὐτῶν ἓν οὐ καταλείπει[3] τὰ ἐνενήκοντα[4] ἐννέα[5] ἐν τῇ ἐρήμῳ καὶ πορεύεται ἐπὶ τὸ ἀπολωλὸς ἕως εὕρῃ αὐτό;

quis ex vobis homo qui habet centum[6] oves et si perdiderit unam ex illis nonne dimittit nonaginta[7] novem[8] in deserto et vadit ad illam quae perierat donec inveniat illam?

1. בָּקַר, piel perf. 1 c. s., *seek*
2. ἑκατόν, *hundred*
3. καταλείπω, pres. act. ind. 3 s., *leave*
4. ἐνενήκοντα, *ninety*
5. ἐννέα, *nine*
6. centum, *hundred*
7. nonaginta, *ninety*
8. novem, *nine*

May 29

Ezekiel 37:5

כֹּ֤ה אָמַר֙ אֲדֹנָ֣י יְהוִ֔ה לָעֲצָמ֖וֹת הָאֵ֑לֶּה הִנֵּ֨ה אֲנִ֜י מֵבִ֥יא
בָכֶ֛ם ר֖וּחַ וִחְיִיתֶֽם׃

Τάδε λέγει κύριος τοῖς ὀστέοις τούτοις Ἰδοὺ ἐγὼ
φέρω εἰς ὑμᾶς πνεῦμα ζωῆς.

Revelation 11:11

Καὶ μετὰ τὰς τρεῖς ἡμέρας καὶ ἥμισυ[1] *πνεῦμα ζωῆς* ἐκ τοῦ θεοῦ *εἰσῆλθεν ἐν αὐτοῖς, καὶ ἔστησαν ἐπὶ τοὺς πόδας αὐτῶν*, καὶ φόβος μέγας ἐπέπεσεν[2] ἐπὶ τοὺς θεωροῦντας αὐτούς.

et post dies tres et dimidium[3] spiritus vitae a Deo intravit in eos et steterunt super pedes suos et timor magnus cecidit super eos qui viderunt eos.

1. ἥμισυς, *half*
2. ἐπιπίπτω, aor. act. ind. 3 s., *fall*
3. dimidium, *half*

John the Baptist

May 30

Judges 13:4[1]

וְעַתָּה֙ הִשָּׁ֣מְרִי נָ֔א וְאַל־תִּשְׁתִּ֖י יַ֣יִן וְשֵׁכָ֑ר[2] וְאַל־
תֹּאכְלִ֖י כָּל־טָמֵֽא׃[3]

καὶ νῦν φύλαξαι καὶ μὴ πίῃς οἶνον καὶ σικερα[4] καὶ μὴ φάγῃς πᾶν ἀκάθαρτον.

Luke 1:15

ἔσται γὰρ μέγας ἐνώπιον [τοῦ] κυρίου, *καὶ οἶνον καὶ σίκερα οὐ μὴ πίῃ*, καὶ πνεύματος ἁγίου πλησθήσεται[5] ἔτι ἐκ κοιλίας[6] μητρὸς αὐτοῦ.

erit enim magnus coram Domino et vinum et sicera[7] non bibet et Spiritu Sancto replebitur[8] adhuc ex utero[9] matris suae.

1. PA: Samson's mother is instructed to do these things, as he will himself become a Nazarite.

2. שֵׁכָר, *strong drink*

3. טָמֵא, *unclean*

4. σίκερα, *strong drink*

5. πίμπλημι, fut. pass. ind. 3 s., *fill*

6. κοιλία, *womb*

7. sicera, *strong drink*

8. repleo, fut. pass. ind. 3 s., *fill*

9. uterus, *womb*

May 31

2 Kings 1:8

וַיֹּאמְרוּ אֵלָיו אִישׁ בַּעַל שֵׂעָר[1] וְאֵזוֹר[2] עוֹר אָזוּר[3] בְּמָתְנָיו[4] וַיֹּאמַר אֵלִיָּה[5] הַתִּשְׁבִּי[6] הוּא׃

καὶ εἶπον πρὸς αὐτόν Ἀνὴρ δασὺς[7] καὶ ζώνην[8] δερματίνην[9] περιεζωσμένος[10] τὴν ὀσφὺν[11] αὐτοῦ. καὶ εἶπεν Ηλιου[12] ὁ Θεσβίτης[13] οὗτός ἐστιν.

Mark 1:6

καὶ ἦν ὁ Ἰωάννης ἐνδεδυμένος[14] τρίχας[15] καμήλου[16] καὶ ζώνην δερματίνην περὶ τὴν ὀσφὺν αὐτοῦ καὶ ἐσθίων ἀκρίδας[17] καὶ μέλι[18] ἄγριον.[19]

et erat Iohannes vestitus[20] pilis[21] cameli[22] et zona[23] pellicia[24] circa lumbos[25] eius et lucustas[26] et mel[27] silvestre[28] edebat.[29]

1. שֵׂעָר, *hair, garment of hair*
2. אֵזוֹר, *skin, leather*
3. אָזַר, qal pass. ptcp. m. abs. s., *gird, go around*
4. מָתְנַיִם, *loins*
5. אֵלִיָּה, *Elijah*
6. תִּשְׁבִּי, *Tishbite*
7. δασύς, *hairy*
8. ζώνη, *belt*
9. δερμάτινος, *leather, made of skin*
10. περιζωννύω, perf. pass, ptcp. m. nom. s., *wrap around*
11. ὀσφύς, *waist*
12. Ηλιου, *Elijah*
13. Θεσβίτης, *Tishbite*
14. ἐνδύω, perf. pass. ptcp. m. nom. s., *wear*
15. θρίξ, *hair*
16. κάμηλος, *camel*
17. ἀκρίς, *locust*
18. μέλι, *honey*
19. ἄγριος, *wild*
20. vestio, perf. pass. ptcp. m. nom. s., *dress, clothe*
21. pilus, *hair*
22. camelus, *camel*
23. zona, *money belt, girdle*

24. pellicius, *made of skin.* **25.** lumbus, *loin.* **26.** lucusta, *locust.* **27.** mel, *honey.* **28.** silvestris, *wild.* **29.** edo, impf. act. ind. 3 s., *eat*

June 1

Isaiah 40:3

קֹ֗ול קֹורֵ֔א בַּמִּדְבָּ֕ר פַּנּ֖וּ דֶּ֣רֶךְ יְהוָ֑ה יַשְּׁרוּ֙[1] בָּעֲרָבָ֔ה[2]
מְסִלָּ֖ה[3] לֵאלֹהֵֽינוּ׃

φωνὴ βοῶντος ἐν τῇ ἐρήμῳ Ἑτοιμάσατε τὴν ὁδὸν κυρίου, εὐθείας[4] ποιεῖτε τὰς τρίβους[5] τοῦ θεοῦ ἡμῶν.

Mark 1:4

ἐγένετο Ἰωάννης [ὁ] βαπτίζων ἐν τῇ ἐρήμῳ καὶ κηρύσσων βάπτισμα[6] μετανοίας[7] εἰς ἄφεσιν[8] ἁμαρτιῶν.

fuit Iohannes in deserto baptizans et praedicans baptismum[9] paenitentiae in remissionem[10] peccatorum.

1. יָשַׁר, piel impf. m. p., *make straight*
2. עֲרָבָה, *wilderness*
3. מְסִלָּה, *highway*
4. εὐθύς, *straight*
5. τρίβος, *path*
6. βάπτισμα, *baptism*
7. μετάνοια, *repentance*
8. ἄφεσις, *forgiveness*
9. baptismus, *baptism*
10. remissio, *forgiveness*

June 2

Leviticus 18:16

עֶרְוַ֛ת[1] אֵֽשֶׁת־אָחִ֖יךָ לֹ֣א תְגַלֵּ֑ה עֶרְוַ֥ת אָחִ֖יךָ הִֽוא׃

ἀσχημοσύνην[2] γυναικὸς ἀδελφοῦ σου οὐκ ἀποκαλύψεις·[3] ἀσχημοσύνη ἀδελφοῦ σού ἐστιν.

Mark 6:17

Αὐτὸς γὰρ ὁ Ἡρῴδης ἀποστείλας ἐκράτησεν τὸν Ἰωάννην καὶ ἔδησεν αὐτὸν ἐν φυλακῇ διὰ Ἡρῳδιάδα[4] τὴν γυναῖκα Φιλίππου τοῦ ἀδελφοῦ αὐτοῦ, ὅτι αὐτὴν ἐγάμησεν.[5]

ipse enim Herodes misit ac tenuit Iohannem et vinxit[6] eum in carcere propter Herodiadem[7] uxorem Philippi fratris sui quia duxerat eam.

1. עֶרְוָה, *nakedness*
2. ἀσχημοσύνη, *nakedness*
3. ἀποκαλύπτω, fut. act. ind. 2 s., *reveal, uncover*
4. Ἡρῳδιάς, *Herodias*
5. γαμέω, aor. act. ind. 3 s., *marry*
6. vincio, perf. act. ind. 3 s., *bind*
7. Herodiades, *Herodias*

June 3

1. אֶסְתֵּר, *Esther*
2. מַלְכָּה, *queen*
3. בַּקָּשָׁה, *request, entreaty*
4. מַלְכוּת, *kingdom*
5. Εσθηρ, *Esther*
6. ἀξίωμα, *petition*
7. ἥμισυς, *half*
8. θυγάτηρ, *daughter*
9. Ἡρῳδιάς, *Herodias*
10. ὀρχέομαι, aor. mid. ptcp. f. g. s., *dance*
11. ἀρέσκω, aor. act. ind. 3 s., *please*
12. κοράσιον, *girl*
13. ὀμνύω, aor. act. ind. 3 s., *swore*
14. Herodias, *Herodias*
15. salto, pluperf. act. subj. 3 s., *dance*
16. recumbo, pres. act. ptcp. m. d. p., *recline*
17. puella, *girl, maiden*
18. iuro, perf. act. ind. 3 s., *swear*
19. quisquis, *whatever*
20. dimidium, *half*

Esther 5:3

וַיֹּ֤אמֶר לָהּ֙ הַמֶּ֔לֶךְ מַה־לָּ֖ךְ אֶסְתֵּ֣ר[1] הַמַּלְכָּ֑ה[2] וּמַה־בַּקָּשָׁתֵ֛ךְ[3] עַד־חֲצִ֥י הַמַּלְכ֖וּת[4] וְיִנָּ֥תֵֽן לָֽךְ׃

καὶ εἶπεν ὁ βασιλεύς Τί θέλεις, Εσθηρ,[5] καὶ τί σού ἐστιν τὸ ἀξίωμα;[6] ἕως τοῦ ἡμίσους[7] τῆς βασιλείας μου καὶ ἔσται σοι.

Mark 6:22–23

καὶ εἰσελθούσης τῆς θυγατρὸς[8] αὐτοῦ Ἡρῳδιάδος[9] καὶ ὀρχησαμένης[10] ἤρεσεν[11] τῷ Ἡρῴδῃ καὶ τοῖς συνανακειμένοις. εἶπεν ὁ βασιλεὺς τῷ κορασίῳ·[12] αἴτησόν με ὃ ἐὰν θέλῃς, καὶ δώσω σοι· καὶ ὤμοσεν[13] αὐτῇ [πολλὰ] ὅ τι ἐάν με αἰτήσῃς δώσω σοι ἕως ἡμίσους τῆς βασιλείας μου.

cumque introisset filia ipsius Herodiadis[14] et saltasset[15] et placuisset Herodi simulque recumbentibus[16] rex ait puellae[17] pete a me quod vis et dabo tibi et iuravit[18] illi quia quicquid[19] petieris dabo tibi licet dimidium[20] regni mei.

June 4

Malachi 3:23 [LXX 3:22]

הִנֵּ֤ה אָֽנֹכִי֙ שֹׁלֵ֣חַ לָכֶ֔ם אֵ֖ת אֵלִיָּ֣ה[1] הַנָּבִ֑יא לִפְנֵ֗י בּ֚וֹא
י֣וֹם יְהוָ֔ה הַגָּד֖וֹל וְהַנּוֹרָֽא׃

καὶ ἰδοὺ ἐγὼ ἀποστέλλω ὑμῖν Ηλιαν[2] τὸν Θεσβίτην[3] πρὶν[4] ἐλθεῖν ἡμέραν κυρίου τὴν μεγάλην καὶ ἐπιφανῆ.[5]

Matthew 11:14

καὶ εἰ θέλετε δέξασθαι, αὐτός ἐστιν Ἠλίας ὁ μέλλων ἔρχεσθαι.

et si vultis recipere ipse est Helias[6] qui venturus est.

1. אֵלִיָּה, *Elijah*
2. Ηλιας, *Elijah*
3. Θεσβίτης, *Tishbite*
4. πρίν, *before*
5. ἐπιφανής, *notable*
6. Helias, *Elijah*

Jesus's Infancy

June 5

Genesis 5:1

זֶ֣ה סֵ֔פֶר תּוֹלְדֹ֖ת[1] אָדָ֑ם[2] בְּי֗וֹם בְּרֹ֤א[3] אֱלֹהִים֙ אָדָ֔ם
בִּדְמ֥וּת[4] אֱלֹהִ֖ים עָשָׂ֥ה אֹתֽוֹ׃

Αὕτη ἡ βίβλος[5] γενέσεως[6] ἀνθρώπων· ᾗ ἡμέρᾳ ἐποίησεν ὁ θεὸς τὸν Αδαμ,[7] κατ᾽ εἰκόνα[8] θεοῦ ἐποίησεν αὐτόν.

Matthew 1:1

Βίβλος γενέσεως Ἰησοῦ Χριστοῦ υἱοῦ Δαυὶδ υἱοῦ Ἀβραάμ.

liber generationis Iesu Christi filii David filii Abraham.

1. תּוֹלֵדוֹת, *genealogy, generation*
2. אָדָם, *Adam, mankind*
3. בָּרָא, qal inf. cons., *create*
4. דְּמוּת, *likeness*
5. βίβλος, *book*
6. γένεσις, *genealogy, genesis*
7. Αδαμ, *Adam*
8. εἰκών, *image, likeness*

June 6

Ruth 4:13

וַיִּקַּ֨ח בֹּ֤עַז[1] אֶת־רוּת֙[2] וַתְּהִי־ל֣וֹ לְאִשָּׁ֔ה וַיָּבֹ֖א אֵלֶ֑יהָ
וַיִּתֵּ֨ן יְהוָ֥ה לָ֛הּ הֵרָי֖וֹן[3] וַתֵּ֥לֶד בֵּֽן׃

καὶ ἔλαβεν Βοος[4] τὴν Ρουθ,[5] καὶ ἐγενήθη αὐτῷ εἰς γυναῖκα, καὶ εἰσῆλθεν πρὸς αὐτήν, καὶ ἔδωκεν αὐτῇ κύριος κύησιν,[6] καὶ ἔτεκεν υἱόν.

Matthew 1:5

Σαλμὼν[7] δὲ ἐγέννησεν τὸν Βόες[8] ἐκ τῆς Ῥαχάβ,[9] Βόες δὲ ἐγέννησεν τὸν Ἰωβὴδ[10] ἐκ τῆς Ῥούθ, Ἰωβὴδ δὲ ἐγέννησεν τὸν Ἰεσσαί.[11]

Salmon[12] autem genuit Booz[13] de Rachab[14] Booz autem genuit Obed[15] ex Ruth[16] Obed autem genuit Iesse[17] Iesse autem genuit David regem.

1. בֹּעַז, *Boaz*
2. רוּת, *Ruth*
3. הֵרָיוֹן, *conception, pregnancy*
4. Βοος, *Boaz*
5. Ῥούθ, *Ruth*
6. κύησις, *pregnancy*
7. Σαλμών, *Salmon*
8. Βόες, *Boaz*
9. Ῥαχάβ, *Rahab*
10. Ἰωβήδ, *Obed*
11. Ἰεσσαί, *Jesse*
12. Salmon, *Salmon*
13. Booz, *Boaz*
14. Rachab, *Rahab*
15. Obed, *Obed*
16. Ruth, *Ruth*
17. Iesse, *Jesse*

June 7

Genesis 18:14

הֲיִפָּלֵ֥א[1] מֵיְהוָ֖ה דָּבָ֑ר לַמּוֹעֵ֞ד אָשׁ֥וּב אֵלֶ֛יךָ כָּעֵ֥ת חַיָּ֖ה
וּלְשָׂרָ֥ה[2] בֵֽן׃

μὴ ἀδυνατεῖ[3] παρὰ τῷ θεῷ ῥῆμα; εἰς τὸν καιρὸν τοῦτον ἀναστρέψω πρὸς σὲ εἰς ὥρας,[4] καὶ ἔσται τῇ Σαρρα[5] υἱός.

Luke 1:37–38

ὅτι οὐκ ἀδυνατήσει[6] παρὰ τοῦ θεοῦ πᾶν ῥῆμα. εἶπεν δὲ Μαριάμ·[7] ἰδοὺ ἡ δούλη[8] κυρίου· γένοιτό μοι κατὰ τὸ ῥῆμά σου. Καὶ ἀπῆλθεν ἀπ᾽ αὐτῆς ὁ ἄγγελος.

quia non erit inpossibile[9] apud Deum omne verbum dixit autem Maria ecce ancilla[10] Domini fiat mihi secundum verbum tuum et discessit ab illa angelus.

1. פלא, niph. impf. 3 m. s., *beyond one's power*
2. שָׂרָה, *Sarah*
3. ἀδυνατέω, pres. act. ind. 3 s., *be impossible*
4. ὥρα, *season, hour*
5. Σαρρα, *Sarah*
6. ἀδυνατέω, fut. act. ind. 3 s., *be impossible*
7. Μαριάμ, *Mary*
8. δούλη, *maidservant, female slave*
9. inpossibilis, *impossible*
10. ancilla, *maidservant, female slave*

June 8

Genesis 37:11

וַיְקַנְאוּ[1]־בוֹ אֶחָיו וְאָבִיו[2] שָׁמַר אֶת־הַדָּבָר׃

ἐζήλωσαν[3] δὲ αὐτὸν οἱ ἀδελφοὶ αὐτοῦ,[4] ὁ δὲ πατὴρ αὐτοῦ διετήρησεν[5] τὸ ῥῆμα.

Luke 2:19

ἡ δὲ Μαριὰμ[6] πάντα συνετήρει[7] τὰ ῥήματα ταῦτα συμβάλλουσα[8] ἐν τῇ καρδίᾳ αὐτῆς.

Maria autem conservabat[9] omnia verba haec conferens[10] in corde suo.

1. קנא, piel wcons. 3 m. p., *be jealous*
2. CH: The pronoun refers to Joseph.
3. ζηλόω, aor. act. ind. 3 p., *be jealous*
4. CH: The pronoun refers to Joseph.
5. διατηρέω, aor. act. ind. 3 s., *keep*
6. Μαριάμ, *Mary*
7. συντηρέω, impf. act. ind. 3 s., *preserve, treasure up*
8. συμβάλλω, pres. act. ptcp. f. nom. s., *consider*
9. conservo, impf. act. ind. 3 s., *keep, preserve*
10. confero, pres. act. ptcp. f. nom. s., *consider*

June 9

Psalm 72:10 [LXX 71:10]

מַלְכֵ֬י תַרְשִׁ֣ישׁ[1] וְ֭אִיִּים[2] מִנְחָ֣ה יָשִׁ֑יבוּ מַלְכֵ֥י שְׁבָ֥א[3]
וּ֝סְבָ֗א[4] אֶשְׁכָּ֥ר[5] יַקְרִֽיבוּ׃

βασιλεῖς Θαρσις[6] καὶ αἱ νῆσοι[7] δῶρα
προσοίσουσιν, βασιλεῖς Ἀράβων[8] καὶ Σαβα[9]
δῶρα[10] προσάξουσιν·

Matthew 2:11

καὶ ἐλθόντες εἰς τὴν οἰκίαν εἶδον τὸ παιδίον
μετὰ Μαρίας[11] τῆς μητρὸς αὐτοῦ, καὶ πεσόντες
προσεκύνησαν αὐτῷ καὶ ἀνοίξαντες τοὺς
θησαυροὺς[12] αὐτῶν προσήνεγκαν αὐτῷ δῶρα,
χρυσὸν[13] καὶ λίβανον[14] καὶ σμύρναν.[15]

et intrantes domum invenerunt puerum cum
Maria matre eius et procidentes[16] adoraverunt
eum et apertis thesauris[17] suis obtulerunt ei
munera[18] aurum[19] tus[20] et murram.[21]

1. תַּרְשִׁישׁ, *Tarshish*
2. אִי, *coastal region*
3. שְׁבָא, *Sheba*
4. סְבָא, *Seba*
5. אֶשְׁכָּר, *gift, tribute*
6. Θαρσις, *Tarshish*
7. νῆσος, *island*
8. Ἄραψ, *Arabian*
9. Σαβα, *Sheba*
10. δῶρον, *gift*
11. Μαρία, *Mary*
12. θησαυρός, *treasure*
13. χρυσός, *gold*
14. λίβανος, *frankincense*
15. σμύρνα, *myrrh*
16. procido, pres. act. ptcp. m. nom. p., *fall down*
17. thesaurus, *treasure*
18. munus, *gift*
19. aurum, *gold*
20. tus, *frankincense*
21. murra, *myrrh*

June 10

Exodus 1:15a, 16

וַיֹּ֨אמֶר֙ מֶ֣לֶךְ מִצְרַ֔יִם לַֽמְיַלְּדֹ֖ת הָֽעִבְרִיֹּ֑ת[1]... בְּיַלֶּדְכֶן֙
אֶת־הָֽעִבְרִיּ֔וֹת וּרְאִיתֶ֖ן עַל־הָאׇבְנָ֑יִם[2] אִם־בֵּ֥ן הוּא֙
וַהֲמִתֶּ֣ן אֹת֔וֹ וְאִם־בַּ֥ת הִ֖יא וָחָֽיָה׃

Καὶ εἶπεν ὁ βασιλεὺς τῶν Αἰγυπτίων ταῖς μαίαις[3] τῶν Εβραίων[4] . . . Ὅταν μαιοῦσθε[5] τὰς Εβραίας καὶ ὦσιν πρὸς τῷ τίκτειν, ἐὰν μὲν ἄρσεν[6] ᾖ, ἀποκτείνατε αὐτό, ἐὰν δὲ θῆλυ,[7] περιποιεῖσθε[8] αὐτό.

Matthew 2:16

Τότε Ἡρῴδης ἰδὼν ὅτι ἐνεπαίχθη[9] ὑπὸ τῶν μάγων[10] ἐθυμώθη[11] λίαν,[12] καὶ ἀποστείλας ἀνεῖλεν[13] πάντας τοὺς παῖδας[14] τοὺς ἐν Βηθλέεμ[15] καὶ ἐν πᾶσιν τοῖς ὁρίοις[16] αὐτῆς ἀπὸ διετοῦς[17] καὶ κατωτέρω,[18] κατὰ τὸν χρόνον ὃν ἠκρίβωσεν[19] παρὰ τῶν μάγων.

tunc Herodes videns quoniam inlusus[20] esset a magis[21] iratus[22] est valde[23] et mittens occidit omnes pueros qui erant in Bethleem[24] et in omnibus finibus eius a bimatu[25] et infra[26] secundum tempus quod exquisierat[27] a magis.

1. עִבְרִי, *Hebrew*

2. אֶ֫בֶן, *stone, (birthstool)*

3. μαῖα, *midwife*

4. Ἑβραῖος, *Hebrew*

5. μαιόομαι, pres. mid. ind. 2 p., *deliver*

6. ἄρσην, *male*

7. θῆλυς, *female*

8. περιποιέω, pres. mid. impv. 2 p., *preserve, keep alive*

9. ἐμπαίζω, aor. pass. ind. 3 s., *trick, mock*

10. μάγος, *magician*

11. θυμόω, aor. pass. ind. 3 s., *become angry, incensed*

12. λίαν, *very, exceedingly*

13. ἀναιρέω, aor. act. ind. 3 s., *destroy, kill*

14. παῖς, *child*

15. Βηθλέεμ, *Bethlehem*

16. ὅριον, *region*

17. διετής, *two years old*

18. κατωτέρω, *under, below*

19. ἀκριβόω, aor. act. ind. 3 s., *ascertain, inquiry*

20. inludo, pluperf. pass. subj. 3 s., *mock, ridicule*

21. magus, *sorcerer, wise man.* **22.** irascor, perf. dep. ind. 3 s., *be angry.* **23.** valde, *very, exceedingly.* **24.** Bethleem, *Bethlehem.* **25.** bimatus, *two years old.* **26.** infra, *under, below.* **27.** exquiro, pluperf. act. ind. 3 s., *examine, search*

June 11

Exodus 4:19

וַיֹּ֨אמֶר יְהוָ֤ה אֶל־מֹשֶׁה֙ בְּמִדְיָ֔ן[1] לֵ֖ךְ שֻׁ֣ב מִצְרָ֑יִם כִּי־
מֵ֙תוּ֙ כָּל־הָ֣אֲנָשִׁ֔ים הַֽמְבַקְשִׁ֖ים אֶת־נַפְשֶֽׁךָ׃

μετὰ δὲ τὰς ἡμέρας τὰς πολλὰς ἐκείνας ἐτελεύτησεν[2] ὁ βασιλεὺς Αἰγύπτου. εἶπεν δὲ κύριος πρὸς Μωυσῆν ἐν Μαδιαμ[3] Βάδιζε[4] ἄπελθε εἰς Αἴγυπτον· τεθνήκασιν[5] γὰρ πάντες οἱ ζητοῦντές σου τὴν ψυχήν.

Matthew 2:20

λέγων· ἐγερθεὶς παράλαβε τὸ παιδίον καὶ τὴν μητέρα αὐτοῦ καὶ πορεύου εἰς γῆν Ἰσραήλ· τεθνήκασιν γὰρ οἱ ζητοῦντες τὴν ψυχὴν τοῦ παιδίου.

dicens surge et accipe puerum et matrem eius et vade in terram Israhel defuncti[6] sunt enim qui quaerebant animam pueri.

1. מִדְיָן, *Midian*
2. τελευτάω, aor. act. ind. 3 s., *die*
3. Μαδιάμ, *Midian*
4. βαδίζω, pres. act. impv. 2 s., *go*
5. θνήσκω, perf. act. ind. 3 p., *die*
6. defungor, perf. dep. ind. 3 p., *die*

June 12

Exodus 13:15

וַיְהִ֗י כִּֽי־הִקְשָׁ֣ה[1] פַרְעֹה֮ לְשַׁלְּחֵנוּ֒ וַיַּהֲרֹ֨ג יְהוָ֤ה
כָּל־בְּכוֹר֙ בְּאֶ֣רֶץ מִצְרַ֔יִם מִבְּכֹ֥ר אָדָ֖ם וְעַד־בְּכ֣וֹר
בְּהֵמָ֑ה עַל־כֵּ֞ן אֲנִ֣י זֹבֵ֣חַ לַֽיהוָ֗ה כָּל־פֶּ֤טֶר[2] רֶ֙חֶם֙[3]
הַזְּכָרִ֔ים[4] וְכָל־בְּכ֥וֹר בָּנַ֖י אֶפְדֶּֽה׃[5]

ἡνίκα δὲ ἐσκλήρυνεν[6] Φαραω ἐξαποστεῖλαι ἡμᾶς, ἀπέκτεινεν πᾶν πρωτότοκον ἐν γῇ Αἰγύπτῳ ἀπὸ πρωτοτόκων ἀνθρώπων ἕως πρωτοτόκων κτηνῶν· διὰ τοῦτο ἐγὼ θύω τῷ κυρίῳ πᾶν διανοῖγον[7] μήτραν,[8] τὰ ἀρσενικά,[9] καὶ πᾶν πρωτότοκον τῶν υἱῶν μου λυτρώσομαι.

Luke 2:22[10]

Καὶ ὅτε ἐπλήσθησαν[11] αἱ ἡμέραι τοῦ καθαρισμοῦ[12] αὐτῶν κατὰ τὸν νόμον Μωϋσέως, ἀνήγαγον[13] αὐτὸν εἰς Ἱεροσόλυμα παραστῆσαι τῷ κυρίῳ.

et postquam[14] impleti sunt dies purgationis[15] eius secundum legem Mosi tulerunt illum in Hierusalem ut sisterent[16] eum Domino.

1. קָשָׁה, hiph. perf. 3 m. s., *harden*
2. פֶּטֶר, *firstborn*
3. רֶחֶם, *womb*
4. זָכָר, *male*
5. פָּדָה, qal impf. 1 c. s., *redeem, ransom*
6. σκληρύνω, aor. act. ind. 3 s., *harden*
7. διανοίγω, pres. act. ptcp. n. a. s., *open*
8. μήτρα, *womb*
9. ἀρσενικός, *male*
10. PA: As Luke 2:23 goes on to explain, part of the reason for their visit to Jerusalem is to provide the sacrifice required for the firstborn male.
11. πίμπλημι, aor. pass. ind. 3 p., *complete, fulfill*
12. καθαρισμός, *purification*
13. ἀνάγω, aor. act. ind. 3 p., *bring*
14. postquam, *after*
15. purgatio, *purification*
16. sisto, impf. act. subj. 3 p., *set, place*

June 13

1 Samuel 2:26

וְהַנַּ֣עַר שְׁמוּאֵ֔ל הֹלֵ֥ךְ וְגָדֵ֖ל וָטֹ֑וב[1] גַּ֚ם עִם־יְהוָ֔ה וְגַ֖ם עִם־אֲנָשִֽׁים׃

καὶ τὸ παιδάριον Σαμουηλ ἐπορεύετο καὶ ἐμεγαλύνετο[2] καὶ ἀγαθὸν καὶ μετὰ κυρίου καὶ μετὰ ἀνθρώπων.

Luke 2:52

Καὶ Ἰησοῦς προέκοπτεν[3] [ἐν τῇ] σοφίᾳ καὶ ἡλικίᾳ[4] καὶ χάριτι παρὰ θεῷ καὶ ἀνθρώποις.

et Iesus proficiebat[5] sapientia aetate[6] et gratia apud Deum et homines.

1. טוֹב, qal perf. 3 m. s., *be pleasing, good*
2. μεγαλύνω, impf. pass. ind. 3 s., *make great, magnify*
3. προκόπτω, impf. act. ind. 3 s., *increase, advance*
4. ἡλικία, *stature*
5. proficio, impf. act. ind. 3 s., *advance, increase*
6. aetas, *age*

Fulfillment of Prophecy

June 14

Hosea 11:1

כִּ֛י נַ֥עַר יִשְׂרָאֵ֖ל וָאֹהֲבֵ֑הוּ וּמִמִּצְרַ֖יִם קָרָ֥אתִי לִבְנִֽי׃

Διότι νήπιος Ισραηλ, καὶ ἐγὼ ἠγάπησα αὐτὸν καὶ ἐξ Αἰγύπτου μετεκάλεσα τὰ τέκνα αὐτοῦ.

Matthew 2:14[1]

ὁ δὲ ἐγερθεὶς παρέλαβεν τὸ παιδίον καὶ τὴν μητέρα αὐτοῦ νυκτὸς καὶ ἀνεχώρησεν[2] εἰς Αἴγυπτον.[3]

qui consurgens[4] accepit puerum et matrem eius nocte et recessit[5] in Aegyptum.[6]

1. PA: The following verse in Matthew then cites Hos 11:1.
2. ἀναχωρέω, aor. act. ind. 3 s., *depart*
3. Αἴγυπτος, *Egypt*
4. consurgo, pres. act. ptcp. m. nom. s., *rise up*
5. recedo, perf. act. ind. 3 s., *depart*
6. Aegyptus, *Egypt*

June 15

Isaiah 9:1

הָעָם֙ הַהֹלְכִ֣ים בַּחֹ֔שֶׁךְ[1] רָא֖וּ א֣וֹר גָּד֑וֹל יֹשְׁבֵי֙ בְּאֶ֣רֶץ
צַלְמָ֔וֶת[2] א֖וֹר נָגַ֥הּ[3] עֲלֵיהֶֽם׃

ὁ λαὸς ὁ πορευόμενος ἐν σκότει, ἴδετε φῶς μέγα· οἱ κατοικοῦντες ἐν χώρᾳ καὶ σκιᾷ[4] θανάτου, φῶς λάμψει[5] ἐφ᾽ ὑμᾶς.

Matthew 4:13[6]

καὶ καταλιπὼν[7] τὴν Ναζαρὰ[8] ἐλθὼν κατῴκησεν εἰς Καφαρναοὺμ[9] τὴν παραθαλασσίαν[10] ἐν ὁρίοις[11] Ζαβουλὼν[12] καὶ Νεφθαλίμ.[13]

et relicta civitate Nazareth[14] venit et habitavit in Capharnaum[15] maritimam[16] in finibus Zabulon[17] et Nepthalim.[18]

1. חֹשֶׁךְ, *darkness*
2. צַלְמָוֶת, *deep darkness*
3. נָגַהּ, qal perf. 3 m. s., *shine*
4. σκιά, *shadow*
5. λάμπω, fut. act. ind. 3 s., *shine*
6. PA: This was done to fulfill the prophecy in Isa 9:1, as it is stated in Matt 4:14.
7. καταλείπω, aor. act. ptcp. m. nom. s., *leave*
8. Ναζαρά, *Nazareth*
9. Καφαρναούμ, *Capernaum*
10. παραθαλάσσιος, *by the sea*
11. ὅριον, *region*
12. Ζαβουλών, *Zebulun*
13. Νεφθαλίμ, *Naphtali*
14. Nazareth, *Nazareth*
15. Capharnaum, *Capernaum*
16. maritimus, *by the sea*
17. Zabulon, *Zebulun*
18. Nepthalim, *Naphtali*

June 16

Isaiah 53:4

אָכֵן[1] חֳלָיֵנוּ[2] הוּא נָשָׂא וּמַכְאֹבֵינוּ[3] סְבָלָם[4] וַאֲנַחְנוּ
חֲשַׁבְנֻהוּ נָגוּעַ מֻכֵּה אֱלֹהִים וּמְעֻנֶּה׃[5]

οὗτος τὰς ἁμαρτίας ἡμῶν φέρει καὶ περὶ ἡμῶν ὀδυνᾶται,[6] καὶ ἡμεῖς ἐλογισάμεθα αὐτὸν εἶναι ἐν πόνῳ[7] καὶ ἐν πληγῇ[8] καὶ ἐν κακώσει.[9]

Matthew 8:16[10]

Ὀψίας[11] δὲ γενομένης προσήνεγκαν αὐτῷ δαιμονιζομένους[12] πολλούς· καὶ ἐξέβαλεν τὰ πνεύματα λόγῳ καὶ πάντας τοὺς κακῶς[13] ἔχοντας ἐθεράπευσεν.

vespere[14] autem facto obtulerunt ei multos daemonia habentes et eiciebat spiritus verbo et omnes male[15] habentes curavit.

1. אָכֵן, *surely*
2. חֳלִי, *sickness, disease*
3. מַכְאוֹב, *pain, suffering*
4. סָבַל, qal perf. 3 m. s., *bear, carry*
5. ענה, pual ptcp. m. s. abs., *be afflicted, humbled*
6. ὀδυνάω, pres. pass. ind. 3 s., *be in pain, suffer*
7. πόνος, *work, toil*
8. πληγή, *blow, wound*
9. κάκωσις, *ill-treatment*
10. PA: In Matt 8:17 the author says Jesus's acts of healing here were to fulfill what is written in Isa 53:4.
11. ὀψία, *evening*
12. δαιμονίζομαι, pres. mid. ptcp. m. a. p., *be possessed by a demon*
13. κακῶς, *illness, sickness;* TH: τοὺς κακῶς ἔχοντας is used idiomatically, meaning *who were sick*
14. vesper, *evening*
15. male, *illness, sickness;* TH: male habentes is used idiomatically, meaning *who were sick*

June 17

Isaiah 35:5

אָז תִּפָּקַחְנָה[1] עֵינֵי עִוְרִים[2] וְאָזְנֵי חֵרְשִׁים[3] תִּפָּתַחְנָה׃

τότε ἀνοιχθήσονται ὀφθαλμοὶ τυφλῶν,[4] καὶ ὦτα κωφῶν[5] ἀκούσονται.

Matthew 11:5

τυφλοὶ ἀναβλέπουσιν[6] καὶ χωλοὶ περιπατοῦσιν, λεπροὶ[7] καθαρίζονται καὶ κωφοὶ ἀκούουσιν, καὶ νεκροὶ ἐγείρονται καὶ πτωχοὶ εὐαγγελίζονται.

caeci vident claudi[8] ambulant leprosi[9] mundantur[10] surdi[11] audiunt mortui resurgunt pauperes[12] evangelizantur.

1. פָּקַח, niph. impf. 3 f. p., *open*
2. עִוֵּר, *blind*
3. חֵרֵשׁ, *deaf*
4. τυφλός, *blind*
5. κωφός, *deaf*
6. ἀναβλέπω, pres. act. ind. 3 p., *see, receive sight*
7. λεπρός, *leper*
8. claudus, *lame*
9. leprosus, *leper*
10. mundo, pres. pass. ind. 3 p., *cleanse*
11. surdus, *deaf*
12. pauper, *poor*

June 18

Ezekiel 37:25

וְיָשְׁב֣וּ עַל־הָאָ֗רֶץ אֲשֶׁ֤ר נָתַ֙תִּי֙ לְעַבְדִּ֣י לְיַעֲקֹ֔ב אֲשֶׁ֥ר
יָֽשְׁבוּ־בָ֖הּ אֲבֽוֹתֵיכֶ֑ם וְיָשְׁב֣וּ עָ֠לֶיהָ הֵ֞מָּה וּבְנֵיהֶ֨ם וּבְנֵ֤י
בְנֵיהֶם֙ עַד־עוֹלָ֔ם וְדָוִ֣ד עַבְדִּ֔י נָשִׂ֥יא לָהֶ֖ם לְעוֹלָֽם׃

καὶ κατοικήσουσιν ἐπὶ τῆς γῆς αὐτῶν, ἣν ἐγὼ δέδωκα τῷ δούλῳ μου Ιακωβ, οὗ κατῴκησαν ἐκεῖ οἱ πατέρες αὐτῶν· καὶ κατοικήσουσιν ἐπ᾽ αὐτῆς αὐτοί, καὶ Δαυιδ ὁ δοῦλός μου ἄρχων αὐτῶν ἔσται εἰς τὸν αἰῶνα.

John 12:34

Ἀπεκρίθη οὖν αὐτῷ ὁ ὄχλος· ἡμεῖς ἠκούσαμεν ἐκ τοῦ νόμου ὅτι ὁ χριστὸς μένει εἰς τὸν αἰῶνα, καὶ πῶς λέγεις σὺ ὅτι δεῖ ὑψωθῆναι[1] τὸν υἱὸν τοῦ ἀνθρώπου; τίς ἐστιν οὗτος ὁ υἱὸς τοῦ ἀνθρώπου;

respondit ei turba nos audivimus ex lege quia Christus manet in aeternum et quomodo tu dicis oportet exaltari[2] Filium hominis quis est iste Filius hominis?

1. ὑψόω, aor. pass. inf., *exalt, lift up*

2. exalto, pres. pass. inf., *lift up*

June 19

Isaiah 53:1

מִ֥י הֶאֱמִ֖ין[1] לִשְׁמֻעָתֵ֑נוּ[2] וּזְר֥וֹעַ[3] יְהוָ֖ה עַל־מִ֥י נִגְלָֽתָה׃

κύριε, τίς ἐπίστευσεν[4] τῇ ἀκοῇ[5] ἡμῶν; καὶ ὁ βραχίων κυρίου τίνι ἀπεκαλύφθη;[6]

John 12:37[7]

Τοσαῦτα[8] δὲ αὐτοῦ σημεῖα πεποιηκότος ἔμπροσθεν αὐτῶν οὐκ ἐπίστευον εἰς αὐτόν.

cum autem tanta[9] signa fecisset coram eis non credebant in eum.

1. אָמַן, hiph. perf. 3 m. s., *trust*
2. שְׁמוּעָה, *report*
3. זְרוֹעַ, *arm*
4. πιστεύω, aor. act. ind. 3 s., *believe*
5. ἀκοή, *report*
6. ἀποκαλύπτω, aor. pass. ind. 3 s., *reveal*
7. PA: John cites Isa 53:1 in John 12:38 as a fulfillment of prophecy.
8. τοσοῦτος, *so much, so many*
9. tantus, *so much, so many*

June 20

Psalm 78:2 [LXX 77:2]

אֶפְתְּחָ֣ה בְמָשָׁ֣ל[1] פִּ֑י אַבִּ֥יעָה[2] חִ֝יד֗וֹת[3] מִנִּי־קֶֽדֶם׃[4]

ἀνοίξω ἐν παραβολαῖς[5] τὸ στόμα μου, φθέγξομαι[6]
προβλήματα[7] ἀπ᾽ ἀρχῆς.

Matthew 13:34

ταῦτα πάντα ἐλάλησεν ὁ Ἰησοῦς ἐν παραβολαῖς τοῖς ὄχλοις καὶ χωρὶς παραβολῆς οὐδὲν ἐλάλει αὐτοῖς.

haec omnia locutus est Iesus in parabolis ad turbas et sine parabolis non loquebatur eis.

1. מָשָׁל, *parable*
2. נָבַע, hiph. impf. 1 c. s. coh., *utter*
3. חִידָה, *riddle*
4. קֶ֫דֶם, *ancient times*
5. παραβολή, *parable*
6. φθέγγομαι, fut. mid. ind. 1 s., *utter*
7. πρόβλημα, *riddle*

June 21

Deuteronomy 21:23

לֹֽא־תָלִ֨ין[1] נִבְלָת֜וֹ[2] עַל־הָעֵ֗ץ כִּֽי־קָב֤וֹר תִּקְבְּרֶ֙נּוּ֙ בַּיּ֣וֹם
הַה֔וּא כִּֽי־קִלְלַ֥ת[3] אֱלֹהִ֖ים תָּל֑וּי[4] וְלֹ֤א תְטַמֵּא֙ אֶת־
אַדְמָ֣תְךָ֔ אֲשֶׁר֙ יְהוָ֣ה אֱלֹהֶ֔יךָ נֹתֵ֥ן לְךָ֖ נַחֲלָֽה׃

οὐκ ἐπικοιμηθήσεται[5] τὸ σῶμα αὐτοῦ ἐπὶ τοῦ ξύλου, ἀλλὰ ταφῇ[6] θάψετε αὐτὸν ἐν τῇ ἡμέρᾳ ἐκείνῃ, ὅτι κεκατηραμένος[7] ὑπὸ θεοῦ πᾶς κρεμάμενος[8] ἐπὶ ξύλου·[9] καὶ οὐ μιανεῖτε τὴν γῆν, ἣν κύριος ὁ θεός σου δίδωσίν σοι ἐν κλήρῳ.

Galatians 3:13

Χριστὸς ἡμᾶς ἐξηγόρασεν[10] ἐκ τῆς κατάρας[11] τοῦ νόμου γενόμενος ὑπὲρ ἡμῶν κατάρα, ὅτι γέγραπται· *ἐπικατάρατος*[12] *πᾶς ὁ κρεμάμενος ἐπὶ ξύλου.*

Christus nos redemit[13] de maledicto[14] legis factus pro nobis maledictum quia scriptum est maledictus[15] omnis qui pendet[16] in ligno.[17]

1. לִין, qal impf. 2 m. s., *remain overnight*
2. נְבֵלָה, *corpse*
3. קְלָלָה, *curse*
4. תָּלָה, qal pass. ptcp. m. s. abs., *hang*
5. ἐπικοιμάω, fut. pass. ind. 3 s., *neglect*
6. ταφή, *burial*
7. καταράομαι, perf. pass. ptcp. m. nom. s., *curse*
8. κρεμάω, pres. pass. ptcp. m. nom. s., *hang*
9. ξύλον, *tree, wood*
10. ἐξαγοράζω, aor. act. ind. 3 s., *redeem*
11. κατάρα, *curse*
12. ἐπικατάρατος, *cursed*
13. redimo, perf. act. ind. 3 s., *redeem*
14. maledictum, *curse*
15. maledico, perf. pass. ptcp. m. nom. s., *curse*
16. pendeo, pres. act. ind. 3 s., *hang*
17. lignum, *wood, tree*

Jesus's Baptism and Temptation

June 22

Isaiah 63:19b

לוּא[1]־קָרַעְתָּ[2] שָׁמַיִם יָרַדְתָּ מִפָּנֶיךָ הָרִים נָזֹלּוּ׃[3]

ἐὰν ἀνοίξῃς τὸν οὐρανόν, τρόμος[4] λήμψεται ἀπὸ
σοῦ ὄρη, καὶ τακήσονται.[5]

Mark 1:10

καὶ εὐθὺς ἀναβαίνων ἐκ τοῦ ὕδατος εἶδεν
σχιζομένους[6] τοὺς οὐρανοὺς καὶ τὸ πνεῦμα ὡς
περιστερὰν[7] καταβαῖνον εἰς αὐτόν.

et statim ascendens de aqua vidit apertos
caelos et Spiritum tamquam columbam[8]
descendentem et manentem in ipso.

1. לוּא, *if only*
2. קָרַע, qal perf. 2 m. s., *tear open, rend*
3. זָלַל, niph. perf. 3 c. p., *quake*
4. τρόμος, *quaking, trembling*
5. τήκω, fut. pass. ind. 3 p., *melt, dissolve*
6. σχίζω, pres. pass. ptcp. m. a. p., *split*
7. περιστερά, *dove*
8. columba, *dove*

June 23

Isaiah 42:1

הֵ֤ן[1] עַבְדִּי֙ אֶתְמָךְ[2]־בּ֔וֹ בְּחִירִ֖י[3] רָצְתָ֣ה[4] נַפְשִׁ֑י נָתַ֤תִּי
ר֙וּחִי֙ עָלָ֔יו מִשְׁפָּ֖ט לַגּוֹיִ֥ם יוֹצִֽיא׃

Ιακωβ ὁ παῖς μου, ἀντιλήμψομαι[5] αὐτοῦ· Ισραηλ ὁ ἐκλεκτός[6] μου, προσεδέξατο[7] αὐτὸν ἡ ψυχή μου· ἔδωκα τὸ πνεῦμά μου ἐπ᾽ αὐτόν, κρίσιν τοῖς ἔθνεσιν ἐξοίσει.[8]

Mark 1:11

καὶ φωνὴ ἐγένετο ἐκ τῶν οὐρανῶν· σὺ εἶ ὁ υἱός μου ὁ ἀγαπητός, ἐν σοὶ εὐδόκησα.[9]

et vox facta est de caelis tu es Filius meus dilectus in te conplacui.[10]

1. הֵן, *behold*
2. תָּמַךְ, qal impf. 1 c. s., *uphold, support*
3. בָּחִיר, *chosen*
4. רָצָה, qal perf. 3 f. s., *be pleased with*
5. ἀντιλαμβάνομαι, fut. mid. ind. 1 s., *take hold, support*
6. ἐκλεκτός, *elect, chosen*
7. προσδέχομαι, aor. mid. ind. 3 s., *receive, wait for*
8. ἐκφέρω, fut. act. ind. 3 s., *carry out*
9. εὐδοκέω, aor. act. ind. 1 s., *be well pleased*
10. conplaceo, perf. act. ind. 1 s., *please*

June 24

Deuteronomy 8:3

וַיְעַנְּךָ[1] וַיַּרְעִבֶךָ[2] וַיַּאֲכִלְךָ אֶת־הַמָּן[3] אֲשֶׁר לֹא־יָדַעְתָּ
וְלֹא יָדְעוּן אֲבֹתֶיךָ לְמַעַן הוֹדִעֲךָ כִּי לֹא עַל־הַלֶּחֶם
לְבַדּוֹ יִחְיֶה הָאָדָם כִּי עַל־כָּל־מוֹצָא[4] פִי־יְהוָה
יִחְיֶה הָאָדָם׃

καὶ ἐκάκωσέν[5] σε καὶ ἐλιμαγχόνησέν[6] σε καὶ ἐψώμισέν[7] σε τὸ μαννα,[8] ὃ οὐκ εἴδησαν οἱ πατέρες σου, ἵνα ἀναγγείλῃ σοι ὅτι οὐκ ἐπ᾽ ἄρτῳ μόνῳ ζήσεται ὁ ἄνθρωπος, ἀλλ᾽ ἐπὶ παντὶ ῥήματι τῷ ἐκπορευομένῳ διὰ στόματος θεοῦ ζήσεται ὁ ἄνθρωπος.

Matthew 4:3[9]

καὶ προσελθὼν ὁ πειράζων εἶπεν αὐτῷ· εἰ υἱὸς εἶ τοῦ θεοῦ, εἰπὲ ἵνα οἱ λίθοι οὗτοι ἄρτοι γένωνται.

et accedens temptator[10] dixit ei si Filius Dei es dic ut lapides isti panes fiant.

1. עָנָה, piel wcons. 3 m. s., *humble*
2. רָעֵב, hiph. wcons. 3 m. s., *be hungry, hunger*
3. מָן, *manna*
4. מוֹצָא, *comes from*
5. κακόω, aor. act. ind. 3 s., *afflict, harm*
6. λιμαγχονέω, aor. act. ind. 3 s., *grow weak due to lack of food, let emaciate*
7. ψωμίζω, aor. act. ind. 3 s., *feed*
8. μάννα, *manna*
9. PA: Jesus answers in Matt 4:4 with the words of Deut 8:3.
10. temptator, *tempter, assailant*

June 25

Deuteronomy 6:16

לֹ֣א תְנַסּ֔וּ[1] אֶת־יְהוָ֖ה אֱלֹהֵיכֶ֑ם כַּאֲשֶׁ֥ר נִסִּיתֶ֖ם[2] בַּמַּסָּֽה׃[3]

Οὐκ ἐκπειράσεις[4] κύριον τὸν θεόν σου, ὃν τρόπον ἐξεπειράσασθε[5] ἐν τῷ Πειρασμῷ.[6]

Matthew 4:5–6a[7]

Τότε παραλαμβάνει αὐτὸν ὁ διάβολος εἰς τὴν ἁγίαν πόλιν καὶ ἔστησεν αὐτὸν ἐπὶ τὸ πτερύγιον[8] τοῦ ἱεροῦ καὶ λέγει αὐτῷ· εἰ υἱὸς εἶ τοῦ θεοῦ, βάλε σεαυτὸν κάτω.[9]

tunc adsumit eum diabolus in sanctam civitatem et statuit[10] eum supra pinnaculum[11] templi et dixit ei si Filius Dei es mitte te deorsum.[12]

1. נָסָה, piel impf. 2 m. p., *test, tempt*
2. נָסָה, piel perf. 2 m. p., *test, tempt*
3. מַסָּה, *Massah, (place of) testing, trial*
4. ἐκπειράζω, fut. act. ind. 2 s., *test, tempt*
5. ἐκπειράζω, aor. mid. ind. 2 p., *test, tempt*
6. πειρασμός, *temptation, test, trial, Peirasmo*
7. PA: Jesus responds with the words of Deut 6:16 in Matt 4:7.
8. πτερυγίον, *apex, pinnacle, tip*
9. κατώ, *down*
10. statuo, pres. act. ind. 3 s., *cause to stand, set*
11. pinnaculum, *pinnacle*
12. deorsum, *down*

June 26

Deuteronomy 6:13

אֶת־יְהוָ֧ה אֱלֹהֶ֛יךָ תִּירָ֖א וְאֹת֣וֹ תַעֲבֹ֑ד וּבִשְׁמ֖וֹ תִּשָּׁבֵֽעַ׃

κύριον τὸν θεόν σου φοβηθήσῃ καὶ αὐτῷ λατρεύσεις[1] καὶ πρὸς αὐτὸν κολληθήσῃ[2] καὶ τῷ ὀνόματι αὐτοῦ ὀμῇ.

Matthew 4:9[3]

καὶ εἶπεν αὐτῷ· ταῦτά[4] σοι πάντα δώσω, ἐὰν πεσὼν προσκυνήσῃς μοι.

et dixit illi haec[5] tibi omnia dabo si cadens adoraveris me.

1. λατρεύω, fut. act. ind. 2 s., *serve, worship*

2. κολλάω, fut. pass. ind. 2 s., *join oneself to, firmly fasten, fix*

3. PA: Jesus responds to the devil in Matt 4:10 with Deut 6:13.

4. CH: This pronoun refers to all the nations of the world.

5. CH: This pronoun refers to all the nations of the world.

June 27

Isaiah 53:3

נִבְזֶה[1] וַחֲדַל[2] אִישִׁים אִישׁ מַכְאֹבוֹת[3] וִידוּעַ חֹלִי[4]
וּכְמַסְתֵּר[5] פָּנִים מִמֶּנּוּ נִבְזֶה[6] וְלֹא חֲשַׁבְנֻהוּ׃

ἀλλὰ τὸ εἶδος[7] αὐτοῦ ἄτιμον ἐκλεῖπον παρὰ πάντας ἀνθρώπους, ἄνθρωπος ἐν πληγῇ[8] ὢν καὶ εἰδὼς φέρειν μαλακίαν,[9] ὅτι ἀπέστραπται τὸ πρόσωπον αὐτοῦ, ἠτιμάσθη[10] καὶ οὐκ ἐλογίσθη.

Hebrews 4:15

οὐ γὰρ ἔχομεν ἀρχιερέα μὴ δυνάμενον συμπαθῆσαι[11] ταῖς ἀσθενείαις[12] ἡμῶν, πεπειρασμένον δὲ κατὰ πάντα καθ᾽ ὁμοιότητα[13] χωρὶς ἁμαρτίας.

non enim habemus pontificem qui non possit conpati[14] infirmitatibus[15] nostris temptatum autem per omnia pro similitudine[16] absque[17] peccato.

1. בָּזָה, niph. ptcp. m. s. abs., *despise*
2. חָדֵל, *rejected*
3. מַכְאֹב, *sorrow*
4. חֳלִי, *grief, sickness*
5. מִסְתָּר, *hiding*
6. בָּזָה, niph. ptcp. m. s. abs., *despise*
7. εἶδος, *appearance, form*
8. πληγή, *blow, wound*
9. μαλακία, *sickness*
10. ἀτιμάζω, aor. pass. ind. 3 s., *dishonor*
11. συμπαθέω, aor. act. inf., *sympathize*
12. ἀσθένεια, *weakness*
13. ὁμοιότης, *as, like*
14. conpatior, pres. dep. inf., *have compassion*
15. infirmitas, *infirmity*
16. similitudo, *likeness*
17. absque, *without*

June 28

Deuteronomy 6:5

וְאָ֣הַבְתָּ֔ אֵ֖ת יְהוָ֣ה אֱלֹהֶ֑יךָ בְּכָל־לְבָבְךָ֥ וּבְכָל־נַפְשְׁךָ֖
וּבְכָל־מְאֹדֶֽךָ׃

καὶ ἀγαπήσεις κύριον τὸν θεόν σου ἐξ ὅλης τῆς καρδίας σου καὶ ἐξ ὅλης τῆς ψυχῆς σου καὶ ἐξ ὅλης τῆς δυνάμεώς σου.

Mark 12:28[1]

Καὶ προσελθὼν εἷς τῶν γραμματέων ἀκούσας αὐτῶν συζητούντων,[2] ἰδὼν ὅτι καλῶς ἀπεκρίθη αὐτοῖς ἐπηρώτησεν αὐτόν· ποία ἐστὶν ἐντολὴ πρώτη πάντων;

et accessit unus de scribis qui audierat illos conquirentes[3] et videns quoniam bene illis responderit interrogavit eum quod esset primum omnium mandatum.

1. PA: Jesus's response in the subsequent verse is taken from Deut 6:5.

2. συζητέω, pres. act. ptcp. m. g. p., *argue, dispute*

3. conquiro, pres. act. ptcp. m. a. p., *inquire*

June 29

Leviticus 19:18

לֹא־תִקֹּם[1] וְלֹא־תִטֹּר[2] אֶת־בְּנֵי עַמֶּךָ וְאָהַבְתָּ לְרֵעֲךָ
כָּמוֹךָ אֲנִי יְהוָה׃

καὶ οὐκ ἐκδικᾶταί[3] σου ἡ χείρ, καὶ οὐ μηνιεῖς[4] τοῖς υἱοῖς τοῦ λαοῦ σου καὶ ἀγαπήσεις τὸν πλησίον[5] σου ὡς σεαυτόν· ἐγώ εἰμι κύριος.

Mark 12:31

δευτέρα αὕτη· *ἀγαπήσεις τὸν πλησίον σου ὡς σεαυτόν.* μείζων τούτων ἄλλη ἐντολὴ οὐκ ἔστιν.

secundum autem simile illi diliges proximum[6] tuum tamquam te ipsum maius horum aliud mandatum non est.

1. נָקַם, qal impf. 2 m. s., *avenge*
2. נָטַר, qal impf. 2 m. s., *keep (a grudge)*
3. ἐκδικάζω, fut. mid. ind. 3 s., *avenge*
4. μηνίω, fut. act. ind. 2 s., *be angry, hold a grudge*
5. πλησίον, *neighbor*
6. propior, *near one, neighbor*

June 30

Exodus 20:13 [LXX 20:15]

לֹ֖א תִּֿרְצָֽח׃[1]

οὐ φονεύσεις.[2]

Matthew 5:22

ἐγὼ δὲ λέγω ὑμῖν ὅτι πᾶς ὁ ὀργιζόμενος[3] τῷ ἀδελφῷ αὐτοῦ ἔνοχος[4] ἔσται τῇ κρίσει· ὃς δ᾽ ἂν εἴπῃ τῷ ἀδελφῷ αὐτοῦ· ῥακά,[5] ἔνοχος ἔσται τῷ συνεδρίῳ·[6] ὃς δ᾽ ἂν εἴπῃ· μωρέ,[7] ἔνοχος ἔσται εἰς τὴν γέενναν[8] τοῦ πυρός.

ego autem dico vobis quia omnis qui irascitur[9] fratri suo reus[10] erit iudicio qui autem dixerit fratri suo racha[11] reus erit concilio[12] qui autem dixerit fatue[13] reus erit gehennae[14] ignis.

1. רָצַח, qal impf. 2 m. s., *murder*
2. φονεύω, fut. act. ind. 2 s., *murder*
3. ὀργίζω, pres. mid. ptcp. m. nom. s., *be angry*
4. ἔνοχος, *guilty, liable*
5. ῥακά, *fool*
6. συνέδριον, *council, Sanhedrin*
7. μωρός, *foolish, stupid*
8. γέεννα, *gehenna*
9. irascor, pres. dep. ind. 3 s., *be angry*
10. reus, *liable, guilty*
11. racha, *fool*
12. concilium, *council*
13. fatuus, *foolish, idiotic*
14. gehenna, *gehenna*

July 1

Exodus 20:14 [LXX 20:13]

לֹ֥א תִּֿנְאָֽף׃[1]

οὐ μοιχεύσεις.[2]

Matthew 5:28

ἐγὼ δὲ λέγω ὑμῖν ὅτι πᾶς ὁ βλέπων γυναῖκα πρὸς τὸ ἐπιθυμῆσαι[3] αὐτὴν ἤδη ἐμοίχευσεν[4] αὐτὴν ἐν τῇ καρδίᾳ αὐτοῦ.

ego autem dico vobis quoniam omnis qui viderit mulierem ad concupiscendum[5] eam iam moechatus[6] est eam in corde suo.

1. נָאַף, qal impf. 2 m. s., *commit adultery*
2. μοιχεύω, fut. act. ind. 2 s., *commit adultery*
3. ἐπιθυμέω, aor. act. inf., *desire*
4. μοιχεύω, aor. act. ind. 3 s., *commit adultery*
5. concupisco, ger. act. n. a. s., *desire, covet*
6. moechor, perf. dep. ind. 3 s., *commit adultery*

July 2

Deuteronomy 24:1

כִּֽי־יִקַּ֥ח אִ֛ישׁ אִשָּׁ֖ה וּבְעָלָ֑הּ[1] וְהָיָ֗ה אִם־לֹ֤א תִֽמְצָא־
חֵן֙[2] בְּעֵינָ֔יו כִּי־מָ֥צָא בָהּ֙ עֶרְוַ֣ת[3] דָּבָ֔ר וְכָ֨תַב לָ֜הּ סֵ֤פֶר
כְּרִיתֻת֙[4] וְנָתַ֣ן בְּיָדָ֔הּ וְשִׁלְּחָ֖הּ מִבֵּיתֽוֹ׃

Ἐὰν δέ τις λάβῃ γυναῖκα καὶ συνοικήσῃ[5] αὐτῇ, καὶ ἔσται ἐὰν μὴ εὕρῃ χάριν ἐναντίον αὐτοῦ, ὅτι εὗρεν ἐν αὐτῇ ἄσχημον[6] πρᾶγμα, καὶ γράψει αὐτῇ βιβλίον ἀποστασίου[7] καὶ δώσει εἰς τὰς χεῖρας αὐτῆς καὶ ἐξαποστελεῖ αὐτὴν ἐκ τῆς οἰκίας αὐτοῦ.

Matthew 5:32

ἐγὼ δὲ λέγω ὑμῖν ὅτι πᾶς ὁ ἀπολύων τὴν γυναῖκα αὐτοῦ παρεκτὸς[8] λόγου πορνείας[9] ποιεῖ αὐτὴν μοιχευθῆναι,[10] καὶ ὃς ἐὰν ἀπολελυμένην γαμήσῃ,[11] μοιχᾶται.[12]

ego autem dico vobis quia omnis qui dimiserit uxorem suam excepta[13] fornicationis[14] causa facit eam moechari[15] et qui dimissam duxerit adulterat.[16]

1. בָּעַל, qal perf. 3 m. s., *marry*

2. חֵן, *favor, acceptance*

3. עֶרְוָה, *indecency, improper behavior*

4. כְּרִיתוּת, *divorce*

5. συνοικέω, aor. act. subj. 3 s., *dwell together*

6. ἀσχήμων, *indecent, unseemly*

7. ἀποστάσιον, *divorce notice*

8. παρεκτός, *except, with the exception of*

9. πορνεία, *fornication, adultery*

10. μοιχεύω, aor. pass. inf., *commit adultery*

11. γαμέω, aor. act. subj. 3 s., *marry*

12. μοιχεύω, aor. mid. ind. 3 s., *commit adultery*

13. excipio, perf. pass. ptcp. f. abl. s., *except, take out*

14. fornicatio, *fornication, prostitution*

15. moechor, pres. dep. inf., *commit adultery*

16. adultero, pres. act. ind. 3 s., *commit adultery*

July 3

Numbers 30:3

אִישׁ כִּי־יִדֹּר[1] נֶדֶר[2] לַיהוָה אוֹ־הִשָּׁבַע שְׁבֻעָה[3]
לֶאְסֹר אִסָּר[4] עַל־נַפְשׁוֹ לֹא יַחֵל דְּבָרוֹ כְּכָל־הַיֹּצֵא
מִפִּיו יַעֲשֶׂה׃

ἄνθρωπος ἄνθρωπος, ὃς ἂν εὔξηται[5] εὐχὴν[6] κυρίῳ ἢ ὀμόσῃ ὅρκον[7] ἢ ὁρίσηται[8] ὁρισμῷ[9] περὶ τῆς ψυχῆς αὐτοῦ, οὐ βεβηλώσει[10] τὸ ῥῆμα αὐτοῦ· πάντα, ὅσα ἐὰν ἐξέλθῃ ἐκ τοῦ στόματος αὐτοῦ, ποιήσει.

Matthew 5:37

ἔστω δὲ ὁ λόγος ὑμῶν ναὶ ναί, οὒ οὔ· τὸ δὲ περισσὸν[11] τούτων ἐκ τοῦ πονηροῦ ἐστιν.

sit autem sermo vester est est non non quod autem his abundantius[12] est a malo est.

1. נָדַר, qal impf. 3 m. s., *vow*
2. נֶדֶר, *vow, oath*
3. שְׁבוּעָה, *oath*
4. אִסָּר, *obligation, pledge*
5. εὔχομαι, aor. mid. subj. 3 s., *vow, pray*
6. εὐχή, *vow, prayer*
7. ὅρκος, *oath, vow*
8. ὁρίζω, aor. mid. subj. 3 s., *determine*
9. ὁρισμός, *fixed course, determination*
10. βεβηλόω, fut. act. ind. 3 s., *desecrate, profane*
11. περισσός, *more than, exceeding*
12. abundans, *abundant, overflowing*

July 4

Exodus 21:24

עַ֚יִן תַּ֣חַת עַ֔יִן שֵׁ֖ן[1] תַּ֣חַת שֵׁ֑ן יָ֚ד תַּ֣חַת יָ֔ד רֶ֖גֶל תַּ֥חַת רָֽגֶל׃

ὀφθαλμὸν ἀντὶ ὀφθαλμοῦ, ὀδόντα[2] ἀντὶ ὀδόντος, χεῖρα ἀντὶ χειρός, πόδα ἀντὶ ποδός.

Matthew 5:39

ἐγὼ δὲ λέγω ὑμῖν μὴ ἀντιστῆναι[3] τῷ πονηρῷ· ἀλλ᾽ ὅστις σε ῥαπίζει[4] εἰς τὴν δεξιὰν σιαγόνα[5] [σου], στρέψον[6] αὐτῷ καὶ τὴν ἄλλην.

ego autem dico vobis non resistere[7] malo sed si quis te percusserit in dextera[8] maxilla[9] tua praebe[10] illi et alteram.

1. שֵׁן, *tooth*
2. ὀδούς, *tooth*
3. ἀνθίστημι, aor. act. inf., *resist*
4. ῥαπίζω, pres. act. ind. 3 s., *slap, hint*
5. σιαγών, *cheek, jaw*
6. στρέφω, aor. act. impv. 2 s., *turn*
7. resisto, pres. act. inf., *resist, oppose*
8. dexter, *right*
9. maxilla, *cheek, jaw*
10. praebeo, pres. act. impv. 2 s., *offer, present*

July 5

Deuteronomy 15:7

כִּֽי־יִהְיֶ֨ה בְךָ֜ אֶבְי֗וֹן[1] מֵאַחַ֤ד אַחֶ֙יךָ֙ בְּאַחַ֣ד שְׁעָרֶ֔יךָ
בְּאַ֨רְצְךָ֔ אֲשֶׁר־יְהוָ֥ה אֱלֹהֶ֖יךָ נֹתֵ֣ן לָ֑ךְ לֹ֧א תְאַמֵּ֣ץ[2] אֶת־
לְבָבְךָ֗ וְלֹ֤א תִקְפֹּץ֙[3] אֶת־יָ֣דְךָ֔ מֵאָחִ֖יךָ הָאֶבְיֽוֹן׃

Ἐὰν δὲ γένηται ἐν σοὶ ἐνδεὴς[4] τῶν ἀδελφῶν σου ἐν μιᾷ τῶν πόλεών σου ἐν τῇ γῇ, ᾗ κύριος ὁ θεός σου δίδωσίν σοι, οὐκ ἀποστέρξεις[5] τὴν καρδίαν σου οὐδ᾽ οὐ μὴ συσφίγξῃς[6] τὴν χεῖρά σου ἀπὸ τοῦ ἀδελφοῦ σου τοῦ ἐπιδεομένου.[7]

Matthew 5:42

τῷ αἰτοῦντί σε δός, καὶ τὸν θέλοντα ἀπὸ σοῦ δανίσασθαι[8] μὴ ἀποστραφῇς.[9]

qui petit a te da ei et volenti mutuari[10] a te ne avertaris.[11]

1. אֶבְיוֹן, *needy, poor*

2. אָמֵץ, piel impf. 2 m. s., *harden*

3. קָפַץ, qal impf. 2 m. s., *shut*

4. ἐνδεής, *needy, lacking*

5. ἀποστέργω, fut. act. ind. 2 s., *harden*

6. συσφίγγω, aor. act. subj. 2 s., *harden, close off*

7. ἐπιδέομαι, pres. mid. ptcp. m. g. s., *be in need*

8. δανείζω, pres. mid. inf., *lend money*

9. ἀποστρέφω, aor. pass. subj. 2 s., *refuse, turn away*

10. mutuor, pres. dep. inf., *borrow*

11. averto, pres. pass. subj. 3 s., *turn away*

July 6

Deuteronomy 18:13

תָּמִים[1] תִּהְיֶה עִם יְהוָה אֱלֹהֶיךָ׃

τέλειος[2] ἔσῃ ἐναντίον κυρίου τοῦ θεοῦ σου.

Matthew 5:48

ἔσεσθε οὖν ὑμεῖς τέλειοι ὡς ὁ πατὴρ ὑμῶν ὁ οὐράνιος[3] τέλειός ἐστιν.

estote ergo vos perfecti sicut et Pater vester caelestis[4] perfectus est.

1. תָּמִים, perfect
2. τέλειος, *perfect*
3. οὐράνιος, *heavenly*
4. caelestis, *heavenly*

July 7

Deuteronomy 23:25

כִּ֤י תָבֹא֙ בְּכֶ֣רֶם[1] רֵעֶ֔ךָ וְאָכַלְתָּ֧ עֲנָבִ֛ים[2] כְּנַפְשְׁךָ֖
שָׂבְעֶ֑ךָ[3] וְאֶֽל־כֶּלְיְךָ֖ לֹ֥א תִתֵּֽן׃

Ἐὰν δὲ εἰσέλθῃς εἰς ἀμητὸν[4] τοῦ πλησίον σου, καὶ συλλέξεις[5] ἐν ταῖς χερσίν σου στάχυς[6] καὶ δρέπανον[7] οὐ μὴ ἐπιβάλῃς[8] ἐπὶ τὸν ἀμητὸν τοῦ πλησίον σου.

Matthew 12:1

Ἐν ἐκείνῳ τῷ καιρῷ ἐπορεύθη ὁ Ἰησοῦς τοῖς σάββασιν διὰ τῶν σπορίμων·[9] οἱ δὲ μαθηταὶ αὐτοῦ ἐπείνασαν[10] καὶ ἤρξαντο τίλλειν[11] στάχυας[12] καὶ ἐσθίειν.

in illo tempore abiit Iesus sabbato per sata[13] discipuli autem eius esurientes[14] coeperunt vellere[15] spicas[16] et manducare.

1. כֶּרֶם, *vineyard*
2. עֵנָב, *grape*
3. שָׂבַע, *satisfy, satiate*
4. ἄμητος, *crop*
5. συλλέγω, fut. act. ind. 2 s., *gather, collect*
6. στάχυς, *ears of grain*
7. δρέπανον, *sickle*
8. ἐπιβάλλω, aor. act. subj. 2 s., *cast, throw*
9. σπόριμος, *grainfield*
10. πεινάω, aor. act. ind. 3 p., *be hungry*
11. τίλλω, pres. act. inf., *pluck*
12. στάχυς, *grain*
13. sero, perf. pass. ptcp. n. a. p., *pluck; plant, sow*
14. esurio, pres. act. ptcp. m. nom. p., *be hungry*
15. vello, pres. act. inf., *pluck*
16. spica, *ear of grain*

July 8

Genesis 38:8

וַיֹּ֤אמֶר יְהוּדָה֙ לְאוֹנָ֔ן[1] בֹּ֛א אֶל־אֵ֥שֶׁת אָחִ֖יךָ וְיַבֵּ֣ם[2]
אֹתָ֑הּ וְהָקֵ֥ם זֶ֖רַע לְאָחִֽיךָ׃

εἶπεν δὲ Ιουδας τῷ Αυναν[3] Εἴσελθε πρὸς τὴν γυναῖκα τοῦ ἀδελφοῦ σου καὶ γάμβρευσαι[4] αὐτὴν καὶ ἀνάστησον σπέρμα τῷ ἀδελφῷ σου.

Mark 12:19[5]

διδάσκαλε, Μωϋσῆς ἔγραψεν ἡμῖν ὅτι ἐάν τινος ἀδελφὸς ἀποθάνῃ καὶ καταλίπῃ[6] γυναῖκα καὶ μὴ ἀφῇ τέκνον, ἵνα λάβῃ ὁ ἀδελφὸς αὐτοῦ τὴν γυναῖκα καὶ ἐξαναστήσῃ[7] σπέρμα τῷ ἀδελφῷ αὐτοῦ.

magister Moses nobis scripsit ut si cuius frater mortuus fuerit et dimiserit uxorem et filios non reliquerit accipiat frater eius uxorem ipsius et resuscitet[8] semen fratri suo.

1. אוֹנָן, *Onan*

2. יבם, piel impf. 2 m. s., *marry one's sister-in-law*

3. Αυναν, *Onan*

4. γαμβρεύω, aor. mid. impv. 2 s., *marry*

5. PA: Here the religious leaders challenge Jesus with his understanding of the law and of the resurrection. They present him with a situation where seven brothers have the same wife. Whose wife is she in the resurrection?

6. καταλείπω, aor. act. subj. 3 s., *leave behind*

7. ἐξανίστημι, aor. act. subj. 3 s., *raise up*

8. resuscito, pres. act. subj. 3 s., *raise up*

Jesus's Ministry

July 9

Ezekiel 34:16

אֶת־הָאֹבֶדֶת אֲבַקֵּשׁ וְאֶת־הַנִּדַּחַת[1] אָשִׁיב וְלַנִּשְׁבֶּרֶת
אֶחֱבֹשׁ[2] וְאֶת־הַחוֹלָה[3] אֲחַזֵּק וְאֶת־הַשְּׁמֵנָה[4] וְאֶת־
הַחֲזָקָה[5] אַשְׁמִיד[6] אֶרְעֶנָּה בְמִשְׁפָּט׃

Τὸ ἀπολωλὸς ζητήσω καὶ τὸ πλανώμενον ἐπιστρέψω καὶ τὸ συντετριμμένον καταδήσω[7] καὶ τὸ ἐκλεῖπον ἐνισχύσω[8] καὶ τὸ ἰσχυρὸν φυλάξω καὶ βοσκήσω[9] αὐτὰ μετὰ κρίματος.

Luke 19:10

ἦλθεν γὰρ ὁ υἱὸς τοῦ ἀνθρώπου ζητῆσαι καὶ σῶσαι τὸ ἀπολωλός.

venit enim Filius hominis quaerere et salvum facere quod perierat.

1. נָדַח, niph. ptcp. f. s. abs., *banish, drive away*
2. חָבַשׁ, qal impf. 1 c. s., *bind*
3. חָלָה, qal ptcp. f. s. abs., *be sick*
4. שָׁמֵן, *fat*
5. חָזָק, *strong*
6. שָׁמַד, hiph. impf. 1 c. s., *destroy*; TC: Notice what verb the LXX uses here.
7. καταδέω, fut. act. ind. 1 s., *bind up*
8. ἐνισχύω, fut. act. ind. 1 s., *strengthen*
9. βόσκω, fut. act. ind. 1 s., *feed, graze*

July 10

Psalm 69:10 [LXX 68:10]

כִּֽי־קִנְאַ֣ת[1] בֵּיתְךָ֣ אֲכָלָ֑תְנִי וְחֶרְפּ֥וֹת[2] ח֝וֹרְפֶ֗יךָ[3] נָפְל֥וּ עָלָֽי׃

ὅτι ὁ ζῆλος[4] τοῦ οἴκου σου κατέφαγέν με, καὶ οἱ ὀνειδισμοὶ[5] τῶν ὀνειδιζόντων[6] σε ἐπέπεσαν[7] ἐπ᾽ ἐμέ.

John 2:15[8]

καὶ ποιήσας φραγέλλιον[9] ἐκ σχοινίων[10] πάντας ἐξέβαλεν ἐκ τοῦ ἱεροῦ τά τε πρόβατα καὶ τοὺς βόας,[11] καὶ τῶν κολλυβιστῶν[12] ἐξέχεεν[13] τὸ κέρμα[14] καὶ τὰς τραπέζας[15] ἀνέτρεψεν.[16]

et cum fecisset quasi flagellum[17] de funiculis[18] omnes eiecit de templo oves quoque[19] et boves[20] et nummulariorum[21] effudit[22] aes[23] et mensas[24] subvertit.[25]

1. קִנְאָה, *zeal*
2. חֶרְפָּה, *reproach*
3. חָרַף, qal ptcp. m. p. cons., *reproach*
4. ζῆλος, *zeal*
5. ὀνειδισμός, *reproach*
6. ὀνειδίζω, pres. act. ptcp. m. g. p., *reproach*
7. ἐπιπίπτω, aor. act. ind. 3 p., *fall*
8. PA: Jesus's disciples recalled the words of this psalm in connection with Jesus's actions in the temple.
9. φραγέλλιον, *whip*
10. σχοινίον, *rope*
11. βοῦς, *ox*
12. κολλυβιστής, *money changer*
13. ἐκχέω, aor. act. ind. 3 s., *pour out*
14. κέρμα, *money, coin*
15. τραπέζα, *table*
16. ἀνατρέπω, aor. act. ind. 3 s., *overturn*
17. flagellum, *whip*
18. funiculus, *small cord*
19. quoque, *also*
20. bos, *ox*

21. nummularius, *money changer.* **22.** effundo, perf. act. ind. 3 s., *pour out.* **23.** aes, *money.* **24.** mensa, *table.* **25.** subverto, pres. act. ind. 3 s., *overturn*

July 11

Proverbs 30:4

מִֽי עָלָֽה־שָׁמַ֨יִם ׀ וַיֵּרַ֡ד מִ֤י אָֽסַף־ר֨וּחַ ׀ בְּחָפְנָ֗יו[1] מִ֤י
צָֽרַר[2]־מַ֨יִם ׀ בַּשִּׂמְלָ֗ה[3] מִ֣י הֵ֭קִים כָּל־אַפְסֵי[4]־אָ֑רֶץ
מַה־שְּׁמ֥וֹ וּמַה־שֶּׁם־בְּ֝נ֗וֹ כִּ֣י תֵדָֽע׃

τίς ἀνέβη εἰς τὸν οὐρανὸν καὶ κατέβη; τίς συνήγαγεν ἀνέμους[5] ἐν κόλπῳ;[6] τίς συνέστρεψεν[7] ὕδωρ ἐν ἱματίῳ; τίς ἐκράτησεν πάντων τῶν ἄκρων[8] τῆς γῆς; τί ὄνομα αὐτῷ, ἢ τί ὄνομα τοῖς τέκνοις αὐτοῦ, ἵνα γνῷς;

John 3:13

καὶ οὐδεὶς ἀναβέβηκεν εἰς τὸν οὐρανὸν εἰ μὴ ὁ ἐκ τοῦ οὐρανοῦ καταβάς, ὁ υἱὸς τοῦ ἀνθρώπου.

et nemo ascendit in caelum nisi qui descendit de caelo Filius hominis qui est in caelo

1. חֹפֶן, *handful*
2. צָרַר, qal perf. 3 m. s., *bind*
3. שִׂמְלָה, *garment*
4. אֶפֶס, *end*
5. ἄνεμος, *wind*
6. κόλπος, *bosom*
7. συστρέφω, aor. act. ind. 3 s., *gather, tie up, wrap*
8. ἄκρος, *highest part*

July 12

Isaiah 57:15

כִּי֩ כֹ֨ה אָמַ֜ר רָ֣ם וְנִשָּׂ֗א שֹׁכֵ֥ן עַד֙[1] וְקָד֣וֹשׁ שְׁמ֔וֹ מָר֥וֹם[2]
וְקָד֖וֹשׁ אֶשְׁכּ֑וֹן וְאֶת־דַּכָּא֙[3] וּשְׁפַל[4]־ר֔וּחַ לְהַחֲיוֹת֙ ר֣וּחַ
שְׁפָלִ֔ים וּֽלְהַחֲי֖וֹת לֵ֥ב נִדְכָּאִֽים׃[5]

Τάδε λέγει κύριος ὁ ὕψιστος ὁ ἐν ὑψηλοῖς κατοικῶν τὸν αἰῶνα, ἅγιος ἐν ἁγίοις ὄνομα αὐτῷ, κύριος ὕψιστος ἐν ἁγίοις ἀναπαυόμενος[6] καὶ ὀλιγοψύχοις[7] διδοὺς μακροθυμίαν[8] καὶ διδοὺς ζωὴν τοῖς συντετριμμένοις τὴν καρδίαν.

Matthew 5:3

Μακάριοι οἱ πτωχοὶ τῷ πνεύματι, ὅτι αὐτῶν ἐστιν ἡ βασιλεία τῶν οὐρανῶν.

beati pauperes[9] spiritu quoniam ipsorum est regnum caelorum.

1. עַד, *eternity, forever*
2. מָרוֹם, *high*
3. דַּכָּא, *crushed, contrite*
4. שָׁפָל, *low, lowly*
5. דָּכָא, niph. ptcp. m. abs. p., *crush;* TH: contrite ones
6. ἀναπαύω, pres. mid. ptcp. m. nom. s., *rest*
7. ὀλιγοψύχος, *fainthearted, discouraged*
8. μακροθυμία, *long-suffering, patient*
9. pauper, *poor*

July 13

Isaiah 61:1a, 2

רוּחַ אֲדֹנָי יְהוִה עָלָי יַעַן[1] מָשַׁח[2] יְהוָה אֹתִי לְבַשֵּׂר[3]
עֲנָוִים[4]. . . לִקְרֹא שְׁנַת־רָצוֹן[5] לַיהוָה וְיוֹם נָקָם[6]
לֵאלֹהֵינוּ לְנַחֵם כָּל־אֲבֵלִים׃[7]

Πνεῦμα κυρίου ἐπ᾽ ἐμέ. . . . εὐαγγελίσασθαι[8] πτωχοῖς ἀπέσταλκέν με . . . καλέσαι ἐνιαυτὸν κυρίου δεκτὸν[9] καὶ ἡμέραν ἀνταποδόσεως,[10] παρακαλέσαι πάντας τοὺς πενθοῦντας.[11]

Matthew 5:4 [Vulgata 5:5]

μακάριοι οἱ πενθοῦντες,[12] ὅτι αὐτοὶ παρακληθήσονται.

beati qui lugent[13] quoniam ipsi consolabuntur.[14]

1. יַעַן, *because*

2. מָשַׁח, qal perf. 3 m. s., *anoint*

3. בָּשַׂר, piel inf. cons., *bring good news*

4. עָנָו, *poor, meek*

5. רָצוֹן, *favor*

6. נָקָם, *vengeance*

7. אֵבֶל, *mourning*

8. εὐαγγελίζω, aor. mid. inf., *proclaim/bring good news*

9. δεκτός, *acceptable*

10. ἀνταπόδοσις, *retribution, repayment*

11. πενθέω, pres. act. ptcp. m. a. p., *mourn, lament*

12. πενθέω, pres. act. ptcp. m. nom. p., *mourn, lament*

13. lugeo, pres. act. ind. 3 s., *mourn, lament*

14. consolor, fut. dep. ind. 3 s., *comfort, console*

July 14

Psalm 37:11 [LXX 36:11]

וַעֲנָוִים[1] יִֽירְשׁוּ־אָ֑רֶץ וְ֝הִתְעַנְּגוּ[2] עַל־רֹ֥ב שָׁלֽוֹם׃

οἱ δὲ πραεῖς[3] κληρονομήσουσιν[4] γῆν καὶ κατατρυφήσουσιν[5] ἐπὶ πλήθει εἰρήνης.

Matthew 5:5 [Vulgata 5:4]

μακάριοι οἱ πραεῖς, ὅτι αὐτοὶ κληρονομήσουσιντὴν γῆν.

beati mites[6] quoniam ipsi possidebunt[7] terram.

1. עָנָו, *poor, meek*
2. עָנֹג, hithpael perf. 3 c. p., *take delight*
3. πραΰς, *gentle, meek*
4. κληρονομέω, fut. act. ind. 3 p., *inherit*
5. κατατρυφάω, fut. act. ind. 3 p., *delight in*
6. mitis, *gentle, mild*
7. possideo, fut. act. ind. 3 p., *possess, inherit*

July 15

Isaiah 55:1

הֹ֤וי[1] כָּל־צָמֵא֙[2] לְכ֣וּ לַמַּ֔יִם וַאֲשֶׁ֥ר אֵין־ל֖וֹ כָּ֑סֶף לְכ֤וּ
שִׁבְרוּ֙[3] וֶֽאֱכֹ֔לוּ וּלְכ֣וּ שִׁבְר֗וּ בְּלוֹא־כֶ֛סֶף וּבְל֥וֹא מְחִ֖יר[4]
יַ֥יִן וְחָלָֽב׃[5]

Οἱ διψῶντες,[6] πορεύεσθε ἐφ᾽ ὕδωρ, καὶ ὅσοι μὴ ἔχετε ἀργύριον, βαδίσαντες[7] ἀγοράσατε[8] καὶ πίετε ἄνευ[9] ἀργυρίου καὶ τιμῆς[10] οἴνου καὶ στέαρ.[11]

Matthew 5:6

μακάριοι οἱ πεινῶντες[12] καὶ διψῶντες[13] τὴν δικαιοσύνην, ὅτι αὐτοὶ χορτασθήσονται.[14]

beati qui esuriunt[15] et sitiunt[16] iustitiam quoniam ipsi saturabuntur.[17]

1. הוֹי, *come*
2. צָמֵא, *thirsty*
3. שָׁבַר, qal impv. m. p., *buy*
4. מְחִיר, *price*
5. חָלָב, *milk*
6. διψάω, pres. act. ptcp. m. nom. p., *thirst*
7. βαδίζω, aor. act. ptcp. m. nom. p., *go*
8. ἀγοράζω, aor. act. impv. 2 p., *buy*
9. ἄνευ, *without*
10. τιμή, *price*
11. στέαρ, *fat*
12. πεινάω, pres. act. ptcp. m. nom. p., *be hungry*
13. διψάω, pres. act. ptcp. m. nom. p., *thirst*
14. χορτάζω, fut. pass. ind. 3 p., *be filled, satisfied*
15. esurio, pres. act. ind. 3 p., *be hungry*
16. sitio, pres. act. ind. 3 p., *be thirsty*
17. saturo, fut. pass. ind. 3 p., *be satisfied, filled*

July 16

Isaiah 51:7

שִׁמְעוּ אֵלַי יֹדְעֵי צֶדֶק עַם תּוֹרָתִי בְלִבָּם אַל־תִּירְאוּ
חֶרְפַּת[1] אֱנוֹשׁ[2] וּמִגִּדֻּפֹתָם[3] אַל־תֵּחָתּוּ׃[4]

ἀκούσατέ μου, οἱ εἰδότες κρίσιν, λαός μου, οὗ ὁ νόμος μου ἐν τῇ καρδίᾳ ὑμῶν· μὴ φοβεῖσθε ὀνειδισμὸν[5] ἀνθρώπων καὶ τῷ φαυλισμῷ[6] αὐτῶν μὴ ἡττᾶσθε.[7]

Matthew 5:11

μακάριοί ἐστε ὅταν ὀνειδίσωσιν[8] ὑμᾶς καὶ διώξωσιν καὶ εἴπωσιν πᾶν πονηρὸν καθ᾽ ὑμῶν [ψευδόμενοι][9] ἕνεκεν[10] ἐμοῦ.

beati estis cum maledixerint[11] vobis et persecuti[12] vos fuerint et dixerint omne malum adversum[13] vos mentientes[14] propter me.

1. חֶרְפָּה, *reproach*
2. אֱנוֹשׁ, *man*
3. גִּדּוּפָה, *taunt, reviling*
4. חָתַת, niph. impf. 2 m. p. juss., *be shattered, dismayed*
5. ὀνειδισμός, *disgrace, insult*
6. φαυλισμός, *contempt, contemptibility*
7. ἡττάω, pres. mid. impv. 2 p., *overcome*
8. ὀνειδίζω, aor. act. subj. 3 p., *reproach, revile*
9. ψεύδομαι, pres. mid. ptcp. m. nom. p., *lie, speak falsehoods*
10. ἕνεκα, *because of, on account of*
11. maledico, futperf. act. ind. 3 p., *speak ill of, revile, curse*
12. persequor, futperf. dep. ind. 3 p., *persecute*
13. adversum, *against*
14. mentior, pres. act. ptcp. m. nom. p., *lie, deceive*

July 17

Leviticus 14:2

זֹ֤את תִּֽהְיֶה֙ תּוֹרַ֣ת הַמְּצֹרָ֔ע[1] בְּי֖וֹם טָהֳרָת֑וֹ[2] וְהוּבָ֖א אֶל־הַכֹּהֵֽן׃

Οὗτος ὁ νόμος τοῦ λεπροῦ,[3] ᾗ ἂν ἡμέρᾳ καθαρισθῇ· καὶ προσαχθήσεται πρὸς τὸν ἱερέα.

Matthew 8:4[4]

καὶ λέγει αὐτῷ ὁ Ἰησοῦς· ὅρα μηδενὶ εἴπῃς, ἀλλ᾽ ὕπαγε σεαυτὸν δεῖξον[5] τῷ ἱερεῖ καὶ προσένεγκον τὸ δῶρον[6] ὃ προσέταξεν[7] Μωϋσῆς, εἰς μαρτύριον[8] αὐτοῖς.

et ait illi Iesus vide nemini dixeris sed vade ostende te sacerdoti et offer munus[9] quod praecepit Moses in testimonium illis.

1. צָרַע, pual perf. ptcp. m. s., *be struck with leprosy*
2. טָהֳרָה, *purifying, cleansing*
3. λεπρός, *leprous*
4. PA: In Matt 8:3, Jesus healed this man of leprosy.
5. δείκνυμι, aor. act. impv. 2 s., *show*
6. δῶρον, *gift*
7. προστάσσω, aor. act. ind. 3 s., *command*
8. μαρτύριον, *testimony*
9. munus, *gift*

July 18

Jonah 1:4

וַיהוָ֗ה הֵטִ֤יל[1] רֽוּחַ־גְּדוֹלָה֙ אֶל־הַיָּ֔ם וַיְהִ֥י סַֽעַר[2]־גָּד֖וֹל
בַּיָּ֑ם וְהָ֣אֳנִיָּ֔ה[3] חִשְּׁבָ֖ה לְהִשָּׁבֵֽר׃

καὶ κύριος ἐξήγειρεν[4] πνεῦμα εἰς τὴν θάλασσαν, καὶ ἐγένετο κλύδων[5] μέγας ἐν τῇ θαλάσσῃ, καὶ τὸ πλοῖον[6] ἐκινδύνευεν[7] συντριβῆναι.

Matthew 8:27

οἱ δὲ ἄνθρωποι ἐθαύμασαν λέγοντες· ποταπός[8] ἐστιν οὗτος ὅτι καὶ οἱ ἄνεμοι καὶ ἡ θάλασσα αὐτῷ ὑπακούουσιν;[9]

porro[10] homines mirati sunt dicentes qualis[11] est hic quia et venti et mare oboediunt[12] ei?

1. טוּל, hiph. perf. 3 m. s., *hurl*
2. סַ֫עַר, *storm*
3. אֳנִיָּה, *ship*
4. ἐξεγείρω, aor. act. ind. 3 s., *raise up*
5. κλύδων, *wave, surge*
6. πλοῖον, *ship*
7. κινδυνεύω, impf. act. ind. 3 s., *be in danger*
8. ποταπός, *what sort of*
9. ὑπακούω, pres. act. ind. 3 p., *obey*
10. porro, *then, but*
11. qualis, *what sort of*
12. oboedio, pres. act. ind. 3 p., *obey*

July 19

1. מַלָּח, *mariner*

2. זָעַק, qal wcons. 3 m. p., *cry out*

3. טוּל, hiph. wcons. 3 m. p., *hurl, cast*

4. אֳנִיָּה, *ship*

5. יוֹנָה, *Jonah*

6. יַרְכָה, *extreme parts, recesses*

7. סְפִינָה, *ship, vessel*

8. רָדַם, niph. wcons. 3 m. s., *sleep soundly*

9. ναυτικός, *mariner*

10. ἀναβοάω, impf. act. ind. 3 p., *cry out*

11. ἐκβολή, *casting overboard*

12. πλοῖον, *ship*

13. κουφίζω, aor. pass. inf., *be lightened*

14. Ιωνας, *Jonah*

15. κοῖλος, *belly*

16. καθεύδω, impf. act. ind. 3 s., *sleep*

17. ῥέγχω, impf. act. ind. 3 s., *snore*

18. δειλός, *afraid, cowardly*

19. ὀλιγόπιστος, *little faith*

20. ἐπιτιμάω, aor. act. ind. 3 s., *rebuke*

Jonah 1:5

וַיִּֽירְא֣וּ הַמַּלָּחִ֗ים[1] וַֽיִּזְעֲקוּ֮[2] אִ֣ישׁ אֶל־אֱלֹהָיו֒ וַיָּטִ֨לוּ[3]
אֶת־הַכֵּלִ֜ים אֲשֶׁ֤ר בָּֽאֳנִיָּה֙[4] אֶל־הַיָּ֔ם לְהָקֵ֖ל מֵעֲלֵיהֶ֑ם
וְיוֹנָ֗ה[5] יָרַד֙ אֶל־יַרְכְּתֵ֣י[6] הַסְּפִינָ֔ה[7] וַיִּשְׁכַּ֖ב וַיֵּרָדַֽם׃[8]

καὶ ἐφοβήθησαν οἱ ναυτικοὶ[9] καὶ ἀνεβόων[10] ἕκαστος πρὸς τὸν θεὸν αὐτῶν καὶ ἐκβολὴν[11] ἐποιήσαντο τῶν σκευῶν τῶν ἐν τῷ πλοίῳ[12] εἰς τὴν θάλασσαν τοῦ κουφισθῆναι[13] ἀπ᾽ αὐτῶν· Ιωνας[14] δὲ κατέβη εἰς τὴν κοίλην[15] τοῦ πλοίου καὶ ἐκάθευδεν[16] καὶ ἔρρεγχεν.[17]

Matthew 8:26

καὶ λέγει αὐτοῖς· τί δειλοί[18] ἐστε, ὀλιγόπιστοι;[19] τότε ἐγερθεὶς ἐπετίμησεν[20] τοῖς ἀνέμοις καὶ τῇ θαλάσσῃ, καὶ ἐγένετο γαλήνη[21] μεγάλη.

et dicit eis quid timidi[22] estis modicae fidei tunc surgens imperavit[23] ventis et mari et facta est tranquillitas[24] magna.

21. γαλήνη, *calm.* **22.** timidus, *fearful, afraid.* **23.** impero, perf. act. ind. 3 s., *command.* **24.** tranquillitas, *calm, tranquility*

July 20

Leviticus 15:25

וְאִשָּׁ֡ה כִּֽי־יָז֩וּב[1] ז֨וֹב[2] דָּמָ֜הּ יָמִ֣ים רַבִּ֗ים בְּלֹא֙ עֶת־
נִדָּתָ֔הּ[3] א֥וֹ כִֽי־תָז֖וּב[4] עַל־נִדָּתָ֑הּ כָּל־יְמֵ֞י ז֣וֹב טֻמְאָתָ֗הּ[5]
כִּימֵ֧י נִדָּתָ֛הּ תִּהְיֶ֖ה טְמֵאָ֥ה[6] הִֽוא׃

Καὶ γυνή, ἐὰν ῥέῃ[7] ῥύσει[8] αἵματος ἡμέρας πλείους οὐκ ἐν καιρῷ τῆς ἀφέδρου[9] αὐτῆς, ἐὰν καὶ ῥέῃ μετὰ τὴν ἄφεδρον αὐτῆς, πᾶσαι αἱ ἡμέραι ῥύσεως ἀκαθαρσίας[10] αὐτῆς καθάπερ[11] αἱ ἡμέραι τῆς ἀφέδρου, ἀκάθαρτος ἔσται.

Matthew 9:20

Καὶ ἰδοὺ γυνὴ αἱμορροοῦσα[12] δώδεκα ἔτη προσελθοῦσα ὄπισθεν[13] ἥψατο τοῦ κρασπέδου[14] τοῦ ἱματίου αὐτοῦ·

et ecce mulier quae sanguinis fluxum[15] patiebatur duodecim annis accessit retro[16] et tetigit fimbriam[17] vestimenti eius.

1. **זוּב**, qal impf. 3 m. s., *flow*
2. **זוֹב**, *discharge*
3. **נִדָּה**, *impurity*
4. **זוּב**, qal impf. 3 f. s., *flow, discharge*
5. **טֻמְאָה**, *uncleanness*
6. **טָמֵא**, *unclean*
7. ῥέω, pres. act. subj. 3 s., *flow*
8. ῥύσις, *flow*
9. ἄφεδρος, *menstruation*
10. ἀκαθαρσία, *uncleanness*
11. καθάπερ, *just as, like*
12. αἱμορροέω, pres. act. ptcp. f. nom. s., *bleed*
13. ὄπισθεν, *behind*
14. κράσπεδον, *fringe, hem*
15. fluxus, *flow*
16. retro, *behind*
17. fimbria, *edge, hem*

July 21

2 Kings 4:43

וַיֹּ֙אמֶר֙ מְשָׁ֣רְת֔וֹ[1] מָ֚ה אֶתֵּ֣ן זֶ֔ה לִפְנֵ֖י מֵ֣אָה אִ֑ישׁ וַיֹּ֗אמֶר
תֵּ֤ן לָעָם֙ וְיֹאכֵ֔לוּ כִּ֣י כֹ֥ה אָמַ֛ר יְהוָ֖ה אָכֹ֥ל וְהוֹתֵֽר׃

καὶ εἶπεν ὁ λειτουργὸς[2] αὐτοῦ Τί δῶ τοῦτο ἐνώπιον ἑκατὸν ἀνδρῶν; καὶ εἶπεν Δὸς τῷ λαῷ καὶ ἐσθιέτωσαν, ὅτι τάδε λέγει κύριος Φάγονται καὶ καταλείψουσιν.

Luke 9:17

καὶ ἔφαγον καὶ ἐχορτάσθησαν[3] πάντες, καὶ ἤρθη τὸ περισσεῦσαν αὐτοῖς κλασμάτων[4] κόφινοι[5] δώδεκα.

et manducaverunt omnes et saturati[6] sunt et sublatum est quod superfuit[7] illis fragmentorum[8] cofini[9] duodecim.

1. שָׁרַת, piel ptcp. m. s. cons., *minister, attend*
2. λειτουργός, *minister, attendant*
3. χορτάζω, aor. pass. ind. 3 p., *fill, satisfy*
4. κλάσμα, *piece*
5. κόφινος, *basket*
6. saturo, perf. pass. ind. 3 p., *satisfy*
7. supersum, perf. act. ind. 3 s., *be left over*
8. fragmentum, *fragment*
9. cofinus, *basket*

July 22

Psalm 91:13 [LXX 90:13]

עַל־שַׁ֣חַל[1] וָפֶ֣תֶן[2] תִּדְרֹ֑ךְ[3] תִּרְמֹ֖ס[4] כְּפִ֣יר[5] וְתַנִּֽין׃[6]

ἐπ᾽ ἀσπίδα[7] καὶ βασιλίσκον[8] ἐπιβήσῃ[9] καὶ καταπατήσεις[10] λέοντα καὶ δράκοντα.[11]

Luke 10:19

ἰδοὺ δέδωκα ὑμῖν τὴν ἐξουσίαν τοῦ πατεῖν[12] ἐπάνω[13] ὄφεων[14] καὶ σκορπίων,[15] καὶ ἐπὶ πᾶσαν τὴν δύναμιν τοῦ ἐχθροῦ, καὶ οὐδὲν ὑμᾶς οὐ μὴ ἀδικήσῃ.[16]

ecce dedi vobis potestatem calcandi[17] supra serpentes[18] et scorpiones[19] et supra omnem virtutem inimici et nihil vobis nocebit.[20]

1. שַׁ֫חַל, *lion*
2. פֶּ֫תֶן, *asp, snake*
3. דָּרַךְ, qal impf. 2 m. s., *walk, tread*
4. רָמַס, qal impf. 2 m. s., *trample*
5. כְּפִיר, *young lion*
6. תַּנִּין, *snake*
7. ἀσπίς, *asp, snake*
8. βασιλίσκος, *cobra*
9. ἐπιβαίνω, fut. mid. ind. 2 s., *walk upon*
10. καταπατέω, fut. act. ind. 3 s., *trample*
11. δράκων, *giant snake, dragon*
12. πατέω, pres. act. inf., *trample, crush*
13. ἐπάνω, *upon*
14. ὄφις, *snake*
15. σκορπίος, *scorpion*
16. ἀδικέω, aor. act. subj. 3 s., *harm*
17. calco, ger. act. n. g. s., *tread on*
18. serpens, *snake*
19. scorpio, *scorpion*
20. noceo, fut. act. ind. 3 s., *harm, injure*

July 23

Ezra 4:3

וַיֹּאמֶר לָהֶם זְרֻבָּבֶל[1] וְיֵשׁוּעַ[2] וּשְׁאָר[3] רָאשֵׁי הָאָבוֹת
לְיִשְׂרָאֵל לֹא־לָכֶם וָלָנוּ לִבְנוֹת בַּיִת לֵאלֹהֵינוּ כִּי
אֲנַחְנוּ יַחַד[4] נִבְנֶה לַיהוָה אֱלֹהֵי יִשְׂרָאֵל כַּאֲשֶׁר צִוָּנוּ
הַמֶּלֶךְ כּוֹרֶשׁ[5] מֶלֶךְ־פָּרָס׃[6]

καὶ εἶπεν πρὸς αὐτοὺς Ζοροβαβελ[7] καὶ Ἰησοῦς καὶ οἱ κατάλοιποι[8] τῶν ἀρχόντων τῶν πατριῶν τοῦ Ισραηλ Οὐχ ἡμῖν καὶ ὑμῖν τοῦ οἰκοδομῆσαι οἶκον τῷ θεῷ ἡμῶν, ὅτι ἡμεῖς αὐτοὶ ἐπὶ τὸ αὐτὸ οἰκοδομήσομεν τῷ κυρίῳ θεῷ ἡμῶν, ὡς ἐνετείλατο ἡμῖν Κῦρος[9] ὁ βασιλεὺς Περσῶν.[10]

John 4:9

λέγει οὖν αὐτῷ ἡ γυνὴ ἡ Σαμαρῖτις·[11] πῶς σὺ Ἰουδαῖος ὢν παρ᾽ ἐμοῦ πεῖν αἰτεῖς γυναικὸς Σαμαρίτιδος οὔσης; οὐ γὰρ συγχρῶνται[12] Ἰουδαῖοι Σαμαρίταις.

dicit ergo ei mulier illa samaritana[13] quomodo tu Iudaeus[14] cum sis bibere a me poscis[15] quae sum mulier samaritana non enim coutuntur[16] Iudaei Samaritanis.

1. זְרֻבָּבֶל, *Zerubbabel*

2. יֵשׁוּעַ, *Jeshua*

3. שְׁאָר, *rest*

4. יַחַד, *together*

5. כּוֹרֶשׁ, *Cyrus*

6. פָּרַס, *Persia*

7. Ζοροβαβέλ, *Zerubbabel*

8. κατάλοιπος, *rest*

9. Κῦρος, *Cyrus*

10. Πέρσης, *Persia*

11. Σαμαρῖτις, *Samaritan*

12. συγχράομαι, pres. mid. ind. 3 p., *have dealings with*

13. Samaritanus, *Samaritan*

14. Iudaeus, *Jew*

15. posco, pres. act. ind. 2 s., *ask*

16. coutor, pres. dep. ind. 3 p., *have dealings with*

July 24

Psalm 105:40 [LXX 104:40]

שָׁאַל[1] וַיָּבֵא שְׂלָו[2] וְלֶחֶם שָׁמַיִם יַשְׂבִּיעֵם׃[3]

ᾔτησαν,[4] καὶ ἦλθεν ὀρτυγομήτρα,[5] καὶ ἄρτον οὐρανοῦ ἐνέπλησεν αὐτούς.

John 6:32

εἶπεν οὖν αὐτοῖς ὁ Ἰησοῦς· ἀμὴν ἀμὴν λέγω ὑμῖν, οὐ Μωϋσῆς δέδωκεν ὑμῖν τὸν ἄρτον ἐκ τοῦ οὐρανοῦ, ἀλλʼ ὁ πατήρ μου δίδωσιν ὑμῖν τὸν ἄρτον ἐκ τοῦ οὐρανοῦ τὸν ἀληθινόν.[6]

dixit ergo eis Iesus amen amen dico vobis non Moses dedit vobis panem de caelo sed Pater meus dat vobis panem de caelo verum.

1. TC: The versions have third person plural.
2. שְׂלָו, *quail*
3. שָׂבַע, hiph. impf. 3 m. s., *satisfy*
4. αἰτέω, aor. act. ind. 3 p., *ask*
5. ὀρτυγομήτρα, *quail*
6. ἀληθινός, *true*

Opposition to Jesus

July 25

Isaiah 49:24

הֲיֻקַּח מִגִּבּוֹר מַלְקוֹחַ[1] וְאִם־שְׁבִי[2] צַדִּיק יִמָּלֵט׃[3]

μὴ λήμψεταί τις παρὰ γίγαντος[4] σκῦλα;[5] καὶ ἐὰν αἰχμαλωτεύσῃ[6] τις ἀδίκως,[7] σωθήσεται;

Matthew 12:29

ἢ πῶς δύναταί τις εἰσελθεῖν εἰς τὴν οἰκίαν τοῦ ἰσχυροῦ[8] καὶ τὰ σκεύη[9] αὐτοῦ ἁρπάσαι,[10] ἐὰν μὴ πρῶτον δήσῃ τὸν ἰσχυρόν; καὶ τότε τὴν οἰκίαν αὐτοῦ διαρπάσει.[11]

aut quomodo potest quisquam intrare in domum fortis[12] et vasa[13] eius diripere[14] nisi prius[15] alligaverit[16] fortem et tunc domum illius diripiat.[17]

1. מַלְקוֹחַ, *prey*
2. שְׁבִי, *captive*
3. מָלַט, niph. impf. 3 m. s., *rescue*
4. γίγας, *giant, strong one*
5. σκῦλον, *plunder*
6. αἰχμαλωτεύω, aor. act. subj. 3 s., *lead captive*
7. ἀδίκως, *unjustly*
8. ἰσχυρός, *strong*
9. σκεῦος, *object, vessel*
10. ἁρπάζω, aor. act. inf., *plunder, snatch*
11. διαρπάζω, fut. act. ind. 3 s., *plunder, despoil, seize*
12. fortis, *strong*
13. vas, *vessel*
14. diripio, pres. act. inf., *plunder, despoil*
15. prius, *first*
16. alligo, perf. act. subj. 3 s., *bind*
17. diripio, pres. act. subj. 3 s., *plunder, despoil*

July 26

Amos 1:9

כֹּה אָמַר יְהוָה עַל־שְׁלֹשָׁה פִּשְׁעֵי[1]־צֹר[2] וְעַל־אַרְבָּעָה
לֹא אֲשִׁיבֶנּוּ עַל־הַסְגִּירָם[3] גָּלוּת[4] שְׁלֵמָה[5] לֶאֱדוֹם[6]
וְלֹא זָכְרוּ בְּרִית אַחִים׃

Τάδε λέγει κύριος Ἐπὶ ταῖς τρισὶν ἀσεβείαις[7] Τύρου[8] καὶ ἐπὶ ταῖς τέσσαρσιν οὐκ ἀποστραφήσομαι αὐτήν, ἀνθ᾽ ὧν συνέκλεισαν[9] αἰχμαλωσίαν τοῦ Σαλωμων εἰς τὴν Ιδουμαίαν[10] καὶ οὐκ ἐμνήσθησαν διαθήκης ἀδελφῶν.

Luke 10:13

Οὐαί σοι, Χοραζίν,[11] οὐαί σοι, Βηθσαϊδά·[12] ὅτι εἰ ἐν Τύρῳ καὶ Σιδῶνι[13] ἐγενήθησαν αἱ δυνάμεις αἱ γενόμεναι ἐν ὑμῖν, πάλαι[14] ἂν ἐν σάκκῳ[15] καὶ σποδῷ[16] καθήμενοι μετενόησαν.

vae tibi Corazain[17] vae tibi Bethsaida[18] quia si in Tyro[19] et Sidone[20] factae fuissent virtutes quae in vobis factae sunt olim[21] in cilicio[22] et cinere[23] sedentes paeniterent.[24]

1. פֶּשַׁע, *transgression*
2. צֹר, *Tyre*
3. סָגַר, hiph. inf. cons., *deliver over*
4. גָּלוּת, *exile(s)*
5. שָׁלֵם, *entire, whole*
6. אֱדוֹם, *Edom*
7. ἀσέβεια, *impious, ungodly*
8. Τύρος, *Tyre*
9. συγκλείω, aor. act. ind. 3 p., *imprison, shut up*
10. Ἰδουμαία, *Edom*
11. Χοραζίν, *Chorazin*
12. Βηθσαϊδά, *Bethsaida*
13. Σιδών, *Sidon*
14. πάλαι, *long ago*
15. σάκκος, sackcloth
16. σποδός, *ashes*
17. Corazain, *Chorazin*
18. Bethsaida, *Bethsaida*
19. Tyrus, *Tyre*
20. Sidon, *Sidon*
21. olim, *long ago*
22. cilicio, *sackcloth*
23. cinis, *ashes*
24. paeniteo, impf. act. subj. 3 p., *repent*

July 27

Micah 7:6

כִּֽי־בֵן֙ מְנַבֵּ֣ל[1] אָ֔ב בַּ֚ת קָמָ֣ה בְאִמָּ֔הּ כַּלָּ֖ה[2] בַּחֲמֹתָ֑הּ[3]
אֹיְבֵ֥י אִ֖ישׁ אַנְשֵׁ֥י בֵיתֽוֹ׃

διότι υἱὸς ἀτιμάζει[4] πατέρα, θυγάτηρ[5] ἐπαναστήσεται[6] ἐπὶ τὴν μητέρα αὐτῆς, νύμφη[7] ἐπὶ τὴν πενθερὰν[8] αὐτῆς, ἐχθροὶ ἀνδρὸς πάντες οἱ ἄνδρες οἱ ἐν τῷ οἴκῳ αὐτοῦ.

Luke 12:53

διαμερισθήσονται[9] πατὴρ ἐπὶ υἱῷ καὶ *υἱὸς ἐπὶ πατρί*, μήτηρ ἐπὶ τὴν θυγατέρα καὶ *θυγάτηρ ἐπὶ τὴν μητέρα*, πενθερὰ ἐπὶ τὴν νύμφην αὐτῆς καὶ *νύμφη ἐπὶ τὴν πενθεράν*.

dividentur[10] pater in filium et filius in patrem suum mater in filiam et filia in matrem socrus[11] in nurum[12] suam et nurus in socrum suam.

1. נָבֵל, piel ptcp. m. s. abs., *regard with contempt*

2. כַּלָּה, *daughter-in-law*

3. חָמוֹת, *mother-in-law*

4. ἀτιμάζω, pres. act. ind. 3 s., *dishonor*

5. θυγάτηρ, *daughter*

6. ἐπανίστημι, fut. mid. ind. 3 s., *rise up, turn against*

7. νύμφη, *bride, daughter*

8. πενθερά, *mother-in-law*

9. διαμερίζω, fut. pass. ind. 3 p., *divide*

10. divido, fut. pass. ind. 3 p., *divide up*

11. socrus, *mother-in-law*

12. nurus, *daughter-in-law*

July 28

Leviticus 12:3

וּבַיּ֖וֹם הַשְּׁמִינִ֑י[1] יִמּ֖וֹל[2] בְּשַׂ֥ר עָרְלָתֽוֹ׃[3]

καὶ τῇ ἡμέρᾳ τῇ ὀγδόῃ[4] περιτεμεῖ[5] τὴν σάρκα τῆς ἀκροβυστίας[6] αὐτοῦ.

John 7:22[7]

διὰ τοῦτο Μωϋσῆς δέδωκεν ὑμῖν τὴν περιτομήν – οὐχ ὅτι ἐκ τοῦ Μωϋσέως ἐστὶν ἀλλ᾽ ἐκ τῶν πατέρων – καὶ ἐν σαββάτῳ περιτέμνετε[8] ἄνθρωπον.

propterea Moses dedit vobis circumcisionem non quia ex Mose est sed ex patribus et in sabbato circumciditis[9] hominem.

1. שְׁמִינִי, *eighth*
2. מוּל, niph. impf. 3 m. s., *circumcise*
3. עָרְלָה, *foreskin*
4. ὄγδοος, *eighth*
5. περιτέμνω, fut. act. ind. 3 s., *circumcise*
6. ἀκροβυστία, *uncircumcision*
7. PA: The religious leaders take issue with Jesus's activities on the Sabbath. Jesus points to circumcision as an activity they transgress the Sabbath to uphold in order to ensure it takes place on the eighth day.
8. περιτέμνω, pres. act. ind. 2 p., *circumcise*
9. circumcido, pres. act. ind. 2 p., *circumcise*

July 29

Leviticus 19:15

לֹא־תַעֲשׂ֥וּ עָ֙וֶל֙[1] בַּמִּשְׁפָּ֔ט לֹא־תִשָּׂ֣א פְנֵי־דָ֔ל[2] וְלֹ֥א
תֶהְדַּ֖ר[3] פְּנֵ֣י גָד֑וֹל בְּצֶ֖דֶק תִּשְׁפֹּ֥ט עֲמִיתֶֽךָ׃[4]

Οὐ ποιήσετε ἄδικον ἐν κρίσει· οὐ λήμψῃ πρόσωπον πτωχοῦ οὐδὲ θαυμάσεις[5] πρόσωπον δυνάστου,[6] ἐν δικαιοσύνῃ κρινεῖς τὸν πλησίον σου.

John 7:24[7]

μὴ κρίνετε κατ᾽ ὄψιν,[8] ἀλλὰ τὴν δικαίαν κρίσιν κρίνετε.

nolite iudicare secundum faciem sed iustum iudicium iudicate.

1. עָ֫וֶל, *injustice*
2. דַּל, *poor*
3. הָדַר, qal impf. 2 m. s., *honor*
4. עָמִית, *fellow, associate, neighbor*
5. θαυμάζω, fut. act. ind. 2 s., *admire, wonder*
6. δυνάστης, *official, ruler*
7. PA: This is Jesus's concluding statement to the crowd concerning work on the Sabbath.
8. ὄψις, *appearance*

July 30

Leviticus 20:8

וּשְׁמַרְתֶּם֙ אֶת־חֻקֹּתַ֔י וַעֲשִׂיתֶ֖ם אֹתָ֑ם אֲנִ֥י יְהוָ֖ה מְקַדִּשְׁכֶֽם׃

καὶ φυλάξεσθε τὰ προστάγματά μου καὶ ποιήσετε αὐτά· ἐγὼ κύριος ὁ ἁγιάζων ὑμᾶς.

Matthew 15:3

ὁ δὲ ἀποκριθεὶς εἶπεν αὐτοῖς· διὰ τί καὶ ὑμεῖς παραβαίνετε[1] τὴν ἐντολὴν τοῦ θεοῦ διὰ τὴν παράδοσιν[2] ὑμῶν;

ipse autem respondens ait illis quare et vos transgredimini[3] mandatum Dei propter traditionem[4] vestram?

1. παραβαίνω, pres. act. ind. 2 p., *transgress*
2. παράδοσις, *tradition*
3. transgredior, pres. dep. ind. 2 p., *transgress*
4. traditio, *tradition*

July 31

Leviticus 20:9

כִּֽי־אִ֣ישׁ אִ֗ישׁ אֲשֶׁ֨ר יְקַלֵּ֧ל[1] אֶת־אָבִ֛יו וְאֶת־אִמּ֖וֹ מ֣וֹת יוּמָ֑ת אָבִ֧יו וְאִמּ֛וֹ קִלֵּ֖ל[2] דָּמָ֥יו בּֽוֹ׃

ἄνθρωπος ἄνθρωπος, ὃς ἂν κακῶς[3] εἴπῃ τὸν πατέρα αὐτοῦ ἢ τὴν μητέρα αὐτοῦ, θανάτῳ θανατούσθω· πατέρα αὐτοῦ ἢ μητέρα αὐτοῦ κακῶς εἶπεν, ἔνοχος[4] ἔσται.

Matthew 15:4

ὁ γὰρ θεὸς εἶπεν· *τίμα*[5] *τὸν πατέρα καὶ τὴν μητέρα*, καί· *ὁ κακολογῶν*[6] *πατέρα ἢ μητέρα θανάτῳ τελευτάτω.*[7]

nam Deus dixit honora[8] patrem et matrem et qui maledixerit[9] patri vel matri morte moriatur.

1. קָלַל, piel impf. 3 m. s., *curse*
2. קָלַל, piel perf. 3 m. s., *curse*
3. κακῶς, *severely, badly*
4. ἔνοχος, *liable*
5. τιμάω, pres. act. impv. 2 s., *honor*
6. κακολογέω, pres. act. ptcp. m. nom. s., *curse, speak evil of*
7. τελευτάω, pres. act. impv. 3 s., *die*
8. honoro, pres. act. impv. 2 s., *honor*
9. maledico, fut-perf. act. ind. 3 s., *curse, speak evil of*

August 1

Leviticus 20:10

וְאִ֗ישׁ אֲשֶׁ֤ר יִנְאַף֙[1] אֶת־אֵ֣שֶׁת אִ֔ישׁ אֲשֶׁ֥ר יִנְאַ֖ף אֶת־
אֵ֣שֶׁת רֵעֵ֑הוּ מֽוֹת־יוּמַ֥ת הַנֹּאֵ֖ף[2] וְהַנֹּאָֽפֶת[3]׃

ἄνθρωπος, ὃς ἂν μοιχεύσηται[4] γυναῖκα ἀνδρὸς ἢ ὃς ἂν μοιχεύσηται γυναῖκα τοῦ πλησίον, θανάτῳ θανατούσθωσαν ὁ μοιχεύων[5] καὶ ἡ μοιχευομένη.[6]

John 8:5[7]

ἐν δὲ τῷ νόμῳ ἡμῖν Μωϋσῆς ἐνετείλατο[8] τὰς τοιαύτας λιθάζειν.[9] σὺ οὖν τί λέγεις;

in lege autem Moses mandavit[10] nobis huiusmodi lapidare[11] tu ergo quid dicis?

7. TC: John 8:5 belongs to the broader well-known and much debated *Pericope Adulterae*. This story has not been preserved in the earliest manuscripts and is viewed as a later addition to the Gospel of John by most textual scholars. Including it in this reader is not a comment about its originality. See David Alan Black and Jacob N. Cerone, *The Pericope of the Adulteress in Contemporary Research*, The Library of New Testament Studies 551 (New York: T&T Clark, 2016). **8.** ἐντέλλω, aor. mid. ind. 3 s., *command*. **9.** λιθάζω, pres. act. inf., *stone*. **10.** mando, perf. act. ind. 3 s., *command*. **11.** lapido, pres. act. inf., *stone*

1. נָאַף, qal impf. 3 m. s., *commit adultery*

2. נָאַף, qal ptcp. f. s. abs., *commit adultery*

3. נָאַף, qal ptcp. m. s. abs., *commit adultery*

4. μοιχεύω, aor. mid. subj. 3 s., *commit adultery*

5. μοιχεύω, pres. act. ptcp. m. nom. s., *commit adultery*

6. μοιχεύω, pres. act. ptcp. f. nom. s., *commit adultery*

August 2

Psalm 51:7 [LXX 50:7]

הֵן[1]־בְּעָו֥וֹן חוֹלָ֑לְתִּי[2] וּ֝בְחֵ֗טְא[3] יֶֽחֱמַ֥תְנִי[4] אִמִּֽי׃

ἰδοὺ γὰρ ἐν ἀνομίαις συνελήμφθην, καὶ ἐν ἁμαρτίαις ἐκίσσησέν[5] με ἡ μήτηρ μου.

John 9:34

ἀπεκρίθησαν καὶ εἶπαν αὐτῷ· ἐν ἁμαρτίαις σὺ ἐγεννήθης ὅλος καὶ σὺ διδάσκεις ἡμᾶς; καὶ ἐξέβαλον αὐτὸν ἔξω.

responderunt et dixerunt ei in peccatis natus es totus et tu doces nos et eiecerunt eum foras.[6]

1. הֵן, *look, behold*
2. חִיל, polal perf. 1 c. s., *bring forth*
3. חֵטְא, *sin*
4. יָחַם, piel perf. 3 f. s., *conceive*
5. κισσάω, aor. act. ind. 3 s., *conceive*
6. foras, *out*

August 3

Leviticus 24:16

וְנֹקֵב[1] שֵׁם־יְהוָה מוֹת יוּמָת רָגוֹם[2] יִרְגְּמוּ[3]־בוֹ כָּל־
הָעֵדָה כַּגֵּר[4] כָּאֶזְרָח[5] בְּנָקְבוֹ[6]־שֵׁם יוּמָת׃

ὀνομάζων[7] δὲ τὸ ὄνομα κυρίου θανάτῳ θανατούσθω· λίθοις λιθοβολείτω[8] αὐτὸν πᾶσα συναγωγὴ Ισραηλ· ἐάν τε προσήλυτος[9] ἐάν τε αὐτόχθων,[10] ἐν τῷ ὀνομάσαι[11] αὐτὸν τὸ ὄνομα κυρίου τελευτάτω.[12]

John 10:33

ἀπεκρίθησαν αὐτῷ οἱ Ἰουδαῖοι· περὶ καλοῦ ἔργου οὐ λιθάζομέν[13] σε ἀλλὰ περὶ βλασφημίας,[14] καὶ ὅτι σὺ ἄνθρωπος ὢν ποιεῖς σεαυτὸν θεόν.

responderunt ei Iudaei de bono opere non lapidamus[15] te sed de blasphemia[16] et quia tu homo cum sis facis te ipsum Deum.

1. נָקַב, qal ptcp. m. s. abs., *curse, misuse*
2. רָגַם, qal inf. abs., *stone (to death)*
3. רגם, *stone*
4. גֵּר, *stranger, foreign resident*
5. אֶזְרָח, *native (citizen)*
6. נָקַב, qal ptcp. m. s. cons., *curse, misuse*
7. ὀνομάζω, pres. act. ptcp. m. nom. s., *name*
8. λιθοβολέω, pres. act. impv. 3 s., *throw stones*
9. προσήλυτος, *resident alien, proselyte*
10. αὐτόχθων, *native (citizen)*
11. ὀνομάζω, aor. act. inf., *name*
12. τελευτάω, pres. act. impv. 3 s., *die*
13. λιθάζω, pres. act. ind. 1 p., *stone (to death)*
14. βλασφημία, *blasphemy*
15. lapido, pres. act. ind. 1 p., *stone (to death)*
16. blasphemia, *blasphemy*

August 4

Psalm 82:6 [LXX 81:6]

אֲנִֽי־אָ֭מַרְתִּי אֱלֹהִ֣ים אַתֶּ֑ם וּבְנֵ֖י עֶלְי֣וֹן[1] כֻּלְּכֶֽם׃

ἐγὼ εἶπα Θεοί ἐστε καὶ υἱοὶ ὑψίστου πάντες.

John 10:34

ἀπεκρίθη αὐτοῖς [ὁ] Ἰησοῦς· οὐκ ἔστιν γεγραμμένον ἐν τῷ νόμῳ ὑμῶν ὅτι *ἐγὼ εἶπα· θεοί ἐστε;*

respondit eis Iesus nonne scriptum est in lege vestra quia ego dixi dii estis?

1. עֶלְיוֹן, *Most High*

August 5

Leviticus 27:30

וְכָל־מַעְשַׂר[1] הָאָרֶץ מִזֶּרַע הָאָרֶץ מִפְּרִי הָעֵץ לַיהוָה
הוּא קֹדֶשׁ לַיהוָה׃

Πᾶσα δεκάτη[2] τῆς γῆς ἀπὸ τοῦ σπέρματος τῆς γῆς καὶ τοῦ καρποῦ τοῦ ξυλίνου[3] τῷ κυρίῳ ἐστίν, ἅγιον τῷ κυρίῳ.

1. מַעֲשֵׂר, *tithe*
2. δέκατος, *tenth*
3. ξύλινος, *wooden thing, tree*

Luke 11:42

ἀλλ᾽ οὐαὶ ὑμῖν τοῖς Φαρισαίοις, ὅτι ἀποδεκατοῦτε[4] τὸ ἡδύοσμον[5] καὶ τὸ πήγανον[6] καὶ πᾶν λάχανον[7] καὶ παρέρχεσθε[8] τὴν κρίσιν καὶ τὴν ἀγάπην τοῦ θεοῦ· ταῦτα δὲ ἔδει ποιῆσαι κἀκεῖνα μὴ παρεῖναι.[9]

sed vae vobis Pharisaeis quia decimatis[10] mentam[11] et rutam[12] et omne holus[13] et praeteritis[14] iudicium et caritatem Dei haec autem oportuit facere et illa non omittere.[15]

4. ἀποδεκατόω, pres. act. ind. 2 p., *tithe*
5. ἡδύοσμον, *mint*
6. πήγανον, *rue*
7. λάχανον, *herb*
8. παρέρχομαι, pres. mid. ind. 2 p., *pass by, neglect*
9. παρίημι, aor. act. inf., *neglect, let go*
10. decimo, pres. act. ind. 2 p., *tithe*
11. menta, *mint*
12. ruta, *rue*
13. holus, *herb*
14. praetereo, pres. act. ind. 2 p., *pass by*
15. omitto, pres. act. inf., *omit, leave undone*

August 6

Psalm 69:5 [LXX 68:5]

רַבּ֤וּ ׀[1] מִשַּׂעֲר֣וֹת[2] רֹאשִׁי֮ שֹׂנְאַ֪י חִ֫נָּ֥ם[3] עָצְמ֣וּ[4] מַ֭צְמִיתַי[5]
אֹיְבַ֣י שֶׁ֑קֶר אֲשֶׁ֥ר לֹא־גָ֝זַ֗לְתִּי[6] אָ֣ז אָשִֽׁיב׃

ἐπληθύνθησαν ὑπὲρ τὰς τρίχας[7] τῆς κεφαλῆς μου οἱ μισοῦντές με δωρεάν,[8] ἐκραταιώθησαν[9] οἱ ἐχθροί μου οἱ ἐκδιώκοντές[10] με ἀδίκως·[11] ἃ οὐχ ἥρπασα,[12] τότε ἀπετίννυον.[13]

John 15:25

ἀλλ᾽ ἵνα πληρωθῇ ὁ λόγος ὁ ἐν τῷ νόμῳ αὐτῶν γεγραμμένος ὅτι *ἐμίσησάν με δωρεάν.*

sed ut impleatur sermo qui in lege eorum scriptus est quia odio[14] me habuerunt gratis.

1. רָבַב, qal perf. 3 c. p., *become numerous*
2. שַׂעֲרָה, *hair*
3. חִנָּם, *without cause*
4. עָצַם, qal perf. 3 c. p., *be mighty*
5. צָמַת, hiph. ptcp. m. p. cons., *destroy*
6. גָּזַל, qal perf. 1 c. s., *rob*
7. θρίξ, *hair*
8. δωρεάν, *freely*; here *without cause*
9. κραταιόω, aor. pass. ind. 3 p., *become strong, prevail*
10. ἐκδιώκω, pres. act. ptcp. m. nom. p., *persecute*
11. ἀδίκως, *wrongfully*
12. ἁρπάζω, aor. act. ind. 1 s., *seize*
13. ἀποτιννύω, impf. act. ind. 1 s., *repay*
14. odium, *hate*

The Passion and Death of Jesus

August 7

Zechariah 9:9

גִּילִי[1] מְאֹד בַּת־צִיּוֹן הָרִיעִי[2] בַּת יְרוּשָׁלַםִ הִנֵּה מַלְכֵּךְ
יָבוֹא לָךְ צַדִּיק וְנוֹשָׁע הוּא עָנִי[3] וְרֹכֵב[4] עַל־חֲמוֹר[5]
וְעַל־עַיִר[6] בֶּן־אֲתֹנוֹת׃[7]

Χαῖρε[8] σφόδρα, θύγατερ Σιων· κήρυσσε,[9] θύγατερ Ιερουσαλημ· ἰδοὺ ὁ βασιλεύς σου ἔρχεταί σοι, δίκαιος καὶ σῴζων αὐτός, πραΰς[10] καὶ ἐπιβεβηκὼς[11] ἐπὶ ὑποζύγιον[12] καὶ πῶλον[13] νέον.

Luke 19:30

. . . ὑπάγετε εἰς τὴν κατέναντι[14] κώμην,[15] ἐν ᾗ εἰσπορευόμενοι[16] εὑρήσετε πῶλον δεδεμένον, ἐφ᾽ ὃν οὐδεὶς πώποτε[17] ἀνθρώπων ἐκάθισεν, καὶ λύσαντες αὐτὸν ἀγάγετε.

. . . ite in castellum[18] quod contra est in quod introeuntes invenietis pullum[19] asinae[20] alligatum[21] cui nemo umquam[22] hominum sedit solvite illum et adducite.

1. גִּיל, qal impv. f. s., *rejoice*

2. רוּעַ, hiph. impv. f. s., *shout*

3. עָנִי, *humble*

4. רָכַב, qal ptcp. m. s. abs., *mount, ride*

5. חֲמוֹר, *donkey*

6. עַיִר, *young donkey*

7. אָתוֹן, *female donkey*

8. χαίρω, pres. act. impv. 2 s., *rejoice*

9. κηρύσσω, pres. act. impv. 2 s., *proclaim*

10. πραΰς, *humble, gentle*

11. ἐπιβαίνω, perf. act. ptcp. m. nom. s., *sit*

12. ὑποζύγιον, *donkey*

13. πῶλος, *young donkey*

14. κατέναντι, *opposite*

15. κώμη, *village*

16. εἰσπορεύομαι, pres. mid. ptcp. m. nom. p., *enter, go in*

17. πώποτε, *ever*

18. castellum, *village*

19. pullus, *young one.* **20.** asina, *female donkey* **21.** alligo, perf. pass. ptcp. m. a. s., *tie, bind.* **22.** umquam, *ever*

August 8

2 Kings 9:13

וַיְמַהֲרוּ[1] וַיִּקְחוּ אִישׁ בִּגְדוֹ וַיָּשִׂימוּ תַחְתָּיו אֶל־גֶּרֶם[2]
הַמַּעֲלוֹת[3] וַיִּתְקְעוּ[4] בַּשּׁוֹפָר[5] וַיֹּאמְרוּ מָלַךְ יֵהוּא׃[6]

καὶ ἀκούσαντες ἔσπευσαν[7] καὶ ἔλαβον ἕκαστος τὸ ἱμάτιον αὐτοῦ καὶ ἔθηκαν ὑποκάτω[8] αὐτοῦ ἐπὶ γαρεμ[9] τῶν ἀναβαθμῶν[10] καὶ ἐσάλπισαν[11] ἐν κερατίνῃ[12] καὶ εἶπον Ἐβασίλευσεν Ιου.[13]

Luke 19:36

πορευομένου δὲ αὐτοῦ ὑπεστρώννυον[14] τὰ ἱμάτια αὐτῶν ἐν τῇ ὁδῷ.

eunte autem illo substernebant[15] vestimenta sua in via.

1. מָהַר, piel wcons. 3 m. p., *hasten*
2. גֶּ֫רֶם, *bare, bone*
3. מַעֲלָה, *step, ascent*
4. תָּקַע, qal wcons. 3 m. p., *blow*
5. שׁוֹפָר, *trumpet*
6. יֵהוּא, *Jehu*
7. σπεύδω, aor. act. ind. 3 s., *hasten*
8. ὑποκάτω, *under*
9. γαρεμ, transliteration of Hebrew; *bare, bone*
10. ἀναβαθμός, *stairway*
11. σαλπίζω, aor. act. ind. 3 p., *sound the trumpet*
12. κερατίνη, *horn*
13. Ιου, *Jehu*
14. ὑποστρωννύω, impf. act. ind. 3 s., *spread under/out*
15. substerno, impf. act. ind. 3 s., *spread beneath*

August 9

Psalm 118:26 [LXX 117:26]

בָּר֣וּךְ הַ֭בָּא בְּשֵׁ֣ם יְהוָ֑ה בֵּ֝רַ֥כְנוּכֶ֗ם מִבֵּ֥ית יְהוָֽה׃

εὐλογημένος ὁ ἐρχόμενος ἐν ὀνόματι κυρίου·
εὐλογήκαμεν ὑμᾶς ἐξ οἴκου κυρίου.

Mark 11:9

καὶ οἱ προάγοντες[1] καὶ οἱ ἀκολουθοῦντες ἔκραζον· *ὡσαννά·*[2] *εὐλογημένος ὁ ἐρχόμενος ἐν ὀνόματι κυρίου.*

et qui praeibant[3] et qui sequebantur clamabant dicentes osanna[4] benedictus qui venit in nomine Domini.

1. προάγω, pres. act. ptcp. m. nom. p., *go before*
2. ὡσαννά, *hosanna, save us*
3. praeeo, impf. act. ind. 3 p., *go before*
4. osanna, *hosanna, save us*

August 10

Ezekiel 34:15

אֲנִ֨י אֶרְעֶ֤ה צֹאנִי֙ וַאֲנִ֣י אַרְבִּיצֵ֔ם[1] נְאֻ֖ם אֲדֹנָ֥י יְהֹוִֽה׃

ἐγὼ βοσκήσω[2] τὰ πρόβατά μου καὶ ἐγὼ ἀναπαύσω[3] αὐτά, καὶ γνώσονται ὅτι ἐγώ εἰμι κύριος. τάδε λέγει κύριος κύριος.

John 10:11

Ἐγώ εἰμι ὁ ποιμὴν[4] ὁ καλός. ὁ ποιμὴν ὁ καλὸς τὴν ψυχὴν αὐτοῦ τίθησιν ὑπὲρ τῶν προβάτων.

ego sum pastor[5] bonus bonus pastor animam suam dat pro ovibus.

1. רָבַץ, hiph. impf. 1 c. s., *lie down*
2. βόσκω, fut. act. ind. 1 s., *feed, graze*
3. ἀναπαύω, fut. act. ind. 1 s., *rest*
4. ποιμήν, *shepherd*
5. pastor, *shepherd*

August 11

Psalm 42:6 [LXX 41:6]

מַה־תִּשְׁתּ֬וֹחֲחִ֨י ׀[1] נַפְשִׁי֮ וַתֶּהֱמִ֪י[2] עָ֫לָ֥י הוֹחִ֣ילִי[3]
לֵ֭אלֹהִים כִּי־ע֣וֹד אוֹדֶ֑נּוּ יְשׁוּע֥וֹת[4] פָּנָֽיו׃

ἵνα τί περίλυπος[5] εἶ, ψυχή, καὶ ἵνα τί συνταράσσεις[6] με; ἔλπισον ἐπὶ τὸν θεόν, ὅτι ἐξομολογήσομαι αὐτῷ· σωτήριον τοῦ προσώπου μου ὁ θεός μου.

John 12:27

Νῦν *ἡ ψυχή μου τετάρακται,*[7] καὶ τί εἴπω; πάτερ, *σῶσόν με* ἐκ τῆς ὥρας ταύτης; ἀλλὰ διὰ τοῦτο ἦλθον εἰς τὴν ὥραν ταύτην.

nunc anima mea turbata[8] est et quid dicam Pater salvifica[9] me ex hora hac sed propterea[10] veni in horam hanc.

1. שׁוּחַ, hithpolel impf. 2 f. s., *despair, cast down, depressed*
2. הָמָה, qal wcons. 2 f. s., *be in distress, turmoil*
3. יָחַל, hiph. impv. f. s., *wait, hope*
4. יְשׁוּעָה, *salvation*
5. περίλυπος, *very sorrowful*
6. συνταράσσω, pres. act. ind. 2 s., *be troubled*
7. ταράσσω, perf. pass. ind. 3 s., *be troubled*
8. turbo, perf. pass. ind. 3 s., *be troubled*
9. salvifico, pres. act. impv. 2 s., *save*
10. propterea, *therefore*

August 12

Psalm 41:10 [LXX 40:10]

גַּם־אִ֤ישׁ שְׁלוֹמִ֨י ׀ אֲשֶׁר־בָּ֣טַחְתִּי ב֭וֹ אוֹכֵ֣ל לַחְמִ֑י הִגְדִּ֖יל עָלַ֣י עָקֵֽב׃[1]

καὶ γὰρ ὁ ἄνθρωπος τῆς εἰρήνης μου, ἐφ᾽ ὃν ἤλπισα, ὁ ἐσθίων ἄρτους μου, ἐμεγάλυνεν[2] ἐπ᾽ ἐμὲ πτερνισμόν.[3]

John 13:18

Οὐ περὶ πάντων ὑμῶν λέγω· ἐγὼ οἶδα τίνας ἐξελεξάμην·[4] ἀλλ᾽ ἵνα ἡ γραφὴ πληρωθῇ· *ὁ τρώγων[5] μου τὸν ἄρτον ἐπῆρεν[6] ἐπ᾽ ἐμὲ τὴν πτέρναν[7]* αὐτοῦ.

non de omnibus vobis dico ego scio quos elegerim sed ut impleatur scriptura qui manducat mecum panem levavit[8] contra me calcaneum[9] suum.

1. עָקֵב, *heel*
2. μεγαλύνω, aor. act. ind. 3 s., *magnify*
3. πτερνισμός, *deception, treachery*
4. ἐκλέγομαι, aor. mid. ind. 1 s., *choose*
5. τρώγω, pres. act. ptcp. m. nom. s., *eat*
6. ἐπαίρω, aor. act. ind. 3 s., *lift up*
7. πτέρνα, *heel*
8. levo, perf. act. ind. 3 s., *lift up*
9. calcaneum, *heel*

August 13

Zechariah 13:7

חֶ֗רֶב עוּרִ֤י[1] עַל־רֹעִי֙ וְעַל־גֶּ֣בֶר[2] עֲמִיתִ֔י[3] נְאֻ֖ם יְהוָ֣ה
צְבָא֑וֹת הַ֤ךְ אֶת־הָֽרֹעֶה֙ וּתְפוּצֶ֣יןָ[4] הַצֹּ֔אן וַהֲשִׁבֹתִ֥י יָדִ֖י
עַל־הַצֹּעֲרִֽים׃[5]

Ῥομφαία, ἐξεγέρθητι[6] ἐπὶ τοὺς ποιμένας[7] μου καὶ ἐπ᾽ ἄνδρα πολίτην[8] μου, λέγει κύριος παντοκράτωρ· πατάξατε τοὺς ποιμένας καὶ ἐκσπάσατε[9] τὰ πρόβατα, καὶ ἐπάξω τὴν χεῖρά μου ἐπὶ τοὺς ποιμένας.

Mark 14:50

Καὶ ἀφέντες αὐτὸν ἔφυγον[10] πάντες.

tunc discipuli eius relinquentes eum omnes fugerunt.

1. עוּר, qal impv. f. s., *awake, rise up*
2. גֶּבֶר, *man*
3. עָמִית, *fellow, associate, neighbor*
4. פּוּץ, qal impf. 3 f. p. juss., *scatter*
5. צָעַר, qal ptcp. m. p. abs., *be little/insignificant*
6. ἐξεγείρω, aor. pass. impv. 2 s., *awake, rise up*
7. ποιμήν, *shepherd*
8. πολίτης, *citizen*
9. ἐκσπάω, aor. act. impv. 2 p., *remove, draw out*
10. φεύγω, aor. act. ind. 3 p., *flee*

August 14

Isaiah 50:6

גֵּוִי[1] נָתַתִּי לְמַכִּים וּלְחָיַי[2] לְמֹרְטִים[3] פָּנַי לֹא הִסְתַּרְתִּי[4]
מִכְּלִמּוֹת[5] וָרֹק׃[6]

τὸν νῶτόν[7] μου δέδωκα εἰς μάστιγας,[8] τὰς δὲ σιαγόνας[9] μου εἰς ῥαπίσματα,[10] τὸ δὲ πρόσωπόν μου οὐκ ἀπέστρεψα ἀπὸ αἰσχύνης[11] ἐμπτυσμάτων.[12]

Matthew 26:67

Τότε ἐνέπτυσαν[13] εἰς τὸ πρόσωπον αὐτοῦ καὶ ἐκολάφισαν[14] αὐτόν, οἱ δὲ ἐράπισαν.[15]

tunc expuerunt[16] in faciem eius et colaphis[17] eum ciciderunt[18] alii autem palmas[19] in faciem ei dederunt.

1. גַּו, *back*
2. לְחִי, *cheek*
3. מָרַט, qal ptcp. m. p. abs., *make smooth/bald*
4. סָתַר, hiph. perf. 1 c. s., *hide, conceal*
5. כְּלִמָּה, *insult, disgrace*
6. רֹק, *spit*
7. νῶτος, *back*
8. μάστιξ, *whip*
9. σιαγών, *cheek*
10. ῥάπισμα, *blow*
11. αἰσχύνη, *shame*
12. ἔμπτυσμα, *spit*
13. ἐμπτύω, aor. act. ind. 3 p., *spit upon*
14. κολαφίζω, aor. act. ind. 3 p., *beat, strike*
15. ῥαπίζω, aor. act. ind. 3 p., *strike*
16. exspuo, perf. act. ind. 3 p., *spit upon*
17. colaphus, *blow*
18. caedo, perf. act. ind. 3 p., *beat, strike*
19. palma, *palm branch*

August 15

Psalm 22:8 [LXX 21:8]

כָּל־רֹ֭אַי יַלְעִ֣גוּ[1] לִ֑י יַפְטִ֥ירוּ[2] בְ֝שָׂפָ֗ה יָנִ֥יעוּ[3] רֹֽאשׁ׃

πάντες οἱ θεωροῦντές[4] με ἐξεμυκτήρισάν[5] με, ἐλάλησαν ἐν χείλεσιν, ἐκίνησαν[6] κεφαλήν.

Mark 15:29

Καὶ οἱ παραπορευόμενοι[7] ἐβλασφήμουν αὐτὸν κινοῦντες[8] τὰς κεφαλὰς αὐτῶν καὶ λέγοντες· οὐὰ[9] ὁ καταλύων[10] τὸν ναὸν καὶ οἰκοδομῶν ἐν τρισὶν ἡμέραις.

et praetereuntes[11] blasphemabant eum moventes[12] capita sua et dicentes va[13] qui destruit[14] templum et in tribus diebus aedificat.

1. לָעַג, hiph. impf. 3 m. p., *mock*
2. פָּטַר, hiph. impf. 3 m. p., *separate*; TH: here used idiomatically with *lip* to mean *mock*.
3. נוּעַ, hiph. impf. 3 m. p., *shake*
4. θεωρέω, pres. act. ptcp. m. nom. p., *see*
5. ἐκμυκτηρίζω, aor. act. ind. 3 p., *mock*
6. κινέω, aor. act. ind. 3 p., *move*
7. παραπορεύομαι, pres. mid. ptcp. m. nom. p., *pass by*
8. κινέω, pres. act. ptcp. m. nom. p., *move*
9. οὐά, *aha*
10. καταλύω, pres. act. ptcp. m. nom. s., *destroy*
11. praetereo, pres. act. ptcp. m. nom. p., *pass by*
12. moveo, pres. act. ptcp. m. nom. p., *move*
13. va, *ah!*
14. destruo, pres. act. ind. 3 s., *destroy*

August 16

Psalm 26:6 [LXX 25:6]

אֶרְחַ֣ץ[1] בְּנִקָּי֣וֹן[2] כַּפָּ֑י וַאֲסֹבְבָ֖ה אֶת־מִזְבַּחֲךָ֣ יְהוָֽה׃

νίψομαι[3] ἐν ἀθῴοις[4] τὰς χεῖράς μου καὶ κυκλώσω[5] τὸ θυσιαστήριόν σου, κύριε.

Matthew 27:24

Ἰδὼν δὲ ὁ Πιλᾶτος ὅτι οὐδὲν ὠφελεῖ[6] ἀλλὰ μᾶλλον θόρυβος[7] γίνεται, λαβὼν ὕδωρ ἀπενίψατο[8] τὰς χεῖρας ἀπέναντι[9] τοῦ ὄχλου λέγων· ἀθῷός εἰμι ἀπὸ τοῦ αἵματος τούτου· ὑμεῖς ὄψεσθε.

videns autem Pilatus quia nihil proficeret[10] sed magis tumultus[11] fieret accepta aqua lavit[12] manus coram populo dicens innocens[13] ego sum a sanguine iusti huius vos videritis.

1. רָחַץ, qal impf. 1 c. s., *wash*
2. נִקָּיוֹן, *pure, innocent*
3. νίπτω, fut. mid. ind. 1 s., *wash*
4. ἀθῷος, *innocent*
5. κυκλόω, fut. act. ind. 1 s., *surround*
6. ὠφελέω, pres. act. ind. 3 s., *gain*
7. θόρυβος, *tumult, riot*
8. ἀπονίπτω, aor. mid. ind. 3 s., *wash*
9. ἀπέναντι, *before*
10. proficio, impf. act. subj. 3 s., *profit*
11. tumultus, *tulmult, riot*
12. lavo, perf. act. ind. 3 s., *wash*
13. innocens, *innocent*

August 17

Psalm 22:9 [LXX 21:9]

גֹּ֣ל[1] אֶל־יְהוָ֣ה יְפַלְּטֵ֑הוּ[2] יַ֝צִּילֵ֗הוּ כִּ֘י חָ֥פֵֽץ[3] בּֽוֹ׃

Ἤλπισεν ἐπὶ κύριον, ῥυσάσθω[4] αὐτόν· σωσάτω αὐτόν, ὅτι θέλει αὐτόν.

Matthew 27:43

πέποιθεν ἐπὶ τὸν θεόν, ῥυσάσθω νῦν εἰ θέλει αὐτόν· εἶπεν γὰρ ὅτι θεοῦ εἰμι υἱός.

confidet[5] in Deo liberet[6] nunc eum si vult dixit enim quia Dei Filius sum.

1. גָּלַל, qal impv. m. s., *rely on, trust*
2. פָּלַט, piel impf. 3 m. s. juss., *deliver*
3. חָפֵץ, qal perf. 3 m. s., *delight*
4. ῥύομαι, aor. mid. impv. 3 s., *deliver*
5. confido, fut. act. ind. 3 s., *be confident*
6. libero, pres. act. subj. 3 s., *set free*

August 18

Psalm 22:19 [LXX 21:19]

יְחַלְּק֣וּ[1] בְגָדַ֣י לָהֶ֑ם וְעַל־לְ֝בוּשִׁ֗י[2] יַפִּ֥ילוּ גוֹרָֽל׃[3]

διεμερίσαντο[4] τὰ ἱμάτιά μου ἑαυτοῖς καὶ ἐπὶ τὸν ἱματισμόν[5] μου ἔβαλον[6] κλῆρον.[7]

Mark 15:24

Καὶ σταυροῦσιν αὐτὸν καὶ *διαμερίζονται*[8] *τὰ ἱμάτια αὐτοῦ βάλλοντες κλῆρον ἐπ᾽ αὐτὰ* τίς τί ἄρῃ.

et crucifigentes eum diviserunt[9] vestimenta eius mittentes sortem[10] super eis quis quid tolleret.

1. חָלַק, piel impf. 3 m. p., *divide*
2. לְבוּשׁ, *clothing*
3. גּוֹרָל, *lot*
4. διαμερίζω, aor. mid. ind. 3 p., *divide*
5. ἱματισμός, *clothing*
6. βάλλω, aor. act. ind. 3 p., *throw, cast*
7. κλῆρος, *lot*
8. διαμερίζω, pres. mid. ind. 3 p., *divide*
9. divido, perf. act. ind. 3 p., *divide up*
10. sors, *lot*

August 19

Psalm 69:22 [LXX 68:22]

וַיִּתְּנוּ בְּבָרוּתִי[1] רֹאשׁ[2] וְלִצְמָאִי[3] יַשְׁקוּנִי[4] חֹמֶץ׃[5]

καὶ ἔδωκαν εἰς τὸ βρῶμά[6] μου χολὴν[7] καὶ εἰς τὴν δίψαν[8] μου ἐπότισάν[9] με ὄξος.[10]

John 19:29

σκεῦος[11] ἔκειτο[12] ὄξους[13] μεστόν·[14] σπόγγον[15] οὖν μεστὸν τοῦ ὄξους ὑσσώπῳ[16] περιθέντες[17] προσήνεγκαν αὐτοῦ τῷ στόματι.

vas[18] ergo positum erat aceto[19] plenum illi autem spongiam[20] plenam aceto hysopo[21] circumponentes[22] obtulerunt ori eius.

1. בָּרוּת, *food*
2. רֹאשׁ, *poison*
3. צָמָא, *thirst*
4. שָׁקָה, hiph. impf. 3 m. p., *give/cause to drink*
5. חֹמֶץ, *vinegar, sour wine*
6. βρῶμα, *food*
7. χολή, *gall*
8. δίψα, *thirst*
9. ποτίζω, aor. act. ind. 3 p., *give a drink*
10. ὄξος, *vinegar*
11. σκεῦος, *vessel, jar*
12. κεῖμαι, impf. mid. ind. 3 s., *lie down*
13. ὄξος, *sour wine, vinegar*
14. μεστός, *full*
15. σπόγγος, *sponge*
16. ὕσσωπος, *hyssop*
17. περιτίθημι, aor. act. ptcp. m. nom. p., *put on*
18. vas, *vessel, jar*
19. acetum, *sour wine, vinegar*
20. spongia, *sponge*
21. hysopus, *hyssop*
22. circumpono, pres. act. ptcp. m. nom. p., *place/wrap around*

August 20

1. רָחוֹק, *distant, far*

2. יְשׁוּעָה, *salvation*

3. שְׁאָגָה, *groaning, cry in distress*

4. ἐγκαταλείπω, aor. act. ind. 2 s., *forsake, desert*

5. μακράν, *far off*

6. παράπτωμα, *transgression*

7. ἔνατος, *ninth*

8. βοάω, aor. act. ind. 3 s., *cry out*

9. TH: *ελωι ελωι λεμα σαβαχθανι* is a transliteration from Aramaic, which is translated in the subsequent clause.

10. μεθερμηνεύω, pres. pass. ptcp. n. nom. s., *translate*

11. nonus, *ninth*

12. exclamo, perf. act. ind. 3 s., *cry aloud*

13. TH: *Heloi Heloi lema sabacthani* is a transliteration from Aramaic, which is translated in the subsequent clause.

14. interpretor, perf. dep. ind. 3 s., *interpret*

15. derelinquo, perf. act. ind. 2 s., *forsake*

Psalm 22:2 [LXX 21:2]

אֵלִ֣י אֵ֭לִי לָמָ֣ה עֲזַבְתָּ֑נִי רָח֥וֹק[1] מִֽ֝ישׁוּעָתִ֗י[2] דִּבְרֵ֥י שַׁאֲגָתִֽי׃[3]

Ὁ θεὸς ὁ θεός μου, πρόσχες μοι· ἵνα τί ἐγκατέλιπές[4] με; μακρὰν[5] ἀπὸ τῆς σωτηρίας μου οἱ λόγοι τῶν παραπτωμάτων[6] μου.

Mark 15:34

καὶ τῇ ἐνάτῃ[7] ὥρᾳ ἐβόησεν[8] ὁ Ἰησοῦς φωνῇ μεγάλῃ· *ελωι ελωι λεμα σαβαχθανι;*[9] ὅ ἐστιν μεθερμηνευόμενον·[10] *ὁ θεός μου ὁ θεός μου, εἰς τί ἐγκατέλιπές με;*

et hora nona[11] exclamavit[12] Iesus voce magna dicens Heloi Heloi lama sabacthani[13] quod est interpretatum[14] Deus meus Deus meus ut quid dereliquisti[15] me?

August 21

Psalm 31:6 [LXX 30:6]

בְּיָדְךָ֮ אַפְקִ֪יד ר֫וּחִ֥י פָּדִ֖יתָה[1] אוֹתִ֥י יְהוָ֗ה אֵ֣ל אֱמֶֽת׃

εἰς χεῖράς σου παραθήσομαι[2] τὸ πνεῦμά μου·
ἐλυτρώσω με, κύριε ὁ θεὸς τῆς ἀληθείας.

Luke 23:46

καὶ φωνήσας φωνῇ μεγάλῃ ὁ Ἰησοῦς εἶπεν· πάτερ, *εἰς χεῖράς σου παρατίθεμαι*[3] *τὸ πνεῦμά μου.* τοῦτο δὲ εἰπὼν ἐξέπνευσεν.[4]

et clamans voce magna Iesus ait Pater in manus tuas commendo[5] spiritum meum et haec dicens exspiravit.[6]

1. פָּדָה, qal perf. 2 m. s., *redeem, rescue*

2. παρατίθημι, fut. mid. ind. 1 s., *commit, commend*

3. παρατίθημι, pres. mid. ind. 1 s., *commit, commend*

4. ἐκπνέω, aor. act. ind. 3 s., *breathe out, die*

5. commendo, pres. act. ind. 1 s., *to commit to the care of*

6. exspiro, perf. act. ind. 3 s., *breathe out*

August 22

Psalm 34:21 [LXX 33:21]

שֹׁמֵ֥ר כָּל־עַצְמוֹתָ֑יו אַחַ֥ת מֵ֝הֵ֗נָּה לֹ֣א נִשְׁבָּֽרָה׃

κύριος φυλάσσει πάντα τὰ ὀστᾶ[1] αὐτῶν, ἓν ἐξ αὐτῶν οὐ συντριβήσεται.[2]

John 19:36

ἐγένετο γὰρ ταῦτα ἵνα ἡ γραφὴ πληρωθῇ· *ὀστοῦν οὐ συντριβήσεται αὐτοῦ.*

facta sunt enim haec ut scriptura impleatur os[3] non comminuetis[4] ex eo.

1. ὀστέον, *bone*

2. συντρίβω, fut. pass. ind. 3 s., *break, crush*

3. os, *bone*

4. comminuo, fut. act. ind. 2 p., *break*

August 23

Leviticus 16:21

וְסָמַ֨ךְ[1] אַהֲרֹ֜ן אֶת־שְׁתֵּ֣י יָדָ֗ו עַ֨ל רֹ֣אשׁ הַשָּׂעִיר֮[2] הַחַי֒
וְהִתְוַדָּ֣ה עָלָ֗יו אֶת־כָּל־עֲוֺנֹת֙ בְּנֵ֣י יִשְׂרָאֵ֔ל וְאֶת־כָּל־
פִּשְׁעֵיהֶ֖ם[3] לְכָל־חַטֹּאתָ֑ם וְנָתַ֤ן אֹתָם֙ עַל־רֹ֣אשׁ
הַשָּׂעִ֔יר וְשִׁלַּ֛ח בְּיַד־אִ֥ישׁ עִתִּ֖י[4] הַמִּדְבָּֽרָה׃

καὶ ἐπιθήσει Ααρων τὰς χεῖρας αὐτοῦ ἐπὶ τὴν κεφαλὴν τοῦ χιμάρου[5] τοῦ ζῶντος καὶ ἐξαγορεύσει[6] ἐπ᾽ αὐτοῦ πάσας τὰς ἀνομίας τῶν υἱῶν Ισραηλ καὶ πάσας τὰς ἀδικίας αὐτῶν καὶ πάσας τὰς ἁμαρτίας αὐτῶν καὶ ἐπιθήσει αὐτὰς ἐπὶ τὴν κεφαλὴν τοῦ χιμάρου τοῦ ζῶντος καὶ ἐξαποστελεῖ ἐν χειρὶ ἀνθρώπου ἑτοίμου[7] εἰς τὴν ἔρημον.

Hebrews 10:4

ἀδύνατον[8] γὰρ αἷμα ταύρων[9] καὶ τράγων[10] ἀφαιρεῖν[11] ἁμαρτίας.

inpossibile[12] enim est sanguine taurorum[13] et hircorum[14] auferri[15] peccata.

1. סָמַךְ, qal perf. 3 m. s., *lay*
2. שָׂעִיר, *male goat*
3. פֶּשַׁע, *transgression*
4. עִתִּי, *ready*
5. χίμαρος, *male goat*
6. ἐξαγορεύω, fut. act. ind. 3 s., *confess*
7. ἕτοιμος, *ready*
8. ἀδύνατος, *impossible*
9. ταῦρος, *bull*
10. τράγος, *goat*
11. ἀφαιρέω, pres. act. inf., *take away*
12. inpossibilis, *impossible*
13. taurus, *bull*
14. hircus, *goat*
15. aufero, pres. pass. inf., *take away, remove*

August 24

Psalm 8:6

וַתְּחַסְּרֵהוּ[1] מְּעַט מֵאֱלֹהִים וְכָבוֹד וְהָדָר[2] תְּעַטְּרֵהוּ׃[3]

ἠλάττωσας[4] αὐτὸν βραχύ[5] τι παρ᾽ ἀγγέλους,
δόξῃ καὶ τιμῇ[6] ἐστεφάνωσας[7] αὐτόν.

Hebrews 2:9

τὸν δὲ βραχύ τι παρ᾽ ἀγγέλους ἠλαττωμένον[8] βλέπομεν Ἰησοῦν διὰ τὸ πάθημα[9] τοῦ θανάτου δόξῃ καὶ τιμῇ ἐστεφανωμένον,[10] ὅπως χάριτι θεοῦ ὑπὲρ παντὸς γεύσηται[11] θανάτου.

eum autem qui modico quam angeli minoratus[12] est videmus Iesum propter passionem[13] mortis gloria et honore coronatum[14] ut gratia Dei pro omnibus gustaret[15] mortem.

1. חָסֵר, piel wcons. 2 s., *lack*
2. הָדָר, *honor*
3. עָטַר, piel impf. 2 m. s., *crown, surround*
4. ἐλαττόω, aor. act. ind. 2 s., *make lower, less than*
5. βραχύς, *little*
6. τιμή, *honor*
7. στεφανόω, aor. act. ind. 2 s., *crown*
8. ἐλαττόω, perf. pass. ptcp. m. a. s., *make less, lower*
9. πάθημα, *suffering*
10. στεφανόω, perf. pass. ptcp. m. a. s., *crown*
11. γεύομαι, aor. mid. subj. 3 s., *taste, experience*
12. minoro, perf. pass. ind. 3 s., *be made less, be in want*
13. passio, *suffering*
14. corono, perf. pass. m. a. s., *crown*
15. gusto, impf. act. subj. 3 s., *taste*

August 25

Numbers 28:3

וְאָמַרְתָּ֣ לָהֶ֔ם זֶ֚ה הָֽאִשֶּׁ֔ה[1] אֲשֶׁ֥ר תַּקְרִ֖יבוּ לַיהוָ֑ה
כְּבָשִׂ֨ים בְּנֵֽי־שָׁנָ֧ה תְמִימִ֛ם[2] שְׁנַ֥יִם לַיּ֖וֹם עֹלָ֥ה תָמִֽיד׃

καὶ ἐρεῖς πρὸς αὐτούς Ταῦτα τὰ καρπώματα,[3] ὅσα προσάξετε κυρίῳ· ἀμνοὺς ἐνιαυσίους[4] ἀμώμους[5] δύο τὴν ἡμέραν εἰς ὁλοκαύτωσιν[6] ἐνδελεχῶς.[7]

Hebrews 7:27

ὃς[8] οὐκ ἔχει καθ᾽ ἡμέραν ἀνάγκην,[9] ὥσπερ οἱ ἀρχιερεῖς, πρότερον[10] ὑπὲρ τῶν ἰδίων ἁμαρτιῶν θυσίας[11] ἀναφέρειν[12] ἔπειτα[13] τῶν τοῦ λαοῦ· τοῦτο γὰρ ἐποίησεν ἐφάπαξ[14] ἑαυτὸν ἀνενέγκας.[15]

qui[16] non habet cotidie[17] necessitatem[18] quemadmodum sacerdotes prius[19] pro suis delictis[20] hostias[21] offerre deinde[22] pro populi hoc enim fecit semel[23] se offerendo.

1. אִשֶּׁה, *offering*
2. תָּמִים, *blameless, without blemish*
3. κάρπωμα, *offering*
4. ἐνιαύσιος, *year old*
5. ἄμωμος, *blameless, without blemish*
6. ὁλοκαύτωσις, *whole burnt offering*
7. ἐνδελεχῶς, *continually*
8. CH: This relative pronoun refers back to Jesus. Simply translate here as *Jesus.*
9. ἀνάγκη, *necessity*
10. πρότερος, *first*
11. θυσία, *sacrifice*
12. ἀναφέρω, pres. act. inf., *offer up*
13. ἔπειτα, *then*
14. ἐφάπαξ, *once for all*
15. ἀναφέρω, aor. act. ptcp. m. nom. s., *offer up*
16. CH: This relative pronoun refers back to Jesus. Simply translate here as *Jesus.*
17. cotidie, *daily*
18. necessitas, *necessity, need*

19. prius, *first.* **20.** delictum, *offence, fault.* **21.** hostia, *offering, sacrifice.* **22.** deinde, *then.* **23.** semel, *once*

August 26

Leviticus 16:27

וְאֵת֩ פַּ֨ר הַֽחַטָּ֜את וְאֵ֣ת ׀ שְׂעִ֣יר[1] הַֽחַטָּ֗את אֲשֶׁ֨ר הוּבָ֤א אֶת־דָּמָם֙ לְכַפֵּ֣ר בַּקֹּ֔דֶשׁ יוֹצִ֖יא אֶל־מִח֣וּץ לַֽמַּחֲנֶ֑ה וְשָׂרְפ֣וּ בָאֵ֔שׁ אֶת־עֹרֹתָ֥ם[2] וְאֶת־בְּשָׂרָ֖ם וְאֶת־פִּרְשָֽׁם׃[3]

καὶ τὸν μόσχον τὸν περὶ τῆς ἁμαρτίας καὶ τὸν χίμαρον[4] τὸν περὶ τῆς ἁμαρτίας, ὧν τὸ αἷμα εἰσηνέχθη[5] ἐξιλάσασθαι ἐν τῷ ἁγίῳ, ἐξοίσουσιν[6] αὐτὰ ἔξω τῆς παρεμβολῆς καὶ κατακαύσουσιν[7] αὐτὰ ἐν πυρί, καὶ τὰ δέρματα[8] αὐτῶν καὶ τὰ κρέα[9] αὐτῶν καὶ τὴν κόπρον[10] αὐτῶν.

Hebrews 13:11

ὧν γὰρ εἰσφέρεται[11] ζῴων[12] τὸ αἷμα περὶ ἁμαρτίας εἰς τὰ ἅγια διὰ τοῦ ἀρχιερέως, τούτων τὰ σώματα κατακαίεται[13] ἔξω τῆς παρεμβολῆς.[14]

quorum enim animalium[15] infertur[16] sanguis pro peccato in sancta[17] per pontificem horum corpora cremantur[18] extra[19] castra.[20]

1. שָׂעִיר, *male goat*
2. עוֹר, *skin*
3. פֶּ֫רֶשׁ, *dung*
4. χίμαρος, *male goat*
5. εἰσφέρω, aor. pass. ind. 3 s., *bring in*
6. ἐκφέρω, fut. act. ind. 3 p., *carry out*
7. κατακαίω, fut. act. ind. 3 p., *burn up*
8. δέρμα, *skin*
9. κρέας, *meat*
10. κόπρος, *excrement, dung*
11. εἰσφέρω, pres. pass. ind. 3 s., *bring in*
12. ζῷον, *animal, living being*
13. κατακαίω, pres. pass. ind. 3 p., *burn up*
14. παρεμβολή, *camp*
15. animal, *animal*
16. infero, pres. pass. ind. 3 s., *bring in*
17. sanctum, *sanctuary*
18. cremo, pres. pass. ind. 3 p., *burn*
19. extra, *outside*
20. castra, *camp*

August 27

Leviticus 16:15

וְשָׁחַ֞ט[1] אֶת־שְׂעִ֣יר[2] הַֽחַטָּאת֮ אֲשֶׁ֣ר לָעָם֒ וְהֵבִיא֙
אֶת־דָּמ֔וֹ אֶל־מִבֵּ֖ית לַפָּרֹ֑כֶת[3] וְעָשָׂ֣ה אֶת־דָּמ֗וֹ כַּאֲשֶׁ֤ר
עָשָׂה֙ לְדַ֣ם הַפָּ֔ר וְהִזָּ֥ה[4] אֹת֛וֹ עַֽל־הַכַּפֹּ֖רֶת[5] וְלִפְנֵ֥י
הַכַּפֹּֽרֶת׃

καὶ σφάξει[6] τὸν χίμαρον[7] τὸν περὶ τῆς ἁμαρτίας τὸν περὶ τοῦ λαοῦ ἔναντι κυρίου καὶ εἰσοίσει[8] ἀπὸ τοῦ αἵματος αὐτοῦ ἐσώτερον[9] τοῦ καταπετάσματος[10] καὶ ποιήσει τὸ αἷμα αὐτοῦ ὃν τρόπον ἐποίησεν τὸ αἷμα τοῦ μόσχου, καὶ ῥανεῖ[11] τὸ αἷμα αὐτοῦ ἐπὶ τὸ ἱλαστήριον[12] κατὰ πρόσωπον τοῦ ἱλαστηρίου.

Hebrews 6:19

ἣν[13] ὡς ἄγκυραν[14] ἔχομεν τῆς ψυχῆς ἀσφαλῆ[15] τε καὶ βεβαίαν[16] καὶ εἰσερχομένην εἰς τὸ ἐσώτερον τοῦ καταπετάσματος,[17]

quam[18] sicut anchoram[19] habemus animae tutam[20] ac firmam[21] et incedentem[22] usque in interiora[23] velaminis,[24]

18. TH: This relative pronoun refers back to "hope." Translate: *We have this [hope].* **19.** anchora, *anchor.* **20.** tutus, *secure.* **21.** firmus, *firm.* **22.** incedo, pres. act. ptcp. m. a. s., *enter.* **23.** interior, *inner.* **24.** velamen, *curtain, veil*

1. שָׁחַט, qal perf. 3 m. s., *slaughter*

2. שָׂעִיר, *male goat*

3. פָּרֹ֫כֶת, *curtain, veil*

4. נָזָה, hiph. perf. 3 m. s., *sprinkle*

5. כַּפֹּרֶת, *atonement*

6. σφάζω, fut. act. ind. 3 s., *slaughter*

7. χίμαρος, *young male goat*

8. εἰσφέρω, fut. act. ind. 3 s., *bring in*

9. ἔσω, *inside*

10. καταπέτασμα, *curtain, veil*

11. ῥαίνω, fut. act. ind. 3 s., *sprinkle*

12. ἱλαστήριον, *place of propitiation/forgiveness*

13. TH: This relative pronoun refers back to "hope." Translate: *We have this [hope].*

14. ἄγκυρα, *anchor*

15. ἀσφαλής, *certain*

16. βέβαιος, *firm*

17. καταπέτασμα, *curtain, veil*

August 28

Leviticus 16:16

וְכִפֶּ֤ר עַל־הַקֹּ֙דֶשׁ֙ מִטֻּמְאֹת֙[1] בְּנֵ֣י יִשְׂרָאֵ֔ל וּמִפִּשְׁעֵיהֶ֖ם[2]
לְכָל־חַטֹּאתָ֑ם וְכֵ֤ן יַעֲשֶׂה֙ לְאֹ֣הֶל מוֹעֵ֔ד הַשֹּׁכֵ֣ן אִתָּ֔ם
בְּת֖וֹךְ טֻמְאֹתָֽם׃

καὶ ἐξιλάσεται τὸ ἅγιον ἀπὸ τῶν ἀκαθαρσιῶν[3] τῶν υἱῶν Ισραηλ καὶ ἀπὸ τῶν ἀδικημάτων[4] αὐτῶν περὶ πασῶν τῶν ἁμαρτιῶν αὐτῶν· καὶ οὕτω ποιήσει τῇ σκηνῇ τοῦ μαρτυρίου τῇ ἐκτισμένῃ[5] ἐν αὐτοῖς ἐν μέσῳ τῆς ἀκαθαρσίας αὐτῶν.

1. טֻמְאָה, *uncleanness, impurity*
2. פֶּשַׁע, *transgression*
3. ἀκαθαρσία, *uncleanness*
4. ἀδίκημα, *sin, unrighteousness*
5. κτίζω, perf. pass. ptcp. f. d. s., *build, found*

Hebrews 6:20

ὅπου[6] πρόδρομος[7] ὑπὲρ ἡμῶν εἰσῆλθεν Ἰησοῦς, κατὰ τὴν τάξιν[8] Μελχισέδεκ[9] ἀρχιερεὺς γενόμενος εἰς τὸν αἰῶνα.

ubi[10] praecursor[11] pro nobis introiit Iesus secundum ordinem[12] Melchisedech[13] pontifex factus in aeternum.

6. CH: This clause is dependent upon verse 19. “Where” refers to the place behind the “curtain.”
7. πρόδρομος, *forerunner*
8. τάξις, *order*
9. Μελχισέδεκ, *Melchizedek*
10. CH: This clause is dependent upon verse 19. “Where” refers to the place behind the “curtain.”
11. praecursor, *forerunner*
12. ordo, *order*
13. Melchisedech, *Melchizedek*

August 29

Psalm 110:1 [LXX 109:1]

... נְאֻ֤ם יְהוָ֨ה ׀ לַֽאדֹנִ֗י שֵׁ֥ב לִֽימִינִ֑י עַד־אָשִׁ֥ית[1] אֹ֝יְבֶ֗יךָ
הֲדֹ֣ם[2] לְרַגְלֶֽיךָ׃

... Εἶπεν ὁ κύριος τῷ κυρίῳ μου Κάθου ἐκ δεξιῶν μου, ἕως ἂν θῶ τοὺς ἐχθρούς σου ὑποπόδιον[3] τῶν ποδῶν σου.

Hebrews 1:3

ὃς[4] ὢν ἀπαύγασμα[5] τῆς δόξης καὶ χαρακτὴρ[6] τῆς ὑποστάσεως[7] αὐτοῦ, φέρων τε τὰ πάντα τῷ ῥήματι τῆς δυνάμεως αὐτοῦ, καθαρισμὸν[8] τῶν ἁμαρτιῶν ποιησάμενος ἐκάθισεν ἐν δεξιᾷ τῆς μεγαλωσύνης[9] ἐν ὑψηλοῖς.[10]

qui[11] cum sit splendor[12] gloriae et figura[13] substantiae[14] eius portansque omnia verbo virtutis suae purgationem[15] peccatorum faciens sedit ad dexteram Maiestatis[16] in excelsis.[17]

1. שִׁית, qal impf. 1 c. s., *put*
2. הֲדֹם, *footstool*
3. ὑποπόδιον, *footstool*
4. CH: This relative pronoun refers to Jesus; TH: ὃς ὢν = *who being* or *he is.*
5. ἀπαύγασμα, *radiance*
6. χαρακτήρ, *mark, imprint, image*
7. ὑπόστασις, *nature*
8. καθαρισμός, *purification*
9. μεγαλωσύνη, *majesty*
10. ὑψηλός, *high*
11. CH: This relative pronoun refers to Jesus; TH: qui cum sit = *who being* or *he is.*
12. splendor, *brilliance*
13. figura, *figure*
14. substantia, *essence*
15. purgatio, *purification*
16. maiestas, *glory*
17. excelsus, *high*

Resurrection

August 30

Exodus 3:6

וַיֹּ֗אמֶר אָנֹכִי֙ אֱלֹהֵ֣י אָבִ֔יךָ אֱלֹהֵ֧י אַבְרָהָ֛ם אֱלֹהֵ֥י יִצְחָ֖ק
וֵאלֹהֵ֣י יַעֲקֹ֑ב וַיַּסְתֵּ֤ר[1] מֹשֶׁה֙ פָּנָ֔יו כִּ֣י יָרֵ֔א מֵהַבִּ֖יט[2]
אֶל־הָאֱלֹהִֽים׃

καὶ εἶπεν αὐτῷ Ἐγώ εἰμι ὁ θεὸς τοῦ πατρός σου, θεὸς Αβρααμ καὶ θεὸς Ισαακ[3] καὶ θεὸς Ιακωβ.[4] ἀπέστρεψεν δὲ Μωυσῆς τὸ πρόσωπον αὐτοῦ· εὐλαβεῖτο[5] γὰρ κατεμβλέψαι[6] ἐνώπιον τοῦ θεοῦ.

Matthew 22:32

ἐγώ εἰμι ὁ θεὸς Ἀβραὰμ καὶ ὁ θεὸς Ἰσαὰκ καὶ ὁ θεὸς Ἰακώβ; οὐκ ἔστιν [ὁ] θεὸς νεκρῶν ἀλλὰ ζώντων.

ego sum Deus Abraham et Deus Isaac[7] et Deus Iacob[8] non est Deus mortuorum sed viventium.

1. סָתַר, hiph. wcons. 3 m. s., *hide, conceal*
2. נָבַט, hiph. inf. cons., *look*
3. Ἰσαάκ, *Isaac*
4. Ἰακώβ, *Jacob*
5. εὐλαβέομαι, impf. mid. ind. 3 s., *be reverent, cautious*
6. κατεμβλέπω, aor. act. inf., *look down*
7. Isaac, *Isaac*
8. Iacob, *Jacob*

August 31

1 Kings 17:21

וַיִּתְמֹדֵד[1] עַל־הַיֶּלֶד[2] שָׁלֹשׁ פְּעָמִים וַיִּקְרָא אֶל־
יְהוָה וַיֹּאמַר יְהוָה אֱלֹהָי תָּשָׁב נָא נֶפֶשׁ־הַיֶּלֶד הַזֶּה
עַל־קִרְבּוֹ׃

καὶ ἐνεφύσησεν[3] τῷ παιδαρίῳ τρὶς[4] καὶ ἐπεκαλέσατο τὸν κύριον καὶ εἶπεν Κύριε ὁ θεός μου, ἐπιστραφήτω δὴ ἡ ψυχὴ τοῦ παιδαρίου τούτου εἰς αὐτόν.

Luke 8:54–55a

αὐτὸς δὲ κρατήσας τῆς χειρὸς αὐτῆς ἐφώνησεν λέγων· ἡ παῖς,[5] ἔγειρε. καὶ ἐπέστρεψεν τὸ πνεῦμα αὐτῆς καὶ ἀνέστη παραχρῆμα.[6]

ipse autem tenens manum eius clamavit dicens puella[7] surge et reversus est spiritus eius et surrexit continuo.[8]

1. מָדַד, hitpolel wcons. 3 m. s., *stretch*
2. יֶלֶד, *child*
3. ἐμφυσάω, aor. act. ind. 3 s., *breathe*
4. τρίς, *three times*
5. παῖς, *child*
6. παραχρῆμα, *immediately*
7. puella, *girl, maiden*
8. continuo, *immediately*

September 1

2 Kings 4:32

וַיָּבֹא אֱלִישָׁע[1] הַבָּיְתָה וְהִנֵּה הַנַּעַר מֵת מֻשְׁכָּב
עַל־מִטָּתוֹ׃[2]

καὶ εἰσῆλθεν Ελισαιε[3] εἰς τὸν οἶκον, καὶ ἰδοὺ τὸ παιδάριον τεθνηκὸς[4] κεκοιμισμένον[5] ἐπὶ τὴν κλίνην[6] αὐτοῦ.

Acts 20:9

καθεζόμενος[7] δέ τις νεανίας[8] ὀνόματι Εὔτυχος[9] ἐπὶ τῆς θυρίδος,[10] καταφερόμενος[11] ὕπνῳ[12] βαθεῖ[13] διαλεγομένου[14] τοῦ Παύλου ἐπὶ πλεῖον, κατενεχθεὶς[15] ἀπὸ τοῦ ὕπνου ἔπεσεν ἀπὸ τοῦ τριστέγου[16] κάτω[17] καὶ ἤρθη νεκρός.

sedens autem quidam adulescens[18] nomine Eutychus[19] super fenestram[20] cum mergeretur[21] somno[22] gravi[23] disputante[24] diu[25] Paulo eductus[26] somno cecidit de tertio cenaculo[27] deorsum[28] et sublatus est mortuus.

1. אֱלִישָׁע, *Elisha*
2. מִטָּה, *couch*
3. Ελισαιε, *Elisha*
4. θνήσκω, perf. act. ptcp. n. nom. s., *die*
5. κοιμίζω, perf. pass. ptcp. n. nom. s., *sleep*
6. κλίνη, *couch*
7. καθέζομαι, pres. mid. ptcp. m. nom. s., *sit*
8. νεανίας, *young man*
9. Εὔτυχος, *Eutychus*
10. θυρίς, *window*
11. καταφέρω, pres. mid. ptcp. m. nom. s., *sink*
12. ὕπνος, *sleep*
13. βαθύς, *deep*
14. διαλέγομαι, pres. mid. ptcp. m. g. s., *discuss*
15. καταφέρω, aor. pass. ptcp. m. nom. s., *sink, bring down*
16. τρίστεγον, *third story*
17. κάτω, *down*
18. adulescens, *young man*
19. Eutychus, *Eutychus*
20. fenestra, *window*

21. mergo, impf. pass. subj. 3 s., *plunge into.* **22.** somnus, *sleep.* **23.** gravis, *deep.* **24.** disputo, pres. act. ptcp. m. abl. s., *discuss.* **25.** diu, *for a long time.* **26.** educo, perf. pass. ptcp. m. nom. s., *lead.* **27.** cenaculum, *upper-room.* **28.** deorsum, *down*

September 2

2 Kings 4:34

וַיַּ֜עַל וַיִּשְׁכַּ֣ב עַל־הַיֶּ֗לֶד[1] וַיָּשֶׂם֩ פִּ֨יו עַל־פִּ֜יו וְעֵינָ֤יו עַל־עֵינָיו֙ וְכַפָּ֣יו עַל־כַּפָּ֔ו וַיִּגְהַ֖ר[2] עָלָ֑יו וַיָּ֖חָם[3] בְּשַׂ֥ר הַיָּֽלֶד׃

καὶ ἀνέβη καὶ ἐκοιμήθη ἐπὶ τὸ παιδάριον καὶ ἔθηκεν τὸ στόμα αὐτοῦ ἐπὶ τὸ στόμα αὐτοῦ καὶ τοὺς ὀφθαλμοὺς αὐτοῦ ἐπὶ τοὺς ὀφθαλμοὺς αὐτοῦ καὶ τὰς χεῖρας αὐτοῦ ἐπὶ τὰς χεῖρας αὐτοῦ καὶ διέκαμψεν[4] ἐπ᾽ αὐτόν, καὶ διεθερμάνθη[5] ἡ σὰρξ τοῦ παιδαρίου.

Acts 20:10

καταβὰς δὲ ὁ Παῦλος ἐπέπεσεν[6] αὐτῷ καὶ συμπεριλαβὼν[7] εἶπεν· μὴ θορυβεῖσθε,[8] ἡ γὰρ ψυχὴ αὐτοῦ ἐν αὐτῷ ἐστιν.

ad quem cum descendisset Paulus incubuit[9] super eum et conplexus[10] dixit nolite turbari[11] anima enim ipsius in eo est.

1. יֶ֫לֶד, *child*
2. גָּהַר, qal wcons. 3 m. s., *stretch*
3. חָמַם, qal wcons. 3 m. s., *warm*
4. διακάμπτω, aor. act. ind. 3 s., *bend*
5. διαθερμαίνω, aor. pass. ind. 3 s., *warm up*
6. ἐπιπίπτω, aor. act. ind. 3 s., *fall/lie upon*
7. συμπεριλαμβάνω, aor. act. ptcp. m. nom. s., *embrace*
8. θορυβέω, pres. mid. impv. 2 p., *be alarmed, troubled*
9. incumbo, perf. act. ind. 3 s., *lie upon*
10. conplector, perf. dep. ptcp. m. nom. s., *wrap around, embrace*
11. turbo, pres. pass. inf., *trouble*

September 3

Jonah 2:1

וַיְמַ֤ן[1] יְהוָה֙ דָּ֣ג[2] גָּד֔וֹל לִבְלֹ֖עַ[3] אֶת־יוֹנָ֑ה[4] וַיְהִ֤י יוֹנָה֙
בִּמְעֵ֣י[5] הַדָּ֔ג שְׁלֹשָׁ֥ה יָמִ֖ים וּשְׁלֹשָׁ֥ה לֵילֽוֹת׃

Καὶ προσέταξεν[6] κύριος κήτει[7] μεγάλῳ καταπιεῖν[8] τὸν Ιωναν·[9] καὶ ἦν Ιωνας ἐν τῇ κοιλίᾳ[10] τοῦ κήτους τρεῖς ἡμέρας καὶ τρεῖς νύκτας.

Mathew 12:40

ὥσπερ γὰρ ἦν Ἰωνᾶς ἐν τῇ κοιλίᾳ τοῦ κήτους τρεῖς ἡμέρας καὶ τρεῖς νύκτας, οὕτως ἔσται ὁ υἱὸς τοῦ ἀνθρώπου ἐν τῇ καρδίᾳ τῆς γῆς τρεῖς ἡμέρας καὶ τρεῖς νύκτας.

sicut enim fuit Ionas[11] in ventre[12] ceti[13] tribus diebus et tribus noctibus sic erit Filius hominis in corde terrae tribus diebus et tribus noctibus.

1. מָנָה, piel wcons. 3 m. s., *appoint, ordain*
2. דָּג, *fish*
3. בָּלַע, qal inf. cons., *swallow*
4. יוֹנָה, *Jonah*
5. מֵעֶה, *belly*
6. προστάσσω, aor. act. ind. 3 s., *command*
7. κῆτος, *sea monster*
8. καταπίνω, aor. act. inf., *swallow*
9. Ιωνας, *Jonah*
10. κοιλία, *stomach, womb*
11. Ionas, *Jonah*
12. venter, *belly, stomach*
13. cetus, *large sea creature*

September 4

Psalm 18:5–6 [LXX 17:5–6]

אֲפָפ֥וּנִי[1] חֶבְלֵי[2]־מָ֑וֶת וְֽנַחֲלֵ֖י בְלִיַּ֣עַל יְבַעֲתֽוּנִי׃ חֶבְלֵ֣י[3]
שְׁא֣וֹל[4] סְבָב֑וּנִי קִ֝דְּמ֗וּנִי[5] מ֣וֹקְשֵׁי[6] מָֽוֶת׃

περιέσχον[7] με ὠδῖνες[8] θανάτου, καὶ χείμαρροι[9] ἀνομίας ἐξετάραξάν[10] με ὠδῖνες ᾄδου περιεκύκλωσάν[11] με, προέφθασάν[12] με παγίδες[13] θανάτου.

Acts 2:23–24

τοῦτον τῇ ὡρισμένῃ[14] βουλῇ[15] καὶ προγνώσει[16] τοῦ θεοῦ ἔκδοτον[17] διὰ χειρὸς ἀνόμων[18] προσπήξαντες[19] ἀνείλατε,[20] ὃν ὁ θεὸς ἀνέστησεν λύσας τὰς ὠδῖνας τοῦ θανάτου, καθότι[21] οὐκ ἦν δυνατὸν κρατεῖσθαι αὐτὸν ὑπ᾽ αὐτοῦ.

hunc definito[22] consilio[23] et praescientia[24] Dei traditum per manus iniquorum[25] adfigentes[26] interemistis[27] quem Deus suscitavit solutis doloribus[28] inferni[29] iuxta[30] quod inpossibile[31] erat teneri illum ab eo.

19. προσπήγνυμι, aor. act. ptcp. m. nom. p., *crucify.* **20.** ἀναιρέω, aor. act. ind. 2 p., *kill.* **21.** καθότι, *since, as.* **22.** definio, perf. pass. ptcp. n. abl. s., *determine.* **23.** consilium, *counsel.* **24.** praescientia, *foreknowledge.* **25.** iniquus, *unrighteous, unjust.* **26.** adfigo, pres. act. ptcp. m. nom. p., *fasten*; TH: here *crucify.* **27.** interimo, perf. act. ind. 2 p., *slay.* **28.** dolor, *pain.* **29.** infernus, *hell, Hades.* **30.** iuxta, *since, according to.* **31.** inpossibilis, *impossible*

1. אָפַף, qal perf. 3 c. p., *surround*

2. חֶ֫בֶל, *cord*

3. בְּלִיַּ֫עַל, *ruin, destruction, chaos*

4. שְׁאוֹל, *Sheol*

5. קדם, piel perf. 3 c. p., *confront, come before*

6. מוֹקֵשׁ, *snare, trap*

7. περιέχω, aor. act. ind. 3 p., *surround*

8. ὠδίν, *pain*

9. χείμαρρος, *brook*

10. ἐκταράσσω, aor. act. ind. 3 p., *trouble, throw into confusion*

11. περικυκλόω, aor. act. ind. 3 p., *surround*

12. προφθάνω, aor. act. ind. 3 p., *outrun*

13. παγίς, *snare, trap*

14. ὁρίζω, perf. mid. ptcp. f. d. s., *determine*

15. βουλή, *plan, will*

16. πρόγνωσις, *foreknowledge*

17. ἔκδοτος, *delivered*

18. ἄνομος, *lawless*

September 5

Psalm 16:10 [LXX 15:10]

כִּ֤י ׀ לֹא־תַעֲזֹ֣ב נַפְשִׁ֣י לִשְׁא֑וֹל[1] לֹֽא־תִתֵּ֥ן חֲ֝סִידְךָ֗[2]
לִרְא֥וֹת שָֽׁחַת׃[3]

ὅτι οὐκ ἐγκαταλείψεις[4] τὴν ψυχήν μου εἰς ᾅδην[5]
οὐδὲ δώσεις τὸν ὅσιόν[6] σου ἰδεῖν διαφθοράν.[7]

Acts 2:31

προϊδὼν[8] ἐλάλησεν περὶ τῆς ἀναστάσεως τοῦ Χριστοῦ ὅτι οὔτε ἐγκατελείφθη[9] εἰς ᾅδην οὔτε ἡ σὰρξ αὐτοῦ εἶδεν διαφθοράν.

providens[10] locutus est de resurrectione Christi quia neque derelictus[11] est in inferno[12] neque caro eius vidit corruptionem.[13]

1. שְׁאוֹל, *Sheol*
2. חָסִיד, *godly, pious one*
3. שַׁ֫חַת, *corruption, pit*
4. ἐγκαταλείπω, fut. act. ind. 3 s., *forsake*
5. ᾅδης, *Hades*
6. ὅσιος, *pious*
7. διαφθορά, *decay, rot*
8. προοράω, aor. act. ptcp. m. nom. s., *foresee*
9. ἐγκαταλείπω, aor. pass. ind. 3 s., *forsake*
10. provideo, pres. act. ptcp. m. nom. s., *foresee*
11. derelinquo, perf. pass. ind. 3 s., *forsake*
12. infernus, *Hades*
13. corruptio, *corruption*

September 6

***Ezekiel* 37:12**

לָכֵן הִנָּבֵא וְאָמַרְתָּ אֲלֵיהֶם כֹּה־אָמַר אֲדֹנָי יְהוִה
הִנֵּה אֲנִי פֹתֵחַ אֶת־קִבְרוֹתֵיכֶם[1] וְהַעֲלֵיתִי אֶתְכֶם
מִקִּבְרוֹתֵיכֶם עַמִּי וְהֵבֵאתִי אֶתְכֶם אֶל־אַדְמַת
יִשְׂרָאֵל׃

διὰ τοῦτο προφήτευσον καὶ εἰπόν Τάδε λέγει κύριος Ἰδοὺ ἐγὼ ἀνοίγω ὑμῶν τὰ μνήματα[2] καὶ ἀνάξω ὑμᾶς ἐκ τῶν μνημάτων ὑμῶν καὶ εἰσάξω ὑμᾶς εἰς τὴν γῆν τοῦ Ισραηλ.

***Matthew* 27:52**

καὶ τὰ μνημεῖα ἀνεῴχθησαν καὶ πολλὰ σώματα τῶν κεκοιμημένων[3] ἁγίων ἠγέρθησαν.

et monumenta aperta sunt et multa corpora sanctorum qui dormierant surrexerunt.

1. קֶבֶר, *grave*
2. μνῆμα, *tomb*
3. κοιμάω, perf. pass. ptcp. m. g. p., *sleep*

September 7

Psalm 68:19 [LXX 67:19]

עָלִ֚יתָ לַמָּר֨וֹם[1] ׀ שָׁ֘בִ֤יתָ[2] שֶּׁ֗בִי[3] לָקַ֣חְתָּ מַ֭תָּנוֹת[4] בָּאָדָ֑ם
וְאַ֥ף ס֝וֹרְרִ֗ים[5] לִשְׁכֹּ֤ן ׀ יָ֬הּ[6] אֱלֹהִֽים׃

ἀνέβης εἰς ὕψος, ᾐχμαλώτευσας[7] αἰχμαλωσίαν, ἔλαβες δόματα[8] ἐν ἀνθρώπῳ, καὶ γὰρ ἀπειθοῦντες[9] τοῦ κατασκηνῶσαι.[10] κύριος ὁ θεὸς εὐλογητός.[11]

Ephesians 4:9[12]

τὸ δὲ *ἀνέβη* τί ἐστιν, εἰ μὴ ὅτι καὶ κατέβη εἰς τὰ κατώτερα[13] [μέρη] τῆς γῆς;

quod autem ascendit quid est nisi quia et descendit primum in inferiores[14] partes terrae?

1. מָרוֹם, *high, height*
2. שָׁבָה, qal perf. 2 m. s., *take captive*
3. שְׁבִי, *captive*
4. מַתָּנָה, *gift*
5. סָרַר, qal ptcp. m. p. abs., *be stubborn, rebellious*
6. יָהּ, *Yah, Yahweh*
7. αἰχμαλωτεύω, aor. act. ind. 2 s., *lead captive*
8. δόμα, *gift*
9. ἀπειθέω, pres. act. ptcp. m. nom. p., *disobey*
10. κατασκηνόω, aor. act. inf., *encamp, settle*
11. εὐλογητός, *blessed*
12. PA: Eph 4:9 represents a brief exposition of the psalm text.
13. κατώτερος, *lower*
14. inferus, *lower*

September 8

Hosea 13:14

מִיַּד שְׁאוֹל[1] אֶפְדֵּם[2] מִמָּוֶת אֶגְאָלֵם אֱהִי[3] דְבָרֶיךָ[4]
מָוֶת אֱהִי קָטָבְךָ[5] שְׁאוֹל נֹחַם[6] יִסָּתֵר[7] מֵעֵינָי׃

ἐκ χειρὸς ᾅδου ῥύσομαι αὐτοὺς καὶ ἐκ θανάτου λυτρώσομαι αὐτούς· ποῦ ἡ δίκη[8] σου, θάνατε; ποῦ τὸ κέντρον[9] σου, ᾅδη; παράκλησις[10] κέκρυπται ἀπὸ ὀφθαλμῶν μου.

1 Corinthians 15:54[11]

ὅταν δὲ τὸ φθαρτὸν[12] τοῦτο ἐνδύσηται[13] ἀφθαρσίαν[14] καὶ τὸ θνητὸν[15] τοῦτο ἐνδύσηται ἀθανασίαν,[16] τότε γενήσεται ὁ λόγος ὁ γεγραμμένος.

cum autem mortale[17] hoc induerit[18] inmortalitatem[19] tunc fiet sermo qui scriptus est absorta[20] est mors in victoria.[21]

1. שְׁאוֹל, *Sheol*
2. פָּדָה, qal impf. 1 c. s., *ransom, redeem*
3. אֱהִי, *where*
4. דֶּבֶר, *plague*
5. קֶטֶב, *pestilence, sting*
6. נֹחַם, *sorrow, compassion*
7. סָתַר, niph. impf. 3 m. s., *hid*
8. δίκη, *punishment*
9. κέντρον, *sting*
10. παράκλησις, *comfort*
11. PA: Paul cites the verse from Hosea in 1 Cor 15:55.
12. φθαρτός, *perishable, corruptible*
13. ἐνδύω, aor. mid. subj. 3 s., *put on, wear*
14. ἀφθαρσία, *incorruptible, imperishable*
15. θνητός, *mortal*
16. ἀθανασία, *immortality*
17. mortalis, *mortal*
18. induo, futperf. act. ind. 3 s., *clothe*
19. immortalitas, *immortality*
20. absorbeo, perf. pass. ind. 3 s., *swallow*
21. victoria, *victory*

Holy Spirit

September 9

Isaiah 32:15

עַד־יֵעָרֶה[1] עָלֵינוּ רוּחַ מִמָּרוֹם[2] וְהָיָה מִדְבָּר לַכַּרְמֶל[3]
וְכַרְמֶל לַיַּעַר[4] יֵחָשֵׁב׃

ἕως ἂν ἐπέλθῃ ἐφ᾽ ὑμᾶς πνεῦμα ἀφ᾽ ὑψηλοῦ. καὶ ἔσται ἔρημος ὁ Χερμελ,[5] καὶ ὁ Χερμελ εἰς δρυμὸν[6] λογισθήσεται.

Acts 1:8

ἀλλὰ λήμψεσθε δύναμιν ἐπελθόντος[7] τοῦ ἁγίου πνεύματος ἐφ᾽ ὑμᾶς καὶ ἔσεσθέ μου μάρτυρες ἔν τε Ἰερουσαλὴμ καὶ [ἐν] πάσῃ τῇ Ἰουδαίᾳ καὶ Σαμαρείᾳ[8] καὶ ἕως ἐσχάτου τῆς γῆς.

sed accipietis virtutem supervenientis[9] Spiritus Sancti in vos et eritis mihi testes in Hierusalem et in omni Iudaea et Samaria[10] et usque ad ultimum[11] terrae.

1. עָרָה, niph. impf. 3 m. s., *pour out, lay bare*
2. מָרוֹם, *high*
3. כַּרְמֶל, *(productive) field*
4. יַעַר, *forest*
5. Χερμελ, Carmel
6. δρυμός, *forest*
7. ἐπέρχομαι, aor. act. ptcp. n. g. s., *come upon*
8. Σαμάρεια, *Samaria*
9. supervenio, pres. act. ptcp. m. g. s., *come upon*
10. Samaria, *Samaria*
11. ulterior, *uttermost, furthest point*

September 10

Joel 3:1

וְהָיָ֣ה אַחֲרֵי־כֵ֗ן אֶשְׁפּ֤וֹךְ אֶת־רוּחִי֙ עַל־כָּל־בָּשָׂ֔ר
וְנִבְּא֖וּ בְּנֵיכֶ֣ם וּבְנוֹתֵיכֶ֑ם זִקְנֵיכֶ֗ם חֲלֹמוֹת֙[1] יַחֲלֹמ֔וּן[2]
בַּח֣וּרֵיכֶ֔ם[3] חֶזְיֹנ֖וֹת[4] יִרְאֽוּ׃

Καὶ ἔσται μετὰ ταῦτα καὶ ἐκχεῶ[5] ἀπὸ τοῦ πνεύματός μου ἐπὶ πᾶσαν σάρκα, καὶ προφητεύσουσιν[6] οἱ υἱοὶ ὑμῶν καὶ αἱ θυγατέρες[7] ὑμῶν, καὶ οἱ πρεσβύτεροι ὑμῶν ἐνύπνια[8] ἐνυπνιασθήσονται,[9] καὶ οἱ νεανίσκοι[10] ὑμῶν ὁράσεις[11] ὄψονται.

Acts 2:17

καὶ ἔσται ἐν ταῖς ἐσχάταις ἡμέραις, λέγει ὁ θεός, ἐκχεῶ ἀπὸ τοῦ πνεύματός μου ἐπὶ πᾶσαν σάρκα, καὶ προφητεύσουσιν οἱ υἱοὶ ὑμῶν καὶ αἱ θυγατέρες ὑμῶν καὶ οἱ νεανίσκοι ὑμῶν ὁράσεις ὄψονται καὶ οἱ πρεσβύτεροι ὑμῶν ἐνυπνίοις ἐνυπνιασθήσονται.

et erit in novissimis diebus dicit Dominus effundam[12] de Spiritu meo super omnem carnem et prophetabunt[13] filii vestri et filiae vestrae et iuvenes[14] vestri visiones[15] videbunt et seniores vestri somnia[16] somniabunt.[17]

1. חֲלוֹם, *dream*
2. חָלַם, qal impf. 3 m. p., *dream*
3. בָּחוּר, *young*
4. חִזָּיוֹן, *vision*
5. ἐκχέω, fut. act. ind. 1 s., *pour out*
6. προφητεύω, fut. act. ind. 3 p., *prophesy*
7. θυγάτηρ, *daughter*
8. ἐνύπνιον, *dream*
9. ἐνυπιάζομαι, fut. pass. ind. 3 p., *dream*
10. νεανίσκος, *young man*
11. ὅρασις, *vision*
12. effundo, fut. act. ind. 1 s., *pour out*
13. propheto, fut. act. ind. 3 p., *prophesy*
14. iuvenis, *young*
15. visio, *vision*
16. somnium, *dream*
17. somnio, fut. act. ind. 3 p., *dream*

September 11

Ezekiel 36:27

וְאֶת־רוּחִי אֶתֵּן בְּקִרְבְּכֶם וְעָשִׂיתִי אֵת אֲשֶׁר־בְּחֻקַּי
תֵּלֵכוּ וּמִשְׁפָּטַי תִּשְׁמְרוּ וַעֲשִׂיתֶם׃

καὶ τὸ πνεῦμά μου δώσω ἐν ὑμῖν καὶ ποιήσω ἵνα ἐν τοῖς δικαιώμασίν μου πορεύησθε καὶ τὰ κρίματά μου φυλάξησθε καὶ ποιήσητε.

1 Thessalonians 4:8

τοιγαροῦν[1] ὁ ἀθετῶν[2] οὐκ ἄνθρωπον ἀθετεῖ[3] ἀλλὰ τὸν θεὸν τὸν [καὶ] διδόντα τὸ πνεῦμα αὐτοῦ τὸ ἅγιον εἰς ὑμᾶς.

itaque qui spernit[4] non hominem spernit sed Deum qui etiam dedit Spiritum suum Sanctum in vobis.

1. τοιγαροῦν, *therefore*
2. ἀθετέω, pres. act. ptcp. m. nom. s., *reject*
3. ἀθετέω, pres. act. ind. 3 s., *reject*
4. sperno, pres. act. ind. 3 s., *reject*

September 12

Isaiah 63:10

וְהֵ֛מָּה מָר֥וּ[1] וְעִצְּב֖וּ[2] אֶת־ר֣וּחַ קָדְשׁ֑וֹ וַיֵּהָפֵ֥ךְ[3] לָהֶ֛ם
לְאוֹיֵ֖ב ה֥וּא נִלְחַם־בָּֽם׃

αὐτοὶ δὲ ἠπείθησαν[4] καὶ παρώξυναν[5] τὸ πνεῦμα τὸ ἅγιον αὐτοῦ· καὶ ἐστράφη[6] αὐτοῖς εἰς ἔχθραν,[7] καὶ αὐτὸς ἐπολέμησεν αὐτούς.

Ephesians 4:30

καὶ μὴ λυπεῖτε[8] τὸ πνεῦμα τὸ ἅγιον τοῦ θεοῦ, ἐν ᾧ ἐσφραγίσθητε[9] εἰς ἡμέραν ἀπολυτρώσεως.[10]

et nolite contristare[11] Spiritum Sanctum Dei in quo signati[12] estis in die redemptionis.[13]

1. מָרָה, qal perf. 3 c. p., *rebel*
2. עָצַב, piel perf. 3 c. p., *grieve*
3. הָפַךְ, niph. wcons. 3 m. s., *turn*
4. ἀπειθέω, aor. act. ind. 3 p., *disobey*
5. παροξύνω, aor. act. ind. 3 p., *provoke*
6. στρέφω, aor. pass. ind. 3 s., *turn*
7. ἔχθρα, *enmity*
8. λυπέω, pres. act. impv. 2 p., *grieve*
9. σφραγίζω, aor. pass. ind. 2 p., *seal*
10. ἀπολύτρωσις, *redemption*
11. contristo, pres. act. inf., *grieve, make sad*
12. signo, perf. pass. ind. 2 p., *seal*
13. redemptio, *redemption, ransom*

Apostolic Age

September 13

Proverbs 16:33[1]

בַּחֵיק[2] יוּטַל[3] אֶת־הַגּוֹרָל[4] וּמֵיְהוָה כָּל־מִשְׁפָּטוֹ׃

εἰς κόλπους[5] ἐπέρχεται πάντα τοῖς ἀδίκοις, παρὰ δὲ κυρίου πάντα τὰ δίκαια.

Acts 1:26

καὶ ἔδωκαν κλήρους[6] αὐτοῖς καὶ ἔπεσεν ὁ κλῆρος ἐπὶ Μαθθίαν[7] καὶ συγκατεψηφίσθη[8] μετὰ τῶν ἕνδεκα[9] ἀποστόλων.

et dederunt sortes[10] eis et cecidit sors super Matthiam[11] et adnumeratus[12] est cum undecim[13] apostolis.

1. PA: Notice that the Hebrew and LXX texts are substantially different; the pairing has been made on the basis of the Hebrew version of Prov 16:33.
2. חֵיק, *lap*
3. טוּל, hoph. impf. 3 m. s., *cast*
4. גּוֹרָל, *lot*
5. κόλπος, *lap*
6. κλῆρος, *lot*
7. Μαθθίας, *Matthias*
8. συγκαταψηφίζομαι, aor. pass. ind. 3 s., *be counted among*
9. ἕνδεκα, *eleven*
10. sors, *lot*
11. Matthias, *Matthias*
12. adnumero, perf. pass. ind. 3 s., *count*
13. undecim, *eleven*

September 14

Numbers 28:26

וּבְי֣וֹם הַבִּכּוּרִ֗ים[1] בְּהַקְרִיבְכֶ֞ם מִנְחָ֤ה חֲדָשָׁה֙[2] לַיהוָ֔ה
בְּשָׁבֻעֹֽתֵיכֶ֑ם[3] מִֽקְרָא[4]־קֹ֙דֶשׁ֙ יִהְיֶ֣ה לָכֶ֔ם כָּל־מְלֶ֥אכֶת
עֲבֹדָ֖ה לֹ֥א תַעֲשֽׂוּ׃

Καὶ τῇ ἡμέρᾳ τῶν νέων, ὅταν προσφέρητε θυσίαν νέαν κυρίῳ τῶν ἑβδομάδων,[5] ἐπίκλητος[6] ἁγία ἔσται ὑμῖν, πᾶν ἔργον λατρευτὸν[7] οὐ ποιήσετε.

Acts 2:1

Καὶ ἐν τῷ συμπληροῦσθαι[8] τὴν ἡμέραν τῆς πεντηκοστῆς[9] ἦσαν πάντες ὁμοῦ[10] ἐπὶ τὸ αὐτό.

et cum conplerentur[11] dies pentecostes[12] erant omnes pariter[13] in eodem loco.

1. בִּכּוּרִים, *firstfruits*
2. חָדָשׁ, *new*
3. שָׁבוּעַ, *week*
4. מִקְרָא, *convocation*
5. ἑβδομάς, *week*
6. ἐπίκλητος, *called, named*
7. λατρευτός, *service*
8. συμπληρόω, pres. pass. inf., *draw near, arrive*
9. πεντηκοστή, *Pentecost*
10. ὁμοῦ, *together*
11. conpleo, impf. pass. subj. 3 p., *complete*
12. pentecoste, *Pentecost*
13. pariter, *together*

September 15

Psalm 118:22 [LXX 117:22]

אֶ֭בֶן מָאֲס֣וּ[1] הַבּוֹנִ֑ים הָ֝יְתָ֗ה לְרֹ֣אשׁ פִּנָּֽה׃[2]

λίθον, ὃν ἀπεδοκίμασαν[3] οἱ οἰκοδομοῦντες, οὗτος ἐγενήθη εἰς κεφαλὴν γωνίας.[4]

Acts 4:11

οὗτός[5] ἐστιν ὁ λίθος, ὁ ἐξουθενηθεὶς[6] ὑφ᾽ ὑμῶν τῶν οἰκοδόμων,[7] ὁ γενόμενος εἰς κεφαλὴν γωνίας.

hic[8] est lapis qui reprobatus[9] est a vobis aedificantibus qui factus est in caput anguli.[10]

1. מָאַס, qal perf. 3 c. p., *reject*
2. פִּנָּה, *cornerstone*
3. ἀποδοκιμάζω, aor. act. ind. 3 p., *reject*
4. γωνία, *cornerstone*
5. CH: This pronoun refers to Jesus.
6. ἐξουθενέω, aor. pass. ptcp. m. nom. s., *despise*
7. οἰκοδόμος, *builder*
8. CH: This pronoun refers to Jesus.
9. reprobo, perf. pass. ind. 3 s., *reject*
10. angulus, *cornerstone*

September 16

Proverbs 14:5

עֵ֣ד[1] אֱ֭מוּנִים[2] לֹ֣א יְכַזֵּ֑ב[3] וְיָפִ֥יחַ[4] כְּ֝זָבִ֗ים[5] עֵ֣ד שָֽׁקֶר׃

μάρτυς[6] πιστὸς[7] οὐ ψεύδεται,[8] ἐκκαίει[9] δὲ ψεύδη[10] μάρτυς ἄδικος.

Acts 6:13

ἔστησάν τε μάρτυρας ψευδεῖς[11] λέγοντας· ὁ ἄνθρωπος οὗτος οὐ παύεται[12] λαλῶν ῥήματα κατὰ τοῦ τόπου τοῦ ἁγίου [τούτου] καὶ τοῦ νόμου.

et statuerunt[13] testes falsos[14] dicentes homo iste non cessat[15] loqui verba adversus locum sanctum et legem.

1. עֵד, *witness*
2. אֱמוּן, *faithful*
3. כָּזַב, piel impf. 3 m. s., *lie*
4. פּוּחַ, hiph. impf. 3 m. s., *breathe out*
5. כָּזָב, *lie*
6. μάρτυς, *witness*
7. πιστός, *faithful*
8. ψεύδομαι, pres. mid. ind. 3 s., *lie*
9. ἐκκαίω, pres. act. ind. 3 s., *burn, kindle*
10. ψεῦδος, *lie*
11. ψευδής, *false*
12. παύω, pres. mid. ind. 3 s., *stop, cease*
13. statuo, perf. act. ind. 3 p., *establish, set up*
14. falsus, *false*
15. cesso, pres. act. ind. 3 s., *cease*

September 17

Jeremiah 4:4

הִמֹּ֣לוּ[1] לַיהוָ֗ה וְהָסִ֙רוּ֙ עָרְל֣וֹת[2] לְבַבְכֶ֔ם אִ֥ישׁ יְהוּדָ֖ה
וְיֹשְׁבֵ֣י יְרוּשָׁלִָ֑ם פֶּן־תֵּצֵ֨א כָאֵ֜שׁ חֲמָתִ֗י וּבָעֲרָה֙[3] וְאֵ֣ין
מְכַבֶּ֔ה[4] מִפְּנֵ֖י רֹ֥עַ[5] מַעַלְלֵיכֶֽם׃[6]

περιτμήθητε[7] τῷ θεῷ ὑμῶν καὶ περιτέμεσθε[8] τὴν σκληροκαρδίαν[9] ὑμῶν, ἄνδρες Ιουδα καὶ οἱ κατοικοῦντες Ιερουσαλημ, μὴ ἐξέλθῃ ὡς πῦρ ὁ θυμός μου καὶ ἐκκαυθήσεται,[10] καὶ οὐκ ἔσται ὁ σβέσων[11] ἀπὸ προσώπου πονηρίας[12] ἐπιτηδευμάτων[13] ὑμῶν.

Acts 7:51

Σκληροτράχηλοι[14] καὶ ἀπερίτμητοι[15] καρδίαις καὶ τοῖς ὠσίν, ὑμεῖς ἀεὶ[16] τῷ πνεύματι τῷ ἁγίῳ ἀντιπίπτετε[17] ὡς οἱ πατέρες ὑμῶν καὶ ὑμεῖς.

dura[18] cervice[19] et incircumcisi[20] cordibus et auribus vos semper Spiritui Sancto resistitis[21] sicut patres vestri et vos.

1. מוּל, niph. impf. m. p., *circumcise*
2. עָרְלָה, *foreskin*
3. בָּעַר, qal perf. 3 f. s., *burn*
4. כָּבָה, piel ptcp. m. s. abs., *quench*
5. רֹעַ, *evil*
6. מַעֲלָל, *deed*
7. περιτέμνω, aor. pass. impv. 2 p., *circumcise*
8. περιτέμνω, aor. mid. impv. 2 p., *circumcise*
9. σκλήροκαρδία, *hard-heartedness*
10. ἐκκαίω, fut. pass. ind. 3 s., *burn*
11. σβέννυμι, fut. act. ptcp. m. nom. s., *quench*
12. πονηρία, *wickedness*
13. ἐπιτήδευμα, *pursuit*
14. σκληροτράχηλος, *stiff-necked*
15. ἀπερίτμητος, *uncircumcised*
16. ἀεί, *always*
17. ἀντιπίπτω, pres. act. ind. 2 p., *resist*
18. durus, *hard*
19. cervix, *neck*
20. incircumcisus, *uncircumcised*
21. resisto, pres. act. ind. 2 p., *resist*

September 18

Psalm 37:12 [LXX 36:12]

זֹמֵ֣ם[1] רָ֭שָׁע לַצַּדִּ֑יק וְחֹרֵ֖ק[2] עָלָ֣יו שִׁנָּֽיו׃[3]

παρατηρήσεται[4] ὁ ἁμαρτωλὸς τὸν δίκαιον καὶ βρύξει[5] ἐπ᾽ αὐτὸν τοὺς ὀδόντας[6] αὐτοῦ.

Acts 7:54[7]

Ἀκούοντες δὲ ταῦτα διεπρίοντο[8] ταῖς καρδίαις αὐτῶν καὶ ἔβρυχον[9] τοὺς ὀδόντας ἐπ᾽ αὐτόν.

audientes autem haec dissecabantur[10] cordibus suis et stridebant[11] dentibus[12] in eum.

1. זָמַם, qal ptcp. m. s. abs., *devise, plot*
2. חָרַק, qal ptcp. m. s. abs., *gnash*
3. שֵׁן, *tooth*
4. παρατηρέω, fut. mid. ind. 3 s., *watch closely*
5. βρύχω, fut. act. ind. 3 s., *gnash*
6. ὀδούς, *tooth*
7. CH: This verse describes the crowd's reaction to Stephen's speech.
8. διαπρίω, impf. mid. ind. 3 p., *enrage*
9. βρύχω, impf. act. ind. 3 p., *gnash*
10. disseco, impf. pass. ind. 3 p., *cut*
11. strideo, impf. act. ind. 3 p., *gnash*
12. dens, *tooth*

September 19

Isaiah 53:7

נִגַּ֨שׂ[1] וְה֣וּא נַעֲנֶה֮[2] וְלֹ֣א יִפְתַּח־פִּיו֒ כַּשֶּׂה֙[3] לַטֶּ֣בַח[4]
יוּבָ֔ל[5] וּכְרָחֵ֕ל[6] לִפְנֵ֥י גֹזְזֶ֖יהָ[7] נֶאֱלָ֑מָה[8] וְלֹ֥א יִפְתַּ֖ח פִּֽיו׃

καὶ αὐτὸς διὰ τὸ κεκακῶσθαι[9] οὐκ ἀνοίγει τὸ στόμα· ὡς πρόβατον ἐπὶ σφαγὴν[10] ἤχθη καὶ ὡς ἀμνὸς ἐναντίον τοῦ κείροντος[11] αὐτὸν ἄφωνος[12] οὕτως οὐκ ἀνοίγει τὸ στόμα αὐτοῦ.

Acts 8:35[13]

ἀνοίξας δὲ ὁ Φίλιππος τὸ στόμα αὐτοῦ καὶ ἀρξάμενος ἀπὸ τῆς γραφῆς ταύτης εὐηγγελίσατο αὐτῷ τὸν Ἰησοῦν.

aperiens autem Philippus os suum et incipiens ab scriptura ista evangelizavit illi Iesum.

1. נָגַשׂ, niph. perf. 3 m. s., *oppress*
2. עָנָה, niph. ptcp. m. s. abs., *afflict*
3. שֶׂה, *lamb*
4. טֶבַח, *slaughter*
5. יָבַל, hoph. impf. 3 m. s., *lead, bring*
6. רָחֵל, *sheep*
7. גָּזַז, qal ptcp. m. p. cons., *shear*
8. אָלַם, niph. perf. 3 f. s., *be silent*
9. κακόω, perf. pass. inf., *harm, do evil*
10. σφαγή, *slaughter*
11. κείρω, pres. act. ptcp. m. g. s., *shear*
12. ἄφωνος, *silent*
13. PA: Philip encounters the Ethiopian eunuch on the road, reading Isa 53:7. Philip asks him whether he understands, and when he says he does not, he interprets the passage in light of Christ.

September 20

Deuteronomy 4:12

וַיְדַבֵּ֧ר יְהוָ֛ה אֲלֵיכֶ֖ם מִתּ֣וֹךְ הָאֵ֑שׁ ק֤וֹל דְּבָרִים֙ אַתֶּ֣ם
שֹׁמְעִ֔ים וּתְמוּנָ֛ה[1] אֵינְכֶ֥ם רֹאִ֖ים זוּלָתִ֥י[2] קֽוֹל׃

καὶ ἐλάλησεν κύριος πρὸς ὑμᾶς ἐκ μέσου τοῦ πυρός· φωνὴν ῥημάτων ὑμεῖς ἠκούσατε καὶ ὁμοίωμα[3] οὐκ εἴδετε, ἀλλ᾿ ἢ φωνήν.

Acts 9:7

οἱ δὲ ἄνδρες οἱ συνοδεύοντες[4] αὐτῷ[5] εἱστήκεισαν ἐνεοί,[6] ἀκούοντες μὲν τῆς φωνῆς μηδένα δὲ θεωροῦντες.

. . . viri autem illi qui comitabantur[7] cum eo[8] stabant stupefacti[9] audientes quidem vocem neminem autem videntes.

1. תְּמוּנָה, *form*
2. זוּלָה, *only*
3. ὁμοίωμα, *form, likeness*
4. συνοδεύω, pres. act. ptcp. m. nom. p., *travel with*
5. CH: The referent of this pronoun is Paul.
6. ἐνεός, *speechless*
7. comitor, impf. dep. ind. 3 p., *accompany*
8. CH: The referent of this pronoun is Paul.
9. stupefacio, perf. pass. ptcp. m. nom. p., *amaze*

September 21

Ezekiel 44:6

וְאָמַרְתָּ֤ אֶל־מֶ֙רִי֙[1] אֶל־בֵּ֣ית יִשְׂרָאֵ֔ל כֹּ֥ה אָמַ֖ר אֲדֹנָ֣י
יְהוִ֑ה רַב־לָכֶ֥ם מִֽכָּל־תּוֹעֲבוֹתֵיכֶ֖ם בֵּ֥ית יִשְׂרָאֵֽל׃

καὶ ἐρεῖς πρὸς τὸν οἶκον τὸν παραπικραίνοντα,[2] πρὸς τὸν οἶκον τοῦ Ισραηλ Τάδε λέγει κύριος ὁ θεός Ἱκανούσθω[3] ὑμῖν ἀπὸ πασῶν τῶν ἀνομιῶν ὑμῶν, οἶκος Ισραηλ.

Acts 21:27

Ὡς δὲ ἔμελλον αἱ ἑπτὰ ἡμέραι συντελεῖσθαι,[4] οἱ ἀπὸ τῆς Ἀσίας[5] Ἰουδαῖοι θεασάμενοι[6] αὐτὸν ἐν τῷ ἱερῷ συνέχεον[7] πάντα τὸν ὄχλον καὶ ἐπέβαλον[8] ἐπ᾽ αὐτὸν τὰς χεῖρας.

dum autem septem dies consummarentur hii qui de Asia[9] erant Iudaei cum vidissent eum in templo concitaverunt[10] omnem populum et iniecerunt[11] ei manus clamantes.

1. מְרִי, *rebellious*
2. παραπικραίνω, pres. act. ptcp. m. a. s., *provoke*
3. ἱκανόω, pres. pass. impv. 3 s., *be sufficient*
4. συντελέω, pres. pass. inf., *complete, finish*
5. Ἀσία, *Asia*
6. θεάομαι, aor. mid. ptcp. m. n. p., *see*
7. συγχέω, impf. act. ind. 3 p., *stir up, agitate*
8. ἐπιβάλλω, aor. act. ind. 3 p., *lay hands on*
9. Asia, *Asia*
10. concito, perf. act. ind. 3 p., *agitate, stir up*
11. inicio, perf. act. ind. 3 p., *lay on*

September 22

Ezekiel 44:7

בַּהֲבִיאֲכֶם בְּנֵי־נֵכָר[1] עַרְלֵי־[2]לֵב וְעַרְלֵי בָשָׂר לִהְיוֹת
בְּמִקְדָּשִׁי[3] לְחַלְּלוֹ אֶת־בֵּיתִי בְּהַקְרִיבְכֶם אֶת־לַחְמִי
חֵלֶב[4] וָדָם וַיָּפֵרוּ[5] אֶת־בְּרִיתִי אֶל כָּל־תּוֹעֲבוֹתֵיכֶם׃

τοῦ εἰσαγαγεῖν ὑμᾶς υἱοὺς ἀλλογενεῖς[6] ἀπεριτμήτους[7] καρδίᾳ καὶ ἀπεριτμήτους σαρκὶ τοῦ γίνεσθαι ἐν τοῖς ἁγίοις μου, καὶ ἐβεβήλουν[8] αὐτὰ ἐν τῷ προσφέρειν ὑμᾶς ἄρτους, στέαρ[9] καὶ αἷμα, καὶ παρεβαίνετε[10] τὴν διαθήκην μου ἐν πάσαις ταῖς ἀνομίαις ὑμῶν.

Acts 21:28

κράζοντες· ἄνδρες Ἰσραηλῖται,[11] βοηθεῖτε·[12] οὗτός ἐστιν ὁ ἄνθρωπος ὁ κατὰ τοῦ λαοῦ καὶ τοῦ νόμου καὶ τοῦ τόπου τούτου πάντας πανταχῇ[13] διδάσκων, ἔτι τε καὶ Ἕλληνας[14] εἰσήγαγεν[15] εἰς τὸ ἱερὸν καὶ κεκοίνωκεν[16] τὸν ἅγιον τόπον τοῦτον.

viri israhelitae[17] adiuvate[18] hic est homo qui adversus populum et legem et locum hunc omnes ubique[19] docens insuper[20] et gentiles[21] induxit[22] in templum et violavit[23] sanctum locum istum.

20. insuper, *moreover, besides.* **21.** gentilis, *gentile.* **22.** induco, perf. act. ind. 3 s., *bring/lead in.* **23.** violo, perf. act. ind. 3 s., *profane*

1. נֵכָר, *foreigner*
2. עָרֵל, *uncircumcised*
3. מִקְדָּשׁ, *sanctuary*
4. חֵלֶב, *fat*
5. פָּרַר, hiph. wcons. 3 m. p., *break*
6. ἀλλογενής, *stranger, foreigner*
7. ἀπερίτμητος, *uncircumcised*
8. βεβηλόω, impf. act. ind. 3 p., *desecrate*
9. στέαρ, *fat*
10. παραβαίνω, impf. act. ind. 2 p., *transgress*
11. Ἰσραηλίτης, *Israelite*
12. βοηθέω, pres. act. impv. 2 p., *help*
13. πανταχῇ, *everywhere*
14. Ἕλλην, *Greek*
15. εἰσάγω, aor. act. ind. 3 s., *bring in*
16. κοινόω, perf. act. ind. 3 s., *defile*
17. Israhelites, *Israelite*
18. adiuvo, pres. act. impv. 2 p., *help, assist*
19. ubique, *everywhere*

September 23

Psalm 44:23 [LXX 43:23]

כִּֽי־עָ֭לֶיךָ הֹרַ֣גְנוּ כָל־הַיּ֑וֹם נֶ֝חְשַׁ֗בְנוּ כְּצֹ֣אן טִבְחָֽה׃[1]

ὅτι ἕνεκα σοῦ θανατούμεθα ὅλην τὴν ἡμέραν,
ἐλογίσθημεν ὡς πρόβατα σφαγῆς.[2]

Romans 8:35[3]

τίς ἡμᾶς χωρίσει[4] ἀπὸ τῆς ἀγάπης τοῦ Χριστοῦ; θλῖψις ἢ στενοχωρία[5] ἢ διωγμὸς[6] ἢ λιμὸς[7] ἢ γυμνότης[8] ἢ κίνδυνος[9] ἢ μάχαιρα;[10]

quis nos separabit[11] a caritate Christi tribulatio an angustia[12] an persecutio[13] an fames[14] an nuditas[15] an periculum[16] an gladius?

1. טִבְחָה, *slaughter*
2. σφαγή, *slaughter*
3. PA: Paul uses Ps 44:23 in Rom 8:36 in support of his statement in 8:35.
4. χωρίζω, fut. act. ind. 3 s., *separate, remove*
5. στενοχωρία, *distress*
6. διωγμός, *persecution*
7. λιμός, *famine*
8. γυμνότης, *nakedness*
9. κίνδυνος, *danger, peril*
10. μάχαιρα, *short-sword*
11. separo, fut. act. ind. 3 s., *separate, sever*
12. angustia, *anguish*
13. persecutio, *persecution*
14. fames, *hunger, famine*
15. nuditas, *nakedness*
16. periculum, *danger*

September 24

Psalm 22:22 [LXX 21:22]

הֽ֭וֹשִׁיעֵנִי מִפִּ֣י אַרְיֵ֑ה[1] וּמִקַּרְנֵ֖י[2] רֵמִ֣ים[3] עֲנִיתָֽנִי׃

σῶσόν με ἐκ στόματος λέοντος[4] καὶ ἀπὸ κεράτων μονοκερώτων[5] τὴν ταπείνωσίν[6] μου.

2 Timothy 4:17

ὁ δὲ κύριός μοι παρέστη καὶ ἐνεδυνάμωσέν[7] με, ἵνα δι᾽ ἐμοῦ τὸ κήρυγμα[8] πληροφορηθῇ[9] καὶ ἀκούσωσιν πάντα τὰ ἔθνη, καὶ ἐρρύσθην[10] ἐκ στόματος λέοντος.

Dominus autem mihi adstitit[11] et confortavit[12] me ut per me praedicatio[13] impleatur et audiant omnes gentes et liberatus[14] sum de ore leonis.[15]

1. אַרְיֵה, *lion*
2. קֶ֫רֶן, *horn*
3. רְאֵם, *wild ox*
4. λέων, *lion*
5. μονόκερως, *unicorn*
6. ταπείνωσις, *humiliation*
7. ἐνδυναμόω, aor. act. ind. 3 s., *make strong*
8. κήρυγμα, *proclamation, preaching*
9. πληροφορέω, aor. pass. subj. 3 s., *bring to completion*
10. ῥύομαι, aor. pass. ind. 1 s., *deliver*
11. adsto, perf. act. ind. 3 s., *stand by*
12. conforto, perf. act. ind. 3 s., *strengthen*
13. praedicatio, *proclamation, preaching*
14. libero, perf. pass. ind. 1 s., *liberate, set free*
15. leo, *lion*

September 25

Jeremiah 20:9

וְאָמַרְתִּי לֹא־אֶזְכְּרֶנּוּ וְלֹא־אֲדַבֵּר עוֹד בִּשְׁמוֹ וְהָיָה
בְלִבִּי כְּאֵשׁ בֹּעֶרֶת[1] עָצֻר[2] בְּעַצְמֹתָי וְנִלְאֵיתִי[3] כַּלְכֵל[4]
וְלֹא אוּכָל׃

καὶ εἶπα Οὐ μὴ ὀνομάσω[5] τὸ ὄνομα κυρίου καὶ οὐ μὴ λαλήσω ἔτι ἐπὶ τῷ ὀνόματι αὐτοῦ· καὶ ἐγένετο ὡς πῦρ καιόμενον[6] φλέγον[7] ἐν τοῖς ὀστέοις μου, καὶ παρεῖμαι[8] πάντοθεν[9] καὶ οὐ δύναμαι φέρειν.

1 Corinthians 9:16

ἐὰν γὰρ εὐαγγελίζωμαι, οὐκ ἔστιν μοι καύχημα·[10] ἀνάγκη[11] γάρ μοι ἐπίκειται·[12] οὐαὶ γάρ μοί ἐστιν ἐὰν μὴ εὐαγγελίσωμαι.

nam si evangelizavero non est mihi gloria necessitas[13] enim mihi incumbit[14] vae enim mihi est si non evangelizavero.

1. בָּעַר, qal ptcp. f. s. abs., *burn*
2. עָצַר, qal pass. ptcp. m. s. abs., *restrain, hold back*
3. לָאָה, niph. perf. 1 c. s., *be weary*
4. כּוּל, pilpel inf. cons., *hold in, contain*
5. ὀνομάζω, fut. act. ind. 1 s., *name*
6. καίω, pres. mid. ptcp. n. nom. s., *burn*
7. φλέγω, pres. act. ptcp. n. nom. s., *set on fire*
8. παρίημι, perf. pass. ind. 1 s., *go limp*
9. πάντοθεν, *on all sides*
10. καύχημα, *reason for boasting*
11. ἀνάγκη, *necessity*
12. ἐπίκειμαι, pres. mid. ind. 3 s., *put upon*
13. necessitas, *need, necessity*
14. incumbo, pres. act. ind. 3 s., *put upon*

September 26

Psalm 106:37 [LXX 105:37]

וַיִּזְבְּח֣וּ אֶת־בְּ֭נֵיהֶם וְאֶת־בְּנֽוֹתֵיהֶ֗ם לַשֵּֽׁדִים׃[1]

καὶ ἔθυσαν[2] τοὺς υἱοὺς αὐτῶν καὶ τὰς θυγατέρας αὐτῶν τοῖς δαιμονίοις.[3]

1 Corinthians 10:20

ἀλλ᾽ ὅτι ἃ θύουσιν,[4] δαιμονίοις καὶ οὐ θεῷ [θύουσιν]· οὐ θέλω δὲ ὑμᾶς κοινωνοὺς[5] τῶν δαιμονίων γίνεσθαι.

sed quae immolant[6] gentes daemoniis immolant et non Deo nolo autem vos socios[7] fieri daemoniorum non potestis calicem Domini bibere et calicem daemoniorum.

1. שֵׁד, *demon*
2. θύω, aor. act. ind. 3 p., *sacrifice*
3. δαιμόνιον, *demon*
4. θύω, pres. act. ind. 3 p., *sacrifice*
5. κοινωνός, *partaker, participant*
6. immolo, pres. act. ind. 3 p., *sacrifice*
7. socius, *partaker, participant*

September 27

Psalm 24:1b [LXX 23:1b]

לַֽיהוָה הָאָרֶץ וּמְלוֹאָהּ[1] תֵּבֵל[2] וְיֹשְׁבֵי בָהּ׃

Τοῦ κυρίου ἡ γῆ καὶ τὸ πλήρωμα[3] αὐτῆς, ἡ οἰκουμένη[4] καὶ πάντες οἱ κατοικοῦντες ἐν αὐτῇ.

1 Corinthians 10:25[5]

Πᾶν τὸ ἐν μακέλλῳ[6] πωλούμενον[7] ἐσθίετε μηδὲν ἀνακρίνοντες[8] διὰ τὴν συνείδησιν.[9]

omne quod in macello[10] venit[11] manducate nihil interrogantes propter conscientiam.

1. מְלֹא, *fullness*
2. תֵּבֵל, *world*
3. πλήρωμα, *fullness*
4. οἰκουμένη, *world*
5. PA: Paul cites the psalm text above as justification for what he says here.
6. μάκελλον, *meat market*
7. πωλέω, pres. pass. ptcp. n. a. s., *sell*
8. ἀνακρίνω, pres. act. ptcp. m. nom. p., *examine, question*
9. συνείδησις, *conscience*
10. macellum, *meat market*
11. veneo, pres. act. ind. 3 s., *be sold*

September 28

Psalm 67:3 [LXX 66:3]

לָדַ֣עַת בָּאָ֣רֶץ דַּרְכֶּ֑ךָ בְּכָל־גּ֝וֹיִ֗ם יְשׁוּעָתֶֽךָ׃[1]

τοῦ γνῶναι ἐν τῇ γῇ τὴν ὁδόν σου, ἐν πᾶσιν ἔθνεσιν τὸ σωτήριόν[2] σου.

Acts 28:28

γνωστὸν[3] οὖν ἔστω ὑμῖν ὅτι τοῖς ἔθνεσιν ἀπεστάλη τοῦτο τὸ σωτήριον τοῦ θεοῦ· αὐτοὶ καὶ ἀκούσονται.

notum ergo sit vobis quoniam gentibus missum est hoc salutare[4] Dei ipsi et audient.

1. יְשׁוּעָה, *salvation*
2. σωτήριον, *salvation*
3. γνωστός, *known*
4. salutare, *salvation*

September 29

Psalm 119:46 [LXX 118:46]

וַאֲדַבְּרָה בְעֵדֹתֶיךָ[1] נֶגֶד מְלָכִים וְלֹא אֵבוֹשׁ׃

καὶ ἐλάλουν ἐν τοῖς μαρτυρίοις σου ἐναντίον βασιλέων καὶ οὐκ ᾐσχυνόμην.[2]

Romans 1:16

Οὐ γὰρ ἐπαισχύνομαι[3] τὸ εὐαγγέλιον, δύναμις γὰρ θεοῦ ἐστιν εἰς σωτηρίαν παντὶ τῷ πιστεύοντι, Ἰουδαίῳ τε πρῶτον καὶ Ἕλληνι.[4]

non enim erubesco[5] evangelium virtus enim Dei est in salutem omni credenti Iudaeo[6] primum et Graeco.[7]

1. עֵדָה, *testimony*
2. αἰσχύνω, impf. pass. ind. 1 s., *be ashamed*
3. ἐπαισχύνομαι, pres. mid. ind. 1 s., *be ashamed*
4. Ἕλλην, *Greek*
5. erubesco, pres. act. ind. 1 s., *blush, be ashamed*
6. Iudaeus, *Jew*
7. Graecus, *Greek*

September 30

Ezekiel 18:23

הֶחָפֹ֤ץ[1] אֶחְפֹּץ֙[2] מ֣וֹת רָשָׁ֔ע נְאֻ֖ם אֲדֹנָ֣י יְהוִ֑ה הֲל֛וֹא
בְּשׁוּב֥וֹ מִדְּרָכָ֖יו וְחָיָֽה׃

μὴ θελήσει[3] θελήσω τὸν θάνατον τοῦ ἀνόμου,
λέγει κύριος, ὡς τὸ ἀποστρέψαι αὐτὸν ἐκ τῆς
ὁδοῦ τῆς πονηρᾶς καὶ ζῆν αὐτόν;

1 Timothy 2:4

ὃς[4] πάντας ἀνθρώπους θέλει σωθῆναι καὶ εἰς ἐπίγνωσιν[5] ἀληθείας ἐλθεῖν.

qui[6] omnes homines vult salvos fieri et ad agnitionem[7] veritatis venire.

1. חָפֵץ, qal inf. abs., *delight*
2. חָפֵץ, qal impf. 1 c. s., *delight*
3. θελήσει, *desire*
4. CH: The referent of this relative pronoun is God. Simply translate as *God.*
5. ἐπίγνωσις, *knowledge*
6. CH: The referent of this relative pronoun is God. Simply translate as *God.*
7. agnitio, *knowledge*

October 1

Psalm 7:13

אִם־לֹ֣א יָ֭שׁוּב חַרְבּ֣וֹ יִלְט֑וֹשׁ[1] קַשְׁתּ֥וֹ[2] דָ֝רַ֗ךְ[3] וַֽיְכוֹנְנֶֽהָ׃

ἐὰν μὴ ἐπιστραφῆτε, τὴν ῥομφαίαν αὐτοῦ στιλβώσει·[4] τὸ τόξον[5] αὐτοῦ ἐνέτεινεν[6] καὶ ἡτοίμασεν αὐτὸ.

Luke 13:3

οὐχί, λέγω ὑμῖν, ἀλλ᾽ ἐὰν μὴ μετανοῆτε πάντες ὁμοίως[7] ἀπολεῖσθε.

non dico vobis sed nisi paenitentiam habueritis omnes similiter peribitis.

1. לָטַשׁ, qal impf. 3 m. s., *sharpen*
2. קֶ֫שֶׁת, *bow*
3. דָּרַךְ, qal perf. 3 m. s., *bend, tread*
4. στιλβόω, fut. act. ind. 3 s., *polish*
5. τόξον, *bow*
6. ἐντείνω, aor. act. ind. 3 s., *stretch tight*
7. ὁμοίως, *likewise*

October 2

Psalm 51:3 [LXX 50:3]

חָנֵּ֣נִי[1] אֱלֹהִ֣ים כְּחַסְדֶּ֑ךָ כְּרֹ֥ב רַ֝חֲמֶ֗יךָ[2] מְחֵ֣ה[3] פְשָׁעָֽי׃[4]

Ἐλέησόν με, ὁ θεός, κατὰ τὸ μέγα ἔλεός σου καὶ κατὰ τὸ πλῆθος τῶν οἰκτιρμῶν[5] σου ἐξάλειψον[6] τὸ ἀνόμημά[7] μου.

Luke 18:13

ὁ δὲ τελώνης[8] μακρόθεν[9] ἑστὼς οὐκ ἤθελεν οὐδὲ τοὺς ὀφθαλμοὺς ἐπᾶραι[10] εἰς τὸν οὐρανόν, ἀλλʼ ἔτυπτεν[11] τὸ στῆθος[12] αὐτοῦ λέγων· ὁ θεός, ἱλάσθητί[13] μοι τῷ ἁμαρτωλῷ.

et publicanus[14] a longe[15] stans nolebat nec oculos ad caelum levare[16] sed percutiebat pectus[17] suum dicens Deus propitius[18] esto mihi peccatori.

1. חָנַן, qal impv. m. s., *show favor*
2. רַחֲמִים, *compassion*
3. מָחָה, qal impv. m. s., *wipe out*
4. פֶּשַׁע, *transgression*
5. οἰκτιρμός, *compassion*
6. ἐξαλείφω, aor. act. impv. 2 s., *wipe out*
7. ἀνόμημα, *lawless*
8. τελώνης, *tax collector*
9. μακρόθεν, *far off*
10. ἐπαίρω, aor. act. inf., *lift up*
11. τύπτω, impf. act. ind. 3 s., *beat*
12. στῆθος, *breast, chest*
13. ἱλάσκομαι, aor. pass. impv. 2 s., *be merciful*
14. publicanus, *tax collector*
15. longe, *far off*
16. levo, pres. act. inf., *lift up*
17. pectus, *breast*
18. propitius, *merciful*

October 3

Jonah 3:10

וַיַּרְא הָאֱלֹהִים אֶת־מַעֲשֵׂיהֶם כִּי־שָׁבוּ מִדַּרְכָּם
הָרָעָה וַיִּנָּחֶם הָאֱלֹהִים עַל־הָרָעָה אֲשֶׁר־דִּבֶּר
לַעֲשׂוֹת־לָהֶם וְלֹא עָשָׂה׃

καὶ εἶδεν ὁ θεὸς τὰ ἔργα αὐτῶν, ὅτι ἀπέστρεψαν ἀπὸ τῶν ὁδῶν αὐτῶν τῶν πονηρῶν, καὶ μετενόησεν[1] ὁ θεὸς ἐπὶ τῇ κακίᾳ, ᾗ ἐλάλησεν τοῦ ποιῆσαι αὐτοῖς, καὶ οὐκ ἐποίησεν.

Luke 11:32

ἄνδρες Νινευῖται[2] ἀναστήσονται ἐν τῇ κρίσει μετὰ τῆς γενεᾶς ταύτης καὶ κατακρινοῦσιν[3] αὐτήν· ὅτι μετενόησαν[4] εἰς τὸ κήρυγμα[5] Ἰωνᾶ,[6] καὶ ἰδοὺ πλεῖον Ἰωνᾶ ὧδε.

viri ninevitae[7] surgent in iudicio cum generatione hac et condemnabunt[8] illam quia paenitentiam egerunt ad praedicationem[9] Ionae[10] et ecce plus Iona hic.

1. μετανοέω, aor. act. ind. 3 s., *repent*
2. Νινευίτης, *Ninevite*
3. κατακρίνω, fut. act. ind. 3 p., *condemn*
4. μετανοέω, aor. act. ind. 3 p., *repent*
5. κήρυγμα, *preaching, proclamation*
6. Ἰωνᾶς, *Jonah*
7. ninevitus, *Ninevite*
8. condemno, fut. act. ind. 3 p., *condemn*
9. praedicatio, *preaching, proclamation*
10. Ionas, *Jonah*

October 4

Jeremiah 34:15 [LXX 41:15]

וַתָּשֻׁ֨בוּ אַתֶּ֜ם הַיּ֗וֹם וַתַּעֲשׂ֤וּ אֶת־הַיָּשָׁר֙ בְּעֵינַ֔י לִקְרֹ֥א דְר֖וֹר[1] אִ֣ישׁ לְרֵעֵ֑הוּ וַתִּכְרְת֤וּ בְרִית֙ לְפָנַ֔י בַּבַּ֕יִת אֲשֶׁר־נִקְרָ֥א שְׁמִ֖י עָלָֽיו׃

καὶ ἐπέστρεψαν σήμερον ποιῆσαι τὸ εὐθὲς[2] πρὸ ὀφθαλμῶν μου τοῦ καλέσαι ἄφεσιν[3] ἕκαστον τοῦ πλησίον αὐτοῦ καὶ συνετέλεσαν διαθήκην κατὰ πρόσωπόν μου ἐν τῷ οἴκῳ, οὗ ἐπεκλήθη τὸ ὄνομά μου ἐπ᾿ αὐτῷ.

Acts 26:20

ἀλλὰ τοῖς ἐν Δαμασκῷ[4] πρῶτόν τε καὶ Ἱεροσολύμοις, πᾶσάν τε τὴν χώραν[5] τῆς Ἰουδαίας καὶ τοῖς ἔθνεσιν ἀπήγγελλον μετανοεῖν καὶ ἐπιστρέφειν ἐπὶ τὸν θεόν, ἄξια τῆς μετανοίας[6] ἔργα πράσσοντας.

sed his qui sunt Damasci[7] primum et Hierosolymis et in omnem regionem Iudaeae et gentibus adnuntiabam ut paenitentiam agerent et converterentur ad Deum digna paenitentiae opera facientes.

1. דְּרוֹר, *liberty*
2. εὐθής, *right*
3. ἄφεσις, *forgiveness, release*
4. Δαμασκός, *Damascus*
5. χώρα, *land, country*
6. μετάνοια, *repentance*
7. Damascus, *Damascus*

October 5

Proverbs 28:13

מְכַסֶּה פְשָׁעָיו[1] לֹא יַצְלִיחַ[2] וּמוֹדֶה וְעֹזֵב יְרֻחָם׃[3]

ὁ ἐπικαλύπτων[4] ἀσέβειαν[5] ἑαυτοῦ οὐκ εὐοδωθήσεται,[6] ὁ δὲ ἐξηγούμενος[7] ἐλέγχους[8] ἀγαπηθήσεται.

1 John 1:9

ἐὰν ὁμολογῶμεν[9] τὰς ἁμαρτίας ἡμῶν, πιστός ἐστιν καὶ δίκαιος, ἵνα ἀφῇ ἡμῖν τὰς ἁμαρτίας καὶ καθαρίσῃ ἡμᾶς ἀπὸ πάσης ἀδικίας.[10]

si confiteamur peccata nostra fidelis est et iustus ut remittat[11] nobis peccata et emundet[12] nos ab omni iniquitate.

1. פֶּשַׁע, *transgression*
2. צָלַח, hiph. impf. 3 m. s., *prosper*
3. רחם, pual impf. 3 m. s., *have compassion/mercy*
4. ἐπικαλύπτω, pres. act. ptcp. m. nom. s, *cover*
5. ἀσέβεια, *impiety*
6. εὐοδόω, fut. pass. ind. 3 s., *prosper*
7. ἐξηγέομαι, pres. mid. ptcp. m. nom. s., *explain*
8. ἔλεγχος, *reproof*
9. ὁμολογέω, pres. act. subj. 1 p., *confess*
10. ἀδικία, *unrighteousness*
11. remitto, pres. act. subj. 3 s., *remit, forgive*
12. emundo, pres. act. subj. 3 s., *cleanse*

October 6

Exodus 19:6

וְאַתֶּם תִּהְיוּ־לִי מַמְלֶכֶת כֹּהֲנִים וְגוֹי קָדוֹשׁ אֵלֶּה הַדְּבָרִים אֲשֶׁר תְּדַבֵּר אֶל־בְּנֵי יִשְׂרָאֵל׃

ὑμεῖς δὲ ἔσεσθέ μοι βασίλειον[1] ἱεράτευμα[2] καὶ ἔθνος ἅγιον. ταῦτα τὰ ῥήματα ἐρεῖς τοῖς υἱοῖς Ισραηλ.

1 Peter 2:9

ὑμεῖς δὲ γένος[3] ἐκλεκτόν,[4] βασίλειον ἱεράτευμα, ἔθνος ἅγιον, λαὸς εἰς *περιποίησιν*,[5] ὅπως τὰς *ἀρετὰς*[6] ἐξαγγείλητε[7] τοῦ ἐκ σκότους ὑμᾶς καλέσαντος εἰς τὸ θαυμαστὸν[8] αὐτοῦ φῶς.

vos autem genus[9] electum regale[10] sacerdotium[11] gens sancta populus adquisitionis[12] ut virtutes adnuntietis eius qui de tenebris vos vocavit in admirabile[13] lumen suum.

1. βασίλειος, *royal*
2. ἱεράτευμα, *priesthood*
3. γένος, *race, generation*
4. ἐκλεκτός, *chosen, elect*
5. περιποίησις, *possession*
6. ἀρετή, *virtue, moral excellence*
7. ἐξαγγέλλω, aor. act. subj. 2 p., *make known, proclaim*
8. θαυμαστός, *marvelous*
9. genus, *generation, descent*
10. regalis, *royal*
11. sacerdotium, *priesthood*
12. adquisitio, *acquisition*
13. admirabilis, *marvelous*

October 7

1. נָטַשׁ, qal impf. 3 m. s., *forsake, abandon*
2. עָבוּר, *for the sake of, because of*
3. יָאַל, hiph. perf. 3 m. s., *be pleased*
4. ἀπωθέω, fut. mid. ind. 3 s., *cast away*
5. ἐπιεικέως, *kindly, graciously*
6. προσλαμβάνω, aor. mid. ind. 3 s., *take, receive*
7. ἀπωθέω, aor. mid. ind. 3 s., *cast away*
8. Ἰσραηλίτης, *Israelite*
9. Βενιαμίν, *Benjamin*
10. προγινώσκω, aor. act. ind. 3 s., *foreknow*
11. repello, perf. act. ind. 3 s., *reject, throw away*
12. absum, pres. act. subj. 3 s., *God forbid, by no means*
13. Israhelita, *Israelite*
14. Beniamin, *Benjamin*
15. praescio, perf. act. ind. 3 s., *foreknow*

1 Samuel 12:22

כִּ֠י לֹֽא־יִטֹּ֤שׁ[1] יְהוָה֙ אֶת־עַמּ֔וֹ בַּעֲב֖וּר[2] שְׁמ֣וֹ הַגָּד֑וֹל כִּ֚י הוֹאִ֣יל[3] יְהוָ֔ה לַעֲשׂ֥וֹת אֶתְכֶ֛ם ל֖וֹ לְעָֽם׃

ὅτι οὐκ ἀπώσεται[4] κύριος τὸν λαὸν αὐτοῦ διὰ τὸ ὄνομα αὐτοῦ τὸ μέγα, ὅτι ἐπιεικέως[5] κύριος προσελάβετο[6] ὑμᾶς αὐτῷ εἰς λαόν.

Romans 11:1–2a

Λέγω οὖν, μὴ ἀπώσατο[7] ὁ θεὸς τὸν λαὸν αὐτοῦ; μὴ γένοιτο· καὶ γὰρ ἐγὼ Ἰσραηλίτης[8] εἰμί, ἐκ σπέρματος Ἀβραάμ, φυλῆς Βενιαμίν.[9] *οὐκ ἀπώσατο ὁ θεὸς τὸν λαὸν αὐτοῦ* ὃν προέγνω.[10]

dico ergo numquid reppulit[11] Deus populum suum absit[12] nam et ego Israhelita[13] sum ex semine Abraham tribu Beniamin[14] non reppulit Deus plebem suam quam praesciit.[15]

October 8

Hosea 1:6[1]

וַתַּ֤הַר[2] עוֹד֙ וַתֵּ֣לֶד בַּ֔ת וַיֹּ֣אמֶר ל֔וֹ קְרָ֥א שְׁמָ֖הּ לֹ֣א
רֻחָ֑מָה[3] כִּי֩ לֹ֨א אוֹסִ֜יף ע֗וֹד אֲרַחֵם֙[4] אֶת־בֵּ֣ית יִשְׂרָאֵ֔ל
כִּֽי־נָשֹׂ֥א אֶשָּׂ֖א לָהֶֽם׃

καὶ συνέλαβεν ἔτι καὶ ἔτεκεν θυγατέρα. καὶ εἶπεν αὐτῷ Κάλεσον τὸ ὄνομα αὐτῆς Οὐκ-ἠλεημένη,[5] διότι οὐ μὴ προσθήσω ἔτι ἐλεῆσαι τὸν οἶκον τοῦ Ισραηλ, ἀλλ᾽ ἢ ἀντιτασσόμενος[6] ἀντιτάξομαι[7] αὐτοῖς.

1 Peter 2:10

οἵ ποτε[8] *οὐ λαός,* νῦν δὲ λαὸς θεοῦ, οἱ *οὐκ ἠλεημένοι,*[9] νῦν δὲ ἐλεηθέντες.[10]

qui aliquando[11] non populus nunc autem populus Dei qui non consecuti[12] misericordiam nunc autem misericordiam consecuti.

1. See also Hos 1:9
2. הָרָה, qal wcons. 3 f. s., *conceive*
3. רֻחָמָה, *Ruhamah, Mercy*
4. רחם, piel impf. 1 c. s., *have mercy/compassion*
5. Οὐκ-ἠλεημένη, trans. of the Hebrew לֹא רֻחָמָה, *Not-Received-Mercy, Not-Pitied*
6. ἀντιτάσσω, pres. mid. ptcp. m. nom. s., *oppose, resist*
7. ἀντιτάσσω, fut. mid. ind. 1 s., *oppose, resist*
8. ποτέ, *when*
9. ἐλεέω, perf. pass. ptcp. m. nom. p., *show mercy*
10. ἐλεέω, aor. pass. ptcp. m. nom. p., *show mercy*
11. aliquando, *once, at one time*
12. consequor, perf. dep. ptcp. m. nom. p., *obtain, attain*

October 9

Ezekiel 34:23

וַהֲקִמֹתִ֨י עֲלֵיהֶ֜ם רֹעֶ֤ה אֶחָד֙ וְרָעָ֣ה אֶתְהֶ֔ן אֵ֖ת עַבְדִּ֣י
דָוִ֑יד ה֚וּא יִרְעֶ֣ה אֹתָ֔ם וְהֽוּא־יִהְיֶ֥ה לָהֶ֖ן לְרֹעֶֽה׃

καὶ ἀναστήσω ἐπ᾽ αὐτοὺς ποιμένα[1] ἕνα καὶ ποιμανεῖ[2] αὐτούς, τὸν δοῦλόν μου Δαυιδ, καὶ ἔσται αὐτῶν ποιμήν.

John 10:16

καὶ ἄλλα πρόβατα ἔχω ἃ οὐκ ἔστιν ἐκ τῆς αὐλῆς[3] ταύτης· κἀκεῖνα δεῖ με ἀγαγεῖν καὶ τῆς φωνῆς μου ἀκούσουσιν, καὶ γενήσονται μία ποίμνη, εἷς ποιμήν.

et alias oves habeo quae non sunt ex hoc ovili[4] et illas oportet me adducere et vocem meam audient et fiet unum ovile unus pastor.[5]

1. ποιμήν, *shepherd*
2. ποιμαίνω, fut. act. ind. 3 s., *shepherd, feed*
3. αὐλή, *sheepfold*
4. ovile, *sheepfold*
5. pastor, *shepherd*

October 10

Ezekiel 37:27

וְהָיָה מִשְׁכָּנִי עֲלֵיהֶם וְהָיִיתִי לָהֶם לֵאלֹהִים וְהֵמָּה
יִהְיוּ־לִי לְעָם׃

καὶ ἔσται ἡ κατασκήνωσίς[1] μου ἐν αὐτοῖς, καὶ ἔσομαι αὐτοῖς θεός, καὶ αὐτοί μου ἔσονται λαός.

2 Corinthians 6:16

τίς δὲ συγκατάθεσις[2] ναῷ θεοῦ μετὰ εἰδώλων;[3] ἡμεῖς γὰρ ναὸς θεοῦ ἐσμεν ζῶντος, καθὼς εἶπεν ὁ θεὸς ὅτι *ἐνοικήσω*[4] *ἐν αὐτοῖς καὶ ἐμπεριπατήσω*[5] *καὶ ἔσομαι αὐτῶν θεὸς καὶ αὐτοὶ ἔσονταί μου λαός.*

qui autem consensus[6] templo Dei cum idolis[7] vos enim estis templum Dei vivi sicut dicit Deus quoniam inhabitabo[8] in illis et inambulabo[9] et ero illorum Deus et ipsi erunt mihi populus.

1. κατασκήνωσις, *dwelling, encamping*
2. συγκατάθεσις, *agreement*
3. εἴδωλον, *idol*
4. ἐνοικέω, fut. act. ind. 1 s., *dwell in*
5. ἐμπεριπατέω, fut. act. ind. 1 s., *walk around in*
6. consensus, *agreement*
7. idolum, *idol*
8. inhabito, fut. act. ind. 1 s., *inhabit*
9. inambulo, fut. act. ind. 1 s., *walk up and down*

October 11

Joel 3:5

וְהָיָה כֹּל אֲשֶׁר־יִקְרָא בְּשֵׁם יְהוָה יִמָּלֵט[1] כִּי בְּהַר־
צִיּוֹן וּבִירוּשָׁלַםִ תִּהְיֶה פְלֵיטָה[2] כַּאֲשֶׁר אָמַר יְהוָה
וּבַשְּׂרִידִים[3] אֲשֶׁר יְהוָה קֹרֵא׃

καὶ ἔσται πᾶς, ὃς ἂν ἐπικαλέσηται τὸ ὄνομα κυρίου, σωθήσεται· ὅτι ἐν τῷ ὄρει Σιων καὶ ἐν Ιερουσαλημ ἔσται ἀνασῳζόμενος,[4] καθότι[5] εἶπεν κύριος, καὶ εὐαγγελιζόμενοι,[6] οὓς κύριος προσκέκληται.[7]

1. מָלַט, niph. impf. 3 m. s., *escape, be delivered*
2. פְּלֵיטָה, *escape*
3. שָׂרִיד, *survivor*
4. ἀνασῴζω, pres. pass. ptcp. m. nom. s., *deliver, preserve, save*
5. καθότι, *because, as*
6. εὐαγγελίζω, pres. pass. ptcp. m. nom. p., *proclaim good news*
7. προσκαλέω, perf. mid. ind. 3 s., *call*

Acts 2:39

ὑμῖν γάρ ἐστιν ἡ ἐπαγγελία καὶ τοῖς τέκνοις ὑμῶν καὶ πᾶσιν τοῖς εἰς μακράν,[8] ὅσους ἂν προσκαλέσηται[9] κύριος ὁ θεὸς ἡμῶν.

vobis enim est repromissio[10] et filiis vestris et omnibus qui longe[11] sunt quoscumque advocaverit[12] Dominus Deus noster.

8. μακράν, *far off*
9. προσκαλέω, aor. mid. subj. 3 s., *call*
10. repromissio, *promise*
11. longe, *far off*
12. advoco, futperf. act. ind. 3 s., *call*

October 12

1 Chronicles 29:15

כִּֽי־גֵרִ֨ים[1] אֲנַ֧חְנוּ לְפָנֶ֛יךָ וְתוֹשָׁבִ֖ים[2] כְּכָל־אֲבֹתֵ֑ינוּ
כַּצֵּ֧ל׀[3] יָמֵ֛ינוּ עַל־הָאָ֖רֶץ וְאֵ֥ין מִקְוֶֽה׃[4]

ὅτι πάροικοί[5] ἐσμεν ἐναντίον σου καὶ παροικοῦντες[6] ὡς πάντες οἱ πατέρες ἡμῶν· ὡς σκιὰ[7] αἱ ἡμέραι ἡμῶν ἐπὶ γῆς, καὶ οὐκ ἔστιν ὑπομονή.[8]

Hebrews 11:13

Κατὰ πίστιν ἀπέθανον οὗτοι πάντες, μὴ λαβόντες τὰς ἐπαγγελίας ἀλλὰ πόρρωθεν[9] αὐτὰς ἰδόντες καὶ ἀσπασάμενοι καὶ ὁμολογήσαντες[10] ὅτι ξένοι[11] καὶ παρεπίδημοί[12] εἰσιν ἐπὶ τῆς γῆς.

iuxta[13] fidem defuncti[14] sunt omnes isti non acceptis repromissionibus[15] sed a longe[16] eas aspicientes[17] et salutantes et confitentes quia peregrini[18] et hospites[19] sunt supra terram.

1. גֵּר, *resident foreigner*
2. תּוֹשָׁב, *sojourner*
3. צֵל, *shadow*
4. מִקְוֶה, *hope*
5. πάροικος, *stranger*
6. παροικέω, pres. act. ptcp. m. nom. p., *live as a stranger*
7. σκιά, *shadow*
8. ὑπομονή, *endurance*
9. πόρρωθεν, *from afar*
10. ὁμολογέω, aor. act. ptcp. m. nom. p., *acknowledge*
11. ξένος, *stranger*
12. παρεπίδημος, *exile, refugee*
13. iuxta, *according to*
14. defungor, perf. dep. ind. 3 p., *die*
15. repromissio, *promise*
16. longe, *far off*
17. aspicio, pres. act. ptcp. m. nom. p., *look at, behold*
18. peregrinus, *pilgrim*
19. hospes, *stranger*

October 13

Isaiah 65:11

וְאַתֶּם֙ עֹזְבֵ֣י יְהוָ֔ה הַשְּׁכֵחִ֖ים[1] אֶת־הַ֣ר קָדְשִׁ֑י
הַֽעֹרְכִ֤ים[2] לַגַּד֙[3] שֻׁלְחָ֔ן[4] וְהַֽמְמַלְאִ֖ים לַמְנִ֣י[5] מִמְסָֽךְ׃[6]

ὑμεῖς δὲ οἱ ἐγκαταλιπόντες με καὶ ἐπιλανθανόμενοι τὸ ὄρος τὸ ἅγιόν μου καὶ ἑτοιμάζοντες τῷ δαίμονι[7] τράπεζαν[8] καὶ πληροῦντες τῇ τύχῃ[9] κέρασμα.[10]

1 Corinthians 10:21

οὐ δύνασθε ποτήριον κυρίου πίνειν καὶ ποτήριον δαιμονίων, οὐ δύνασθε τραπέζης κυρίου μετέχειν[11] καὶ τραπέζης δαιμονίων.

non potestis mensae[12] Domini participes[13] esse et mensae daemoniorum.

1. שָׁכֵחַ, *forgetful*
2. עָרַךְ, qal ptcp. m. p. abs., *arrange, set*
3. גַּד, *fortune*
4. שֻׁלְחָן, *table*
5. מְנִי, *destiny*
6. מִמְסָךְ, *wine, mixed drink*
7. δαίμων, *demon*
8. τράπεζα, *table*
9. τύχη, *fortune*
10. κέρασμα, *mixture*
11. μετέχω, pres. act. inf., *partake*
12. mensa, *table*
13. particeps, *partaker, participant*

October 14

Proverbs 26:11

כְּכֶלֶב[1] שָׁב עַל־קֵאוֹ[2] כְּסִיל[3] שׁוֹנֶה[4] בְאִוַּלְתּוֹ׃[5]

ὥσπερ κύων[6] ὅταν ἐπέλθῃ ἐπὶ τὸν ἑαυτοῦ ἔμετον[7] καὶ μισητὸς[8] γένηται, οὕτως ἄφρων τῇ ἑαυτοῦ κακίᾳ ἀναστρέψας ἐπὶ τὴν ἑαυτοῦ ἁμαρτίαν. ἔστιν αἰσχύνη[9] ἐπάγουσα ἁμαρτίαν, καὶ ἔστιν αἰσχύνη δόξα καὶ χάρις.

2 Peter 2:21[10]

κρεῖττον[11] γὰρ ἦν αὐτοῖς μὴ ἐπεγνωκέναι τὴν ὁδὸν τῆς δικαιοσύνης ἢ ἐπιγνοῦσιν ὑποστρέψαι ἐκ τῆς παραδοθείσης αὐτοῖς ἁγίας ἐντολῆς.

melius enim erat illis non cognoscere viam iustitiae quam post agnitionem[12] retrorsum[13] converti ab eo quod illis traditum est sancto mandato.

1. כֶּלֶב, *dog*
2. קֵא, *vomit*
3. כְּסִיל, *fool*
4. שָׁנָה, qal ptcp. m. s. abs., *repeat*
5. אִוֶּלֶת, *folly*
6. κύων, *dog*
7. ἔμετος, *vomit*
8. μισητός, *hated, detested*
9. αἰσχύνη, *shame*
10. PA: This passage is about those who apostate; 2 Pet 2:22 applies Prov 26:11 to these people.
11. κρείττων, *better*
12. agnitio, *knowledge*
13. retrorsum, *back, behind*

October 15

Isaiah 30:10

אֲשֶׁר[1] אָמְרוּ לָרֹאִים[2] לֹא תִרְאוּ וְלַחֹזִים[3] לֹא תֶחֱזוּ־[4]
לָנוּ נְכֹחוֹת[5] דַּבְּרוּ־לָנוּ חֲלָקוֹת[6] חֲזוּ[7] מַהֲתַלּוֹת׃[8]

οἱ λέγοντες τοῖς προφήταις Μὴ ἀναγγέλλετε ἡμῖν, καὶ τοῖς τὰ ὁράματα[9] ὁρῶσιν Μὴ λαλεῖτε ἡμῖν, ἀλλὰ ἡμῖν λαλεῖτε καὶ ἀναγγέλλετε ἡμῖν ἑτέραν πλάνησιν.[10]

Romans 16:18

οἱ γὰρ τοιοῦτοι τῷ κυρίῳ ἡμῶν Χριστῷ οὐ δουλεύουσιν[11] ἀλλὰ τῇ ἑαυτῶν κοιλίᾳ,[12] καὶ διὰ τῆς χρηστολογίας[13] καὶ εὐλογίας[14] ἐξαπατῶσιν[15] τὰς καρδίας τῶν ἀκάκων.[16]

huiusmodi enim Christo Domino nostro non serviunt sed suo ventri[17] et per dulces[18] sermones et benedictiones[19] seducunt corda innocentium.[20]

1. CH: The relative pronoun here refers back to the rebellious people. TH: Translate here as *they*.
2. רֹאֶה, *visionary*
3. חֹזֶה, *seer*
4. חָזָה, qal impf. 2 m. p., *see*
5. נָכֹחַ, *right*
6. חֵלֶק, *smooth, pleasant*
7. חָזָה, qal impv. m. p., *see*
8. מַהֲתַלָּה, *deceitful (thing)*
9. ὅραμα, *vision*
10. πλάνησις, *error*
11. δουλεύω, pres. act. ind. 3 p., *serve*
12. κοιλία, *belly*
13. χρηστολογία, *smooth talk*
14. εὐλογία, *flattery*
15. ἐξαπατάω, pres. act. ind. 3 p., *deceive*
16. ἄκακος, *naive*
17. venter, *belly*
18. dulcis, *sweet*
19. benedictio, *blessing*
20. innocens, *innocent*

October 16

Isaiah 59:17

וַיִּלְבַּ֤שׁ[1] צְדָקָה֙ כַּשִּׁרְיָ֔ן[2] וְכ֥וֹבַע[3] יְשׁוּעָ֖ה[4] בְּרֹאשׁ֑וֹ
וַיִּלְבַּ֞שׁ בִּגְדֵ֤י נָקָם֙[5] תִּלְבֹּ֔שֶׁת[6] וַיַּ֥עַט[7] כַּמְעִ֖יל[8] קִנְאָֽה׃[9]

καὶ ἐνεδύσατο δικαιοσύνην ὡς θώρακα[10] καὶ περιέθετο[11] περικεφαλαίαν[12] σωτηρίου ἐπὶ τῆς κεφαλῆς καὶ περιεβάλετο[13] ἱμάτιον ἐκδικήσεως[14] καὶ τὸ περιβόλαιον.[15]

Ephesians 6:17

καὶ τὴν περικεφαλαίαν τοῦ σωτηρίου[16] δέξασθε καὶ τὴν μάχαιραν[17] τοῦ πνεύματος, ὅ ἐστιν ῥῆμα θεοῦ.

et galeam[18] salutis adsumite et gladium Spiritus quod est verbum Dei.

1. לָבַשׁ, qal wcons. 3 m. s., *wear*
2. שִׁרְיוֹן, *breastplate, body armor*
3. כּוֹבַע, *helmet*
4. יְשׁוּעָה, *salvation*
5. נָקָם, *vengeance*
6. תִּלְבֹּשֶׁת, *garment*
7. עָטָה, qal wcons. 3 m. s., *wrap, cover*
8. מְעִיל, *robe*
9. קִנְאָה, *zeal*
10. θώραξ, *breastplate*
11. περιτίθημι, aor. mid. ind. 3 s., *put on*
12. περικεφαλαία, *helmet*
13. περιβάλλω, aor. mid. ind. 3 s., *put on, clothe*
14. ἐκδίκησις, *vengeance*
15. περιβόλαιον, *cloak, robe*
16. σωτήριον, *salvation*
17. μάχαιρα, *short-sword*
18. galea, *helmet*

October 17

1. יְהוֹנָתָן, *Jonathan*

2. שֻׁלְחָן, *table*

3. חֳרִי, *fierce, burning*

4. עָצַב, niph. perf. 3 m. s., *grieve*

5. כָּלַם, hiph. perf. 3 m. s., *disgrace, humiliate*

6. ἀναπηδάω, aor. act. ind. 3 s., *leap up*

7. τράπεζα, *table*

8. θραύω, aor. pass. ind. 3 s., *shatter, break into pieces*

9. παροργίζω, pres. act. impv. 2 p., *make angry*

10. ἐκτρέφω, pres. act. impv. 2 p., *raise, nourish*

11. παιδεία, *discipline, instruction*

12. νουθεσία, *admonition, warning*

13. iracundia, *anger, wrath*

14. provoco, pres. act. inf., *provoke, stir up*

15. educo, pres. act. impv. 2 p., *bring up, educate, train*

16. disciplina, *discipline, instruction*

17. correptio, *admonition, correction*

1 Samuel 20:34

וַיָּקָם יְהוֹנָתָן[1] מֵעִם הַשֻּׁלְחָן[2] בָּחֳרִי[3]־אָף וְלֹא־אָכַל
בְּיוֹם־הַחֹדֶשׁ הַשֵּׁנִי לֶחֶם כִּי נֶעְצַב[4] אֶל־דָּוִד כִּי
הִכְלִמוֹ[5] אָבִיו׃

καὶ ἀνεπήδησεν[6] Ιωναθαν ἀπὸ τῆς τραπέζης[7] ἐν ὀργῇ θυμοῦ καὶ οὐκ ἔφαγεν ἐν τῇ δευτέρᾳ τοῦ μηνὸς ἄρτον, ὅτι ἐθραύσθη[8] ἐπὶ τὸν Δαυιδ, ὅτι συνετέλεσεν ἐπ᾽ αὐτὸν ὁ πατὴρ αὐτοῦ.

Ephesians 6:4

Καὶ οἱ πατέρες, μὴ παροργίζετε[9] τὰ τέκνα ὑμῶν ἀλλ᾽ ἐκτρέφετε[10] αὐτὰ ἐν παιδείᾳ[11] καὶ νουθεσίᾳ[12] κυρίου.

et patres nolite ad iracundiam[13] provocare[14] filios vestros sed educate[15] illos in disciplina[16] et correptione[17] Domini.

October 18

Amos 5:15

שִׂנְאוּ־רָע֙ וְאֶ֣הֱבוּ ט֔וֹב וְהַצִּ֥יגוּ[1] בַשַּׁ֖עַר מִשְׁפָּ֑ט אוּלַ֗י[2]
יֶחֱנַ֛ן[3] יְהוָ֥ה אֱלֹהֵֽי־צְבָא֖וֹת שְׁאֵרִ֥ית[4] יוֹסֵֽף׃

Μεμισήκαμεν τὰ πονηρὰ καὶ ἠγαπήκαμεν τὰ καλά· καὶ ἀποκαταστήσατε[5] ἐν πύλαις κρίμα, ὅπως ἐλεήσῃ κύριος ὁ θεὸς ὁ παντοκράτωρ τοὺς περιλοίπους[6] τοῦ Ιωσηφ.

Romans 12:9

Ἡ ἀγάπη ἀνυπόκριτος.[7] ἀποστυγοῦντες[8] τὸ πονηρόν, κολλώμενοι[9] τῷ ἀγαθῷ.

dilectio[10] sine simulatione[11] odientes[12] malum adherentes[13] bono.

1. יָצַג, hiph. impv. m. p., *establish*

2. אוּלַי, *perhaps*

3. חָנַן, qal impf. 3 m. s., *show/have mercy*

4. שְׁאֵרִית, *remnant*

5. ἀποκαθίστημι, aor. act. impv. 2 p., *restore*

6. περίλοιπος, *remnant*

7. ἀνυπόκριτος, *sincere, genuine*

8. ἀποστυγέω, pres. act. ptcp. m. nom. p., *abhor*

9. κολλάω, pres. mid. ptcp. m. nom. p., *labor for, cleave to*

10. dilectio, *love*

11. simulatio, *hypocrisy*

12. odi, perf. act. ptcp. m. nom. p., *hate*

13. adhaereo, pres. act. ptcp. m. nom. p., *adhere to, cling to*

October 19

Proverbs 10:12

שִׂ֭נְאָה[1] תְּעוֹרֵ֣ר[2] מְדָנִ֑ים[3] וְעַ֥ל כָּל־פְּ֝שָׁעִ֗ים[4] תְּכַסֶּ֥ה
אַהֲבָֽה׃[5]

μῖσος[6] ἐγείρει[7] νεῖκος,[8] πάντας δὲ τοὺς μὴ φιλονεικοῦντας[9] καλύπτει[10] φιλία.[11]

1 Peter 4:8

πρὸ πάντων τὴν εἰς ἑαυτοὺς ἀγάπην ἐκτενῆ[12] ἔχοντες, ὅτι *ἀγάπη καλύπτει πλῆθος ἁμαρτιῶν.*

ante omnia mutuam[13] in vosmet[14] ipsos caritatem continuam[15] habentes quia caritas operit[16] multitudinem peccatorum.

1. שִׂנְאָה, *hatred*

2. עוּר, polel impf. 3 f. s., *stir up*

3. מָדוֹן, *strife*

4. פֶּשַׁע, *transgression, rebellion*

5. אַהֲבָה, *love*

6. μῖσος, *hate*

7. ἐγείρω, pres. act. ind. 3 s., *raise, lift up*

8. νεῖκος, *strife*

9. φιλονεικέω, pres. act. ptcp. m. a. p., *be fond of strife*

10. καλύπτω, pres. act. ind. 3 s., *cover*

11. φιλία, *friendship*

12. ἐκτενής, *earnestly, constantly*

13. mutuus, *mutual*

14. tumet, *yourself*

15. continuus, *continual*

16. operio, pres. act. ind. 3 s., *cover*

October 20

Job 31:32

בַּחוּץ לֹא־יָלִין[1] גֵּר[2] דְּלָתַי[3] לָאֹרַח[4] אֶפְתָּח׃

ἔξω δὲ οὐκ ηὐλίζετο[5] ξένος,[6] ἡ δὲ θύρα μου παντὶ ἐλθόντι ἀνέῳκτο.

Romans 12:13

ταῖς χρείαις τῶν ἁγίων κοινωνοῦντες,[7] τὴν φιλοξενίαν[8] διώκοντες.

necessitatibus[9] sanctorum communicantes[10] hospitalitatem[11] sectantes.[12]

1. לִין, qal impf. 3 m. s., *lodge, stay the night*
2. גֵּר, *stranger, resident foreigner*
3. דֶּלֶת, *door*
4. אֹרַח, *traveler*
5. αὐλίζομαι, impf. mid. ind. 3 s., *spend the night*
6. ξένος, *stranger*
7. κοινωνέω, pres. act. ptcp. m. nom. p., *share*
8. φιλοξενία, *hospitality*
9. necessitas, *need*
10. communico, pres. act. ptcp. m. nom. p., *share*
11. hospitalitas, *hospitality*
12. sector, pres. act. ptcp. m. nom. p., *pursue, follow*

October 21

Proverbs 11:24

יֵשׁ מְפַזֵּר[1] וְנוֹסָף עוֹד וְחוֹשֵׂךְ[2] מִיֹּשֶׁר[3] אַךְ־לְמַחְסוֹר׃[4]

εἰσὶν οἳ τὰ ἴδια[5] σπείροντες[6] πλείονα ποιοῦσιν, εἰσὶν καὶ οἳ συνάγοντες ἐλαττονοῦνται.[7]

2 Corinthians 9:6

Τοῦτο δέ, ὁ σπείρων[8] φειδομένως[9] φειδομένως καὶ θερίσει,[10] καὶ ὁ σπείρων[11] ἐπ' εὐλογίαις[12] ἐπ' εὐλογίαις καὶ θερίσει.

hoc autem qui parce[13] seminat parce et metet[14] et qui seminat in benedictionibus[15] de benedictionibus et metet.

1. פָּזַר, piel ptcp. m. s. abs., *scatter*; TH: *give freely*
2. חָשַׂךְ, qal ptcp. m. s. abs., *spare, withhold*
3. יֹשֶׁר, *right*
4. מַחְסוֹר, *poverty*
5. ἴδιος, *possession, one's own*
6. σπείρω, pres. act. ptcp. m. nom. p., *sow*; TH: *give freely*
7. ἐλαττονέω, pres. mid. ind. 3 p., *be in need*
8. σπείρω, pres. act. ptcp. m. nom. s., *sow*
9. φειδομένως, *sparingly*
10. θερίζω, fut. act. ind. 3 s., *reap*
11. σπείρω, pres. act. ptcp. m. nom. s., *sow*
12. εὐλογία, *bountifully*
13. parce, *sparingly*
14. meto, fut. act. ind. 3 s., *reap*
15. benedictio, *blessing*

October 22

Psalm 109:28 [LXX 108:28]

יְקַֽלְלוּ[1]־הֵמָּה֮ וְאַתָּ֪ה תְבָ֫רֵ֥ךְ קָ֤מוּ׀ וַיֵּבֹ֗שׁוּ וְֽעַבְדְּךָ֥
יִשְׂמָֽח׃

καταράσονται[2] αὐτοί, καὶ σὺ εὐλογήσεις· οἱ ἐπανιστανόμενοί[3] μοι αἰσχυνθήτωσαν,[4] ὁ δὲ δοῦλός σου εὐφρανθήσεται.

Romans 12:14

εὐλογεῖτε τοὺς διώκοντας [ὑμᾶς], εὐλογεῖτε καὶ μὴ καταρᾶσθε.[5]

benedicite persequentibus[6] benedicite et nolite maledicere.[7]

1. קָלַל, piel impf. 3 m. p., *curse*
2. καταράομαι, fut. mid. ind. 3 p., *curse*
3. ἐπανιστάνω, pres. mid. ptcp. m. nom. p., *rise, turn against*
4. αἰσχύνω, aor. pass. impv. 3 p., *be ashamed*
5. καταράομαι, pres. mid. impv. 2 p., *curse*
6. persequor, pres. act. ptcp. m. d. p., *persecute*
7. maledico, pres. act. inf., *curse*

October 23

Job 30:25

אִם־לֹ֣א בָ֭כִיתִי לִקְשֵׁה[1]־י֑וֹם[2] עָֽגְמָ֥ה[3] נַ֝פְשִׁ֗י לָאֶבְיֽוֹן׃[4]

ἐγὼ δὲ ἐπὶ παντὶ ἀδυνάτῳ[5] ἔκλαυσα, ἐστέναξα[6] δὲ
ἰδὼν ἄνδρα ἐν ἀνάγκαις.[7]

Romans 12:15

χαίρειν μετὰ χαιρόντων, κλαίειν μετὰ κλαιόντων.

gaudere cum gaudentibus flere[8] cum flentibus.[9]

1. קָשֶׁה, *hard*
2. TH: Literally *for the hard of day; for the unfortunate*
3. עָגַם, qal perf. 3 f. s., *grieve*
4. אֶבְיוֹן, *needy, poor*
5. ἀδύνατος, *powerless*
6. στενάζω, aor. act. ind. 1 s., *mourn, groan*
7. ἀνάγκη, *distress*
8. fleo, pres. act. inf., *weep*
9. fleo, pres. act. ptcp. m. abl. p., *weep*

October 24

Psalm 112:9 [LXX 111:9]

פִּזַּ֤ר ׀[1] נָ֘תַ֤ן לָֽאֶבְיוֹנִ֗ים[2] צִ֭דְקָתוֹ עֹמֶ֣דֶת לָעַ֑ד[3] קַ֝רְנ֗וֹ[4]
תָּר֥וּם בְּכָבֽוֹד׃

ἐσκόρπισεν,[5] ἔδωκεν τοῖς πένησιν·[6] ἡ δικαιοσύνη αὐτοῦ μένει[7] εἰς τὸν αἰῶνα τοῦ αἰῶνος, τὸ κέρας αὐτοῦ ὑψωθήσεται ἐν δόξῃ.

2 Corinthians 9:8[8]

δυνατεῖ[9] δὲ ὁ θεὸς πᾶσαν χάριν περισσεῦσαι εἰς ὑμᾶς, ἵνα ἐν παντὶ πάντοτε πᾶσαν αὐτάρκειαν[10] ἔχοντες περισσεύητε εἰς πᾶν ἔργον ἀγαθόν.

potens[11] est autem Deus omnem gratiam abundare facere in vobis ut in omnibus semper omnem sufficientiam[12] habentes abundetis in omne opus bonum.

1. פִּזַּר, piel perf. 3 m. s., *scatter*

2. אֶבְיוֹן, *needy*

3. עַד, *forever*

4. קֶרֶן, *horn*

5. σκορπίζω, aor. act. ind. 3 s., *scatter*

6. πένης, *poor person, day laborer*

7. μένω, pres. act. ind. 3 s., *remain, endure*

8. PA: The psalm text is used as evidence in support of the statement made in 2 Cor 9:8.

9. δυνατέω, pres. act. ind. 3 s., *be able*

10. αὐτάρκεια, *sufficiency*

11. potens, *able, strong*

12. sufficientia, *sufficiency*

October 25

Isaiah 5:21

הֹ֥וי[1] חֲכָמִ֖ים בְּעֵֽינֵיהֶ֑ם וְנֶ֥גֶד פְּנֵיהֶ֖ם נְבֹנִֽים׃

οὐαὶ[2] οἱ συνετοὶ[3] ἐν ἑαυτοῖς καὶ ἐνώπιον ἑαυτῶν ἐπιστήμονες.[4]

Romans 12:16

τὸ αὐτὸ εἰς ἀλλήλους φρονοῦντες,[5] μὴ τὰ ὑψηλὰ[6] φρονοῦντες ἀλλὰ τοῖς ταπεινοῖς[7] συναπαγόμενοι.[8] μὴ γίνεσθε φρόνιμοι[9] παρ᾽ ἑαυτοῖς.

id ipsum invicem sentientes[10] non alta[11] sapientes[12] sed humilibus[13] consentientes[14] nolite esse prudentes[15] apud vosmet[16] ipsos.

1. הוֹי, *woe*
2. οὐαί, *woe*
3. συνετός, *wise, intelligent*
4. ἐπιστήμων, *understanding*
5. φρονέω, pres. act. ptcp. m. nom. p., *be wise*
6. ὑψηλός, *proud*
7. ταπεινός, *humble*
8. συναπάγω, pres. mid. ptcp. m. nom. p., *condescend, associate*
9. φρόνιμος, *wise*
10. sentio, pres. act. ptcp. m. nom. p., *think*
11. altus, *high*
12. sapio, pres. act. ptcp. m. nom. p., *consider*
13. humilis, *humble*
14. consentio, pres. act. ptcp. m. nom. p., *consent, agree*
15. prudens, *wise*
16. tumet, *yourself*

October 26

Proverbs 29:23

גַּאֲוַת[1] אָדָם תַּשְׁפִּילֶנּוּ[2] וּשְׁפַל[3]־רוּחַ יִתְמֹךְ[4] כָּבוֹד׃

ὕβρις[5] ἄνδρα ταπεινοῖ, τοὺς δὲ ταπεινόφρονας[6] ἐρείδει[7] δόξῃ κύριος.

Matthew 23:12

ὅστις δὲ ὑψώσει[8] ἑαυτὸν ταπεινωθήσεται[9] καὶ ὅστις ταπεινώσει[10] ἑαυτὸν ὑψωθήσεται.[11]

qui autem se exaltaverit[12] humiliabitur[13] et qui se humiliaverit[14] exaltabitur.[15]

1. גַּאֲוָה, *pride*
2. שָׁפֵל, hiph. impf. 3 f. s., *be low/abased*
3. שֵׁפֶל, *low estate*
4. תָּמַךְ, qal impf. 3 m. s., *attain*
5. ὕβρις, *pride*
6. ταπεινόφρων, *humble*
7. ἐρείδω, pres. act. ind. 3 s., *support*
8. ὑψόω, fut. act. ind. 3 s., *exalt*
9. ταπεινόω, fut. pass. ind. 3 s., *humble*
10. ταπεινόω, fut. act. ind. 3 s., *humble*
11. ὑψόω, fut. pass. ind. 3 s., *exalt*
12. exalto, futperf. act. ind. 3 s., *exalt*
13. humilio, fut. pass. ind. 3 s., *humble*
14. humilio, fut-perf. act. ind. 3 s., *humble*
15. exalto, fut. pass. ind. 3 s., *exalt*

October 27

1. לֵץ, *scoffer*
2. לִיץ, hiph. impf. 3 m. s., *scoff*
3. עָנָו, *poor, afflicted*
4. חֵן, *grace*
5. ὑπερήφανος, *proud*
6. ἀντιτάσσω, pres. mid. ind. 3 s., *resist*
7. ταπεινός, *humble*
8. ὁμοίως, *likewise*
9. νέος, *young*
10. ταπεινοφροσύνη, *humility*
11. ἐγκομβόομαι, aor. mid. impv. 2 p., *put on, clothe*
12. adulescens, *young man*
13. subdo, perf. pass. ptcp. m. nom. p., *subject*
14. humilitas, *humility*
15. insinuo, pres. act. impv. 2 p., *insinuate, make known*
16. superbus, *proud*
17. resisto, pres. act. ind. 3 s., *resist*
18. humilis, *humble*

Proverbs 3:34

אִם־לַלֵּצִים[1] הֽוּא־יָלִ֑יץ[2] וְ֝לַעֲנָוִים[3] יִתֶּן־חֵֽן׃[4]

κύριος ὑπερηφάνοις[5] ἀντιτάσσεται,[6] ταπεινοῖς[7] δὲ δίδωσιν χάριν.

1 Peter 5:5

ὁμοίως,[8] νεώτεροι,[9] ὑποτάγητε πρεσβυτέροις· πάντες δὲ ἀλλήλοις τὴν ταπεινοφροσύνην[10] ἐγκομβώσασθε,[11] ὅτι ὁ θεὸς *ὑπερηφάνοις ἀντιτάσσεται, ταπεινοῖς δὲ δίδωσιν χάριν.*

similiter adulescentes[12] subditi[13] estote senioribus omnes autem invicem humilitatem[14] insinuate[15] quia Deus superbis[16] resistit[17] humilibus[18] autem dat gratiam.

October 28

Proverbs 8:15

בִּי מְלָכִים יִמְלֹכוּ וְרוֹזְנִים[1] יְחֹקְקוּ[2] צֶדֶק׃

δι᾽ ἐμοῦ βασιλεῖς βασιλεύουσιν, καὶ οἱ δυνάσται[3] γράφουσιν δικαιοσύνην.

Romans 13:1

Πᾶσα ψυχὴ ἐξουσίαις ὑπερεχούσαις[4] ὑποτασσέσθω. οὐ γὰρ ἔστιν ἐξουσία εἰ μὴ ὑπὸ θεοῦ, αἱ δὲ οὖσαι ὑπὸ θεοῦ τεταγμέναι[5] εἰσίν.

omnis anima potestatibus sublimioribus[6] subdita[7] sit non est enim potestas nisi a Deo quae autem sunt a Deo ordinatae[8] sunt.

1. רָזַן, qal ptcp. m. p. abs., *rule*
2. חָקַק, poel impf. 3 m. p., *decree*
3. δυνάστης, *ruler*
4. ὑπερέχω, pres. act. ptcp. f. d. p., *be in control*; TH: here *higher powers*
5. τάσσω, perf. pass. ptcp. f. nom. p., *appoint*
6. sublimis, *high*
7. subdo, perf. pass. subj. 3 s., *submit*
8. ordino, perf. pass. ind. 3 p., *appoint*

October 29

1. רֵיחַ, *scent, aroma*

2. נִיחוֹחַ, *soothing*

3. אִשֶּׁה, *offering*

4. κριός, *ram*

5. ὁλοκαύτωμα, *whole burnt offering*

6. ὀσμή, *smell*

7. εὐωδία, *fragrant aroma*

8. θυσίασμα, *sacrificial victim*

9. PA: Christian service (monetary gifts offered by the Philippians) is described here with priestly language.

10. ἀπέχω, pres. act. ind. 1 s., *receive*

11. Ἐπαφρόδιτος, *Epaphroditus*

12. θυσία, *sacrifice*

13. δεκτός, *acceptable*

14. εὐάρεστος, *well-pleasing*

15. repleo, perf. pass. ind. 1 s., *fill, satisfy*

16. Epafroditus, *Epaphroditus*

17. odor, *smell, odor*

18. suavitas, *sweetness*

19. hostia, *offering*

Exodus 29:18

וְהִקְטַרְתָּ֣ אֶת־כָּל־הָאַ֙יִל֙ הַמִּזְבֵּ֔חָה עֹלָ֥ה ה֖וּא לַֽיהוָ֑ה
רֵ֣יחַ[1] נִיח֔וֹחַ[2] אִשֶּׁ֥ה[3] לַֽיהוָ֖ה הֽוּא׃

καὶ ἀνοίσεις ὅλον τὸν κριὸν[4] ἐπὶ τὸ θυσιαστήριον ὁλοκαύτωμα[5] κυρίῳ εἰς ὀσμὴν[6] εὐωδίας·[7] θυσίασμα[8] κυρίῳ ἐστίν.

Philippians 4:18[9]

ἀπέχω[10] δὲ πάντα καὶ περισσεύω· πεπλήρωμαι δεξάμενος παρὰ Ἐπαφροδίτου[11] τὰ παρ᾽ ὑμῶν, ὀσμὴν εὐωδίας, θυσίαν[12] δεκτήν,[13] εὐάρεστον[14] τῷ θεῷ.

habeo autem omnia et abundo repletus[15] sum acceptis ab Epafrodito[16] quae misistis odorem[17] suavitatis[18] hostiam[19] acceptam placentem Deo,

October 30

Psalm 62:11 [LXX 61:11]

אַל־תִּבְטְח֬וּ בְעֹ֡שֶׁק[1] וּבְגָזֵ֗ל[2] אַל־תֶּ֫הְבָּ֥לוּ[3] חַ֤יִל ׀ כִּֽי־
יָנ֑וּב[4] אַל־תָּשִׁ֥יתוּ[5] לֵֽב׃

μὴ ἐλπίζετε ἐπὶ ἀδικίαν καὶ ἐπὶ ἅρπαγμα[6] μὴ ἐπιποθεῖτε·[7] πλοῦτος[8] ἐὰν ῥέῃ,[9] μὴ προστίθεσθε καρδίαν.

1 Timothy 6:17

Τοῖς πλουσίοις[10] ἐν τῷ νῦν αἰῶνι παράγγελλε μὴ ὑψηλοφρονεῖν[11] μηδὲ ἠλπικέναι ἐπὶ πλούτου ἀδηλότητι[12] ἀλλ᾽ ἐπὶ θεῷ τῷ παρέχοντι[13] ἡμῖν πάντα πλουσίως[14] εἰς ἀπόλαυσιν.[15]

divitibus huius saeculi praecipe non sublime[16] sapere[17] neque sperare in incerto[18] divitiarum[19] sed in Deo qui praestat[20] nobis omnia abunde[21] ad fruendum.[22]

1. עֹשֶׁק, *oppression*
2. גָּזֵל, *robbery*
3. הָבַל, qal impf. 2 m. p. juss., *become vain*
4. נוּב, qal impf. 3 m. s., *bear fruit*
5. שִׁית, qal impf. 2 m. p. juss., *set*
6. ἅρπαγμα, *stolen goods*
7. ἐπιποθέω, pres. act. ind. 2 p., *desire, long for*
8. πλοῦτος, *riches*
9. ῥέω, pres. act. subj. 3 s., *flow*
10. πλούσιος, *rich*
11. ὑψηλοφρονέω, pres. act. inf., *be arrogant*
12. ἀδηλότης, *uncertainty*
13. παρέχω, pres. act. ptcp. m. d. s., *provide*
14. πλουσίως, *richly*
15. ἀπόλαυσις, *enjoyment*
16. sublimis, *lofty*
17. sapio, pres. act. inf., *think, consider*
18. incertum, *uncertain*
19. divitiae, *riches*
20. praesto, pres. act. ind. 3 s., *furnish, give*

21. abunde, *abundantly.* 22. fruor, ger. dep. n. a. s., *enjoy*

October 31

Job 1:8

וַיֹּ֤אמֶר יְהוָה֙ אֶל־הַשָּׂטָ֔ן[1] הֲשַׂ֥מְתָּ לִבְּךָ֖ עַל־עַבְדִּ֣י
אִיּ֑וֹב[2] כִּ֣י אֵ֤ין כָּמֹ֙הוּ֙ בָּאָ֔רֶץ אִ֣ישׁ תָּ֧ם[3] וְיָשָׁ֛ר יְרֵ֥א[4]
אֱלֹהִ֖ים וְסָ֥ר מֵרָֽע׃

καὶ εἶπεν αὐτῷ ὁ κύριος Προσέσχες τῇ διανοίᾳ[5] σου κατὰ τοῦ παιδός μου Ιωβ,[6] ὅτι οὐκ ἔστιν κατʼ αὐτὸν τῶν ἐπὶ τῆς γῆς ἄνθρωπος ἄμεμπτος,[7] ἀληθινός,[8] θεοσεβής,[9] ἀπεχόμενος[10] ἀπὸ παντὸς πονηροῦ πράγματος;

1 Thessalonians 5:22

ἀπὸ παντὸς εἴδους[11] πονηροῦ ἀπέχεσθε.[12]

ab omni specie[13] mala abstinete[14] vos.

1. שָׂטָן, *adversary, Satan*
2. אִיּוֹב, *Job*
3. תֹּם, *blameless*
4. יָרֵא, *fear*
5. διάνοια, *thought*
6. Ἰώβ, *Job*
7. ἄμεμπτος, *blameless*
8. ἀληθινός, *truthful*
9. θεοσεβής, *God-fearing, godly*
10. ἀπέχω, pres. mid. ptcp. m. nom. s., *be far off, abstain*
11. εἶδος, *appearance, form*
12. ἀπέχω, pres. mid. impv. 2 p., *be far off, abstain*
13. species, *appearance, form*
14. abstineo, pres. act. impv. 2 p., *abstain*

November 1

Leviticus 25:43

לֹא־תִרְדֶּ֥ה[1] בֹ֖ו[2] בְּפָ֑רֶךְ[3] וְיָרֵ֖אתָ מֵאֱלֹהֶֽיךָ׃

οὐ κατατενεῖς[4] αὐτὸν[5] ἐν τῷ μόχθῳ[6] καὶ
φοβηθήσῃ κύριον τὸν θεόν σου.

Colossians 4:1

Οἱ κύριοι, τὸ δίκαιον καὶ τὴν ἰσότητα[7] τοῖς
δούλοις παρέχεσθε,[8] εἰδότες ὅτι καὶ ὑμεῖς ἔχετε
κύριον ἐν οὐρανῷ.

domini quod iustum est et aequum[9] servis
praestate[10] scientes quoniam et vos Dominum
habetis in caelo.

1. רָדָה, qal impf. 2 m. s., *rule, have dominion over*

2. This pronoun is a referent to a slave.

3. פֶּרֶךְ, *violence*

4. κατατείνω, fut. act. ind. 2 s., *stretch,*

5. This pronoun is a referent to a slave.

6. μόχθος, *labor, trouble*

7. ἰσότης, *fairly*

8. παρέχω, pres. mid. impv. 2 p., *treat, render*

9. aequus, *just, right*

10. praesto, pres. act. impv. 2 p., *do, perform*

November 2

Proverbs 2:6

כִּֽי־יְ֭הוָה יִתֵּ֣ן חָכְמָ֑ה מִ֝פִּ֗יו דַּ֣עַת[1] וּתְבוּנָֽה׃[2]

ὅτι κύριος δίδωσιν σοφίαν, καὶ ἀπὸ προσώπου αὐτοῦ γνῶσις[3] καὶ σύνεσις.

James 1:5

Εἰ δέ τις ὑμῶν λείπεται[4] σοφίας, αἰτείτω παρὰ τοῦ διδόντος θεοῦ πᾶσιν ἁπλῶς[5] καὶ μὴ ὀνειδίζοντος,[6] καὶ δοθήσεται αὐτῷ.

si quis autem vestrum indiget[7] sapientiam postulet[8] a Deo qui dat omnibus affluenter[9] et non inproperat[10] et dabitur ei.

1. דַּ֣עַת, *knowledge*
2. תְּבוּנָה, *understanding*
3. γνῶσις, *knowledge*
4. λείπω, pres. mid. ind. 3 s., *lack*
5. ἁπλῶς, *generously*
6. ὀνειδίζω, pres. act. ptcp. m. g. s., *reproach*
7. indigeo, pres. act. ind. 3 s., *lack*
8. postulo, pres. act. subj. 3 s., *ask*
9. affluenter, *generously, abundantly*
10. inpropero, pres. act. ind. 3 s., *reproach*

November 3

Proverbs 15:29

רָח֣וֹק[1] יְ֭הוָה מֵרְשָׁעִ֑ים וּתְפִלַּ֖ת[2] צַדִּיקִ֣ים יִשְׁמָֽע׃

μακρὰν[3] ἀπέχει[4] ὁ θεὸς ἀπὸ ἀσεβῶν, εὐχαῖς[5] δὲ δικαίων ἐπακούει.

John 9:31

οἴδαμεν ὅτι ἁμαρτωλῶν ὁ θεὸς οὐκ ἀκούει, ἀλλ᾽ ἐάν τις θεοσεβὴς[6] ᾖ καὶ τὸ θέλημα αὐτοῦ ποιῇ τούτου ἀκούει.

scimus autem quia peccatores Deus non audit sed si quis Dei cultor[7] est et voluntatem eius facit hunc exaudit.[8]

1. רָחוֹק, *distant, far*
2. תְּפִלָּה, *prayer*
3. μακράν, *far off*
4. ἀπέχω, pres. act. ind. 3 s., *be far off*
5. εὐχή, *prayer*
6. θεοσεβής, *God-fearing*
7. cultor, *worshipper*
8. exaudio, pres. act. ind. 3 s., *hear*

November 4

Proverbs 3:11

מוּסַ֣ר[1] יְ֭הוָה בְּנִ֣י אַל־תִּמְאָ֑ס[2] וְאַל־תָּ֝קֹ֗ץ[3] בְּתוֹכַחְתּֽוֹ׃[4]

Υἱέ, μὴ ὀλιγώρει[5] παιδείας[6] κυρίου μηδὲ ἐκλύου[7] ὑπ᾽ αὐτοῦ ἐλεγχόμενος.[8]

Hebrews 12:7

εἰς παιδείαν ὑπομένετε,[9] ὡς υἱοῖς ὑμῖν προσφέρεται ὁ θεός. τίς γὰρ υἱὸς ὃν οὐ παιδεύει[10] πατήρ;

in disciplina[11] perseverate[12] tamquam filiis vobis offert Deus quis enim filius quem non corripit[13] pater?

1. מוּסָר, *discipline*
2. מָאַס, qal impf. 2 m. s. juss., *reject*
3. קוּץ, qal impf. 2 m. s. juss., *loathe*
4. תּוֹכַ֫חַת, *reproof*
5. ὀλιγωρέω, pres. act. impv. 2 s., *despise*
6. παιδεία, *discipline*
7. ἐκλύω, pres. pass. impv. 2 s., *weaken*
8. ἐλέγχω, pres. pass. ptcp. m. nom. s., *reprove*
9. ὑπομένω, pres. act. ind. 2 p., *endure*
10. παιδεύω, pres. act. ind. 3 s., *discipline, instruct*
11. disciplina, *discipline, instruction*
12. persevero, pres. act. impv. 2 p., *endure*
13. corripio, pres. act. ind. 3 s., *reprove*

November 5

Proverbs 3:12

כִּ֤י אֶ֥ת אֲשֶׁ֣ר יֶאֱהַ֣ב יְהוָ֣ה יוֹכִ֑יחַ[1] וּ֝כְאָ֗ב אֶת־בֵּ֥ן יִרְצֶֽה׃[2]

ὃν γὰρ ἀγαπᾷ κύριος παιδεύει,[3] μαστιγοῖ[4] δὲ πάντα υἱὸν ὃν παραδέχεται.[5]

Hebrews 12:8

εἰ δὲ χωρίς ἐστε παιδείας ἧς μέτοχοι[6] γεγόνασιν πάντες, ἄρα νόθοι[7] καὶ οὐχ υἱοί ἐστε.

quod si extra[8] disciplinam estis cuius participes[9] facti sunt omnes ergo adulteri[10] et non filii estis.

1. יָכַח, hiph. impf. 3 m. s., *reprove*
2. רָצָה, qal impf. 3 m. s., *be pleased with*
3. παιδεύω, pres. act. ind. 3 s., *discipline*
4. μαστιγόω, pres. act. ind. 3 s., *beat, whip*
5. παραδέχομαι, pres. mid. ind. 3 s., *receive*
6. μέτοχος, *participant, partaker*
7. νόθος, *illegitimate*
8. extra, *except*
9. particeps, *participant*
10. adulter, *illegitimate*

November 6

Psalm 34:14 [LXX 33:14]

נְצֹ֣ר[1] לְשׁוֹנְךָ֣ מֵרָ֑ע וּ֝שְׂפָתֶ֗יךָ מִדַּבֵּ֥ר מִרְמָֽה׃[2]

παῦσον[3] τὴν γλῶσσάν σου ἀπὸ κακοῦ καὶ χείλη σου τοῦ μὴ λαλῆσαι δόλον.[4]

James 1:26

Εἴ τις δοκεῖ θρησκὸς[5] εἶναι μὴ χαλιναγωγῶν[6] γλῶσσαν αὐτοῦ ἀλλ᾽ ἀπατῶν[7] καρδίαν αὐτοῦ, τούτου μάταιος[8] ἡ θρησκεία.

si quis autem putat se religiosum[9] esse non refrenans[10] linguam suam sed seducens cor suum huius vana[11] est religio.

1. נָצַר, qal impv. m. s., *keep, watch*

2. מִרְמָה, *deceit*

3. παύω, aor. act. impv. 2 s., *cease, stop*

4. δόλος, *deceit*

5. θρῆσκος, *religious*

6. χαλιναγωγέω, pres. act. ptcp. m. nom. s., *bridle*

7. ἀπατάω, pres. act. ptcp. m. nom. s., *deceive*

8. μάταιος, *vain, empty*

9. religiosus, *religious*

10. refreno, pres. act. ptcp. m. nom. s., *bridle, rein back*

11. vanus, *vain, profitless*

November 7

Isaiah 53:12

לָכֵ֞ן אֲחַלֶּק[1]־ל֣וֹ בָרַבִּ֗ים וְאֶת־עֲצוּמִים֮[2] יְחַלֵּ֣ק[3] שָׁלָל֒[4]
תַּ֗חַת אֲשֶׁ֨ר הֶעֱרָ֤ה[5] לַמָּ֙וֶת֙ נַפְשׁ֔וֹ וְאֶת־פֹּשְׁעִ֖ים[6]
נִמְנָ֑ה[7] וְהוּא֙ חֵטְא[8]־רַבִּ֣ים נָשָׂ֔א וְלַפֹּשְׁעִ֖ים יַפְגִּֽיעַ׃[9]

διὰ τοῦτο αὐτὸς κληρονομήσει πολλοὺς καὶ τῶν ἰσχυρῶν μεριεῖ[10] σκῦλα,[11] ἀνθ᾽ ὧν παρεδόθη εἰς θάνατον ἡ ψυχὴ αὐτοῦ, καὶ ἐν τοῖς ἀνόμοις ἐλογίσθη· καὶ αὐτὸς ἁμαρτίας πολλῶν ἀνήνεγκεν καὶ διὰ τὰς ἁμαρτίας αὐτῶν παρεδόθη.

Hebrews 9:28

οὕτως καὶ ὁ Χριστὸς ἅπαξ[12] προσενεχθεὶς εἰς τὸ πολλῶν ἀνενεγκεῖν[13] ἁμαρτίας ἐκ δευτέρου χωρὶς ἁμαρτίας ὀφθήσεται τοῖς αὐτὸν ἀπεκδεχομένοις[14] εἰς σωτηρίαν.

sic et Christus semel[15] oblatus ad multorum exhaurienda[16] peccata secundo sine peccato apparebit expectantibus se in salutem.

1. חָלַק, piel impf. 1 c. s., *divide*
2. עָצוּם, *strong, mighty*
3. חָלַק, piel impf. 3 m. s., *divide*
4. שָׁלָל, *spoil, plunder*
5. עָרָה, hiph. perf. 3 m. s., *empty, pour out*
6. פֹּשֵׁעַ, *transgressor*
7. מָנָה, niph. perf. 3 m. s., *number, count*
8. חֵטְא, *sin*
9. פָּגַע, hiph. impf. 3 m. s., *intercede*
10. μερίζω, fut. act. ind. 3 s., *divide*
11. σκῦλον, *plunder*
12. ἅπαξ, *once*
13. ἀναφέρω, aor. act. inf., *bear*
14. ἀπεκδέχομαι, pres. mid. ptcp. m. d. p., *await*
15. semel, *once*
16. exhaurio, ger. pass. n. a. p., *remove, take away*

November 8

Ezekiel 32:7

וְכִסֵּיתִ֤י בְכַבּֽוֹתְךָ֙[1] שָׁמַ֔יִם וְהִקְדַּרְתִּ֖י[2] אֶת־כֹּכְבֵיהֶ֑ם[3]
שֶׁ֚מֶשׁ בֶּעָנָ֣ן[4] אֲכַסֶּ֔נּוּ וְיָרֵ֖חַ[5] לֹא־יָאִ֥יר אוֹרֽוֹ׃[6]

καὶ κατακαλύψω[7] ἐν τῷ σβεσθῆναί[8] σε οὐρανὸν καὶ συσκοτάσω[9] τὰ ἄστρα[10] αὐτοῦ, ἥλιον ἐν νεφέλῃ καλύψω,[11] καὶ σελήνη[12] οὐ μὴ φάνῃ[13] τὸ φῶς αὐτῆς.

Matthew 24:29

Εὐθέως δὲ μετὰ τὴν θλῖψιν τῶν ἡμερῶν ἐκείνων *ὁ ἥλιος σκοτισθήσεται,*[14] *καὶ ἡ σελήνη οὐ δώσει τὸ φέγγος*[15] *αὐτῆς, καὶ οἱ ἀστέρες πεσοῦνται ἀπὸ* τοῦ οὐρανοῦ, καὶ αἱ δυνάμεις τῶν οὐρανῶν σαλευθήσονται.[16]

statim autem post tribulationem dierum illorum sol obscurabitur[17] et luna[18] non dabit lumen suum et stellae[19] cadent de caelo et virtutes caelorum commovebuntur.[20]

1. כָּבָה, piel inf. cons., *extinguish*
2. קָדַר, hiph. perf. 1 c. s., *be dark*
3. כּוֹכָב, *star*
4. עָנָן, *cloud*
5. יָרֵחַ, *moon*
6. אוֹר, hiph. impf. 3 m. s., *be light*
7. κατακαλύπτω, fut. act. ind. 1 s., *cover*
8. σβέννυμι, aor. pass. inf., *extinguish*
9. συσκοτάζω, fut. act. ind. 1 s., *darken*
10. ἄστρον, *star*
11. καλύπτω, fut. act. ind. 1 s., *cover*
12. σελήνη, *moon*
13. φαίνω, aor. act. subj. 3 s., *shine*
14. σκοτίζω, fut. pass. ind. 3 s., *darken*
15. φέγγος, *light*
16. σαλεύω, fut. pass. ind. 3 p., *shake*
17. obscuro, fut. pass. ind. 3 s., *darken*
18. luna, *moon*
19. stella, *star*
20. commoveo, fut. pass. ind. 3 p., *shake, move*

November 9

Daniel 7:13

חָזֵה[1] הֲוֵית[2] בְּחֶזְוֵי[3] לֵילְיָא[4] וַאֲרוּ[5] עִם[6]־עֲנָנֵי[7] שְׁמַיָּא[8]
כְּבַר[9] אֱנָשׁ[10] אָתֵה[11] הֲוָה[12] וְעַד[13]־עַתִּיק[14] יוֹמַיָּא[15]
מְטָה[16] וּקְדָמוֹהִי[17] הַקְרְבוּהִי׃[18]

ἐθεώρουν[19] ἐν ὁράματι[20] τῆς νυκτὸς καὶ ἰδοὺ ἐπὶ τῶν νεφελῶν[21] τοῦ οὐρανοῦ ὡς υἱὸς ἀνθρώπου ἤρχετο, καὶ ὡς παλαιὸς[22] ἡμερῶν παρῆν,[23] καὶ οἱ παρεστηκότες[24] παρῆσαν[25] αὐτῷ.

Matthew 24:30

καὶ τότε φανήσεται τὸ σημεῖον τοῦ υἱοῦ τοῦ ἀνθρώπου ἐν οὐρανῷ, καὶ τότε κόψονται[26] πᾶσαι αἱ φυλαὶ τῆς γῆς καὶ ὄψονται *τὸν υἱὸν τοῦ ἀνθρώπου ἐρχόμενον ἐπὶ τῶν νεφελῶν τοῦ οὐρανοῦ* μετὰ δυνάμεως καὶ δόξης πολλῆς.

et tunc parebit[27] signum Filii hominis in caelo et tunc plangent[28] omnes tribus terrae et videbunt Filium hominis venientem in nubibus[29] caeli cum virtute multa et maiestate.[30]

1. חֲזָה, peal ptcp. m. s. abs., *see*
2. הֲוָה, peal perf. 1 c. s., *be, become*
3. חֵזוּ, *vision*
4. לֵילֵי, *night*
5. אֲרוּ, *behold*
6. עִם, *with*
7. עֲנָן, *cloud*
8. שְׁמַיִן, *heavens*
9. בַּר, *son*
10. אֱנָשׁ, *man*
11. אֲתָה, peal ptcp. m. s. abs., *come*
12. הֲוָה, peal perf. 3 m. s., *be, become*
13. עַד, *to*
14. עַתִּיק, *ancient one*
15. יוֹם, *day*
16. מְטָא, peal perf. 3 m. s., *reach, attain, come*
17. קֳדָם, *before*
18. קְרֵב, haphel perf. 3 m. p., *approach, bring near*
19. θεωρέω, impf. act. ind. 1 s., *see*
20. ὅραμα, *vision*
21. νεφέλη, *cloud*
22. παλαιός, *old*
23. πάρειμι, impf. act. ind. 3 s., *be present*

24. παρίστημι, perf. act. ptcp. m. nom. p., *stand near.* **25.** πάρειμι, impf. act. ind. 3 p., *be present.* **26.** κόπτω, fut. mid. ind. 3 p., *mourn.* **27.** pareo, fut. act. ind. 3 s., *appear.* **28.** plango, fut. act. ind. 3 p., *lament.* **29.** nubes, *cloud.* **30.** maiestas, *majesty, glory*

November 10

Jeremiah 6:14

וַיְרַפְּא֞וּ[1] אֶת־שֶׁ֤בֶר[2] עַמִּי֙ עַל־נְקַלָּ֔ה[3] לֵאמֹ֖ר שָׁל֣וֹם ׀
שָׁל֑וֹם וְאֵ֖ין שָׁלֽוֹם׃

καὶ ἰῶντο[4] τὸ σύντριμμα[5] τοῦ λαοῦ μου ἐξουθενοῦντες[6] καὶ λέγοντες Εἰρήνη εἰρήνη· καὶ ποῦ ἐστιν εἰρήνη;

1 Thessalonians 5:3

ὅταν λέγωσιν· εἰρήνη καὶ ἀσφάλεια,[7] τότε αἰφνίδιος[8] αὐτοῖς ἐφίσταται[9] ὄλεθρος[10] ὥσπερ ἡ ὠδὶν[11] τῇ ἐν γαστρὶ[12] ἐχούσῃ, καὶ οὐ μὴ ἐκφύγωσιν.[13]

cum enim dixerint pax et securitas[14] tunc repentinus[15] eis superveniet[16] interitus[17] sicut dolor[18] in utero[19] habenti et non effugient.[20]

1. רָפָא, niph. ptcp. f. s. abs., *heal*

2. שֶׁבֶר, *wound, harm, break*

3. קָלַל, niph. ptcp. f. s. abs., *be trifling, slight*

4. ἰάομαι, impf. mid. ind. 3 p., *heal*

5. σύντριμμα, *fracture, wound*

6. ἐξουθενέω, pres. act. ptcp. m. nom. p., *despise, treat with contempt*

7. ἀσφάλεια, *security*

8. αἰφνίδιος, *sudden*

9. ἐφίστημι, pres. mid. ind. 3 s., *come upon*

10. ὄλεθρος, *destruction*

11. ὠδίν, *birth pain*

12. γαστήρ, *womb*

13. ἐκφεύγω, aor. act. subj. 3 p., *escape*

14. securitas, *safety, security*

15. repentinus, *sudden*

16. supervenio, fut. act. ind. 3 s., *come upon*

17. interitus, *destruction*

18. dolor, *pain, grief*

19. uterus, *womb.* **20.** effugio, fut. act. ind. 3 p., *escape*

November 11

2 Chronicles 15:6

וְכֻתְּת֥וּ[1] גוֹי־בְּג֖וֹי וְעִ֣יר בְּעִ֑יר כִּֽי־אֱלֹהִ֥ים הֲמָמָ֖ם[2]
בְּכָל־צָרָֽה׃[3]

καὶ πολεμήσει ἔθνος πρὸς ἔθνος καὶ πόλις πρὸς πόλιν, ὅτι ὁ θεὸς ἐξέστησεν[4] αὐτοὺς ἐν πάσῃ θλίψει.

Mark 13:8

ἐγερθήσεται γὰρ ἔθνος ἐπ᾽ ἔθνος καὶ βασιλεία ἐπὶ βασιλείαν, ἔσονται σεισμοὶ[5] κατὰ τόπους, ἔσονται λιμοί·[6] ἀρχὴ ὠδίνων[7] ταῦτα.

exsurget[8] autem gens super gentem et regnum super regnum et erunt terraemotus[9] per loca et fames[10] initium dolorum[11] haec.

1. כָּתַת, pual perf. 3 c. p., *beat, crush*
2. הָמַם, qal perf. 3 m. s., *make a noise, confuse*
3. צָרָה, *turmoil*
4. ἐξίστημι, aor. act. ind. 3 s., *amaze, confuse*
5. σεισμός, *earthquake*
6. λιμός, *famine*
7. ὠδίν, *pain*
8. exsurgo, fut. act. ind. 3 s., *rise up*
9. terraemotus, *earthquake*
10. fames, *hunger, famine*
11. dolor, *pain, sorrow*

November 12

Genesis 49:10

לֹֽא־יָס֥וּר שֵׁ֙בֶט֙ מִֽיהוּדָ֔ה וּמְחֹקֵ֖ק[1] מִבֵּ֣ין רַגְלָ֑יו עַ֚ד כִּֽי־יָבֹ֣א שִׁילֹ֔ה[2] וְל֖וֹ יִקְּהַ֥ת[3] עַמִּֽים׃

οὐκ ἐκλείψει ἄρχων ἐξ Ιουδα καὶ ἡγούμενος ἐκ τῶν μηρῶν[4] αὐτοῦ, ἕως ἂν ἔλθῃ τὰ ἀποκείμενα[5] αὐτῷ, καὶ αὐτὸς προσδοκία[6] ἐθνῶν.

Revelation 5:5

καὶ εἷς ἐκ τῶν πρεσβυτέρων[7] λέγει μοι· μὴ κλαῖε,[8] ἰδοὺ ἐνίκησεν[9] ὁ λέων[10] ὁ ἐκ τῆς φυλῆς[11] Ἰούδα,[12] ἡ ῥίζα[13] Δαυίδ,[14] ἀνοῖξαι τὸ βιβλίον[15] καὶ τὰς ἑπτὰ σφραγῖδας[16] αὐτοῦ.

et unus de senioribus dicit mihi ne fleveris[17] ecce vicit[18] leo[19] de tribu Iuda radix[20] David aperire librum et septem signacula[21] eius.

1. חָקַק, poel ptcp. m. s. abs., *ruler's staff*
2. שִׁילֹה, *that which is his, tribute*
3. יְקָהָה, *obedience*
4. μηρός, *thigh*
5. ἀπόκειμαι, pres. pass. ptcp. n. nom. p., *store away*
6. προσδοκία, *expectation*
7. πρεσβύτερος, *elder*
8. κλαίω, pres. act. impv. 2 s., *weep, cry*
9. νικάω, aor. act. ind. 3 s., *conquer*
10. λέων, *lion*
11. φυλή, *tribe*
12. Ἰούδας, *Judah*
13. ῥίζα, *root*
14. Δαυίδ, *David*
15. βιβλίον, *little book*
16. σφραγίς, *seal*
17. fleo, perf. act. subj. 2 s., *weep*
18. vinco, perf. act. ind. 3 s., *conquer, overcome*
19. leo, *lion*
20. radix, *root*
21. signaculum, *seal*

November 13

Psalm 2:2

יִ֥תְיַצְּב֨וּ ׀[1] מַלְכֵי־אֶ֗רֶץ וְרוֹזְנִ֥ים[2] נֽוֹסְדוּ[3]־יָ֑חַד[4] עַל־יְ֝הוָ֗ה
וְעַל־מְשִׁיחֽוֹ׃

παρέστησαν[5] οἱ βασιλεῖς τῆς γῆς, καὶ οἱ ἄρχοντες συνήχθησαν ἐπὶ τὸ αὐτὸ κατὰ τοῦ κυρίου καὶ κατὰ τοῦ χριστοῦ[6] αὐτοῦ.

Revelation 19:19

Καὶ εἶδον τὸ θηρίον καὶ τοὺς βασιλεῖς τῆς γῆς καὶ τὰ στρατεύματα[7] αὐτῶν συνηγμένα ποιῆσαι τὸν πόλεμον[8] μετὰ τοῦ καθημένου ἐπὶ τοῦ ἵππου[9] καὶ μετὰ τοῦ στρατεύματος αὐτοῦ.

et vidi bestiam et reges terrae et exercitus[10] eorum congregatos ad faciendum proelium[11] cum illo qui sedebat in equo[12] et cum exercitu eius.

1. יָצַב, hitpael impf. 3 m. p., *set oneself against, stand*

2. רָזַן, qal ptcp. m. p. abs., *rule*

3. יָסַד, niph. perf. 3 c. p., *take counsel*

4. יַ֫חַד, *together, united*

5. παρίστημι, aor. act. ind. 3 p., *stand side by side*

6. χριστός, *anointed one*

7. στράτευμα, *army*

8. πόλεμος, *war, battle*

9. ἵππος, *horse*

10. exercitus, *army*

11. proelium, *battle, war*

12. equus, *horse*

Judgment

November 14

Psalm 9:9

וְהוּא יִשְׁפֹּט־תֵּבֵל[1] בְּצֶדֶק יָדִין[2] לְאֻמִּים[3] בְּמֵישָׁרִים׃[4]

καὶ αὐτὸς κρινεῖ τὴν οἰκουμένην[5] ἐν δικαιοσύνῃ, κρινεῖ λαοὺς ἐν εὐθύτητι.[6]

Acts 17:31

καθότι[7] ἔστησεν ἡμέραν ἐν ᾗ μέλλει κρίνειν τὴν οἰκουμένην ἐν δικαιοσύνῃ, ἐν ἀνδρὶ ᾧ ὥρισεν,[8] πίστιν παρασχὼν[9] πᾶσιν ἀναστήσας αὐτὸν ἐκ νεκρῶν.

eo quod statuit[10] diem in qua iudicaturus est orbem[11] in aequitate[12] in viro in quo statuit fidem praebens[13] omnibus suscitans eum a mortuis.

1. תֵּבֵל, *world*
2. דִּין, qal impf. 3 m. s., *judge*
3. לְאֹם, *people*
4. מֵישָׁר, *uprightness, justice*
5. οἰκουμένη, *world*
6. εὐθύτης, *upright*
7. καθότι, *just as*
8. ὁρίζω, aor. act. ind. 3 s., *appoint*
9. παρέχω, aor. act. ptcp. m. nom. s., *grant, give*
10. statuo, perf. act. ind. 3 s., *determine*
11. orbis, *world*
12. aequitas, *righteousness*
13. praebeo, pres. act. ptcp. m. nom. s., *present*

November 15

Genesis 6:13

וַיֹּאמֶר אֱלֹהִים לְנֹחַ[1] קֵץ[2] כָּל־בָּשָׂר בָּא לְפָנַי כִּי־
מָלְאָה הָאָרֶץ חָמָס[3] מִפְּנֵיהֶם וְהִנְנִי מַשְׁחִיתָם
אֶת־הָאָרֶץ׃

καὶ εἶπεν ὁ θεὸς πρὸς Νωε[4] Καιρὸς παντὸς ἀνθρώπου ἥκει ἐναντίον μου, ὅτι ἐπλήσθη ἡ γῆ ἀδικίας ἀπ᾽ αὐτῶν, καὶ ἰδοὺ ἐγὼ καταφθείρω[5] αὐτοὺς καὶ τὴν γῆν.

Matthew 24:37[6]

Ὥσπερ γὰρ αἱ ἡμέραι τοῦ Νῶε, οὕτως ἔσται ἡ παρουσία[7] τοῦ υἱοῦ τοῦ ἀνθρώπου.

sicut autem in diebus Noe[8] ita erit et adventus[9] Filii hominis.

1. נֹחַ, *Noah*
2. קֵץ, *end*
3. חָמָס, *violence*
4. Νῶε, *Noah*
5. καταφθείρω, pres. act. ind. 1 s., *corrupt, ruin*
6. PA: Jesus's use of the flood narrative in comparison with the coming of the Son of Man highlights not the violence and destruction of the flood but the imminent coming of the Son of Man and the ensuing judgment.
7. παρουσία, *coming, arrival, advent*
8. Noe, *Noah*
9. adventus, *coming, arrival, advent*

November 16

Genesis 19:24

וַיהוָה הִמְטִיר[1] עַל־סְדֹם[2] וְעַל־עֲמֹרָה[3] גָּפְרִית[4] וָאֵשׁ
מֵאֵת יְהוָה מִן־הַשָּׁמָיִם׃

καὶ κύριος ἔβρεξεν[5] ἐπὶ Σοδομα[6] καὶ Γομορρα[7] θεῖον[8] καὶ πῦρ παρὰ κυρίου ἐκ τοῦ οὐρανοῦ.

Luke 10:10a, 12

εἰς ἣν δ᾽ ἂν πόλιν εἰσέλθητε καὶ μὴ δέχωνται ὑμᾶς . . . λέγω ὑμῖν ὅτι Σοδόμοις ἐν τῇ ἡμέρᾳ ἐκείνῃ ἀνεκτότερον[9] ἔσται ἢ τῇ πόλει ἐκείνῃ.

in quamcumque civitatem intraveritis et non receperint vos exeuntes . . . dico vobis quia Sodomis[10] in die illa remissius[11] erit quam illi civitat.

1. מָטָר, hiph. perf. 3 m. s., *rain*
2. סְדֹם, *Sodom*
3. עֲמֹרָה, *Gomorrah*
4. גָּפְרִית, *sulfur, brimstone*
5. βρέχω, aor. act. ind. 3 s., *rain*
6. Σόδομα, *Sodom*
7. Γομορρα, *Gomorrah*
8. θεῖον, *sulfur*
9. ἀνεκτός, *tolerable, bearable*
10. Sodoma, *Sodom*
11. remissus, *tolerable, gentle*

November 17

Genesis 19:28

וַיַּשְׁקֵף[1] עַל־פְּנֵי סְדֹם[2] וַעֲמֹרָה[3] וְעַל־כָּל־פְּנֵי אֶרֶץ
הַכִּכָּר[4] וַיַּרְא וְהִנֵּה עָלָה קִיטֹר[5] הָאָרֶץ כְּקִיטֹר
הַכִּבְשָׁן׃[6]

καὶ ἐπέβλεψεν ἐπὶ πρόσωπον Σοδομων[7] καὶ Γομορρας[8] καὶ ἐπὶ πρόσωπον τῆς γῆς τῆς περιχώρου[9] καὶ εἶδεν, καὶ ἰδοὺ ἀνέβαινεν φλὸξ[10] τῆς γῆς ὡσεὶ ἀτμὶς[11] καμίνου.[12]

Revelation 9:2

καὶ ἤνοιξεν τὸ φρέαρ[13] τῆς ἀβύσσου,[14] καὶ ἀνέβη καπνὸς[15] ἐκ τοῦ φρέατος ὡς καπνὸς καμίνου μεγάλης, καὶ ἐσκοτώθη[16] ὁ ἥλιος[17] καὶ ὁ ἀὴρ[18] ἐκ τοῦ καπνοῦ τοῦ φρέατος.

et aperuit puteum[19] abyssi[20] et ascendit fumus[21] putei sicut fumus fornacis[22] magnae et obscuratus[23] est sol et aer[24] de fumo putei.

1. שָׁקַף, hiph. wcons. 3 m. s., *look*
2. סְדֹם, *Sodom*
3. עֲמֹרָה, *Gomorrah*
4. כִּכָּר, *valley*
5. קִיטוֹר, *thick smoke*
6. כִּבְשָׁן, *furnace, kiln*
7. Σόδομα, *Sodom*
8. Γομορρα, *Gomorrah*
9. περίχωρος, *surrounding region*
10. φλόξ, *flame*
11. ἀτμίς, *smoke, vapor*
12. κάμινος, *furnace*
13. φρέαρ, *well, shaft*
14. ἄβυσσος, *pit, abyss*
15. καπνός, *smoke*
16. σκοτόω, aor. pass. ind. 3 m. s., *darken*
17. ἥλιος, *sun*
18. ἀήρ, *air*
19. puteus, *pit, well*
20. abyssus, *abyss, bottomless pit*
21. fumus, *smoke*
22. fornax, *furnace*
23. obscuro, perf. pass. ind. 3 s., *darken*
24. aer, *air*

November 18

Isaiah 2:19

וּבָ֗אוּ בִּמְעָר֣וֹת[1] צֻרִ֔ים[2] וּבִמְחִלּ֖וֹת[3] עָפָ֑ר מִפְּנֵי֙ פַּ֣חַד[4]
יְהוָ֔ה וּמֵהֲדַ֣ר[5] גְּאוֹנ֔וֹ בְּקוּמ֖וֹ לַעֲרֹ֥ץ[6] הָאָֽרֶץ׃

εἰσενέγκαντες[7] εἰς τὰ σπήλαια[8] καὶ εἰς τὰς σχισμὰς[9] τῶν πετρῶν[10] καὶ εἰς τὰς τρώγλας[11] τῆς γῆς ἀπὸ προσώπου τοῦ φόβου κυρίου καὶ ἀπὸ τῆς δόξης τῆς ἰσχύος[12] αὐτοῦ, ὅταν ἀναστῇ θραῦσαι[13] τὴν γῆν.

Revelation 6:16b–17

πέσετε ἐφ᾽ ἡμᾶς καὶ *κρύψατε*[14] *ἡμᾶς* ἀπὸ προσώπου τοῦ καθημένου ἐπὶ τοῦ θρόνου καὶ ἀπὸ τῆς ὀργῆς τοῦ ἀρνίου,[15] ὅτι ἦλθεν ἡ ἡμέρα ἡ μεγάλη τῆς ὀργῆς αὐτῶν, καὶ τίς δύναται σταθῆναι;

cadite super nos et abscondite nos a facie sedentis super thronum et ab ira agni quoniam venit dies magnus irae ipsorum et quis poterit stare?

1. מְעָרָה, *cave*
2. צוּר, *rock*
3. מְחִלָּה, *hole*
4. פַּחַד, *terror*
5. הָדָר, *splendor, majesty*
6. עָרַץ, qal inf. cons., *make tremble*
7. εἰσφέρω, aor. act. ptcp. m. nom. p., *bring in*
8. σπήλαιον, *cave*
9. σχισμή, *fissure, crack*
10. πέτρος, *rock*
11. τρώγλη, *hole, cave*
12. ἰσχύς, *strength, might*
13. θραύω, aor. act. inf., *crush, break down*
14. κρύπτω, aor. act. impv. 2 p., *hide*
15. ἀρνίον, *lamb*

November 19

Psalm 28:4 [LXX 27:4]

תֶּן־לָהֶ֣ם כְּפָעֳלָם֮[1] וּכְרֹ֪עַ[2] מַעַלְלֵ֫יהֶ֥ם[3] כְּמַעֲשֵׂ֣ה יְ֭דֵיהֶם
תֵּ֣ן לָהֶ֑ם הָשֵׁ֖ב גְּמוּלָ֣ם[4] לָהֶֽם׃

δὸς αὐτοῖς κατὰ τὰ ἔργα αὐτῶν καὶ κατὰ τὴν πονηρίαν[5] τῶν ἐπιτηδευμάτων[6] αὐτῶν· κατὰ τὰ ἔργα τῶν χειρῶν αὐτῶν δὸς αὐτοῖς, ἀπόδος τὸ ἀνταπόδομα[7] αὐτῶν αὐτοῖς.

Revelation 22:12

Ἰδοὺ ἔρχομαι ταχύ,[8] καὶ ὁ μισθός[9] μου μετ᾽ ἐμοῦ ἀποδοῦναι ἑκάστῳ ὡς τὸ ἔργον ἐστὶν αὐτοῦ.

ecce venio cito[10] et merces mea mecum est reddere unicuique secundum opera sua.

1. פֹּעַל, *work, deed*
2. רֹעַ, *evil*
3. מַעֲלָל, *deed*
4. גְּמוּל, *recompense*
5. πονηρία, *wickedness, evil*
6. ἐπιτήδευμα, *practice*
7. ἀνταπόδομα, *repayment*
8. ταχύς, *quickly, soon*
9. μισθός, *recompense*
10. cito, *quickly*

November 20

Nahum 1:6

לִפְנֵ֤י זַעְמוֹ֙[1] מִ֣י יַֽעֲמ֔וֹד וּמִ֥י יָק֖וּם בַּחֲר֣וֹן[2] אַפּ֑וֹ חֲמָתוֹ֙
נִתְּכָ֣ה[3] כָאֵ֔שׁ וְהַצֻּרִ֖ים[4] נִתְּצ֥וּ[5] מִמֶּֽנּוּ׃

ἀπὸ προσώπου ὀργῆς αὐτοῦ τίς ὑποστήσεται;[6] καὶ τίς ἀντιστήσεται[7] ἐν ὀργῇ θυμοῦ αὐτοῦ; ὁ θυμὸς αὐτοῦ τήκει[8] ἀρχάς, καὶ αἱ πέτραι[9] διεθρύβησαν[10] ἀπ᾽ αὐτοῦ.

1. זַעַם, *indignation*
2. חָרוֹן, *fury*
3. נָתַךְ, niph. perf. 3 f. s., *pour out*
4. צוּר, *rock*
5. נָתַץ, niph. perf. 3 c. p., *break down*
6. ὑφίστημι, fut. mid. ind. 3 s., *withstand*
7. ἀνθίστημι, fut. mid. ind. 3 s., *resist*
8. τήκω, pres. act. ind. 3 s., *melt*
9. πέτρα, *rock*
10. διαθρύπτω, aor. pass. ind. 3 p., *break in pieces*

2 Thessalonians 1:9

οἵτινες δίκην[11] τίσουσιν[12] ὄλεθρον[13] αἰώνιον ἀπὸ προσώπου τοῦ κυρίου καὶ ἀπὸ τῆς δόξης τῆς ἰσχύος αὐτοῦ.

qui poenas[14] dabunt in interitu[15] aeternas a facie Domini et a gloria virtutis eius.

11. δίκη, *punishment*
12. τίνω, fut. act. ind. 3 p., *pay, suffer punishment*
13. ὄλεθρος, *destruction*
14. poena, *penalty, punishment*
15. interitus, *destruction*

November 21

Psalm 2:9

תְּרֹעֵם בְּשֵׁבֶט בַּרְזֶל[1] כִּכְלִי יוֹצֵר[2] תְּנַפְּצֵם׃[3]

ποιμανεῖς[4] αὐτοὺς ἐν ῥάβδῳ[5] σιδηρᾷ,[6] ὡς σκεῦος[7] κεραμέως[8] συντρίψεις[9] αὐτούς.

Revelation 2:27

καὶ ποιμανεῖ αὐτοὺς ἐν ῥάβδῳ σιδηρᾷ ὡς τὰ σκεύη τὰ κεραμικὰ συντρίβεται.

et reget[10] illas in virga[11] ferrea[12] tamquam vas[13] figuli[14] confringentur.[15]

1. בַּרְזֶל, *iron*
2. יָצַר, *potter*
3. נָפַץ, piel impf. 2 m. s., *shatter, dash, beat*
4. ποιμαίνω, fut. act. ind. 2 s., *shepherd, feed*
5. ῥάβδος, *staff, scepter*
6. σιδηροῦς, *iron, made of iron*
7. σκεῦος, *vessel*
8. κεραμεύς, *potter*
9. συντρίβω, fut. act. ind. 2 s., *crush, break*
10. rego, fut. act. ind. 3 s., *rule, govern*
11. virga, *staff, scepter*
12. ferreus, *iron, made of iron*
13. vas, *vessel*
14. figulus, *potter*
15. confringo, fut. pass. ind. 3 p., *break to pieces*

New Heavens and New Earth

November 22

Isaiah 65:17

כִּֽי־הִנְנִ֥י בוֹרֵ֛א[1] שָׁמַ֥יִם חֲדָשִׁ֖ים[2] וָאָ֣רֶץ חֲדָשָׁ֑ה וְלֹ֤א תִזָּכַ֙רְנָה֙ הָרִ֣אשֹׁנ֔וֹת וְלֹ֥א תַעֲלֶ֖ינָה עַל־לֵֽב׃

ἔσται γὰρ ὁ οὐρανὸς καινὸς[3] καὶ ἡ γῆ καινή, καὶ οὐ μὴ μνησθῶσιν τῶν προτέρων, οὐδ᾽ οὐ μὴ ἐπέλθῃ αὐτῶν ἐπὶ τὴν καρδίαν.

2 Corinthians 5:17

ὥστε εἴ τις ἐν Χριστῷ, καινὴ κτίσις·[4] τὰ ἀρχαῖα[5] παρῆλθεν,[6] ἰδοὺ γέγονεν καινά.

si qua[7] ergo in Christo nova creatura[8] vetera[9] transierunt ecce facta sunt nova.

1. בָּרָא, qal ptcp. m. s. abs., *create*
2. חָדָשׁ, *new*
3. καινός, *new*
4. κτίσις, *creation*
5. ἀρχαῖος, *old, ancient*
6. παρέρχομαι, aor. act. ind. 3 s., *pass away*
7. qui, *any*
8. creatura, *creation*
9. vetus, *old*

November 23

Ezekiel 48:35b

...וְשֵׁם־הָעִיר מִיּוֹם יְהוָה ׀ שָׁמָּה׃

καὶ τὸ ὄνομα τῆς πόλεως, ἀφ᾽ ἧς ἂν ἡμέρας γένηται, ἔσται τὸ ὄνομα αὐτῆς.

Revelation 3:12

Ὁ νικῶν[1] ποιήσω αὐτὸν στῦλον[2] ἐν τῷ ναῷ τοῦ θεοῦ μου καὶ ἔξω οὐ μὴ ἐξέλθῃ ἔτι καὶ γράψω ἐπ᾽ αὐτὸν τὸ ὄνομα τοῦ θεοῦ μου καὶ τὸ ὄνομα τῆς πόλεως τοῦ θεοῦ μου, τῆς καινῆς Ἰερουσαλὴμ ἡ καταβαίνουσα ἐκ τοῦ οὐρανοῦ ἀπὸ τοῦ θεοῦ μου, καὶ τὸ ὄνομά μου τὸ καινόν.

qui vicerit[3] faciam illum columnam[4] in templo Dei mei et foras[5] non egredietur amplius et scribam super eum nomen Dei mei et nomen civitatis Dei mei novae Hierusalem quae descendit de caelo a Deo meo et nomen meum novum.

1. νικάω, pres. act. ptcp. m. nom. s., *conquer*
2. στῦλος, *pillar*
3. vinco, futperf. act. ind. 3 s., *conquer*
4. columna, *pillar*
5. foras, *out*

November 24

Psalm 23:2 [LXX 22:2]

בִּנְא֣וֹת[1] דֶּ֭שֶׁא[2] יַרְבִּיצֵ֑נִי[3] עַל־מֵ֖י מְנֻח֣וֹת[4] יְנַהֲלֵֽנִי׃[5]

εἰς τόπον χλόης,[6] ἐκεῖ με κατεσκήνωσεν,[7] ἐπὶ ὕδατος ἀναπαύσεως[8] ἐξέθρεψέν[9] με.

Revelation 7:17a

ὅτι τὸ ἀρνίον[10] τὸ ἀνὰ[11] μέσον τοῦ θρόνου ποιμανεῖ[12] αὐτοὺς καὶ ὁδηγήσει[13] αὐτοὺς ἐπὶ ζωῆς πηγὰς[14] ὑδάτων.

quoniam agnus qui in medio throni est reget[15] illos et deducet[16] eos ad vitae fontes[17] aquarum.

1. נָוֶה, *pasture*
2. דֶּשֶׁא, *grass*
3. רָבַץ, hiph. impf. 3 m. s., *lie down*
4. מְנוּחָה, *still, rest*
5. נָהַל, piel impf. 3 m. s., *lead*
6. χλόη, *grass*
7. κατασκηνόω, aor. act. ind. 3 s., *pitch a tent*
8. ἀνάπαυσις, *rest*
9. ἐκτρέφω, aor. act. ind. 3 s., *nourish*
10. ἀρνίον, *lamb*
11. ἀνά, here with μέσον = *in the middle*
12. ποιμαίνω, fut. act. ind. 3 s., *shepherd*
13. ὁδηγέω, fut. act. ind. 3 s., *lead, guide*
14. πηγή, *spring*
15. rego, fut. act. ind. 3 s., *rule*
16. deduco, fut. act. ind. 3 s., *lead*
17. fons, *spring*

November 25

Psalm 89:28 [LXX 88:28]

אַף־אָנִי בְּכוֹר אֶתְּנֵהוּ עֶלְיוֹן[1] לְמַלְכֵי־אָרֶץ׃

κἀγὼ πρωτότοκον[2] θήσομαι αὐτόν, ὑψηλὸν παρὰ τοῖς βασιλεῦσιν τῆς γῆς.

Revelation 1:5

καὶ ἀπὸ Ἰησοῦ Χριστοῦ, ὁ μάρτυς, ὁ πιστός, ὁ πρωτότοκος τῶν νεκρῶν καὶ ὁ ἄρχων τῶν βασιλέων τῆς γῆς. Τῷ ἀγαπῶντι ἡμᾶς καὶ λύσαντι ἡμᾶς ἐκ τῶν ἁμαρτιῶν ἡμῶν ἐν τῷ αἵματι αὐτοῦ.

et ab Iesu Christo qui est testis fidelis primogenitus[3] mortuorum et princeps regum terrae qui dilexit nos et lavit[4] nos a peccatis nostris in sanguine suo.

1. עֶלְיוֹן, *most high*
2. πρωτότοκος, *firstborn*
3. primogenitus, *firstborn*
4. lavo, perf. act. ind. 3 s., *wash*

November 26

Obadiah 21

וְעָלוּ מֽוֹשִׁעִים[1] בְּהַר צִיּוֹן לִשְׁפֹּט אֶת־הַר עֵשָׂו[2]
וְהָיְתָה לַיהוָה הַמְּלוּכָה׃[3]

καὶ ἀναβήσονται ἄνδρες σεσῳσμένοι ἐξ ὄρους Σιων τοῦ ἐκδικῆσαι[4] τὸ ὄρος Ησαυ, καὶ ἔσται τῷ κυρίῳ ἡ βασιλεία.

Revelation 11:15

Καὶ ὁ ἕβδομος[5] ἄγγελος ἐσάλπισεν·[6] καὶ ἐγένοντο φωναὶ μεγάλαι ἐν τῷ οὐρανῷ λέγοντες· ἐγένετο ἡ βασιλεία τοῦ κόσμου τοῦ κυρίου ἡμῶν καὶ τοῦ χριστοῦ αὐτοῦ, καὶ βασιλεύσει[7] εἰς τοὺς αἰῶνας τῶν αἰώνων.

et septimus[8] angelus tuba[9] cecinit[10] et factae sunt voces magnae in caelo dicentes factum est regnum huius mundi Domini nostri et Christi eius et regnabit[11] in saecula saeculorum.

1. מוֹשִׁיעַ, *savior*; TC: the text should probably read מוּשָׁעִים = *those who have been delivered.*
2. עֵשָׂו, *Esau*
3. מְלוּכָה, *kingdom*
4. ἐκδικέω, aor. act. inf., *avenge, punish*
5. ἕβδομος, *seventh*
6. σαλπίζω, aor. act. ind. 3 s., *sound the trumpet*
7. βασιλεύω, fut. act. ind. 3 s., *rule, reign*
8. septimus, *seventh*
9. tuba, *trumpet*
10. cano, perf. act. ind. 3 s., *play (an instrument)*
11. regno, fut. act. ind. 3 s., *reign*

November 27

Leviticus 26:12

וְהִתְהַלַּכְתִּי֙ בְּת֣וֹכְכֶ֔ם וְהָיִ֥יתִי לָכֶ֖ם לֵֽאלֹהִ֑ים וְאַתֶּ֖ם
תִּֽהְיוּ־לִ֥י לְעָֽם׃

καὶ ἐμπεριπατήσω[1] ἐν ὑμῖν καὶ ἔσομαι ὑμῶν θεός, καὶ ὑμεῖς ἔσεσθέ μου λαός.

Revelation 21:3

καὶ ἤκουσα φωνῆς μεγάλης ἐκ τοῦ θρόνου λεγούσης· ἰδοὺ ἡ σκηνὴ[2] τοῦ θεοῦ μετὰ τῶν ἀνθρώπων, καὶ σκηνώσει[3] μετ᾽ αὐτῶν, καὶ αὐτοὶ λαοὶ αὐτοῦ ἔσονται, καὶ αὐτὸς ὁ θεὸς μετ᾽ αὐτῶν ἔσται [αὐτῶν θεός].

et audivi vocem magnam de throno dicentem ecce tabernaculum[4] Dei cum hominibus et habitabit cum eis et ipsi populus eius erunt et ipse Deus cum eis erit eorum Deus.

1. ἐμπεριπατέω, fut. act. ind. 1 s., *walk around*

2. σκηνή, *tent, dwelling, tabernacle*

3. σκηνόω, fut. act. ind. 3 s., *dwell (in a tent)*

4. tabernaculum, *tent, tabernacle*

November 28

Ezekiel 40:2

בְּמַרְא֣וֹת אֱלֹהִ֔ים הֱבִיאַ֖נִי אֶל־אֶ֣רֶץ יִשְׂרָאֵ֑ל וַיְנִיחֵ֗נִי
אֶל־הַ֤ר גָּבֹ֙הַּ֙[1] מְאֹ֔ד וְעָלָ֥יו כְּמִבְנֵה[2]־עִ֖יר מִנֶּֽגֶב׃

ἐν ὁράσει θεοῦ εἰς τὴν γῆν τοῦ Ισραηλ καὶ ἔθηκέν με ἐπ᾽ ὄρους ὑψηλοῦ[3] σφόδρα, καὶ ἐπ᾽ αὐτοῦ ὡσεὶ οἰκοδομὴ[4] πόλεως ἀπέναντι.[5]

Revelation 21:10

καὶ ἀπήνεγκέν[6] με ἐν πνεύματι ἐπὶ ὄρος μέγα καὶ ὑψηλόν, καὶ ἔδειξέν[7] μοι τὴν πόλιν τὴν ἁγίαν Ἰερουσαλὴμ καταβαίνουσαν ἐκ τοῦ οὐρανοῦ ἀπὸ τοῦ θεοῦ.

et sustulit me in spiritu in montem magnum et altum[8] et ostendit mihi civitatem sanctam Hierusalem descendentem de caelo a Deo.

1. גָּבֹהַּ, *high*
2. מִבְנֶה, *structure*
3. ὑψηλός, *high*
4. οἰκοδομή, *building*
5. ἀπέναντι, *opposite, against*
6. ἀποφέρω, aor. act. ind. 3 s., *carry*
7. δείκνυμι, aor. act. ind. 3 s., *show*
8. altus, *high*

November 29

Ezekiel 47:1

וַיְשִׁבֵנִי֮ אֶל־פֶּ֣תַח הַבַּיִת֒ וְהִנֵּה־מַ֣יִם יֹצְאִ֗ים מִתַּ֨חַת
מִפְתַּ֤ן[1] הַבַּ֙יִת֙ קָדִ֔ימָה[2] כִּֽי־פְנֵ֥י הַבַּ֖יִת קָדִ֑ים וְהַמַּ֣יִם
יֹרְדִ֗ים מִתַּ֜חַת מִכֶּ֤תֶף[3] הַבַּ֙יִת֙ הַיְמָנִ֔ית[4] מִנֶּ֖גֶב לַמִּזְבֵּֽחַ׃

Καὶ εἰσήγαγέν με ἐπὶ τὰ πρόθυρα[5] τοῦ οἴκου, καὶ ἰδοὺ ὕδωρ ἐξεπορεύετο ὑποκάτωθεν[6] τοῦ αἰθρίου[7] κατ᾽ ἀνατολάς, ὅτι τὸ πρόσωπον τοῦ οἴκου ἔβλεπεν κατ᾽ ἀνατολάς, καὶ τὸ ὕδωρ κατέβαινεν ἀπὸ τοῦ κλίτους[8] τοῦ δεξιοῦ ἀπὸ νότου[9] ἐπὶ τὸ θυσιαστήριον.

Revelation 22:1

Καὶ ἔδειξέν[10] μοι ποταμὸν[11] ὕδατος ζωῆς λαμπρὸν[12] ὡς κρύσταλλον,[13] ἐκπορευόμενον ἐκ τοῦ θρόνου τοῦ θεοῦ καὶ τοῦ ἀρνίου.[14]

et ostendit mihi fluvium[15] aquae vitae splendidum[16] tamquam cristallum[17] procedentem de sede Dei et agni.

1. מִפְתָּן, *threshold*
2. קָדִים, *east*
3. כָּתֵף, *opposite side*
4. יְמָנִי, *right*
5. πρόθυρον, *doorway*
6. ὑποκάτωθεν, *from beneath, below*
7. αἴθριος, *atrium*
8. κλίτος, *side*
9. νότος, *south*
10. δείκνυμι, aor. act. ind. 3 s., *show*
11. ποταμός, *river*
12. λαμπρός, *bright*
13. κρύσταλλος, *crystal*
14. ἀρνίον, *lamb*
15. fluvius, *river*
16. splendidus, *bright*
17. cristallus, *crystal*

November 30

Ezekiel 47:12

וְעַל־הַנַּחַל יַעֲלֶה עַל־שְׂפָתוֹ מִזֶּה | וּמִזֶּה |[1] כָּל־עֵץ־
מַאֲכָל[2] לֹא־יִבּוֹל[3] עָלֵהוּ[4] וְלֹא־יִתֹּם[5] פִּרְיוֹ לָחֳדָשָׁיו
יְבַכֵּר[6] כִּי מֵימָיו מִן־הַמִּקְדָּשׁ[7] הֵמָּה יוֹצְאִים וְהָיוּ פִרְיוֹ
לְמַאֲכָל וְעָלֵהוּ לִתְרוּפָה׃[8]

καὶ ἐπὶ τοῦ ποταμοῦ ἀναβήσεται ἐπὶ τοῦ χείλους αὐτοῦ ἔνθεν καὶ ἔνθεν[9] πᾶν ξύλον[10] βρώσιμον,[11] οὐ μὴ παλαιωθῇ[12] ἐπ᾽ αὐτοῦ, οὐδὲ μὴ ἐκλίπῃ ὁ καρπὸς αὐτοῦ· τῆς καινότητος[13] αὐτοῦ πρωτοβολήσει,[14] διότι τὰ ὕδατα αὐτῶν ἐκ τῶν ἁγίων ταῦτα ἐκπορεύεται, καὶ ἔσται ὁ καρπὸς αὐτῶν εἰς βρῶσιν καὶ ἀνάβασις[15] αὐτῶν εἰς ὑγίειαν.[16]

Revelation 22:2

ἐν μέσῳ τῆς πλατείας[17] αὐτῆς καὶ τοῦ ποταμοῦ[18] ἐντεῦθεν καὶ ἐκεῖθεν[19] ξύλον ζωῆς ποιοῦν καρποὺς δώδεκα, κατὰ μῆνα[20] ἕκαστον ἀποδιδοῦν τὸν καρπὸν αὐτοῦ, καὶ τὰ φύλλα[21] τοῦ ξύλου εἰς θεραπείαν[22] τῶν ἐθνῶν.

in medio plateae[23] eius et ex utraque[24] parte fluminis[25] lignum[26] vitae adferens fructus duodecim per menses[27] singula reddentia fructum suum et folia[28] ligni ad sanitatem[29] gentium.

24. uterque, *each of two.* **25.** flumen, *river.* **26.** lignum, *tree.* **27.** mensis, *month.* **28.** folium, *leaf.* **29.** sanitas, *health*

1. TH: מִזֶּה | וּמִזֶּה *= on both sides*

2. מַאֲכָל, *food*

3. נָבֵל, qal impf. 3 m. s., *wither, fade*

4. עָלֶה, *leaf*

5. תָּמַם, qal impf. 3 m. s., *finish, complete;* here *fail*

6. בָּכַר, piel impf. 3 m. s., *bear*

7. מִקְדָּשׁ, *sanctuary*

8. תְּרוּפָה, *healing*

9. TH: ἔνθεν καὶ ἔνθεν *= on both sides*

10. ξύλον, *tree*

11. βρώσιμος, *food*

12. παλαιόω, aor. pass. subj. 3 s., *become old, wear out*

13. καινότης, *newness*

14. πρωτοβολέω, fut. act. ind. 3 s., *produce new fruit*

15. ἀνάβασις, *ascent*

16. ὑγίεια, *health*

17. πλατεῖα, *street*

18. ποταμός, *river*

19. TH: ἐντεῦθεν καὶ ἐκεῖθεν *= on this side . . . on that side*

20. μήν, *month*

21. φύλλον, *leaf*

22. θεραπεία, *healing*

23. platea, *street*

December 1

1 Samuel 2:1[1]

וַתִּתְפַּלֵּ֤ל[2] חַנָּה֙[3] וַתֹּאמַ֔ר עָלַ֤ץ[4] לִבִּי֙ בַּֽיהוָ֔ה רָ֥מָה
קַרְנִ֖י[5] בַּֽיהוָ֑ה רָ֤חַב[6] פִּי֙ עַל־א֣וֹיְבַ֔י כִּ֥י שָׂמַ֖חְתִּי
בִּישׁוּעָתֶֽךָ׃[7]

Καὶ εἶπεν Ἐστερεώθη[8] ἡ καρδία μου ἐν κυρίῳ, ὑψώθη κέρας μου ἐν θεῷ μου· ἐπλατύνθη[9] ἐπὶ ἐχθροὺς τὸ στόμα μου, εὐφράνθην ἐν σωτηρίᾳ σου.

Luke 1:46

Καὶ εἶπεν Μαριάμ·[10] Μεγαλύνει[11] ἡ ψυχή μου τὸν κύριον.

et ait Maria magnificat[12] anima mea Dominum.

1. PA: For the first ten days of the advent, as mentioned in the introduction, we have paired Mary's Magnificat with Hannah's prayer. Structurally, Mary's prayer has clearly been modeled off of Hannah's prayer, even though you will find that only two or three of the days have true parallels.
2. פָּלַל, hitpael wcons. 3 f. s., *pray*
3. חַנָּה, *Hannah*
4. עָלַץ, qal perf. 3 m. s., *exalt, rejoice*
5. קֶ֫רֶן, *horn*
6. רָחַב, qal perf. 3 m. s., *enlarge, make wide*
7. יְשׁוּעָה, *salvation*
8. στερεόω, aor. pass. ind. 3 s., *make strong*
9. πλατύνω, aor. pass. ind. 3 s., *enlarge*
10. Μαριάμ, *Mary*
11. μεγαλύνω, pres. act. ind. 3 s., *magnify, exalt*
12. magnifico, pres. act. ind. 3 s., *magnify*

December 2

1 Samuel 2:2

אֵין־קָדוֹשׁ כַּיהוָה כִּי אֵין בִּלְתֶּךָ וְאֵין צוּר[1] כֵּאלֹהֵינוּ׃

ὅτι οὐκ ἔστιν ἅγιος ὡς κύριος, καὶ οὐκ ἔστιν δίκαιος ὡς ὁ θεὸς ἡμῶν· οὐκ ἔστιν ἅγιος πλὴν σοῦ.

Luke 1:47

καὶ ἠγαλλίασεν[2] τὸ πνεῦμά μου ἐπὶ τῷ θεῷ τῷ σωτῆρί[3] μου.

et exultavit[4] spiritus meus in Deo salutari[5] meo.

1. צוּר, *rock*
2. ἀγαλλιάω, aor. act. ind. 3 s., *rejoice, exalt*
3. σωτήρ, *savior*
4. exsulto, perf. act. ind. 3 s., *rejoice*
5. salutaris, *savior*

December 3

1 Samuel 2:3

אַל־תַּרְבּ֤וּ תְדַבְּרוּ֙ גְּבֹהָ֣ה גְבֹהָ֔ה[1] יֵצֵ֥א עָתָ֖ק[2] מִפִּיכֶ֑ם
כִּ֣י אֵ֤ל דֵּעוֹת֙[3] יְהוָ֔ה וְלֹ֥א[4] נִתְכְּנ֖וּ[5] עֲלִלֽוֹת׃[6]

μὴ καυχᾶσθε[7] καὶ μὴ λαλεῖτε ὑψηλά, μὴ ἐξελθάτω μεγαλορρημοσύνη[8] ἐκ τοῦ στόματος ὑμῶν, ὅτι θεὸς γνώσεων[9] κύριος καὶ θεὸς ἑτοιμάζων ἐπιτηδεύματα[10] αὐτοῦ.

Luke 1:48

ὅτι ἐπέβλεψεν[11] ἐπὶ τὴν ταπείνωσιν[12] τῆς δούλης[13] αὐτοῦ. ἰδοὺ γὰρ ἀπὸ τοῦ νῦν μακαριοῦσίν[14] με πᾶσαι αἱ γενεαί.

quia respexit[15] humilitatem[16] ancillae[17] suae ecce enim ex hoc beatam me dicent omnes generationes.

1. גָּבֹהַּ, *high, exalted*
2. עָתָק, *arrogance*
3. דֵּעָה, *knowledge*
4. TC: The *qere* reading is לוֹ = *by him.*
5. תָּכַן, niph. perf. 3 c. p., *measure, estimate*
6. עֲלִילָה, *action, deed*
7. καυχάομαι, pres. mid. impv. 2 p., *boast*
8. μεγαλορρημοσύνη, *boasting*
9. γνῶσις, *knowledge*
10. ἐπιτήδευμα, *way (of living)*
11. ἐπιβλέπω, aor. act. ind. 3 s., *look on with care*
12. ταπείνωσις, *humble estate*
13. δούλη, *servant, slave*
14. μακαρίζω, fut. act. ind. 3 p., *call blessed*
15. respicio, perf. act. ind. 3 s., *regard, see*
16. humilitas, *humility*
17. ancilla, *maidservant*

December 4

1 Samuel 2:4

קֶ֫שֶׁת[1] גִּבֹּרִ֣ים חַתִּ֑ים[2] וְנִכְשָׁלִ֖ים[3] אָ֥זְרוּ[4] חָֽיִל׃

τόξον[5] δυνατῶν ἠσθένησεν,[6] καὶ ἀσθενοῦντες[7]
περιεζώσαντο[8] δύναμιν.

Luke 1:49

ὅτι ἐποίησέν μοι μεγάλα ὁ δυνατός. καὶ ἅγιον τὸ
ὄνομα αὐτοῦ.

quia fecit mihi magna qui potens[9] est et
sanctum nomen eius.

1. קֶ֫שֶׁת, *bow*
2. חַת, *shattered*
3. כָּשַׁל, niph. ptcp. m. p. abs., *stumble*
4. אָזַר, qal perf. 3 c. p., *gird, put on*
5. τόξον, *bow*
6. ἀσθενέω, aor. act. ind. 3 s., *be weak*
7. ἀσθενέω, aor. act. ptcp. m. nom. p., *be weak*
8. περιζωννύω, aor. mid. ind. 3 p., *wrap around, gird*
9. potens, *strong, powerful*

December 5

1 Samuel 2:5

שְׂבֵעִים[1] בַּלֶּחֶם נִשְׂכָּרוּ[2] וּרְעֵבִים[3] חָדֵלּוּ[4] עַד־עֲקָרָה[5] יָלְדָה שִׁבְעָה וְרַבַּת בָּנִים אֻמְלָלָה׃[6]

πλήρεις ἄρτων ἠλαττώθησαν,[7] καὶ οἱ πεινῶντες[8] παρῆκαν[9] γῆν· ὅτι στεῖρα[10] ἔτεκεν ἑπτά, καὶ ἡ πολλὴ ἐν τέκνοις ἠσθένησεν.[11]

Luke 1:50

καὶ τὸ ἔλεος[12] αὐτοῦ εἰς γενεὰς καὶ γενεὰς τοῖς φοβουμένοις αὐτόν.

et misericordia eius in progenies[13] et progenies timentibus eum.

1. שָׂבֵעַ, *full, satisfied*
2. שָׂכַר, niph. perf. 3 c. p., *hire*
3. רָעֵב, *hungry*
4. חָדַל, qal perf. 3 c. p., *cease, lack*
5. עָקָר, *barren*
6. אָמַל, pulal perf. 3 f. s., *languish*
7. ἐλαττόω, aor. pass. ind. 3 p., *decrease, make lower*
8. πεινάω, pres. act. ptcp. m. nom. p., *be hungry*
9. παρίημι, aor. act. ind. 3 p., *neglect, forsake*
10. στεῖρα, *barren*
11. ἀσθενέω, aor. act. ind. 3 s., *be weak*
12. ἔλεος, *mercy*
13. progenies, *generation*

December 6

1 Samuel 2:6

יְהוָה מֵמִית וּמְחַיֶּה מוֹרִיד שְׁאוֹל[1] וַיָּעַל׃

κύριος θανατοῖ καὶ ζωογονεῖ,[2] κατάγει[3] εἰς ᾅδου καὶ ἀνάγει.

Luke 1:51

Ἐποίησεν κράτος[4] ἐν βραχίονι[5] αὐτοῦ, διεσκόρπισεν[6] ὑπερηφάνους[7] διανοίᾳ[8] καρδίας αὐτῶν.

fecit potentiam[9] in brachio[10] suo dispersit[11] superbos[12] mente[13] cordis sui.

1. שְׁאוֹל, *Sheol*
2. ζῳογονέω, pres. act. ind. 3 s., *keep alive*
3. κατάγω, pres. act. ind. 3 s., *bring down*
4. κράτος, *strength*
5. βραχίων, *arm*
6. διασκορπίζω, aor. act. ind. 3 s., *scatter*
7. ὑπερήφανος, *proud*
8. διάνοια, *thought*
9. potentia, *power, strength*
10. brachium, *arm*
11. dispergo, perf. act. ind. 3 s., *scatter*
12. superbus, *proud*
13. mens, *mind*

December 7

1 Samuel 2:7

יְהוָ֖ה מוֹרִ֣ישׁ וּמַעֲשִׁ֑יר[1] מַשְׁפִּ֖יל[2] אַף־מְרוֹמֵֽם׃

κύριος πτωχίζει[3] καὶ πλουτίζει,[4] ταπεινοῖ καὶ ἀνυψοῖ.[5]

Luke 1:52

καθεῖλεν[6] δυνάστας[7] ἀπὸ θρόνων καὶ ὕψωσεν[8] ταπεινούς.[9]

deposuit[10] potentes[11] de sede et exaltavit[12] humiles.[13]

1. עָשַׁר, hiph. ptcp. m. s. abs., *be rich*
2. שָׁפֵל, hiph. ptcp. m. s. abs., *be low, humble*
3. πτωχίζω, pres. act. ind. 3 s., *make poor*
4. πλουτίζω, pres. act. ind. 3 s., *enrich*
5. ἀνυψόω, pres. act. ind. 3 s., *lift up, raise*
6. καθαιρέω, aor. act. ind. 3 s., *bring down*
7. δυνάστης, *ruler, official*
8. ὑψόω, aor. act. ind. 3 s., *exalt, lift up*
9. ταπεινός, *humble*
10. depono, perf. act. ind. 3 s., *lay down, put down*
11. potens, *strong*
12. exalto, perf. act. ind. 3 s., *lift up, exalt*
13. humilis, *humble, lowly*

December 8

1 Samuel 2:8

מֵקִ֨ים מֵעָפָ֜ר דָּ֗ל[1] מֵֽאַשְׁפֹּת֮[2] יָרִ֣ים אֶבְיוֹן֒[3] לְהוֹשִׁיב֙
עִם־נְדִיבִ֔ים[4] וְכִסֵּ֥א כָב֖וֹד יַנְחִלֵ֑ם[5] כִּ֤י לַֽיהוָה֙ מְצֻ֣קֵי[6]
אֶ֔רֶץ וַיָּ֥שֶׁת[7] עֲלֵיהֶ֖ם תֵּבֵֽל׃[8]

ἀνιστᾷ ἀπὸ γῆς πένητα[9] καὶ ἀπὸ κοπρίας[10] ἐγείρει[11] πτωχὸν καθίσαι μετὰ δυναστῶν[12] λαῶν καὶ θρόνον δόξης κατακληρονομῶν[13] αὐτοῖς.

Luke 1:53

πεινῶντας[14] ἐνέπλησεν[15] ἀγαθῶν καὶ πλουτοῦντας[16] ἐξαπέστειλεν[17] κενούς.[18]

esurientes[19] implevit bonis et divites dimisit inanes.[20]

1. דַּל, *weak, poor*
2. אַשְׁפֹּת, *refuse*
3. אֶבְיוֹן, *needy*
4. נָדִיב, *prince, noble*
5. נחל, hiph. impf. 3 m. s., *bestow*
6. מָצוּק, *pillar, foundation*
7. שִׁית, qal wcons. 3 m. s., *place, set*
8. תֵּבֵל, *world*
9. πένης, *poor*
10. κοπρία, *dung heap*
11. ἐγείρω, pres. act. ind. 3 s., *raise, lift up*
12. δυνάστης, *ruler*
13. κατακληρονομέω, pres. act. ptcp. m. nom. s., *divide by lot*
14. πεινάω, pres. act. ptcp. m. a. p., *be hungry*
15. ἐμπίπλημι, aor. act. ind. 3 s., *fill*
16. πλουτέω, pres. act. ptcp. m. a. p., *be rich*
17. ἐξαποστέλλω, aor. act. ind. 3 s., *send away*
18. κενός, *empty*
19. esurio, pres. act. ptcp. m. a. p., *be hungry*
20. inanis, *empty*

December 9

1 Samuel 2:9

רַגְלֵ֤י חֲסִידָו֙[1] יִשְׁמֹ֔ר וּרְשָׁעִ֖ים בַּחֹ֣שֶׁךְ[2] יִדָּ֑מּוּ[3] כִּֽי־לֹ֥א
בְכֹ֖חַ יִגְבַּר[4]־אִֽישׁ׃

διδοὺς εὐχὴν[5] τῷ εὐχομένῳ[6] καὶ εὐλόγησεν ἔτη
δικαίου· ὅτι οὐκ ἐν ἰσχύι δυνατὸς ἀνήρ.

Luke 1:54

ἀντελάβετο[7] Ἰσραὴλ παιδὸς[8] αὐτοῦ, μνησθῆναι[9]
ἐλέους.[10]

suscepit Israhel puerum suum memorari[11]
misericordiae.

1. חָסִיד, *faithful*
2. חֹשֶׁךְ, *darkness*
3. דָּמַם, niph. impf. 3 m. p., *make silent*
4. גָּבַר, qal impf. 3 m. s., *be strong, prevail*
5. εὐχή, *vow, prayer*
6. εὔχομαι, pres. mid. ptcp. m. d. s., *vow, pray*
7. ἀντιλαμβάνω, aor. mid. ind. 3 s., *aid, assist*
8. παῖς, *servant*
9. μιμνήσκομαι, aor. pass. inf., *remember, remind*
10. ἔλεος, *mercy*
11. memoror, pres. dep. inf., *call to mind, make mention of*

1. חָתַת, niph. impf. 3 m. p., *shatter*

2. רִיב, hiph. ptcp. m. s. cons., *strive, contend*

3. רעם, hiph. impf. 3 m. s. juss., *thunder*

4. דִּין, qal impf. 3 m. s., *judge*

5. אֶ֫פֶס, *end*

6. עֹז, *strength, might*

7. קֶ֫רֶן, *horn*

8. מָשִׁיחַ, *anointed one*

9. ἀσθενής, *weak*

10. ἀντίδικος, *adversary*

11. καυχάομαι, pres. mid. impv. 3 s., *boast*

12. φρόνιμος, *wise, clever*

13. φρόνησις, *wisdom, cleverness*

14. πλούσιος, *rich*

15. πλοῦτος, *riches*

16. καυχάομαι, pres. mid. ptcp. m. nom. s., *boast*

17. συνίημι, pres. act. inf., *understand*

18. βροντάω, aor. act. ind. 3 s., *thunder*

19. ἄκρος, *highest*

20. χριστός, *anointed*

December 10

1 Samuel 2:10

יְהוָ֞ה יֵחַ֣תּוּ[1] מְרִיבָ֗ו[2] עָלָו֙ בַּשָּׁמַ֣יִם יַרְעֵ֔ם[3] יְהוָ֖ה יָדִ֣ין[4]
אַפְסֵי[5]־אָ֑רֶץ וְיִתֶּן־עֹ֣ז[6] לְמַלְכּ֔וֹ וְיָרֵ֖ם קֶ֥רֶן[7] מְשִׁיחֽוֹ׃[8]

κύριος ἀσθενῆ[9] ποιήσει ἀντίδικον[10] αὐτοῦ, κύριος ἅγιος. μὴ καυχάσθω[11] ὁ φρόνιμος[12] ἐν τῇ φρονήσει[13] αὐτοῦ, καὶ μὴ καυχάσθω ὁ δυνατὸς ἐν τῇ δυνάμει αὐτοῦ, καὶ μὴ καυχάσθω ὁ πλούσιος[14] ἐν τῷ πλούτῳ[15] αὐτοῦ, ἀλλ᾽ ἢ ἐν τούτῳ καυχάσθω ὁ καυχώμενος,[16] συνίειν[17] καὶ γινώσκειν τὸν κύριον καὶ ποιεῖν κρίμα καὶ δικαιοσύνην ἐν μέσῳ τῆς γῆς. κύριος ἀνέβη εἰς οὐρανοὺς καὶ ἐβρόντησεν,[18] αὐτὸς κρινεῖ ἄκρα[19] γῆς καὶ δίδωσιν ἰσχὺν τοῖς βασιλεῦσιν ἡμῶν καὶ ὑψώσει κέρας χριστοῦ[20] αὐτοῦ.

Luke 1:55

καθὼς ἐλάλησεν πρὸς τοὺς πατέρας ἡμῶν, τῷ Ἀβραὰμ καὶ τῷ σπέρματι αὐτοῦ εἰς τὸν αἰῶνα.

sicut locutus est ad patres nostros Abraham et semini eius in saecula.

December 11

Deuteronomy 22:22

כִּֽי־יִמָּצֵ֨א אִ֜ישׁ שֹׁכֵ֣ב ׀ עִם־אִשָּׁ֣ה בְעֻֽלַת[1]־בַּ֗עַל[2] וּמֵ֙תוּ֙
גַּם־שְׁנֵיהֶ֔ם הָאִ֛ישׁ הַשֹּׁכֵ֥ב עִם־הָאִשָּׁ֖ה וְהָאִשָּׁ֑ה
וּבִֽעַרְתָּ֥[3] הָרָ֖ע מִיִּשְׂרָאֵֽל׃

Ἐὰν δὲ εὑρεθῇ ἄνθρωπος κοιμώμενος μετὰ γυναικὸς συνῳκισμένης[4] ἀνδρί, ἀποκτενεῖτε ἀμφοτέρους, τὸν ἄνδρα τὸν κοιμώμενον μετὰ τῆς γυναικὸς καὶ τὴν γυναῖκα· καὶ ἐξαρεῖς τὸν πονηρὸν ἐξ Ισραηλ.

Matthew 1:19

Ιωσὴφ δὲ ὁ ἀνὴρ αὐτῆς, δίκαιος ὢν καὶ μὴ θέλων αὐτὴν δειγματίσαι,[5] ἐβουλήθη λάθρᾳ[6] ἀπολῦσαι αὐτήν.

Ioseph autem vir eius cum esset iustus et nollet eam traducere[7] voluit occulte[8] dimittere eam.

1. בָּעַל, qal pass. ptcp. f. s. cons., *marry*
2. בַּעַל, *husband*
3. בָּעַר, piel perf. 2 m. s., *remove, purge, burn*
4. συνοικίζω, perf. pass. ptcp. f. g. s., *marry*
5. δειγματίζω, aor. act. inf., *disgrace, make a show of*
6. λάθρᾳ, *quietly*
7. traduco, pres. act. inf., *disgrace*
8. occulte, *secretly*

December 12

Psalm 130:8 [LXX 129:8]

וְהוּא יִפְדֶּה[1] אֶת־יִשְׂרָאֵל מִכֹּל עֲוֺנֹתָיו׃

καὶ αὐτὸς λυτρώσεται τὸν Ισραηλ ἐκ πασῶν τῶν ἀνομιῶν αὐτοῦ.

Matthew 1:21

τέξεται[2] δὲ υἱόν, καὶ καλέσεις τὸ ὄνομα αὐτοῦ Ἰησοῦν· αὐτὸς γὰρ σώσει τὸν λαὸν αὐτοῦ ἀπὸ τῶν ἁμαρτιῶν αὐτῶν.

pariet[3] autem filium et vocabis nomen eius Iesum ipse enim salvum faciet populum suum a peccatis eorum.

1. פָּדָה, qal impf. 3 m. s., *redeem*
2. τίκτω, fut. mid. ind. 3 s., *bear*
3. pario, fut. act. ind. 3 s., *bear*

December 13

Isaiah 7:14

לָכֵ֗ן יִתֵּ֨ן אֲדֹנָ֥י ה֛וּא לָכֶ֖ם א֑וֹת[1] הִנֵּ֣ה הָעַלְמָ֗ה[2] הָרָה֙[3]
וְיֹלֶ֣דֶת בֵּ֔ן וְקָרָ֥את שְׁמ֖וֹ עִמָּ֥נוּ אֵֽל׃[4]

διὰ τοῦτο δώσει κύριος αὐτὸς ὑμῖν σημεῖον· ἰδοὺ ἡ παρθένος[5] ἐν γαστρὶ[6] ἕξει καὶ τέξεται[7] υἱόν, καὶ καλέσεις τὸ ὄνομα αὐτοῦ Εμμανουηλ.[8]

Matthew 1:23

ἰδοὺ ἡ παρθένος ἐν γαστρὶ ἕξει καὶ τέξεται υἱόν, καὶ καλέσουσιν τὸ ὄνομα αὐτοῦ Ἐμμανουήλ, ὅ ἐστιν μεθερμηνευόμενον[9] *μεθ᾽ ἡμῶν ὁ θεός.*

ecce virgo[10] in utero[11] habebit et pariet[12] filium et vocabunt nomen eius Emmanuhel[13] quod est interpretatum[14] Nobiscum Deus.

1. אוֹת, *sign*
2. עַלְמָה, *young woman, virgin*
3. הָרָה, *conceive, pregnant*
4. עִמָּנוּ אֵל, *Immanuel*
5. παρθένος, *virgin*
6. γαστήρ, *womb*
7. τίκτω, fut. mid. ind. 3 s., *bear children*
8. Εμμανουηλ, *Immanuel*
9. μεθερμηνεύω, pres. pass. ptcp. n. nom. s., *translate, interpret*
10. virgo, *virgin*
11. uterus, *womb*
12. pario, fut. act. ind. 3 s., *bear*
13. Emmanuhel, *Immanuel*
14. interpretor, perf. dep. ind. 3 s., *interpret*

December 14

Psalm 111:9 [LXX 110:9]

פְּד֤וּת׀[1] שָׁ֘לַ֤ח לְעַמּ֗וֹ צִוָּֽה־לְעוֹלָ֥ם בְּרִית֑וֹ קָד֖וֹשׁ וְנוֹרָ֣א שְׁמֽוֹ׃

λύτρωσιν[2] ἀπέστειλεν τῷ λαῷ αὐτοῦ, ἐνετείλατο εἰς τὸν αἰῶνα διαθήκην αὐτοῦ· ἅγιον καὶ φοβερὸν[3] τὸ ὄνομα αὐτοῦ.

Luke 1:68

Εὐλογητὸς[4] κύριος ὁ θεὸς τοῦ Ἰσραήλ, ὅτι ἐπεσκέψατο[5] καὶ ἐποίησεν λύτρωσιν τῷ λαῷ αὐτοῦ.

benedictus Deus Israhel quia visitavit[6] et fecit redemptionem[7] plebi suae.

1. פְּדוּת, *redemption*
2. λύτρωσις, *redemption*
3. φοβερός, *terrible, awesome*
4. εὐλογητός, *blessed*
5. ἐπισκέπτομαι, aor. mid. ind. 3 s., *visit, care for*
6. visito, perf. act. ind. 3 s., *visit*
7. redemptio, *ransom, redemption*

December 15

Psalm 18:3 [LXX 17:3]

יְהוָ֤ה ׀ סַֽלְעִ֥י[1] וּמְצוּדָתִ֗י[2] וּמְפַ֫לְטִ֥י[3] אֵלִ֣י צ֭וּרִי[4] אֶֽחֱסֶה[5]־
בּ֑וֹ מָֽגִנִּ֥י[6] וְקֶֽרֶן[7]־יִ֝שְׁעִ֗י[8] מִשְׂגַּבִּֽי׃[9]

κύριος στερέωμά[10] μου καὶ καταφυγή[11] μου καὶ ῥύστης[12] μου, ὁ θεός μου βοηθός[13] μου, καὶ ἐλπιῶ ἐπ᾽ αὐτόν, ὑπερασπιστής[14] μου καὶ κέρας[15] σωτηρίας μου, ἀντιλήμπτωρ[16] μου.

Luke 1:69

καὶ ἤγειρεν[17] κέρασσωτηρίας ἡμῖν ἐν οἴκῳ Δαυὶδ παιδὸς[18] αὐτοῦ.

et erexit[19] cornu[20] salutis nobis in domo David pueri sui.

1. סֶ֫לַע, *cliff, crag, high ridge*

2. מְצוּדָה, *fortress, stronghold*

3. פלט, piel ptcp. m. s. cons., *deliver*

4. צוּר, *rock*

5. חָסָה, qal impf. 1 c. s., *seek refuge*

6. מָגֵן, *shield*

7. קֶ֫רֶן, *horn*

8. יֵ֫שַׁע, *salvation*

9. מִשְׂגָּב, *stronghold*

10. στερέωμα, *fortified place*

11. καταφυγή, *refuge*

12. ῥύστης, *deliverer*

13. βοηθός, *helper*

14. ὑπερασπιστής, *defender*

15. κέρας, *horn*

16. ἀντιλήμπτωρ, *supporter*

17. CH: The implied subject is *God.*

18. παῖς, *servant, child*

19. erigo, perf. act. ind. 3 s., *set up, raise up*; CH: The implied subject is *God.*

20. cornu, *horn*

December 16

Malachi 3:1

הִנְנִ֤י שֹׁלֵחַ֙ מַלְאָכִ֔י וּפִנָּה־דֶ֖רֶךְ לְפָנָ֑י וּפִתְאֹם֩[1] יָב֨וֹא
אֶל־הֵיכָל֜וֹ[2] הָאָד֣וֹן ׀ אֲשֶׁר־אַתֶּ֣ם מְבַקְשִׁ֗ים וּמַלְאַ֨ךְ
הַבְּרִ֜ית אֲשֶׁר־אַתֶּ֤ם חֲפֵצִים֙[3] הִנֵּה־בָ֔א אָמַ֖ר
יְהוָ֥ה צְבָאֽוֹת׃

ἰδοὺ ἐγὼ ἐξαποστέλλω τὸν ἄγγελόν μου, καὶ ἐπιβλέψεται ὁδὸν πρὸ προσώπου μου, καὶ ἐξαίφνης[4] ἥξει εἰς τὸν ναὸν ἑαυτοῦ κύριος, ὃν ὑμεῖς ζητεῖτε, καὶ ὁ ἄγγελος τῆς διαθήκης, ὃν ὑμεῖς θέλετε· ἰδοὺ ἔρχεται, λέγει κύριος παντοκράτωρ.

Luke 1:76

Καὶ σὺ δέ, παιδίον, προφήτης ὑψίστου[5] κληθήσῃ· προπορεύσῃ[6] γὰρ ἐνώπιον κυρίου ἑτοιμάσαι ὁδοὺς αὐτοῦ.

et tu puer propheta Altissimi[7] vocaberis praeibis[8] enim ante faciem Domini parare vias eius.

1. פִּתְאֹם, *suddenly*
2. הֵיכָל, *temple*
3. חָפֵץ, *delight*
4. ἐξαίφνης, *suddenly*
5. ὕψιστος, *most high, highest*
6. προπορεύομαι, fut. mid. ind. 2 s., *go beforehand*
7. altus, *high*
8. praeeo, fut. act. ind. 2 s., *go before*

December 17

Isaiah 9:1

הָעָם֙ הַהֹלְכִ֣ים בַּחֹ֔שֶׁךְ[1] רָא֖וּ א֣וֹר גָּד֑וֹל יֹשְׁבֵי֙ בְּאֶ֣רֶץ
צַלְמָ֔וֶת[2] א֖וֹר נָגַ֥הּ[3] עֲלֵיהֶֽם׃

ὁ λαὸς ὁ πορευόμενος ἐν σκότει, ἴδετε φῶς μέγα· οἱ κατοικοῦντες ἐν χώρᾳ καὶ σκιᾷ[4] θανάτου, φῶς λάμψει[5] ἐφ᾽ ὑμᾶς.

Luke 1:78b–79

ἐπισκέψεται[6] ἡμᾶς ἀνατολὴ[7] ἐξ ὕψους,[8] ἐπιφᾶναι τοῖς ἐν σκότει καὶ σκιᾷ θανάτου καθημένοις, τοῦ κατευθῦναι[9] τοὺς πόδας ἡμῶν εἰς ὁδὸν εἰρήνης.

visitavit[10] nos oriens[11] ex alto[12] inluminare[13] his qui in tenebris et in umbra[14] mortis sedent ad dirigendos[15] pedes nostros in viam pacis.

1. חֹשֶׁךְ, *darkness*
2. צַלְמָוֶת, *deep darkness*
3. נָגַהּ, qal perf. 3 m. s., *shine*
4. σκιά, *shadow*
5. λάμπω, fut. act. ind. 3 s., *shine*
6. ἐπισκέπτομαι, fut. mid. ind. 3 s., *visit, care for*
7. ἀνατολή, *sunrise*
8. ὕψος, *high*
9. κατευθύνω, aor. act. inf., *direct, keep straight*
10. visito, perf. act. ind. 3 s., *visit*
11. oriens, *sunrise*
12. altum, *high*
13. inlumino, pres. act. inf., *light up, illuminate*
14. umbra, *shadow*
15. dirigo, ger. pass. m. a. p., *make straight*

December 18

Psalm 87:6 [LXX 86:6]

יְהוָ֗ה יִסְפֹּ֣ר בִּכְת֣וֹב עַמִּ֑ים זֶ֓ה יֻלַּד־שָׁ֣ם סֶֽלָה׃[1]

κύριος διηγήσεται[2] ἐν γραφῇ[3] λαῶν καὶ ἀρχόντων τούτων τῶν γεγενημένων ἐν αὐτῇ. διάψαλμα.[4]

Luke 2:1

Ἐγένετο δὲ ἐν ταῖς ἡμέραις ἐκείναις ἐξῆλθεν δόγμα[5] παρὰ Καίσαρος[6] Αὐγούστου[7] ἀπογράφεσθαι[8] πᾶσαν τὴν οἰκουμένην.[9]

factum est autem in diebus illis exiit edictum[10] a Caesare[11] Augusto[12] ut describeretur[13] universus orbis.[14]

1. סֶלָה, *selah*
2. διηγέομαι, fut. mid. ind. 3 s., *recount, explain*
3. γραφή, *list, document*
4. διάψαλμα, *musical interlude*
5. δόγμα, *decree*
6. Καῖσαρ, *Caesar*
7. Αὔγουστος, *Augustus*
8. ἀπογράφω, pres. pass. inf., *register*
9. οἰκουμένη, *world*
10. edictum, *edict, decree*
11. Caesar, *Caesar*
12. Augustus, *Augustus*
13. describo, impf. pass. subj. 3 s., *enroll*
14. orbis, *world*

December 19

Numbers 24:17a

אֶרְאֶנּוּ וְלֹא עַתָּה אֲשׁוּרֶנּוּ[1] וְלֹא קָרוֹב[2] דָּרַךְ[3] כּוֹכָב[4]
מִיַּעֲקֹב וְקָם שֵׁבֶט מִיִּשְׂרָאֵל. . . .

Δείξω αὐτῷ, καὶ οὐχὶ νῦν· μακαρίζω,[5] καὶ οὐκ ἐγγίζει· ἀνατελεῖ[6] ἄστρον[7] ἐξ Ιακωβ, καὶ ἀναστήσεται ἄνθρωπος ἐξ Ισραηλ. . . .

Matthew 2:2

. . . ποῦ ἐστιν ὁ τεχθεὶς[8] βασιλεὺς τῶν Ἰουδαίων; εἴδομεν γὰρ αὐτοῦ τὸν ἀστέρα ἐν τῇ ἀνατολῇ[9] καὶ ἤλθομεν προσκυνῆσαι αὐτῷ.

. . . ubi est qui natus est rex Iudaeorum vidimus enim stellam[10] eius in oriente[11] et venimus adorare eum.

1. שׁוּר, qal impf. 1 c. s., *behold, regard*
2. קָרוֹב, *near*
3. דָּרַךְ, qal perf. 3 m. s., *come*
4. כּוֹכָב, *star*
5. μακαρίζω, pres. act. ind. 1 s., *bless, call happy*
6. ἀνατέλλω, fut. act. ind. 3 s., *rise up, arise*
7. ἄστρον, *star*
8. τίκτω, aor. pass. ptcp. m. nom. s., *bear (a child), give birth*; TH: In the passive voice, *be born.*
9. ἀνατολή, *sunrise, east*
10. stella, *star*
11. oriens, *east, sunrise*

1. אֶתְמוֹל, *formerly*

2. שִׁלְשׁוֹם, *in former times*

3. CH: This pronoun refers to David.

4. נָגִיד, *prince*

5. ἐχθές, *yesterday*

6. CH: This pronoun refers to David.

7. ποιμαίνω, fut. act. ind. 2 s., *shepherd*

8. ἡγέομαι, pres. mid. ptcp. m. a. s., *lead*

9. Βηθλεεμ, *Bethlehem*

10. οὐδαμῶς, *by no means*

11. ἐλάχιστος, *least*

12. ἡγεμών, *leader, ruler*

13. ἡγέομαι, pres. mid. ptcp. m. nom. s., *lead*

14. ποιμαίνω, fut. act. ind. 3 s., *shepherd*

15. Bethleem, *Bethlehem*

16. Iuda, *Judah*

17. nequaquam, *by no means*

18. parvus, *small*

19. dux, *leader*

20. rego, fut. act. ind. 3 s., *rule*

December 20

2 Samuel 5:2

גַּם־אֶתְמ֣וֹל[1] גַּם־שִׁלְשׁ֗וֹם[2] בִּֽהְי֨וֹת שָׁא֥וּל מֶ֙לֶךְ֙ עָלֵ֔ינוּ
אַתָּ֗ה[3] הָיִ֛יתָה מוֹצִ֥יא וְהַמֵּבִ֖י אֶת־יִשְׂרָאֵ֑ל וַיֹּ֨אמֶר
יְהוָ֜ה לְךָ֗ אַתָּ֨ה תִרְעֶ֤ה אֶת־עַמִּי֙ אֶת־יִשְׂרָאֵ֔ל וְאַתָּ֛ה
תִּהְיֶ֥ה לְנָגִ֖יד[4] עַל־יִשְׂרָאֵֽל׃

καὶ ἐχθὲς[5] καὶ τρίτην ὄντος Σαουλ βασιλέως ἐφ᾿ ἡμῖν σὺ[6] ἦσθα ὁ ἐξάγων καὶ εἰσάγων τὸν Ισραηλ, καὶ εἶπεν κύριος πρὸς σέ Σὺ ποιμανεῖς[7] τὸν λαόν μου τὸν Ισραηλ, καὶ σὺ ἔσει εἰς ἡγούμενον[8] ἐπὶ τὸν Ισραηλ.

Matthew 2:6

καὶ σὺ Βηθλέεμ,[9] *γῆ Ἰούδα, οὐδαμῶς*[10] *ἐλαχίστη*[11] *εἶ ἐν τοῖς ἡγεμόσιν*[12] *Ἰούδα· ἐκ σοῦ γὰρ ἐξελεύσεται ἡγούμενος,*[13] *ὅστις ποιμανεῖ*[14] *τὸν λαόν μου τὸν Ἰσραήλ.*

et tu Bethleem[15] terra Iuda[16] nequaquam[17] minima[18] es in principibus Iuda ex te enim exiet dux[19] qui reget[20] populum meum Israhel.

December 21

Micah 5:1

וְאַתָּ֞ה בֵּֽית־לֶ֣חֶם אֶפְרָ֗תָה[1] צָעִיר֙[2] לִהְיוֹת֙ בְּאַלְפֵ֣י[3]
יְהוּדָ֔ה מִמְּךָ֙ לִ֣י יֵצֵ֔א לִהְי֥וֹת מוֹשֵׁ֖ל[4] בְּיִשְׂרָאֵ֑ל
וּמוֹצָאֹתָ֥יו[5] מִקֶּ֖דֶם[6] מִימֵ֥י עוֹלָֽם׃

Καὶ σύ, Βηθλεεμ[7] οἶκος τοῦ Εφραθα,[8] ὀλιγοστὸς[9] εἶ τοῦ εἶναι ἐν χιλιάσιν Ιουδα· ἐκ σοῦ μοι ἐξελεύσεται τοῦ εἶναι εἰς ἄρχοντα ἐν τῷ Ισραηλ, καὶ αἱ ἔξοδοι[10] αὐτοῦ ἀπ᾽ ἀρχῆς ἐξ ἡμερῶν αἰῶνος.

John 7:42

οὐχ ἡ γραφὴ εἶπεν ὅτι ἐκ τοῦ σπέρματος Δαυὶδ καὶ ἀπὸ Βηθλέεμ τῆς κώμης[11] ὅπου ἦν Δαυὶδ ἔρχεται ὁ χριστός;

nonne scriptura dicit quia ex semine David et Bethleem[12] castello[13] ubi erat David venit Christus?

1. אֶפְרָ֫תָה, *Ephrath*
2. צָעִיר, *little, small*
3. אֶ֫לֶף, *thousand;* TH: here, *clans*
4. מָשַׁל, qal ptcp. m. s. abs., *rule*
5. מוֹצָאָה, *origin, going out*
6. קֶ֫דֶם, *ancient time*
7. Βηθλεεμ, *Bethlehem*
8. Εφραθα, *Ephrath*
9. ὀλιγοστός, *few in number*
10. ἔξοδος, *going out*
11. κώμη, *village*
12. Bethleem, *Bethlehem*
13. castellum, *town, village*

December 22

1 Samuel 20:6

אִם־פָּקֹד יִפְקְדֵנִי אָבִיךָ וְאָמַרְתָּ נִשְׁאֹל נִשְׁאַל
מִמֶּנִּי דָוִד לָרוּץ בֵּית־לֶחֶם עִירוֹ כִּי זֶבַח הַיָּמִים שָׁם
לְכָל־הַמִּשְׁפָּחָה׃

ἐὰν ἐπισκεπτόμενος ἐπισκέψηταί με ὁ πατήρ σου, καὶ ἐρεῖς Παραιτούμενος[1] παρῃτήσατο[2] ἀπ᾽ ἐμοῦ Δαυιδ δραμεῖν[3] ἕως εἰς Βηθλεεμ[4] τὴν πόλιν αὐτοῦ, ὅτι θυσία τῶν ἡμερῶν ἐκεῖ ὅλῃ τῇ φυλῇ.

Luke 2:4

Ἀνέβη δὲ καὶ Ἰωσὴφ ἀπὸ τῆς Γαλιλαίας ἐκ πόλεως Ναζαρὲθ[5] εἰς τὴν Ἰουδαίαν εἰς πόλιν Δαυὶδ ἥτις καλεῖται Βηθλέεμ, διὰ τὸ εἶναι αὐτὸν ἐξ οἴκου καὶ πατριᾶς[6] Δαυίδ.

ascendit autem et Ioseph a Galilaea de civitate Nazareth[7] in Iudaeam civitatem David quae vocatur Bethleem[8] eo quod esset de domo et familia[9] David.

1. παραιτέομαι, pres. mid. ptcp. m. nom. s., *ask*
2. παραιτέομαι, aor. mid. ind. 3 s., *ask*
3. τρέχω, aor. act. inf., *run*
4. Βηθλεεμ, *Bethlehem*
5. Ναζαρά, *Nazareth*
6. πατριά, *family*
7. Nazareth, *Nazareth*
8. Bethleem, *Bethlehem*
9. familia, *family*

December 23

Genesis 25:24

וַיִּמְלְאוּ יָמֶיהָ לָלֶדֶת וְהִנֵּה תוֹמִם[1] בְּבִטְנָהּ׃[2]

καὶ ἐπληρώθησαν αἱ ἡμέραι τοῦ τεκεῖν αὐτήν, καὶ τῇδε ἦν δίδυμα[3] ἐν τῇ κοιλίᾳ αὐτῆς.

Luke 2:6

Ἐγένετο δὲ ἐν τῷ εἶναι αὐτοὺς ἐκεῖ ἐπλήσθησαν[4] αἱ ἡμέραι τοῦ τεκεῖν[5] αὐτήν.

factum est autem cum essent ibi impleti sunt dies ut pareret.[6]

1. תּוֹאָם, *twin*
2. בֶּ֫טֶן, *womb*
3. δίδυμος, *twin*
4. πίμπλημι, aor. pass. ind. 3 p., *fulfill, be complete*
5. τίκτω, aor. act. inf., *bear children*
6. pareo, impf. act. subj. 3 s., *complete, come*

December 24

Isaiah 1:3

יָדַ֥ע שׁוֹר֙[1] קֹנֵ֔הוּ[2] וַחֲמ֖וֹר[3] אֵב֣וּס[4] בְּעָלָ֑יו יִשְׂרָאֵל֙ לֹ֣א
יָדַ֔ע עַמִּ֖י לֹ֥א הִתְבּוֹנָֽן׃

ἔγνω βοῦς τὸν κτησάμενον καὶ ὄνος τὴν φάτνην[5] τοῦ κυρίου αὐτοῦ· Ισραηλ δέ με οὐκ ἔγνω, καὶ ὁ λαός με οὐ συνῆκεν.[6]

Luke 2:7

καὶ ἔτεκεν[7] τὸν υἱὸν αὐτῆς τὸν πρωτότοκον,[8] καὶ ἐσπαργάνωσεν[9] αὐτὸν καὶ ἀνέκλινεν[10] αὐτὸν ἐν φάτνῃ, διότι[11] οὐκ ἦν αὐτοῖς τόπος ἐν τῷ καταλύματι.[12]

et peperit[13] filium suum primogenitum[14] et pannis[15] eum involvit[16] et reclinavit[17] eum in praesepio[18] quia non erat eis locus in diversorio.[19]

1. שׁוֹר, *ox*
2. קנה, *owner*
3. חֲמוֹר, *donkey*
4. אֵבוּס, *feeding trough, manger*
5. φάτνη, *manger*
6. συνίημι, aor. act. ind. 3 s., *understand*
7. τίκτω, aor. act. ind. 3 s., *bear children*
8. πρωτότοκος, *firstborn*
9. σπαργανόω, aor. act. ind. 3 s., *wrap in baby cloths*
10. ἀνακλίνω, aor. act. ind. 3 s., *recline*
11. διότι, *because*
12. κατάλυμα, *inn, guest room*
13. pario, perf. act. ind. 3 s., *bring forth*
14. primogenitus, *firstborn*
15. pannus, *cloth*
16. involvo, perf. act. ind. 3 s., *wrap*
17. reclino, perf. act. ind. 3 s., *lay down*
18. praesepium, *manger*
19. diversorium, *guest room, lodging place*

December 25

Habakkuk 3:18

וַאֲנִי בַּיהוָה אֶעְלוֹזָה[1] אָגִילָה[2] בֵּאלֹהֵי יִשְׁעִי׃[3]

ἐγὼ δὲ ἐν τῷ κυρίῳ ἀγαλλιάσομαι,[4] χαρήσομαι[5] ἐπὶ τῷ θεῷ τῷ σωτῆρί[6] μου.

Luke 2:11

ὅτι ἐτέχθη[7] ὑμῖν σήμερον σωτὴρ ὅς ἐστιν χριστὸς κύριος ἐν πόλει Δαυίδ.

quia natus est vobis hodie salvator[8] qui est Christus Dominus in civitate David.

1. עָלַז, qal impf. 1 c. s. coh., *rejoice, exult*
2. גִּיל, qal impf. 1 c. s. coh., *rejoice, exult*
3. יֶשַׁע, *salvation*
4. ἀγαλλιάομαι, fut. mid. ind. 1 s., *exult, rejoice*
5. χαίρω, fut. pass. ind. 1 s., *rejoice*
6. σωτήρ, *salvation*
7. τίκτω, aor. pass. ind. 3 s., *bear a child*
8. salvator, *savior*

God's Reign

December 26

Psalm 8:7

תַּמְשִׁילֵהוּ[1] בְּמַעֲשֵׂי יָדֶיךָ כֹּל שַׁתָּה[2] תַחַת־רַגְלָיו׃

καὶ κατέστησας αὐτὸν ἐπὶ τὰ ἔργα τῶν χειρῶν σου, πάντα ὑπέταξας[3] ὑποκάτω[4] τῶν ποδῶν αὐτοῦ.

Hebrews 2:8

πάντα ὑπέταξας ὑποκάτω τῶν ποδῶν αὐτοῦ. ἐν τῷ γὰρ ὑποτάξαι[5] [αὐτῷ] τὰ πάντα οὐδὲν ἀφῆκεν αὐτῷ ἀνυπότακτον.[6] Νῦν δὲ οὔπω[7] ὁρῶμεν αὐτῷ τὰ πάντα ὑποτεταγμένα.[8]

omnia subiecisti sub pedibus eius in eo enim quod ei omnia subiecit[9] nihil dimisit non subiectum[10] ei nunc autem necdum[11] videmus omnia subiecta[12] ei.

1. מָשַׁל, hiph. impf. 2 m. s., *rule, have dominion*
2. שִׁית, qal perf. 2 m. s., *put, set*
3. ὑποτάσσω, aor. act. ind. 2 s., *subject*
4. ὑποκάτω, *beneath*
5. ὑποτάσσω, aor. act. inf., *subject*
6. ἀνυπότακτος, *independent*
7. οὔπω, *not yet*
8. ὑποτάσσω, perf. pass. ptcp. n. a. p., *subject*
9. subicio, perf. act. ind. 3 s., *subject*
10. subicio, perf. pass. ptcp. n. a. s., *subject*
11. necdum, *not yet*
12. subicio, perf. pass. ptcp. n. a. p., *subject*

December 27

Exodus 15:18

יְהוָ֥ה ׀ יִמְלֹ֖ךְ לְעֹלָ֥ם וָעֶֽד׃[1]

κύριος βασιλεύων τὸν αἰῶνα καὶ ἐπ᾽ αἰῶνα καὶ ἔτι.

Revelation 19:6

Καὶ ἤκουσα ὡς φωνὴν ὄχλου πολλοῦ καὶ ὡς φωνὴν ὑδάτων πολλῶν καὶ ὡς φωνὴν βροντῶν[2] ἰσχυρῶν[3] λεγόντων· ἀλληλουϊά,[4] ὅτι ἐβασίλευσεν[5] κύριος ὁ θεὸς [ἡμῶν] ὁ παντοκράτωρ.[6]

et audivi quasi vocem turbae magnae et sicut vocem aquarum multarum et sicut vocem tonitruum[7] magnorum dicentium alleluia[8] quoniam regnavit[9] Dominus Deus noster omnipotens.[10]

1. עַד, *forever*
2. βροντή, *thunder*
3. ἰσχυρός, *mighty, strong*
4. ἀλληλουϊά, *hallelujah*
5. βασιλεύω, aor. act. ind. 3 s., *reign, rule*
6. παντοκράτωρ, *almighty*
7. tonitrus, *thunder*
8. alleluia, *hallelujah*
9. regno, perf. act. ind. 3 s., *reign, rule*
10. omnipotens, *almighty*

December 28

Psalm 45:7 [LXX 44:7]

כִּסְאֲךָ אֱלֹהִים עוֹלָם וָעֶד[1] שֵׁבֶט מִישֹׁר[2] שֵׁבֶט
מַלְכוּתֶךָ׃[3]

ὁ θρόνος σου, ὁ θεός, εἰς τὸν αἰῶνα τοῦ αἰῶνος,
ῥάβδος[4] εὐθύτητος[5] ἡ ῥάβδος τῆς βασιλείας σου.

Hebrews 1:8

πρὸς δὲ τὸν υἱόν·[6] *ὁ θρόνος σου ὁ θεὸς εἰς τὸν αἰῶνα τοῦ αἰῶνος, καὶ ἡ ῥάβδος τῆς εὐθύτητος ῥάβδος τῆς βασιλείας σου.*

ad Filium autem[7] thronus tuus Deus in saeculum saeculi et virga[8] aequitatis[9] virga regni tui.

1. עַד, *forever*
2. מִישׁוֹר, *uprightness*
3. מַלְכוּת, *kingdom*
4. ῥάβδος, *scepter*
5. εὐθύτης, *uprightness*
6. CH: The verb "he says" elided and can be inferred from context. Here, the author of Hebrews contrasts the angels with Jesus.
7. CH: See CH note above.
8. virga, *scepter*
9. aequitas, *righteousness*

December 29

Psalm 45:8 [LXX 44:8]

אָהַ֣בְתָּ צֶּדֶק֮ וַתִּשְׂנָ֫א רֶ֥שַׁע[1] עַל־כֵּ֤ן ׀ מְשָׁחֲךָ֡[2] אֱלֹהִ֣ים
אֱ֭לֹהֶיךָ שֶׁ֥מֶן שָׂשׂ֗וֹן[3] מֵֽחֲבֵרֶֽיךָ׃[4]

ἠγάπησας δικαιοσύνην καὶ ἐμίσησας ἀνομίαν·[5]
διὰ τοῦτο ἔχρισέν[6] σε ὁ θεὸς ὁ θεός σου ἔλαιον[7]
ἀγαλλιάσεως[8] παρὰ τοὺς μετόχους[9] σου.

Hebrews 1:9

ἠγάπησας δικαιοσύνην καὶ ἐμίσησας ἀνομίαν·
διὰ τοῦτο ἔχρισέν σε ὁ θεὸς ὁ θεός σου ἔλαιον
ἀγαλλιάσεως παρὰ τοὺς μετόχους σου.

dilexisti iustitiam et odisti[10] iniquitatem
propterea[11] unxit[12] te Deus Deus tuus oleo[13]
exultationis[14] prae[15] participibus[16] tuis.

1. רֶשַׁע, *wickedness*
2. מָשַׁח, qal perf. 3 m. s., *anoint*
3. שָׂשׂוֹן, *joy, gladness*
4. חָבֵר, *associate, companion*
5. ἀνομία, *lawlessness*
6. χρίω, aor. act. ind. 3 s., *anoint*
7. ἔλαιον, *olive oil*
8. ἀγαλλίασις, *gladness*
9. μέτοχος, *companion, associate*
10. odi, perf. act. ind. 2 s., *hate*
11. propterea, *therefore*
12. unguo, perf. act. ind. 3 s., *anoint*
13. oleum, *olive oil*
14. exsultatio, *exultation, joy*
15. prae, *in front of*
16. particeps, *fellow, partner*

December 30

Isaiah 37:16

יְהוָ֨ה צְבָא֜וֹת אֱלֹהֵ֤י יִשְׂרָאֵל֙ יֹשֵׁ֣ב הַכְּרֻבִ֔ים[1] אַתָּה־
ה֤וּא הָֽאֱלֹהִים֙ לְבַדְּךָ֔ לְכֹ֖ל מַמְלְכ֣וֹת הָאָ֑רֶץ אַתָּ֣ה
עָשִׂ֔יתָ אֶת־הַשָּׁמַ֖יִם וְאֶת־הָאָֽרֶץ׃

Κύριε σαβαωθ[2] ὁ θεὸς Ισραηλ ὁ καθήμενος ἐπὶ τῶν χερουβιν,[3] σὺ θεὸς μόνος εἶ πάσης βασιλείας τῆς οἰκουμένης,[4] σὺ ἐποίησας τὸν οὐρανὸν καὶ τὴν γῆν.

Acts 4:24

οἱ δὲ ἀκούσαντες ὁμοθυμαδὸν[5] ἦραν φωνὴν πρὸς τὸν θεὸν καὶ εἶπαν· δέσποτα,[6] *σὺ ὁ ποιήσας τὸν οὐρανὸν καὶ τὴν γῆν καὶ τὴν θάλασσαν καὶ πάντα τὰ ἐν αὐτοῖς.*

qui cum audissent unianimiter[7] levaverunt[8] vocem ad Deum et dixerunt Domine tu qui fecisti caelum et terram et mare et omnia quae in eis sunt.

1. כְּרוּב, *cherub*
2. σαβαωθ, *Sabaoth*
3. χερούβ, *cherub*
4. οἰκουμένη, *world*
5. ὁμοθυμαδόν, *of one accord*
6. δεσπότης, *master*
7. unianimiter, *unanimously*
8. levo, perf. act. ind. 3 p., *raise up, lift up*

December 31

Isaiah 44:6

כֹּה־אָמַ֨ר יְהוָ֧ה מֶֽלֶךְ־יִשְׂרָאֵ֛ל וְגֹאֲל֖וֹ יְהוָ֣ה צְבָא֑וֹת אֲנִ֤י
רִאשׁוֹן֙ וַאֲנִ֣י אַחֲר֔וֹן[1] וּמִבַּלְעָדַ֖י[2] אֵ֥ין אֱלֹהִֽים׃

Οὕτως λέγει ὁ θεὸς ὁ βασιλεὺς τοῦ Ισραηλ ὁ ῥυσάμενος αὐτὸν θεὸς σαβαωθ[3] Ἐγὼ πρῶτος καὶ ἐγὼ μετὰ ταῦτα, πλὴν ἐμοῦ οὐκ ἔστιν θεός.

Revelation 1:17

Καὶ ὅτε εἶδον αὐτόν, ἔπεσα πρὸς τοὺς πόδας αὐτοῦ ὡς νεκρός, καὶ ἔθηκεν τὴν δεξιὰν αὐτοῦ ἐπ᾽ ἐμὲ λέγων· μὴ φοβοῦ· ἐγώ εἰμι ὁ πρῶτος καὶ ὁ ἔσχατος.

et cum vidissem eum cecidi ad pedes eius tamquam mortuus et posuit dexteram suam super me dicens noli timere ego sum primus et novissimus.

1. אַחֲרוֹן, *last*
2. בִּלְעֲדֵי, *besides, without*
3. σαβαωθ, *Sabaoth*

Bibliography

Beale, G. K., and D. A. Carson, eds. *Commentary on the New Testament Use of the Old Testament*. Grand Rapids: Baker Academic; Nottingham: Apollos, 2007.

Black, David Alan, and Jacob N. Cerone. *The Pericope of the Adulteress in Contemporary Research*. The Library of New Testament Studies 551. New York: T&T Clark, 2016.

Brown, Francis, Samuel Rolles Driver, and Charles Augustus Briggs. *Enhanced Brown-Driver-Briggs Hebrew and English Lexicon*. Oxford: Clarendon Press, 1977.

Clines, David J. A., ed. *The Dictionary of Classical Hebrew*. Sheffield: Sheffield Academic; Sheffield Phoenix, 1993–2011.

Collins Latin Dictionary Plus Grammar. Glasgow: HarperCollins, 1997.

Danker, Frederick William, Walter Bauer, W. F. Arndt, and F. W. Gingrich. *A Greek-English Lexicon of the New Testament and Other Early Christian Literature*. 3rd ed. Revised and edited by Frederick William Danker. Chicago: University of Chicago Press, 2000.

Glare, P. G. W. *Oxford Latin Dictionary*. Oxford: Oxford University Press, 1968.

Harnack, Adolf von. *The Letter of the Roman Church to the Corinthian Church from the Era of Domitian*. Edited and translated by Jacob N. Cerone. Eugene, OR: Pickwick, 2021.

Koehler, Ludwig, Walter Baumgartner, M. E. J. Richardson, and Johann Jakob Stamm. *The Hebrew and Aramaic Lexicon of the Old Testament*. Leiden: Brill, 1994–2000.

Lewis, Charlton T., and Charles Short. *Harpers' Latin Dictionary*. New York: Harper & Brothers; Oxford: Clarendon, 1891.

Liddell, Henry George, and Robert Scott. *A Greek-English Lexicon*. Revised and augmented by Henry Stuart Jones. Oxford: Clarendon, 1996.

Lust, Johan, Erik Eynikel, and Katrin Hauspie. *A Greek-English Lexicon of the Septuagint*. Rev. ed. Deutsche Bibelgesellschaft: Stuttgart, 2003.

Muraoka, Takamitsu. *A Greek-English Lexicon of the Septuagint*. Leuven: Peeters Publishers, 2009.

Old Testament to New Testament Index

Versification follows that of the original languages and not the English versions of the Bible. Where the LXX diverges from the BHS, note is made of the appropriate LXX reference within brackets.

Leviticus

Numbers

Deuteronomy

New Testament to Old Testament Index

Versification follows that of the original languages and not the English versions of the Bible. Where the LXX diverges from the BHS, note is made of the appropriate LXX reference within brackets.

Rev 4:8	Isa 6:3	15	Rev 15:3	Exod 15:11	83
Rev 5:5	Gen 49:10	318	Rev 15:4	Ps 86:9 [85:9]	14
Rev 6:8	Ezek 14:21	147	Rev 16:2	Exod 9:10	75
Rev 6:16b–17	Isa 2:19	324	Rev 16:10	Exod 10:21	78
Rev 7:17a	Ps 23:2 [22:2]	330	Rev 16:16	Judg 5:19	119
Rev 9:2	Gen 19:28	323	Rev 16:21	Exod 9:24	76
Rev 9:3	Exod 10:12	77	Rev 19:6	Exod 15:18	363
Rev 9:4	Ezek 9:4	144	Rev 19:11	Ezek 1:1	142
Rev 10:9	Ezek 3:1	143	Rev 19:19	Ps 2:2	319
Rev 11:6	Exod 7:17	74	Rev 21:3	Lev 26:12	333
Rev 11:11	Ezek 37:5	151	Rev 21:10	Ezek 40:2	334
Rev 11:12	2 Kgs 2:11	137	Rev 22:1	Ezek 47:1	335
Rev 11:15	Obad 21	332	Rev 22:2	Ezek 47:12	336
Rev 11:19	2 Chr 5:7	130	Rev 22:12	Ps 28:4 [27:4]	325